Econometric Society Monographs No. 15

Axioms of cooperative decision making

Econometric Society Monographs

Editors:

Avinash K. Dixit   *Princeton University*
Alain Monfort   *Institut National de la Statistique et des
   Etudes Economiques*

The Econometric Society is an international society for the
advancement of economic theory in relation to statistics and
mathematics. The Econometric Society Monograph Series
is designed to promote the publication of original research
contributions of high quality in Economic theory, Econometrics,
and Quantitative Economics.

Axioms of cooperative decision making

HERVÉ MOULIN
Virginia Polytechnic Institute and State University

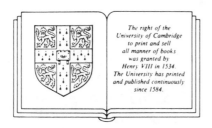

The right of the
University of Cambridge
to print and sell
all manner of books
was granted by
Henry VIII in 1534.
The University has printed
and published continuously
since 1584.

CAMBRIDGE UNIVERSITY PRESS

Cambridge
New York   Port Chester   Melbourne   Sydney

Published by the Press Syndicate of the University of Cambridge
The Pitt Building, Trumpington Street, Cambridge CB2 1RP
40 West 20th Street, New York, NY 10011, USA
10 Stamford Road, Oakleigh, Melbourne 3166, Australia

First published 1988
First paperback edition 1991

Printed in the United States of America

Library of Congress Cataloging-in-Publication Data

Moulin, Hervé.
Axioms of cooperative decision making / Hervé Moulin.
p.   cm. – (Econometric Society monographs ; no. 15)
Bibliography: p.
Includes index.
ISBN 0-521-36055-2 (hbk.)
1. Social sciences – Mathematical models.   2. Game theory.
3. Social choice.   I. Title.   II. Series.
H61.25.M677   1988
658.4′0353 – dc19   88-17056
                                                            CIP

British Library Cataloguing in Publication Data

Moulin, H. (Hervé)
Axioms of cooperative decision making –
(Econometric Society monographs, no. 15)
1. Groups. Decision making
I. Title
302.3

ISBN 0-521-36055-2 hardback
ISBN 0-521-42458-5 paperback

To Marie

Contents

Foreword

Amartya Sen

Two of the main developments in social analysis, broadly defined, since World War II have been the emergence of social choice theory and the blossoming of the theory of games. Each development was characterized by a major contribution that set the stage for further explorations. John von Neumann and Oskar Morgenstern established the fruitfulness of using the theory of games as a tool for the analysis of economic behavior, social cooperation, and strategic analysis.[1] Kenneth Arrow's analysis of social choice and individual values established a new approach to the understanding and investigation of social aggregation, political mechanisms, and normative economic judgments.[2] Both made extensive and elegant use of mathematical reasoning and, inter alia, demonstrated the fruitfulness of formal, axiomatic methods for substantive analysis of problems of practical importance. Each of these lines of investigation led to the development of a vast - often rather technical - literature.

Given the close connections between the subject matters of the two fields of investigation, it would have been natural to expect that there would be a lot of interchange between the two and a good deal of cross-fertilization. There have, in fact, been a number of attempts at drawing lessons from one field for the other, but it is fair to say that much of social choice theory and the bulk of game theory tend to proceed on their own, without even a side glance at the other field. There are, of course, exceptions.[3]

---

[1] J. von Neumann and O. Morgenstern, *Theory of Games and Economic Behavior* (Princeton University Press, 1944).

[2] K. J. Arrow, *Social Choice and Individual Values* (New York: Wiley, 1951; second edition, 1963).

[3] The literature on the manipulability of social choice mechanisms has to be inescapably concerned with game-theoretic issues in social-choice-theoretic contexts. Beginning with early contributions from such authors as Robin Farquharson and Michael Dummett, the literature received a tremendous boost when the powerful Gibbard–Satterthwaite theorem

Hervé Moulin has, in fact, been at the forefront of both social choice theory and game theory, and this monograph is a remarkably illuminating account of the uses that can be made of formal social choice theory and formal game theory in understanding and analyzing the nature and the process of cooperative decision making. Most problems of social interaction involve both conflict and congruence of interests. The elements of congruence make it important to have cooperation, but there are many forms that cooperation can take, and the interests of the different parties may diverge in the choice between different cooperative arrangements. Moulin discusses these problems with remarkable lucidity as well as reach.

Moulin begins with a clear exposition of a particular approach, namely, "welfarism," which has been extensively used in social choice theory, in which social welfare is taken to be a function of – and only of – individual utilities. The utilities can be combined in different ways (e.g., by adding, as under utilitarianism, or by concentrating on the utility of the worst-off individual, as under egalitarian rules), but they share the same concentration on individual utilities only. Part I of the book provides an exploration of this approach and its connections with the problem of bargaining, leading to the selection of a particular outcome from a class of alternative cooperative outcomes that are differentially beneficial to different parties. Moulin's approach here – as elsewhere in the book – is axiomatic, and he makes excellent use of clarifying the principles involved in the different axioms that can be employed to systematize, analyze, and critically evaluate alternative solutions.

In Part II Moulin shifts his focus from social choice theory to game theory, dealing specifically with problems of cooperation. The insights to be gained from game-theoretic analysis are fully used, supplementing what had been learned from the use of axiomatic social choice theory.

In Parts III and IV Moulin discusses, respectively, the problem of public decision making and that of voting and social choice. The former includes important problems of public economics (such as the choice of taxation systems, the regulation of monopolies, problems of decentralization), and the latter is concerned with different political mechanisms, involving various types of voting systems and other ways of dealing

---

Footnote 3 *(cont.)*
on the impossibility of nonmanipulable social choice mechanisms (more generally, game forms) was established. Results very similar to those of Gibbard were also established around that time by Pattanaik, with some variations. The subsequent literature has been extensive, with many interesting impossibility and positive possibility results. See particularly Hervé Moulin, *The Strategy of Social Choice* (Amsterdam: North Holland, 1983), and Bezalel Peleg, *Game Theoretic Analysis of Voting in Committees* (Cambridge: Cambridge University Press, 1984).

with aggregation of partially conflicting preferences of different parties. Throughout these analyses, Moulin makes efficient and elegant use of lessons learned from social choice theory as well as game theory. The overall result is to leave the reader immensely better informed about the issues involved in cooperative decision making and how they might be handled, with an eye both to substantive relevance and to the possibility of using formal reasoning in analyzing problems that may initially look too complex and messy.

There are two features of the book I would particularly like to draw attention to in this preliminary statement. First, a good deal of social choice theory has been concerned primarily with presenting impossibility results, showing what cannot be done rather than what can be. Even though the subject began with the stunning impossibility theorem presented by Kenneth Arrow, to concentrate primarily on deriving impossibility results is quite the wrong way of seeing social choice theory. One object of noting an impossibility is to question the initial choice of axioms and to suggest what variations in the axiomatic structure should be considered. This leads to positive possibilities – what can be done and how. Moulin's approach is constructive throughout, and in this respect the monograph must be seen as an important contribution to creative formal thinking, using social choice theory as well as game theory.

Second, in fields that involve a good deal of formal reasoning, the extent of communication is severely limited by the difficulty of mastering exactly what is going on in the process of deduction that may look remote and unduly abstract. Moulin's method of dealing with this problem is to enrich the analysis with an enormous number of examples, which bring out precisely what is involved. He also supplements his presentations by a number of useful and well-chosen exercises, making sure that the reader has got to the bottom of the problem. As a pedagogic exercise this strategy of presentation is quite excellent, and the book should be praised for that reason as well.

It should be clear to the reader that I am an unashamed admirer of what Moulin has done. His efforts will undoubtedly be well rewarded if the readers pay attention to this work and benefit from it. I do not doubt at all that this will happen in abundance.

Acknowledgments

This book emerged from several graduate classes on collective decisions, social choice, and cooperative games, taught mostly at the Université de Paris Dauphine, Princeton University, and the Virginia Polytechnic Institute. I wish to thank all my students for their patience and criticisms. Three of my colleagues provided invaluable advice at various stages of this manuscript, for which I am most grateful. They are John Roemer, William Thomson, and Peyton Young.

Special thanks are due to Jean-Michel Grandmont for his constant encouragement and to Professor Amartya Sen who accepted to write the Foreword.

Finally, the National Science Foundation has very effectively supported this project by two successive grants (SES8419465 and SES8618600).

Introduction

Many decisions of public concern cannot be left to the market because cooperative opportunities will not be efficiently utilized by decentralized actions of the agents. The most prominent examples include the provision of public goods, pricing of a natural monopoly, as well as all decisions taken by vote. To remedy these market failures, welfare economists have come up with a variety of normative solutions and tried to convince the decision makers of their relevance.

The theoretical foundation of these normative arguments is axiomatic. This point was clearly made in Amartya Sen's landmark book (*Collective Choice and Social Welfare,* first published in 1970). Since then the axiomatic literature has considerably expanded its scope and refined its methods: The whole theory of cooperative games has played a central role in the analysis of cost sharing when there are increasing returns to scales; our understanding of voting rules now encompasses the impact of strategic manipulations; several refined measurements of inequality have been constructed and abundantly tested; and so on.

This book describes the recent successes of the axiomatic method in four areas: welfarism (the construction of collective utility functions and inequality measures as well as the axiomatic bargaining approach); cooperative games (the core and the two most popular value operators – Shapley value and nucleolus); public decision making (cost sharing of a public good and pricing of a regulated monopoly, in both the first-best and strategic-second-best perspectives); and voting and social choice (majority voting à la Condorcet and scoring methods à la Borda; the impossibility of aggregating individual preferences into a social preference).

I attempt to provide a comprehensive and unified presentation of these technically heterogeneous subjects. The link between them is the collection of axioms (in total, about 30 of them are discussed). Many of them are so versatile that they apply, with very little modification, to radically different problems. A good example is the core property that profoundly

1

Table I.1. *Interprofile axioms*

Independence[a]	Monotonicity[a]
Anonymity: all chapters	
Neutrality: 8, 9, 11	
Variable preferences	
Arrow IIA: 11	Pigou–Dalton principle: 2
Zero independence: 2, 5	Monotonicity: 9, 11
Scale independence: 2, 3	Strategyproofness: 8, 10
Independence of common utility pace: 2	Strong monotonicity: 10
Independence of common zero: 2	
Independence of common scale: 2	
Marginalist (value operator): 5	
Decentralizability: 6	
Variable issues	
Nash IIA: 3, 11	Issue monotonicity: 3
Aizerman: 11	Coalition monotonicity: 5
Expansion: 11	Technological monotonicity: 7
Path independence: 11	
Additivity: 3, 5, 6	
Variable population	
Separability: 2, 3	Population monotonicity: 3
Reduced-game properties: 5	Participation: 9
Consistency: 6	Reinforcement: 9

[a] Numbers refer to chapters.

influences the discussion of surplus-sharing methods in Chapters 6 and 7 as well as that of strategic voting in Chapter 10. Or consider the separability axiom, which plays an important role in the analysis of collective utility functions (Chapters 2 and 3), in values of cooperative games (Chapter 5), as well as in cost- and surplus-sharing methods (Chapter 6). Many more such connections exist, as will become clear from the classification outlined in Table I.1.

Throughout the book we utilize the axiomatic method to guide decision making. Of course, each microeconomic problem that we will examine has more than one plausible solution: There are many "good" voting rules, several plausible "values" for cooperative games, many useful inequality indices, and so on. Ideally, the axiomatic method can help our choice by, first, reducing the number of plausible solutions as much as possible and, second, providing us with a specific axiomatic characterization of each of these plausible solutions. For instance, we find essentially two interesting value operators for cooperative games and provide a characterization of each (Part II, Chapter 5). See also the discussion of collective utility functions in Part I (Chapter 2), built on the two polar examples of egalitarianism and classical utilitarianism; or, in Part IV, see the two focal families of voting rules based, respectively, on scoring systems and on majority comparisons.

As a rule, we pay little attention to the innumerable impossibility results that the axiomatic approach generates too easily. The only exceptions are the impossibility theorems of Arrow (Chapter 11) and Gibbard–Satterthwaite (Chapter 10), of which the mathematical content is so rich.

We cover many different economic models where the axiomatic method has scored significant successes. Our choice of topics is, however, not exhaustive. One notable missing subject is the allocation of private goods, whether through exchange or as a pure distribution issue (cake division problems). Despite a substantial normative literature on these questions, the existing results (surveyed in Thomson and Varian [1985]) do not appear sufficiently focused upon particular solutions to justify a textbook presentation. The only (major) exception is the "Edgeworth proposition," characterizing the competitive equilibrium by means of the core property when the agents become vanishingly small. But the allocation of private goods between a small, fixed number of agents has not yet found clear-cut axiomatic answers except in some very special cases such as matching problems.

We now propose a categorization of the many axioms populating this book. The one and only axiom that pervades through the entire book is Pareto optimality (also called unanimity or efficiency). This should come as no surprise since 40 years ago the new welfare economists agreed that it was the only indisputable principle on which legitimate welfare analysis could ever develop. Note that Pareto optimality is an *intraprofile* property, in the sense that it can be defined for one single preference profile for one particular problem. The only other intraprofile axioms are those placing lower or upper bounds (mostly lower) on the welfare of individual agents and/or coalitions of agents. The main examples are the individual rationality and core properties (Chapters 4–8 and 10).

The *interprofile* axioms consider a specific change in the parameters of the model and state some condition on the induced change of the solution. If the condition says that the solution must not change as the parameter changes, we have an *independence* axiom; if it says that the solution must shift in a certain direction related to the shift of the parameter, we have a *monotonicity* axiom.

The most popular independence axiom is anonymity. It says that the solution should treat agents equally (one person, one vote): Specifically, when the problem is altered by exchanging the characteristics of two agents (including their preferences), its solution should not change. This basic equity principle appears explicitly in most chapters and is implicit in all. A related equity property for voting rules is neutrality, requiring that no candidate should be a priori discriminated against. Neutrality plays an important role in Part IV.

The bulk of the interprofile axioms falls into six classes corresponding to the variations of different parameters of the model. The parameters can be (a) the agents' preferences, (b) the set of feasible outcomes (the issue), or (c) the set of concerned agents (the population). In each case the axiom can be either an independence or a monotonicity property, so that, as stated, we have six classes of axioms.

Variable preferences

This is by far the most frequent parameter variation since Arrow's pioneer discussion of the independence of irrelevant alternatives (IIA; an independence axiom) as well as of positive responsiveness (a monotonicity axiom). In the welfarist theory (Part I), Sen [1977] pointed to the paramount importance of independence axioms that economize on information gathering. Indeed, these axioms are all over Part I (see the independence of individual utility scale or common zero of utility). In the analysis of public decision making, monotonicity of the solution with respect to (w.r.t.) preferences is the key to incentive compatibility (see the equivalence between strategyproofness and strong monotonicity in Chapter 10).

Variable issues

The issue monotonicity property in axiomatic bargaining (Chapter 3) says that when the set of feasible outcomes expands, the welfare of no agent should decrease. A similar axiom applies to production economies (Chapter 7) and values of cooperative games (Chapter 5).

On the other hand, abstract choice functions (Chapter 11) are classified by means of independence axioms where the variable parameter is the issue. See Nash's version of the IIA (in Chapters 3 and 11).

Variable population

The prominent independence axiom is separability. A collective utility function is separable if it can compare two utility distributions restricted to a subgroup of agents independently of the rest of the utility distribution. Separability in various forms is also defined for inequality indices (Chapter 2), axiomatic bargaining solutions (Chapter 3), cooperative games (see the reduced-game properties in Chapter 5), and surplus-sharing problems (see the consistency axiom in Chapter 6). In each of these contexts, it drives a very powerful functional equation.

Several population monotonicity properties play an important role in voting (Chapter 9) and in axiomatic bargaining (Chapter 3).

Table I.1 gives the detail of the foregoing classification.

Overview

Two broad categories of models are considered: sharing divisible surplus (Parts I, II, and III) and collective choice of an indivisible public decision (Part IV).

Part I presents the *welfarist* theory of utilitarianism. The central postulate is that only the individual utility levels matter when comparing any two outcomes, and those levels are intercomparable across agents. The main concept is that of a social welfare ordering (or the almost equivalent concept of a collective utility function) aggregating individual utilities into a social preference. The two principal examples are the classical utilitarian collective utility (the sum of individual utilities) and the egalitarian collective utility (the minimal individual utility), which are contrasted in Chapter 1. The next step is to construct collective utility functions that compromise between these two, thereby generating a family of reasonable indices to measure inequality (Chapter 2). Finally, the model of axiomatic bargaining generalizes the welfarist approach by making the feasibility constraint an ingredient of the choice method itself (Chapter 3).

The main limitation of welfarism is that it deliberately ignores ethical considerations suggested by the very nature of the economic decisions at stake. One such consideration is the protection of cooperative opportunities open to individual and to coalitions of agents. The theory of *cooperative games,* to which Part II is devoted, extends the welfarist model by taking those opportunities into account.

The stand-alone test is a general equity principle for cost sharing, translated in Chapter 4 as the *core* property. It prevents a coalition from getting a surplus share below its own cooperative opportunities. Although in most of Part II we make the simplifying assumption that money is available to transfer utility across agents, the search for a value solution (a deterministic surplus sharing defined for all cooperative games) is anything but simple. In Chapter 5 we contrast the two main solutions, one of them picking a central point of the core (nucleolus) and the other assigning to an agent the average of his marginal contribution to various coalitions (Shapley value).

The economic applications of cooperative games are very diverse. In Part III we discuss two especially important ones in the more general perspective of public decision mechanisms. These are the pricing of a regulated monopoly and the provision and cost sharing of a public good.

We start with two deceptively simple binary decision problems in Chapter 6: the cost sharing of an indivisible public good and the surplus sharing of an indivisible cooperative venture. Guided by the core property, we find no less than five reasonable solutions for the cost-sharing problem only. In Chapter 7 we consider in full generality a one-input, one-output regulated monopoly, producing either a public or a private good. We find the traditional marginal pricing methods challenged by two simple welfare egalitarian solutions.

In Chapter 8 we discuss the incentive properties of public good mechanisms. In general, a mechanism is called incentive compatible if its outcome is robust against strategic manipulations of selfish agents. The easiest manipulation consists of misreporting one's preference. A mechanism is strategyproof if such misreport does not occur. The pivotal mechanism was invented in the early seventies as an example of strategyproof mechanism. We discuss its incentive and axiomatic properties and compare it with other strategyproof mechanisms. We also look at the incentive properties of some familiar first-best mechanisms.

Part IV studies the *voting* problem: A pure public decision must be selected from the conflicting opinions of a given set of agents. The key difference with all earlier models is the absence of some *numéraire,* a transferable good allowing compensation for those agents who dislike the chosen decision at the expense of those who like it. In voting, we typically have finitely many outcomes and purely ordinal preferences only. In spite of this, the axioms for voting rules are fairly similar to those used in earlier parts.

The two-centuries-old debate of Condorcet versus Borda inspires the discussion of Chapter 9. We contrast voting rules based on majority comparisons with methods assigning scores to candidates from each voter's ballot. In Chapter 10 we discuss the two main incentive properties, strategyproofness (it turns out that no reasonable rule can be strategyproof if at least three candidates compete) and the core property. The latter leads to the minority principle, attentive to preserve some decision power for all coalitions however small. Finally, in Chapter 11 we survey the main results of Kenneth Arrow's aggregation-of-preferences approach. As in Part I in the cardinal context, one seeks to derive from the profile of individual preferences a collective ordering of all candidates. Despite many impossibility results limiting the scope for practical applications, this line of research provides useful insights into the logics of collective action.

We provide an average of nine exercises at the end of each chapter, many of them establishing some fine points alluded to in the course of the chapter; the exercises are also used to draw more links across chapters with the help of "continued" examples.

The complete bibliography is gathered at the end of the volume. The literature provides some good surveys to complement many of our chapters. We list them here for the benefit of the teaching-oriented reader.

Chapters 1 and 2: The classical books of Sen [1970] and Kolm [1972] can be complemented by the survey of d'Aspremont [1985]. On inequality indices, see Shorrocks [1985] and Foster [1985].

Chapter 3: The monograph by Roth [1979] is slightly outdated and should be supplemented by the recent survey of Kalaï [1985] and the forthcoming book by Thomson. The latter covers many quite recent results and all classical ones.

Chapters 4 and 5: The game theory textbooks typically do not cover the cost allocation applications; the best references seem to be the article by Young [1985b] for the transferable utility (TU) games and the monograph by Sharkey [1982] for the applications to the pricing problem; see also Ichiishi [1983] for a thorough exposition of nontransferable utility (NTU) games.

Chapters 7 and 8: A good elementary introduction is in the books of Feldman [1980] and Mueller [1979]; the monograph by Green and Laffont [1979] gives a more advanced account of the demand-revealing mechanisms (Chapter 8).

Chapter 9: The small book of Straffin [1980] is a remarkable introduction to voting rules (it also discusses the pivotal mechanism). See also the survey by Moulin [1985a]. The book by Mueller [1979] gives a detailed account of the applications of the voting model to public choice.

Chapter 10: A good introduction is in Feldman [1980]; for a systematical presentation of strategic voting, see the books of Peleg [1984a] and Moulin [1983].

Chapter 11: Expositions of the aggregation of preferences approach are easy to find in the literature; for instance, among the preceding texts cited see Sen [1970], Feldman [1980], Mueller [1979], Moulin [1983], and Peleg [1984a]. See also Suzumura [1983].

PART I

Welfarism

CHAPTER 1

Egalitarianism versus utilitarianism

Overview

Utilitarianism is a philosophical thesis two centuries old. It judges collective action on the basis of the utility levels enjoyed by the individual agents and of those levels only. This is literally justice by the ends rather than by the means. Welfarism is the name, coined by Amartya Sen, of the theoretical formulation of utilitarianism, especially useful in economic theory and other social sciences. Its axiomatic presentation, developed in the last three decades, is the subject of Chapters 2 and 3.

For the utilitarianist, social cooperation is good only inasmuch as it improves upon the welfare of individual members of society. The means of cooperation (social and legal institutions, such as private contracts and public firms) do not carry any ethical value; they are merely technical devices – some admittedly more efficient than others – to promote individual welfares. For instance, protecting certain rights – say, freedom of speech – is not a moral imperative; it should be enforced only if the agents derive enough utility from it.

This very dry social model rests entirely upon the concept of individual preferences determined by the agents *"libre-arbitre"* while deliberately ignoring all its mitigating factors (among them education and the shaping of individual opinion by the social environment, as well as kinship, friendship, or any specific interpersonal relation). Ever since Bentham, utilitarianists have been aware of these limitations. Yet, oversimplified as it is, the utilitarian model is easily applicable, and its "liberal" ideology has the force of simplicity. The philosophical debate on utilitarianism is still quite active (see, e.g., Sen and Williams [1982]).

Axiomatic welfarism idealizes a collective decision problem by attaching to each feasible alternative (to each possible decision) the vector $(u_1, \ldots, u_n)$ of individual utility levels, where u_i is agent i's utility. All relevant information is contained in the set of those feasible utility vectors.

11

Any information about specific decisions implementing various utility vectors is systematically erased.

Given the set of feasible utility vectors, the collective decision results from a mathematical and deterministic rule that pinpoints one vector as society's choice. This rule conveys the whole ethical policy of the society under consideration. No wonder that its definition raises fierce arguments: It is nothing less than an exhaustive solution of the social problem, a formula computing from the "arithmetics of pleasures and pains" the final outcome that society should enforce. In this chapter we discuss the two main rules advocated by utilitarianists, namely, egalitarianism (seeking to equalize individual utilities) and classical utilitarianism (maximizing the sum of individual utilities).

Egalitarianism is discussed first (Section 1.1). It derives from the oldest and most popular principle of justice: Equal agents must be treated equally. When utility is the only variable of control, application of the principle amounts to equalizing individual utilities. Yet, simple as this may appear, it may conflict with another basic postulate of collective decision making, known as the unanimity principle.

Whenever every concerned agent prefers decision a to decision b, the unanimity principle rejects decision b (we say that b is Pareto inferior to a). Unanimity is the single most important concept of welfare economics and the only axiom that will play a role in each and every chapter of this book. In the welfarist model, unanimity says that the chosen utility vector must be Pareto optimal (that is to say, it should not be Pareto inferior to any feasible utility vector).

The unanimity principle may conflict with the plain equalization of individual utilities. This somehow counterintuitive fact is known as the equality–efficiency dilemma. Its solution takes a more careful definition of the egalitarian program as the maximization of the leximin preordering (see Section 1.1 for details).

Egalitarianism is a very sturdy social glue. When all agents share equally the benefits of cooperation, there is no room for envy or frustration (except, of course, when some agents feel that their contribution to those benefits has been above average, but that is beyond the scope of the welfarist model; see the models of Chapters 6 and 7). The distributive consequences of egalitarianism, however, are sometimes hard to accept: For the sake of bringing one more unit of utility to a single agent, it may forfeit vast amounts of aggregate utility. Think of the distribution of medical care among patients who have subscribed to the same insurance. Say that the announced objective is to provide them with a level of health as equal as possible. This may mean that we must deny forever aspirin and antibiotics to all agents but one in order to pay for expensive equipment that will prolong the life of the last one for one more day. When the marginal value (in terms of added health) of a dollar spent on the more healthy agents is very much higher than that of a dollar spent on the unhealthy one, most people would have the reflex to spend it in the more "useful" way, thereby implicitly rejecting the egalitarian program.

The classical utilitarian program consists of maximizing the sum of the individual agents' utilities. It was supported by the fathers of the welfarist approach (Bentham and Stuart Mill) and is still the main alternative to egalitarianism. The key to classical utilitarianism is to regard utility increments from different agents (with different total utility levels) as equivalent and fully comparable. Individual agents are thought of as production units producing (individual) welfare, and the role of the social planner is simply to maximize social output (viz., joint utility) under the given feasibility constraints. For instance, in the medical care example, if expected lifetime is taken to measure health level, the classical utilitarian would spend the marginal dollar so as to maximize its return in expected added days of life. In turn, those born with a defect impairing severely their life expectation will be neglected, a quite unacceptable consequence as well.

The egalitarian and classical utilitarian programs are contrasted in Section 1.2 by means of examples. Those examples elaborate on the fundamental tension between two viewpoints. The egalitarian sees individual utility levels as the irreducible and final concern of society's welfare and forbids any compensation across agents; lots of extra utility for all agents but one are not worth the tiny disutility suffered by this last agent if he happens to be already the least happy of all. At the other extreme the classical utilitarian views individual utilities as merely the means of producing social welfare, never hesitating to sacrifice an individual agent for the sake of (aggregate) collective utility. The tension between these two ethics will be developed throughout Part I (see in particular the inequality measures in Section 2.6).

1.1   Egalitarianism

"Les hommes ont pour l'égalité une passion ardente, insatiable, eternelle, invincible" (The passion of men for equality is ardent, insatiable, eternal, invincible; de Tocqueville [1860]). Equally sharing the proceeds of cooperation is a simple and fundamental equity principle. In the welfarist model it amounts to equalizing individual utilities.

Consider next the unanimity principle: If all agents are better off with decision x than with decision y, then decision y should not be taken. The unanimity principle is also called the Pareto optimality principle because

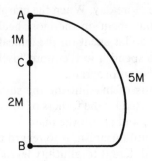

Figure 1.1.

the Italian economist W. Pareto first formulated it. A Pareto-optimal decision is a decision x such that, for any other decision z, if someone (one agent at least) prefers z to x, then someone else prefers x to z. A Pareto-optimal decision is also called, somewhat loosely, an efficient decision; we shall use indifferently both terminologies. The unanimity principle says that an efficient decision must be chosen; why, indeed, should we bother with a Pareto-inferior decision that will be unanimously rejected? The unanimity principle is the single most important concept of welfare economics. It is defined as soon as ordinal preferences are (whereas egalitarianism requires cardinal, interpersonally comparable utilities), and it conveys the convincing idea of welfare efficiency: Some welfare would be wasted if a Pareto-inferior decision were taken. Throughout the many examples discussed in this book, we will always look first for the Pareto-optimal outcomes.

That the two principles of unanimity and equality may not be compatible is a somewhat surprising fact known as the *equality–efficiency dilemma*.

Example 1.1. Location of a facility
Two towns of equal size choose the location of a joint facility (financed exogenously). Two roads connect town A to town B. The long road is 5 miles long and the short road only 3 miles. Let C be 1 mile away from A on the short road. The mountain road between C and B allows no feasible location. Thus, feasible locations are anywhere on the long road and between A and C on the short road (Figure 1.1). The disutility of a town is measured by the distance to the facility; for instance, with the facility at C we have $(u_1, u_2) = (-1, -2)$. In Figure 1.2 we have drawn the set of feasible disutility vectors. The segment $\beta\epsilon$ corresponds to locations on the long road no more than 1 mile away from B. Segment $\epsilon\delta$ is for locations

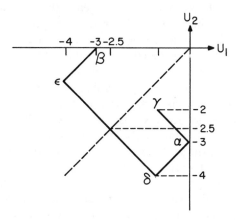

Figure 1.2.

on the long road at least 1 mile away from both towns. Segment $\delta\alpha$ is for locations on the long road no more than 1 mile away from A. Finally $\alpha\gamma$ is for locations between A and C on the short road.

The Pareto-optimal efficient locations are between A and C on the short road, or at B. Plain equality of (dis)utilities obtains only halfway between A and B on the long road. The corresponding disutilities are $(-2.5, -2.5)$ and are hence Pareto inferior to $(-1, -2)$ for location C. Whence the dilemma: We can pick a location either to be Pareto optimal or to equalize utilities but not both.

Note that the dilemma may arise even when the set of feasible utility vectors is convex, as exemplified in Exercise 1.4.

In Example 1.1 the way out of the dilemma is clear: The efficient location C is the most egalitarian within the set of efficient locations (i.e., the difference $|u_1 - u_2|$ is smallest at C among all efficient locations). Alternatively, at C the utility level of the least happy agent [i.e., the level $\min(u_1, u_2)$] is largest among all feasible utility vectors:

$$\min(-1, -2) = -1 \geq \min(u_1, u_2) \quad \text{for all feasible } (u_1, u_2)$$

The two approaches happen to select the same outcome C in our example, but they do not coincide in general. Indeed, suppose the feasible set contains only two vectors $u = (1, 2)$ and $u' = (4, 1.5)$. Both are efficient, u minimizes $|u_1 - u_2|$, whereas u' maximizes $\min\{u_1, u_2\}$. But u' is the most sensible outcome if we treat the two agents symmetrically (i.e., if we comply with the anonymity principle – see Section 2.1). Indeed, anonymity implies that $u = (1, 2)$ is socially indifferent to $u'' = (2, 1)$, and u'' is Pareto inferior to u'. Exercise 1.8 shows that with two agents, the difference between the two methods (maximize $\min\{u_1, u_2\}$ or minimize $|u_1 - u_2|$ among efficient vectors) arises only with nonconvex feasible sets; but with three agents or more, it is easy to construct a convex feasible set where the two programs – (a) maximize $\min(u_i)$ among all feasible utility vectors and (b) minimize $\max|u_i - u_j|$ among all *efficient* utility vectors – yield radically different solutions [see Exercise 1.8, question (c)].

The name of the philosopher John Rawls is attached to the collective utility function $W_e(u_1, \ldots, u_n) = \min_{1 \le i \le n}\{u_i\}$ and the corresponding program of maximizing W_e over the set of feasible utility vectors. This is tantamount to making the least happy agent as happy as possible and is also called the maximin utility program. Note that in his influential book, Rawls [1971] calls for maximin over primary goods rather than maximin over utility, but the difference is beyond the scope of this introduction. The point is that by taking the utility level of the least happy agent for the index of collective utility, we carry out the egalitarian program without contradicting the unanimity principle. Indeed, a decision maximizing W_e over the feasible set is Pareto optimal but only in a weak sense (see Lemma 1.1). Moreover, if a Pareto-optimal decision exists where every agent enjoys the same utility (viz., there is no equality–efficiency dilemma), this decision is uniquely selected by W_e as well. A formal statement of these properties is given in Lemma 1.1.

The correct formulation of the egalitarian principle goes one step beyond the egalitarian utility W_e. The function W_e focuses on the utility level of the least happy agent only. Once this level is maximized, there may be further redistributive opportunities among the remaining agents to which we can again apply egalitarian standards. Here is an example.

Example 1.2. Location of a facility on a loop
The joint facility is used by five towns located at A, B, C, D, and E, respectively, and the road network is the loop shown in Figure 1.3. Disutility is again measured by distance from the facility, and all locations are feasible. The maximin utility program has two solutions, namely x (1 mile away from A on AE) and y (halfway between C and D). Indeed, the corresponding vectors of disutilities are

$$u(x) = (-1, -6, -6, -4, -3) \quad \text{so} \quad W_e(x) = -6$$
$$u(y) = (-6, -6, -1, -1, -2) \quad \text{so} \quad W_e(y) = -6$$

One checks easily that every other location z has $W_e(z) < -6$. Exercise 1.2 gives the general method for solving the maximin utility program on a loop.

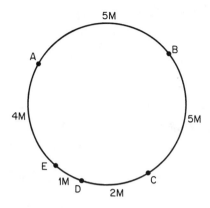

Figure 1.3.

Now consider the choice between x and y with an egalitarian eye: In both we have two towns with disutility -6; beyond this, the least happy in x (town D) has -4, whereas the least happy in y (town E) has -2. We conclude for y against x. Note that y is not Pareto superior to x, but after reordering the utility levels increasingly, it is

$$y^* = (-6, -6, -2, -1, -1) \text{ Pareto dominates } x^* = (-6, -6, -4, -3, -1)$$

The leximin social welfare ordering is a complete ordering of the utility vectors in E^n (we denote by E the set of real numbers). It refines the egalitarian collective utility function W_e whenever the latter has several feasible utility vectors tied. We use the following notation to define it: Given two utility vectors u, v in E^n, denote by u^*, v^* the vectors obtained by rearranging the coordinates of u, v, respectively, in increasing order. For instance, if $u = (5, 3, 2, 4, 3)$, then $u^* = (2, 3, 3, 4, 5)$.

Definition 1.1. *For the **leximin ordering**, we say that u and v are indifferent if $u^* = v^*$; we say that u is preferred to v if there exists an integer k, $k = 0, 1, \ldots, n-1$, such that*

$$u_i^* = v_i^* \text{ for } i = 1, \ldots, k \quad u_{k+1}^* > v_{k+1}^*$$

In particular, if $W_e(u) > W_e(v)$ (namely $u_1^* > v_1^*$), then u is leximin preferred to v.

The leximin ordering works by comparing first the utilities of the "poorest" agent in both distributions and, in case they coincide, by comparing those of the "next poorest" agents, and so on. Its properties are better than those of the egalitarian collective utility W_e as the following result shows.

For any two vectors u, v in E^n, denote

$$u \geq v \quad \text{if } u_i \geq v_i \quad \text{for all } i = 1, \ldots, n$$
$$u > v \quad \text{if } u \geq v \text{ and } u \neq v$$
$$u \gg v \quad \text{if } u_i > v_i \quad \text{for all } i = 1, \ldots, n$$

In Lemma 1.1, we denote by S the given set of feasible utility vectors. It is a closed subset of E^n and is bounded above (there exists $\bar{x}$ such that $\bar{x} \geq u$ for all $u \in S$). Say that a vector $u \in S$ is Pareto optimal in S if, for all $v \in E^n$,

$$v > u \Rightarrow v \notin S$$

Say that u is weakly Pareto optimal in S if, for all v,

$$v \gg u \Rightarrow v \notin S$$

Lemma 1.1. (a) *Consider the egalitarian collective utility function* $W_e(u) = \min\{u_i\}_{1 \leq i \leq n}$. *Denote by S_0 the set of solutions to the program* $\max W_e(u)_{u \in S}$. *Then S_0 is nonempty and any element of S_0 is weakly Pareto optimal in S. Moreover, the set S_0 contains at least one Pareto optimum of S.*

Suppose finally that S contains a Pareto-optimal vector u^0 (a weakly Pareto-optimal vector u_0) such that $u_i^0 = u_j^0$ for all $i, j = 1, \ldots, n$ [$(u_0)_i = (u_0)_j$ for all i, j]. Then $S_0 = \{u^0\}$ (S_0 contains u_0).

(b) *Consider the leximin social welfare ordering (Definition 1.1) and denote by S_o the set of vectors maximizing it on S. Then S_o is nonempty and every element of S_o is Pareto optimal in S. Next if u, v are both in S_o, then $u^* = v^*$ and hence S_o is finite. Moreover, if S is convex, S contains a single element.*

Proof: Statement (a). For every real number t denote $A_t = \{u \in E^n / u_i \geq t$ for all $i = 1, \ldots, n\}$. Maximizing the function W_e on S amounts to finding the highest t such that $A_t \cap S$ is nonempty. Note that $A_t \cap S$ is compact whenever it is nonempty (since A_t and S are both closed, A_t is bounded from below and S is bounded from above). Thus, there exists a largest value t^* such that $A_{t^*} \cap S$ is nonempty (by a standard limit argument using compactness) and is precisely the set S_0 of statement (a).

Suppose v, u are two elements of S and $v \gg u$. Then $W_e(v) > W_e(u)$, and therefore every element of S_0 is weakly Pareto optimal. Observe next that S_0 contains the set S_o of elements maximizing the leximin preordering on S; thus S_0 contains some Pareto-optimal utility vector.

Suppose that S contains the vector u^0, $u_i^0 = t$ for all i, and u^0 is Pareto optimal. Then for every distinct element u of S, there is a coordinate i such that $u_i < u_i^0 = t$. Therefore, $W_e(u) \leq u_i < t = W_e(u^0)$, and we conclude $S_0 = \{u^0\}$. If u^0 is only weakly Pareto optimal, there does not exist another vector u in S such that

$$\text{for all } i, \quad u_i > u_i^0 = t \Leftrightarrow W_e(u) > W_e(u^0) = t$$

Hence, u_0 belongs to S_0.

Statement (b). If two vectors u, v are such that $W_e(u) > W_e(v)$, then $u_1^* > v_1^*$, so u is preferred to v by the leximin ordering. Thus, S_o is a subset of S_0. Within S_0, all vectors u^* have the same coordinate u_1^*. As S_0 is closed and bounded above, we can pick its subset S_{00} where u_2^* is maximized, then the subset S_{000} of S_{00} where u_3^* is maximized, and so on. After repeating this operation n times, we end up with the desired set S_o. By construction, any two elements u, v of S_o are such that $u^* = v^*$. Note that for any two vectors u, v, if $u > v$ then $u^* > v^*$ as well, so that S_o contains only Pareto-optimal elements.

It remains to show that S_o is a singleton if S is convex. Indeed, pick two distinct vectors u, v such that $u^* = v^*$. It is enough to prove that $w = \frac{1}{2}(u+v)$ is leximin superior to both u and v. For all i, we have

$$u_i \geq u_1^*, v_i \geq v_1^* \Rightarrow w_i \geq u_1^* = v_1^*$$

Hence, $w_1^* \geq u_1^* = v_1^*$. If the latter inequality is strict, our statement is proven. Suppose now that $w_1^* = u_1^* = v_1^*$. Let i be a coordinate such that $w_1^* = w_i$. Then $u_i = v_i = u_1^*$ as well. For any $j \neq i$ we have then

$$u_j \geq u_2^*, v_j \geq v_2^* \Rightarrow w_j \geq u_2^* = v_2^*$$

Hence, $w_2^* \geq u_2^* = v_2^*$. If this inequality is strict, we are through; otherwise, there is a coordinate j such that $j \neq i$ and $u_j = v_j = w_2^*$. Repeating this argument we must find an index k such that $w_k^* > u_k^* = v_k^*$; otherwise, $u = v$, a contradiction.   Q.E.D.

1.2   Classical utilitarianism

Cooperation is a fragile enterprise. It is vulnerable in at least two ways. First every agent must recognize that he is fairly treated, namely, he receives his fair share of the cooperative surplus. This guarantees the consensus of the cooperating agent. If an agent or subgroup agent does not accept the division rule, the consensus will eventually break down. We may call internal stability the consequence of a lasting consensus. Most models analyzed in this book pertain to the means of achieving internal stability.

A second threat against the stability of cooperation is low returns. If the surplus produced above and beyond the noncooperative state of the world is too small, nobody will find it worthwhile to cooperate (why tie your hands in a cooperative venture, when you would be almost as well off without giving away your independence?). If the returns from cooperation are even negative, then cooperation will, a fortiori, fall apart. We can call external stability the consequence of sustained high returns of cooperation.

Clearly, egalitarianism brings internal stability: Who can feel exploited when the surplus is equally shared among equal agents? Yet it does not pay any attention to external stability; for the sake of equalizing surplus shares, the egalitarianist is ever ready to compress everyone's share to a point where cooperative surplus winds down to almost nothing. Classical utilitarianism goes in the opposite direction. It maximizes aggregate returns from cooperation (measured in joint utility), thereby guaranteeing external stability, but it ignores internal stability altogether, as the examples that follow (especially Example 1.4) demonstrate.

Consider first the location of a joint facility. This time we have a linear city – say, the interval $[0, 1]$ – where the continuous density of population is $f(x)$, $0 \leq x \leq 1$. Thus, the total population is $\int_0^1 f(x)\,dx$. Assume that the disutility of an agent located at x is the distance from x to the facility. The egalitarian planner – using the collective utility W_e – unambiguously recommends to locate the facility at $\frac{1}{2}$ (assuming that the density of the population is positive at both ends of town). This guarantees maximal disutility $\frac{1}{2}$ to everyone. The utilitarian planner, on the other hand, chooses a location a solving the program:

$$\min_{0 \leq a \leq 1} \int_0^1 |x - a| f(x)\,dx$$

The solution of this program is at the median a^* of f, where half of the population is to the left of a^* and half to its right:

$$\int_0^{a^*} f(x)\,dx = \int_{a^*}^1 f(x)\,dx = \frac{1}{2}\int_0^1 f(x)\,dx$$

To show this, compute

$$\left[\int_0^1 |x - a| f(x) = \int_0^a (a - x) \cdot f(x) + \int_a^1 (x - a) \cdot f(x) \right.$$

$$\left. = 2a \int_0^a f(x) - a - 2\int_0^a x \cdot f(x) + \int_0^1 x \cdot f(x) \right]$$

and check that the derivative of this quantity is zero at a^*, positive before a^*, and negative after a^*.

In this example, the egalitarian solution is quite independent of the population density, provided that some agents live at each end point. The utilitarian solution, on the contrary, depends heavily upon this density: If the density shifts to the left, so does its median. Which solution is more appealing clearly depends upon the context. The utilitarian choice, minimizing overall transportation costs, is quite convincing if the facility is a theater. If 90 percent of the population is concentrated on $[\frac{3}{4}, 1]$, then the agents on $[0, \frac{1}{4}]$ end up with high transportation costs, but this is a fair price to pay for the sake of aggregated welfare maximization. On the other hand, if the facility is a paramedic emergency unit, the egalitarian location at $\frac{1}{2}$ has more appeal because it minimizes the highest risk.

The (classical) *utilitarian collective utility function* will be denoted W_*:

$$W_*(u) = \sum_{i=1}^{n} u_i$$

The utilitarian program consists of maximizing W_* over the feasible utility vectors. This respects the unanimity principle: Any utility vector maximizing W_* within the feasible set must be Pareto optimal. [Exercise: Why?]

This program expresses the mechanical solidarity of the agents. Each agent produces some utility; if agent 1 is a more efficient process for transforming resources into utility than agent 2, then, and only then, will agent 1 end up with more utility than agent 2. In this sense, utilitarianism is justice according to merits, as egalitarianism is justice according to needs. Our next example stresses this interpretation.

Example 1.3. Sharing a homogeneous cake (Sen [1977])
One unit of a divisible, homogeneous cake must be divided between two brothers. Brother 1 is twice as hungry as brother 2; from any piece of cake x, he derives twice as much utility, $u_1(x) = 2u_2(x)$. Assume that u_1, u_2 are both increasing, concave, and differentiable.

The utilitarian program

$$\max_{0 \le x \le 1} \{u_1(x) + u_2(1-x)\}$$

is a concave program. Its solution is found by solving the first-order conditions:

$$u_1'(x^*) = u_2'(1-x^*)$$

As $u_1 = 2u_2$ and u_1' is nonincreasing in x, we get

$$u_1'(x^*) = \tfrac{1}{2}u_1'(1-x^*) \Rightarrow u_1'(x^*) < u_1'(1-x^*) \Rightarrow x^* > \tfrac{1}{2}$$

Thus, classical utilitarianism gives a bigger piece of cake to the hungry brother, who is more productive of social welfare. By contrast, the egalitarian program will compensate brother 2 for his lack of appetite by giving him a bigger piece than to brother 1. Indeed, there is no equality-efficiency dilemma in this problem, so the egalitarian distribution solves

$$u_1(\bar{x}) = u_2(1-\bar{x}) \Rightarrow u_1(\bar{x}) = \tfrac{1}{2}u_1(1-\bar{x}) \Rightarrow u_1(\bar{x}) < u_1(1-\bar{x}) \Rightarrow \bar{x} < \tfrac{1}{2}$$

The egalitarian program may have extreme consequences, as in the location problem described previously. If a single agent settles at location 3, the egalitarian location shifts from $\tfrac{1}{2}$ to $\tfrac{3}{2}$, thereby increasing transportation costs for all agents but one. Symmetrically, the utilitarian program may yield strikingly inequitable outcomes.

Example 1.4. Where productivity is penalized (Mirrlees [1974])
Two agents transform labor into corn by a constant-returns-to-scale (CRS) technology. Agent 2 is twice as productive as agent 1; one hour of labor by agent 2 (respectively agent 1) yields 2 bushels of corn (respectively 1 bushel). Initial endowments are 10 hours of labor for each agent and no corn. Their utility functions coincide (x = hours of labor spent; y = bushels of corn earned):

$$u(x,y) = y^{1/3}(10-x)^{1/3}$$

The utilitarian program suggests a precise outcome for this economy:

$$\max\{y_1^{1/3}(10-x_1)^{1/3} + y_2^{1/3}(10-x_2)^{1/3}\}$$

where x_i, y_i are all nonnegative, and $y_1 + y_2 = x_1 + 2x_2$. Because this is a concave program, we simply solve the system of first-order conditions:

$$\frac{1}{3}\frac{y_1^{1/3}}{(10-x_1)^{2/3}} = \frac{1}{3}\frac{(10-x_1)^{1/3}}{y_1^{2/3}}$$

$$= \frac{1}{3}\frac{y_2^{1/3}}{2(10-x_2)^{2/3}} = \frac{1}{3}\frac{(10-x_2)^{1/3}}{y_2^{2/3}} \tag{1}$$

This implies that $y_1 = 10 - x_1$ and $y_2 = 2(10 - x_2)$; by plugging those back into (1) we obtain

$$(10-x_1) = 4(10-x_2); \qquad y_1 = 2y_2$$

Thus, the more productive agent 2 ends up with four times less leisure and half less corn than agent 1! In this example the utilitarian outcome is quite unfair *and* unrealistic since the productive agent will no doubt conceal his talents; see Mirrlees [1974]. Exercise 1.7 generalizes this example. See also Chapter 7, where other outcomes are proposed.

The key difference between egalitarianism and (classical) utilitarianism is the comparability and interchangeability of utility increments across agents. Under these premises, utilitarianism is viable and meaningful. Indeed, certain social situations urge us to think of our fellow agents in this way.

Mirrlees tells the story of two cars burning after an accident. The first car has four passengers, and the second car has only one; all five are unconscious. The only witness has time to rescue one car only. By choosing to rescue the first car, as most of us would choose, one is willy-nilly utilitarian: The goal is to maximize the expected number of survivors among the five endangered persons. An egalitarian rescuer, on the contrary, would choose which car to help by tossing a fair coin, thereby giving everyone a 50 percent chance of surviving.

Other situations strongly suggest an egalitarian approach, as when we allocate primary goods – such as basic health care, education, or freedom of speech – for which individual utilities are normally viewed as noninterchangeable. To support the egalitarian ethics, one must view utility levels as final, forbidding ulterior compensations among agents.

The debate between egalitarianism and (classical) utilitarianism is old. The most recent contributions by social philosophers are Rawls [1971], supporting egalitarianism, and Harsanyi [1955, 1975], arguing for utilitarianism. Both authors invent a metawelfarist story. An agent is about to join a given society but does not know which seat will be his. Behind this veil of ignorance his own preferences about society's choice method reflect his ethical opinion; not knowing whether he ends up rich or poor, his choice can hardly be a selfish one. Behind the veil, the Rawlsian agent has risk-averse preferences; he fears to end up poorest and therefore strives for the egalitarian utility function. The Harsanyian agent, on the other hand, has Bayesian preferences based on expected utility maximization, whence his choice of the utilitarian collective utility.

These two stories are metaprobabilistic: An agent views himself behind the veil, waiting for the lottery of life to assign his seat in the social body. In this pristine state, he exhibits precise preferences about a random event (his social position), of which the probability distribution is, to say the least, a fragile intellectual construction.

Within a welfarist society, namely, one where the ultimate welfare level of each agent is well defined and observable, only the egalitarian program (maximin utility, or leximin ordering if necessary) guarantees the consensus of individualistic agents. Indeed, the agent with the lowest welfare, say, i, knows that the existing inequalities have emerged for his own sake. Under less inequality, agent i would enjoy a lower welfare, or some other agent would be lower than agent i was originally. Of course, the privileged

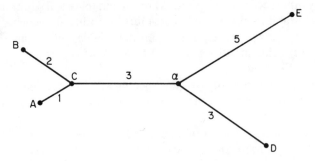

Figure 1.4.

agents (those with the highest welfare) have less relative advantage than under another program (say, classical utilitarianism). But those privileges, however small, are guaranteed to them by the consensus of even the least favored. By contrast, under the utilitarian program, the agents with the lowest welfare have no compelling reason to agree with the chosen decision. We expect them, at least, to *manipulate* (in the senses given to this word in Part III) the decision mechanism. Experimental evidence strongly supports egalitarianism when utilities are perceived as representing objective needs; see Yaari and Bar-Hillel [1984], where utilities are measured by the amount of certain vitamins metabolized by the agents. When utilities represent different tastes, the experimental outcome is much less easy to read.

EXERCISES

1.1 Location of a facility on a tree. Suppose there are n towns located on the vertices of a tree (a tree is a connected graph with no cycle). Moreover, every edge (connecting two adjacent vertices) has a given length. Disutility of a town for a location is taken to be the distance. The problem is to locate a facility somewhere on the tree. Here is an example. In Figure 1.4 we have a tree with six vertices; five of them are occupied by a town, namely, A, B, C, D, and E (vertex α is not a town). Numbers are for the distances in miles.

(a) Consider the maximin utility program. In our example, show that its unique solution is at location α. For an arbitrary tree show that all solutions to the maximin program are found by taking the midpoint(s) of the longest path(s) joining two towns.

(b) Consider the (classical) utilitarian program. In our example, show that its solution is at C. In a general tree, show that all solutions to the utilitarian program are the *Condorcet winners*.

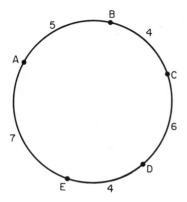

Figure 1.5.

A location x is a Condorcet winner if on every branch starting at x (but excluding location x) there are no more than one-half of the towns. See Section 10.1 for a general definition of Condorcet winners. For instance, with two towns, the whole interval joining them, including the two towns, is the set of Condorcet winners. With any odd number of towns, there is a unique Condorcet winner. See also Exercise 11.4.

1.2 **Location of a facility on a loop.** The road network is a circle along which our towns are located. An example with five towns is given in Figure 1.5.

(a) Consider the egalitarian (maximin utility) program. In our example, show that its solution is between C and D, 0.5 mile away from C (5.5 miles away from D). For an arbitrary loop, find the longest interval(s) and pick the location(s) diametrically symmetrical to its (their) middle point. Show that this is (these are) the egalitarian location(s).

(b) Consider the (classical) utilitarian program. Show that in our example its solution is at C. Next consider an arbitrary loop with an odd number n of towns. Show that a utilitarian solution is at the location x^* of a town.

Denote by $P(x)$ the set of locations y, $y \neq x$, such that the shortest path from x to y is unique and positive (trigonometric orientation). Denote by $N(x)$ the set of those y, $y \neq x$, such that the shortest path from y to x is unique and negative. Show that x^* is a location such that $P(x^*)$ and $N(x^*)$ each contain less than $n/2$ towns. Actually, x^* can again be interpreted as a Condorcet winner (see Exercise 11.4).

Generalize to an arbitrary loop with an even number of towns.

1.3 **An equality–efficiency dilemma.** Three towns (A_1, A_2, A_3) are located in the plane E^2. Every location in E^2 is feasible. The disutility of town A_i for a facility located at x is the Euclidean distance from A_i to x. Show that the Pareto-optimal locations are those within the triangle whose vertices are the three towns. Show that we have an equality–efficiency dilemma if and only if the triangle is obtuse angled. In this case find the optimum of the egalitarian collective utility function.

1.4   One more equality–efficiency dilemma. Two agents can produce the public good at any level x, $x \geq 0$, for a cost $c(x) = 1 + x$. They *must* share equally the variable cost x, but the fixed cost 1 can be split in two arbitrary nonnegative shares:

$$1 = c_1 + c_2 \quad c_1 \geq 0, \ c_2 \geq 0$$

When x units of public goods are produced and their cost is shared as $c_i + (x/2)$ for agent i, $i = 1, 2$, the final utilities are

$$u_1 = 3\sqrt{x} - (c_1 + \tfrac{1}{2}x), \qquad u_2 = \sqrt{x} - (c_2 + \tfrac{1}{2}x)$$

Compute the set of feasible utility vectors (using the two parameters $x \geq 0$ and c_1, $0 \leq c_1 \leq 1$) and check that it is convex. Show that we have an equality–efficiency dilemma. Compute the cost sharing suggested by the egalitarian utility function (maximin utility program).

1.5   Sharing divisible goods. This is an application of the egalitarian collective utility function. It illustrates the role of the utility scale and zero of utility in an egalitarian method.

   Two agents jointly receive a gift made of 3 pounds of cookies and 1 liter of wine to be divided between the two of them. Both agents have linear preferences (indifference curves are straight and parallel), and their marginal rates of substitution differ: Agent 1 is indifferent between 1 pound of cookies and 1 liter of wine, and agent 2 is indifferent between 4 pounds of cookies and 1 liter of wine.

(a)   Take the cookies as *numéraire* and the zero of utility where the agents receive nothing. This yields the cardinal utilities

$$u_1 = c_1 + w_1, \qquad u_2 = c_2 + 4w_2$$

where c_i is agent i's share of cookies, and w_i is that of wine. Show that the efficient and egalitarian allocation of the goods is

$$c_1 = 3, \quad c_2 = 0, \quad w_1 = 0.2, \quad w_2 = 0.8$$

(b)   On the market, 1 pound of cookies is worth a half liter of wine. Take the vector $(2,1)$ as *numéraire* and show that the efficient and egalitarian allocation of the goods is

$$c_1 = 2.33, \quad c_2 = 0.67, \quad w_1 = 0, \quad w_2 = 1$$

(c)   Change the zero of utilities to the physically egalitarian allocation of the goods (viz., the Pareto-inferior allocation $c_i = 1.5$, $w_i = 0.5$). This amounts to taking

$$\tilde{u}_1 = c_1 - (1.5) + w_1 - (0.5), \qquad \tilde{u}_2 = c_2 - (1.5) + 4(w_2 - (0.5))$$

Show that the egalitarian and efficient allocation is then $c_1 = 2.75$, $w_1 = 0$ with the cookies as *numéraire* and $c_1 = 2.5$, $w_1 = 0$ with the market value as *numéraire*.

1.6 Cost sharing of a public project. This is an application of the leximin ordering.

A public project costs c, $c > 0$, and its consumption is worth b_i, $b_i \geq 0$, to agent i, $i = 1, 2, \ldots, n$. We suppose that undertaking the project is the efficient decision $\sum_{i=1}^{n} b_i > c$. We seek to share its cost among the n agents in an egalitarian way. Suppose first that any cost sharing $(x_1, \ldots, x_n)$ such that $\sum_{i=1}^{n} x_i = c$ is feasible regardless of the signs of x_i. To a cost sharing of c, associate the final utility $u_i = b_i - x_i$ for agent i. The following cost sharing equalizes the agents' utilities:

$$x_i = b_i - \frac{1}{n} \left(\sum_{j=1}^{n} b_j - c \right) \tag{2}$$

(a) Suppose that no agent can be subsidized, that is, his cost share cannot be negative: $x_i \geq 0$. Then consider the maximin utility program

$$\max_{x_1, \ldots, x_n} \{ \min_{i=1, \ldots, n} \{ b_i - x_i \} \} \tag{3}$$

where $(x_1, \ldots, x_n)$ are all nonnegative and $\sum_{i=1}^{n} x_i = c$. Show that its optimal solution is (2) if

$$\min_{j=1, \ldots, n} \{ b_j \} \geq \frac{1}{n} \left(\sum_{j=1}^{n} b_j - c \right) \tag{4}$$

If (4) fails, show that a cost sharing $(x_1, \ldots, x_n)$ is a solution of (3) if and only if

$$0 \leq x_i \leq b_i - \min_j \{ b_j \} \quad \text{for all } i \text{ and } \sum_{i=1}^{n} x_i = c$$

For instance, take five agents with $b_1 = 5$, $b_2 = 10$, $b_3 = 20$, $b_4 = 22$, $b_5 = 27$, and $c = 30$. The maximin utility program suggests any cost sharing:

$$x_1 = 0, \quad 0 \leq x_2 \leq 5, \quad 0 \leq x_3 \leq 15, \quad 0 \leq x_4 \leq 17, \quad 0 \leq x_5 \leq 22,$$

and $\sum_{i=2}^{5} x_i = 30$

This calls for the leximin ordering to break ties.

(b) Consider the program "leximin ordering" applied to the vectors $(b_1 - x_1, \ldots, b_n - x_n)$. Show that it recommends a unique cost sharing, where as many agents as possible, starting with those who like the project least, pay nothing, whereas those who pay end up with the same net utility, this net utility being no smaller than that of the "free riders."

Formally, order the agents in such a way that $b_1 \leq b_2 \leq \cdots \leq b_n$. The leximin optimum is

$$x_i = \begin{cases} 0 & \text{for } i = 1, \ldots, k, \\ b_i - \dfrac{1}{n-k} \left(\sum_{j \geq k+1} b_j - c \right) & \text{for } i = k+1, \ldots, n \end{cases} \tag{5}$$

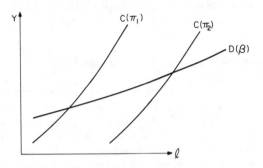

Figure 1.6.

where k is the unique solution of

$$1 \le k \le n-1, \qquad b_k \le \frac{1}{n-k}\left(\sum_{j \ge k+1} b_j - c\right) < b_{k+1} \tag{6}$$

In the numerical example of question (a), we find

$$x_1 = x_2 = 0, \quad x_3 = 7, \quad x_4 = 9, \quad x_5 = 14$$

In Chapter 6 (Lemma 6.1) we give another expression for the cost sharing (5) and (6).

1.7 Generalization of Example 1.4 (Mirrlees [1974]). The two agents have productivities π_1 and π_2, respectively, to transform labor into corn. We assume $\pi_1 > \pi_2$. They have the same utility function $u(x, y)$ over leisure and corn. We suppose u is concave and twice differentiable. Moreover, $\partial^2 u / \partial x\, \partial y > 0$. The utilitarian program is

$$\max u(\omega_1 - x_1, y_1) + u(\omega_2 - x_2, y_2)$$

under constraints $y_1 + y_2 = \pi_1 x_1 + \pi_2 x_2$, $y_i, x_i \ge 0$. Here, as in Example 1.4, x_i denotes agent i's labor, and ω_i is initial endowment of leisure.

(a) Show that the curves $C(\alpha)\colon \partial u / \partial x / \partial u / \partial y (x, y) = \alpha$ are monotonically increasing (for any fixed α) and so are the curves $D(\beta)\colon \partial u / \partial y (x, y) = \beta$ (for any fixed β). Moreover, at any point (x, y) the slope $dy/d\ell$ of the current $D(\beta)$ is smaller than that of the current $C(\alpha)$. Finally, when α increases, the curve $C(\alpha)$ shifts upward (see Figure 1.6).

(b) Write the first-order optimality conditions of the utilitarian program as

$$(x_i, y_i) \in C(\pi_i) \quad \text{for } i = 1, 2$$

(x_1, y_1) and (x_2, y_2) belong to the same curve $D(\beta)$

Deduce from question (a) that in the utilitarian solution the more productive agent works harder and gets less corn.

1.8 The most egalitarian among efficient decisions. As in Lemma 1.1, we start with the set S of feasible utility vectors and assume that S is closed and bounded above in E^n. We denote by $P(S)$ the (nonempty) set of Pareto optima of S. Consider the program

$$\min_{u \in P(S)} \left\{ \max_{1 \le i,j \le n} |u_i - u_j| \right\} \tag{7}$$

(a) If there is a vector u Pareto optimal in S such that $u_i = u_j$ for all i, j, then it is the unique solution of (7). However, even for $n = 2$, the program (7) may have no optimal solution, as the following example in E^2 shows:

$$(u_1, u_2) \in S \Leftrightarrow u_1 \ge 0, \ u_2 \ge 0, \ (\{u_1 + u_2 \le 2\} \text{ and/or } \{u_2 \le 1, u_1 + u_2 \le 3\})$$

(b) If S is convex and $n = 2$, program (7) has a unique solution, and this solution maximizes the leximin social welfare ordering (Definition 1.1).

(c) If $n \ge 3$, the solution to program (7) can be quite different from those of the maximin utility program. An example is the interval

$$S = [(0, 0, 1), (2, \tfrac{1}{2}, \tfrac{1}{2})]$$

Here program (7) is solved at $(\tfrac{4}{5}, \tfrac{1}{5}, \tfrac{4}{5})$, whereas the maximin utility program is solved at $(2, \tfrac{1}{2}, \tfrac{1}{2})$.

CHAPTER 2

Social welfare orderings

Overview

The egalitarian and classical utilitarian programs, in spite of all their differences, have one common functional feature. Both utilize a collective utility function (CUF) aggregating individual utilities into a single utility index representing the social welfare. Within the feasible utility set, they then select the socially *optimum* utility vector by maximizing the CUF. This function is the sum of individual utilities for classical utilitarianism and their minimum for egalitarianism (see Chapter 1).

The welfarist axioms considered in this chapter develop this anthropomorphic idea. Society's welfare is described by a collective utility index computed mechanically from individual utilities. Thus, collective choice follows the same rationale as individual choice: "Il faut que les méthodes d'une assemblée délibérante se rapprochent autant qu'il est possible de celles des individus qui la composent" (Condorcet [1785]; the methods of a deliberating assembly must be as close as possible to those of its individual members). In particular, any two vectors of individual utilities can be compared, and those comparisons are transitive.

The primary economic application of CUFs is to the measurement of inequality. Estimating the welfare consequences of the distribution of incomes (or of that of any variable related to individual welfare) is an important task of public economics. Doing this systematically means that we must be able to compare any two income distributions and tell which one yields the highest social welfare. In other words, we must choose a social welfare ordering (SWO). This choice will be guided by additional ethical postulates. The consequences of those postulates on the mathematical form of the SWO is the subject of this chapter.

The Pigou–Dalton principle is the basic postulate of inequality measurement. It says that a transfer of utility from agent i to agent j increases (or at least does not decrease) social welfare if agent i's utility is higher than agent j's before and after the transfer (of course, the difference in their utilities is smaller after the transfer). Both the egalitarian and the utilitarian CUFs satisfy the principle (the latter in the weak sense that it is indifferent to any redistribution of utility).

The SWOs used to derive actual inequality measurements achieve a compromise between the utilitarian and egalitarian ethics. To explain this, one has to analyze two fundamental axioms satisfied by both, the Pigou–Dalton principle (Section 2.5) and separability (Section 2.4). We give some intuition for these after reviewing the first three sections.

We formally define CUFs and SWOs in Section 2.1. A SWO is the ordinal counterpart of a CUF, just as a preference preordering is the ordinal analog of a cardinal utility function. A general representation theorem (Theorem 2.1) says that under very mild topological assumptions every SWO can be represented by some CUF. Thus, we can use both objects almost indifferently to represent social welfare.

Throughout Chapter 2 we assume that all SWOs (as well as all CUFs) meet two basic requirements, anonymity and respect of unanimity. The latter says that if the utility vector u is Pareto superior to v, society also prefers u to v. Thus, the optimal utility vector will be efficient. Anonymity, on the other hand, expresses equal treatment of the individual agents: Social welfare is unaffected if we exchange the utilities of any two agents. An anonymous SWO cannot discriminate between two agents on the basis of their names only. This is a very weak equity property. A fair amount of the theory of SWOs and CUFs can be generalized without the anonymity axiom. For instance, the utilitarian CUF $\sum_{i=1}^{n} u_i$ generalizes as the weighted sum $\sum_{i=1}^{n} \lambda_i u_i$, where the fixed parameters λ_i give different weights to different agents. Yet we choose for simplicity to present only the anonymous case, while providing references of more detailed articles where nonanonymous SWOs are also discussed.

The (classical) utilitarian CUF ($\sum_i u_i$) and the egalitarian CUF ($\min_i u_i$) play a focal role in the welfarist theory. In addition to their ethical appeal (discussed in Chapter 1), they are relatively easy to characterize by means of two particular independence properties. A CUF is independent of a given transformation of utilities if it compares in the same way two arbitrary vectors whether or not we apply this transformation to both vectors. Examples of such transformations include adding the same constant to all utilities (independence of the common zero; Definition 2.5) or multiplying all utilities by the same (positive) constant (independence of the common scale; Definition 2.5). For instance, think of utilities measured in money. If we use a SWO *not* independent of the common scale, then it *does* matter whether the unit of money is taken to be the U.S. dollar or the French franc. Or consider utilities representing temperatures. If we compare distributions of temperatures with a SWO independent of both the common scale and the common zero, then it does not matter whether those temperatures are all measured in Celsius degrees or (all) in Fahrenheit degrees.

Of course, the utilitarian and the egalitarian CUF are both independent of the common zero and of the common scale. To characterize the utilitarian CUF we need a much stronger independence property, namely, independence of the zero of each individual utility (Definition 2.1). This says that to compare two utility vectors u and v, all that matters is the vector $u - v$. The utilitarian CUF is essentially the only SWO satisfying this property (Theorem 2.2). If we consider instead independence of the scale of each individual utility, we characterize the celebrated CUF proposed by Nash that takes the product of individual utilities (while classical utilitarianism takes their sum). See Theorem 2.3.

The egalitarian (maximin) CUF is independent of the common utility pace. This means that we can transform individual utilities by means of any monotonic transformation (provided the same transformation is used for each utility) without affecting the social preferences. In other words, to compare two vectors u and v, the list of inequalities $u_i \geq v_j$ or $v_i \geq u_j$ contains all the necessary information (Definition 2.3). This property characterizes the family of rank dictatorships. The egalitarian CUF is the dictatorship of the last rank, since we maximize the utility of the agent ranked last; another member of the family is the dictatorship of the median, maximizing the utility of the agent whose welfare is ranked exactly halfway between first and last. See Theorem 2.4 for details.

In Section 2.4 we discuss the powerful separability axiom. Suppose we wish to compare two utility distributions u, v that differ only over a subset T of agents (in other words, all agents in $N \setminus T$ get the same utility in u and in v). With a separable SWO it is not necessary to know the utilities of the agents in $N \setminus T$ (as long as they are the same in u and in v) in order to compare u and v. Separability is a decentralization property. To judge the impact of a change in the utility distribution, we can restrict ourselves to the agents concerned by the change. The leximin and utilitarian SWO are both separable. By combining separability with independence of the common scale, we characterize the family of CUFs that take the sum of some fixed power of the individual utilities (Theorem 2.6). The utilitarian CUF corresponds, of course, to power 1; the leximin SWO obtains in the limit when the exponent of individual utilities goes to $-\infty$.

Section 2.5 is devoted to the Pigou–Dalton principle. We discuss several equivalent formulations of the principle. One of them uses the concept of Lorenz domination (Lemma 2.3), a weakening of Pareto domination. Within a given set of feasible utility vectors, the Lorenz optima consist of those Pareto optima where no Pigou–Dalton redistribution is feasible. Any inequality index (as defined in Section 2.6) is minimized within a given set of Pareto-optimal utility vectors at a Lorenz-optimal utility distribution. Section 2.6 presents the most popular inequality indices, the Gini index and the family of Atkinson indices. The latter are essentially characterized by the combination of the Pigou–Dalton principle and a weak version of the separability axiom (Theorem 2.8). It is beyond the scope of this book to survey the growing applications of inequality indices. The interested reader can consult the survey articles by Foster [1985] and Shorrocks [1985].

2.1 Social welfare orderings and collective utility functions

We shall denote by $N = \{1, 2, \ldots, n\}$ the "society," namely, the fixed set of participating agents, so that a distribution of utilities is a member $u = (u_1, \ldots, u_n)$ of E^N (E is the set of real numbers). A *social welfare ordering* (SWO) is a preordering R of E^N (a complete, reflexive, and transitive relation on E^N). We denote by P its strict component and by I its indifference relation:

$$u P v \quad \text{iff } \{u R v \text{ and no } v R u\}$$
$$u I v \quad \text{iff } \{u R v \text{ and } v R u\}$$

We always assume that a SWO satisfies two additional properties:

(a) *Anonymity* (symmetry across agents). If u is obtained from v by exchanging coordinates, u is indfferent to v: $u I v$.
(b) *Unanimity*. If $u, v \in E^N$ are such that $u_i \geq v_i$, all $i \in N$ (denoted $u \geq v$), then $u R v$. Moreover, if $u_i > v_i$, all $i \in N$ (denoted $u \gg v$), then u is strictly preferred to v: $u P v$.

The leximin ordering (Definition 1.1) is a SWO. We leave it to the reader to check that it satisfies anonymity and unanimity.

Notice that for the binary relation R to be a SWO, it is necessary that both its strict component P and its indifference relation I are transitive. For instance, consider the relation

$$u T v \Leftrightarrow_{\text{def}} \text{no} \{v_i > u_i \text{ for all } i \in N\}$$

It is *not* a SWO (yet it satisfies anonymity and unanimity) because its indifference relation is not transitive [$(1, 2)$ is indifferent to $(3, 1)$, $(3, 1)$ is indifferent to $(2, 3)$, yet $(1, 2)$ is not indifferent to $(2, 3)$]. Note that the strict component of T is just Pareto domination.

A *collective utility function* (CUF) is a real-valued function W defined on E^N that satisfies two properties:

(i)   *Anonymity.* W is symmetrical in its variables $u_1, ..., u_n$.
(ii) *Unanimity.* If $u, v \in E^N$ are such that $u \geq v$ ($u \gg v$), then $W(u) \geq W(v)$ [$W(u) > W(v)$].

Two examples are the egalitarian CUF, $W_e(u) = \min u_i$, and the utilitarian CUF, $W_*(u) = \sum_{i=1}^n u_i$.

To an arbitrary CUF W is associated a unique SWO defined as follows:

$$u R v \Leftrightarrow_{\text{def}} W(u) \geq W(v)$$

Then we say that W represents R. Of course, if W represents R, so do the CUFs $W+3$, $2W$, e^w, and in general $\sigma(W)$, where σ is any increasing function of a real variable.

Given a SWO R, it is very convenient to represent it by a CUF, just as it is to represent the preference preordering of an individual agent by a utility function. But not all SWOs can be represented by CUFs. The simplest is the leximin SWO (Definition 1.1).

Lemma 2.1.   *The leximin SWO is not representable by a CUF.*

Proof: Consider the case $n = 2$ and suppose that $W(u_1, u_2)$ is a CUF representing the leximin ordering. To any number x, $1 \leq x \leq 2$, attach a number $\epsilon_x = W(x, 4) - W(x, 3)$. Since $(x, 4)$ is leximin superior to $(x, 3)$, the number ϵ_x is positive. For any integer n, denote by $A(n)$ the set of those x in $[1, 2]$ such that $\epsilon_x \geq 1/n$. As the sets $A(n)$, $n = 1, 2, ...$, cover the interval $[1, 2]$, one of them is infinite. Thus, we can pick an integer n_0 such that

$$1, 2 \in A(n_0) \quad \text{and} \quad A(n_0) \text{ is infinite}$$

Now consider two elements x, y of $A(n_0)$ such that $y < x$. Since $(x, 3)$ is leximin superior to $(y, 4)$, we have

$$W(y, 4) < W(x, 3) \Rightarrow \frac{1}{n} \leq W(y, 4) - W(y, 3) < W(x, 3) - W(y, 3)$$

Thus, for any finite, increasing sequence $x_1 = 1 < x_2 < \cdots < x_{K-1} < x_K = 2$ in $A(n_0)$, we have

$$W(2, 3) - W(1, 3) = \sum_{k=2}^K (W(x_k, 3) - W(x_{k-1}, 3)) \geq \frac{K-1}{n}$$

Since K can be chosen arbitrarily large, the number $W(2, 3) - W(1, 3)$ is not finite; a contradiction.   Q.E.D.

The difficulty uncovered by Lemma 2.1 can be overcome in two ways. First, we can restrict attention to *continuous* SWOs (those whose upper and lower contour sets are all closed; see Section 2.2), whereby a classical theorem by Debreu [1960] guarantees that a continuous SWO is representable by a continuous CUF. By this restriction, however, we lose the important leximin SWO.

The second way is to content oneself with a weaker notion of representation of a SWO by a CUF. Say that a CUF W *weakly represents* the SWO R if we have

$$W(u) > W(v) \Rightarrow u P v \quad \text{for all } u, v \in E^N \tag{1}$$

In particular, property (1) implies

$$u R v \Rightarrow W(u) \geq W(v) \quad \text{and} \quad u I v \Rightarrow W(u) = W(v)$$

For instance, the egalitarian CUF W_e [$W_e(u) = \min\{u_i\}_{1 \leq i \leq n}$] weakly represents the leximin SWO. All usual SWOs (in particular, all those discussed in this book) are weakly represented by some *continuous* CUF. A very mild continuity assumption of the SWO is sufficient to guarantee this:

Theorem 2.1 (Roberts [1980b]). *Suppose the SWO R satisfies the following property.*

> *For all $u, v \in E^N$ such that $u P v$, there exist u', v' as close as we want to u, v, respectively, and such that $u' \gg u$, $v' \gg v$, and $u' P v'$. Similarly, there exist u'', v'' as close as we want to u, v, respectively, and such that $u'' \ll u$, $v'' \ll v$, and $u'' P v''$.* (2)

Then R can be weakly represented by a continuous CUF.

The proof of Theorem 2.1 is the subject of Exercise 2.9. In the next two sections we characterize the two fundamental CUFs (utilitarian and egalitarian) by means of independence properties.

2.2 Scale and zero independence

The utilitarian CUF is $W_*(u) = \sum_{i=1}^n u_i$. It is independent of the individual zero of utility. Think, for instance, of the location of a facility (Examples 1.1 and 1.2). The facility is a new post office that is going to replace the old post office located at x_0. The natural zero of the utility corresponds to the distance from a given town t_i to the initial position x_0. If we locate the new facility at x, the utility increment of town t_i is $d(t_i, x_0) - d(t_i, x)$. This is a better index of town i's welfare than $-d(t_i, x)$ because the actual decision is a switch from x_0 to x. Hence, the utility vector attached to a decision x is $u(x) = (d(t_i, x_0) - d(t_1, x), \ldots, d(t_n, x_0) - d(t_n, x))$ rather than $v(x) = (-d(t_1, x), \ldots, -d(t_n, x))$ as before. This recalibration of individual utilities changes the solution proposed by most SWOs, but it does *not* affect that proposed by the utilitarian CUF. Indeed, we have

$$W(u(x)) = \sum_{i=1}^{n} [d(t_i, x_0) - d(t_i, x)] = \left\{ \sum_{i=1}^{n} d(t_i, x_0) \right\} - \left\{ \sum_{i=1}^{n} d(t_i, x) \right\}$$
$$= -W(v(x_o)) + W(v(x))$$

The change of individual utility zeros simply adds a constant to the collective utility, whence the maximization of collective utility has the same solutions.

To take one more example, suppose that we compare several tax policies by looking at their after-tax income distributions $(r_1, ..., r_n)$. The taxed income r_i is only one component of an agent's welfare. At the very least, we must take into account some aggregate measure s_i of his nontaxable welfare parameters (fringe benefits, vacations, etc.) and write his global welfare as $u_i = r_i + s_i$. Of course, the nonincome component of welfare s_i is quite hard to measure or even to estimate. This does not matter if we use the utilitarian CUF, for comparing distributions of after-tax income $(r_1, ..., r_n)$ is equivalent to comparing distributions of global welfare $(u_1, ..., u_n)$ provided the distribution of nontaxable welfare components $(s_1, ..., s_n)$ remains fixed.

In short, the utilitarian CUF compares two utility distributions by means of the vector of absolute utility variations. This property is characteristic.

Definition 2.1.   *The SWO R is zero independent (ZI) if it satisfies one of the two equivalent properties:*

(i)   *For all $u, v, w \in E^N$: $u R v \Leftrightarrow (u + w) R (v + w)$.*
(ii) *For all $u, v \in E^N$: $u R v \Leftrightarrow (u - v) R 0$.*

In the following statement, by a *continuous* SWO we mean a SWO R such that for all $u \in E^n$ the upper contour at $u(\{v/v R u\})$ and the lower contour at $u(\{v/u R v\})$ are closed in E^n.

Theorem 2.2 (d'Aspremont and Gevers [1977]).   *The utilitarian CUF W_* is zero independent. Conversely, a zero-independent SWO is weakly represented by the utilitarian CUF. In particular, there is only one SWO zero independent and continuous: It is represented by the utilitarian CUF.*

Proof: Let R be a zero-independent SWO. First, it satisfies (2). Indeed, $u P v$ implies $(u + \epsilon e) P (v + \epsilon e)$ and $(u - \epsilon e) P (v - \epsilon e)$, where e is the vector $e = (1, ..., 1)$. Thus, we may apply Theorem 2.1 and weakly represent R by a continuous CUF W. Fix a vector w and define two open sets A, B:

$$A = \{u \in E^N / W(u) > W(w)\}, \qquad B = \{u \in E^N / W(u) < W(w)\}$$

We claim that A, B are both convex. Indeed, pick any two $u^1, u^2 \in A$ and define $u = \frac{1}{2}u^1 + \frac{1}{2}u^2$. Then check $W(u) > W(w)$ as well, that is, $u \in A$, and hence the convexity of A since A is open. If we have $W(u) \geq W(u^2)$, the conclusion follows at once. On the other hand, if $W(u) < W(u^2)$, then $u^2 P u$, so zero independence implies $u^2 + (u - u^2) P u + (u - u^2)$, namely, $u P u_1$, whence $W(u) \geq W(u_1)$ and the desired conclusion. The proof that B is convex is similar.

Thus, A, B are open, convex, and disjoint. Furthermore, by unanimity, the indifference curve of W through w [namely, $E \setminus (A \cup B)$] has empty interior. It follows by a separation argument that this indifference curve is a hyperplane separating A from B. Thus, all indifference curves of W are hyperplanes. By anonymity, they are all parallel to the simplex (consider the indifference curves through the multiples of e). This in turn means that W represents the same ordering as the utilitarian CUF.   Q.E.D.

A variant of Theorem 2.2 considers independence of individual utility scales. The corresponding SWO, instead of depending upon absolute variations of utilities, now depends upon relative variations.

Definition 2.2. *Consider a SWO R defined over the **positive orthant** E_{++}^N ($u_i > 0$ for all i). Say that R is **scale independent (SI)** if it satisfies one of two equivalent properties:*

   (i)   *For all $u, v, w \in E_{++}^N$: $u R v \Leftrightarrow (u \cdot w) R (v \cdot w)$.*
   (ii) *For all $u, v \in E_{++}^N$: $u R v \Leftrightarrow (u : v) R e$.*

Here we denote $u \cdot v = (u_1 v_1, u_2 v_2, \ldots, u_n v_n)$, $u : v = (u_1/v_1, u_2/v_2, \ldots, u_n/v_n)$, and $e = (1, \ldots, 1)$.

Theorem 2.3. *The Nash CUF W_N (defined over E_{++}^N),*

$$W_N(u) = u_1 u_2 \cdots u_n$$

is scale independent. Conversely, any SWO defined over E_{++}^N and scale independent is weakly represented by the Nash CUF. In particular, there is only one SWO on E_{++}^N that is scale independent and continuous; it is represented by the Nash CUF.

Proof: To a SWO R defined on E_{++}^N, associate the SWO R^* on E^N:

$$u R^* v \Leftrightarrow (e^{u_1}, \ldots, e^{u_n}) R (e^{v_1}, \ldots, e^{v_n})$$

Check that R is scale independent if and only if R^* is zero independent. Moreover, R is represented by Nash's CUF if and only if R^* is represented by classical utilitarianism. Thus, Theorem 2.3 is a corollary of Theorem 2.2.   Q.E.D.

Remark 2.1:   Given the anonymity assumption, the continuity assumption can be dropped in Theorem 2.2 (and Theorem 2.3). See Exercise 2.11.

Example 2.1. Sharing divisible goods
This is a variant of Exercise 1.5. Two agents receive jointly a gift made of *a* units of good A and *b* units of good B to be divided between the two of them. Both agents have linear preferences with different marginal rates of substitution. Specifically,

$$u_1(a_1, b_1) = 2a_1 + b_1 \qquad u_2(a_2, b_2) = a_2 + 2b_2$$

Note that we choose the zero of utilities at the zero allocation. Another natural zero is at the physically egalitarian allocation $a_i = a/2$, $b_i = b/2$; see Exercise 1.5.

The feasible allocations share the bundle (a, b) in nonnegative quantities: $a_i, b_i \geq 0$, $a_1 + a_2 = a$, and $b_1 + b_2 = b$.

By maximizing Nash's CUF over the feasible set, we select an efficient (Pareto-optimal) allocation by purely ordinal arguments. Indeed, Nash's CUF is independent of the particular choice of a *numéraire* to cardinalize utilities (by contrast, see Exercise 1.5 for the influence of the *numéraire* on egalitarian allocation methods).

The optimal allocation is a solution of

$$\max_{\substack{0 \leq a_1 \leq a \\ 0 \leq b_1 \leq b}} (2a_1 + b_1)((a - a_1) + 2(b - b_1)) \tag{3}$$

Figure 2.1 describes the set S of feasible utility vectors for $a = 1.2$, $b = 1$. Pareto-optimal utility vectors are on the interval $[C, D]$, corresponding to $b_1 = 0$, or on $[D, E]$, corresponding to $a_1 = a$. Depending on the slope of $0D$ – namely, b/a – the Nash CUF, whose indifference curves are symmetrical with respect to the 45° line, is maximal between C and D, at D, or between D and E. Routine computations yield the precise formulas:

Case 1: $2b \leq a$. The optimal utility vector is on $[C, D]$. Optimal allocation: $a_1 = \frac{1}{2}(a + 2b)$, $a_2 = \frac{1}{2}(a - 2b)$; $b_1 = 0$, $b_2 = b$.

Case 2: $\frac{1}{2} \leq b/a \leq 2$. The optimal utility vector is at D. Optimal allocation: $a_1 = a$, $a_2 = 0$; $b_1 = 0$, $b_2 = b$.

Case 3: $2a \leq b$. The optimal utility vector is on $[D, E]$. Optimal allocation: $a_1 = a$, $a_2 = 0$; $b_1 = \frac{1}{2}(b - 2a)$, $b_2 = \frac{1}{2}(b + 2a)$.

The justification and generalization of those formulas is the subject of Exercise 2.1.

A consequence of Theorems 2.2 and 2.3 is that no SWO is both scale and zero independent. Thus, every SWO is dependent on individual zeros and/or individual scales. This opens the way to two familiar manipulations by artificially inflating or deflating one's utility scale (respectively

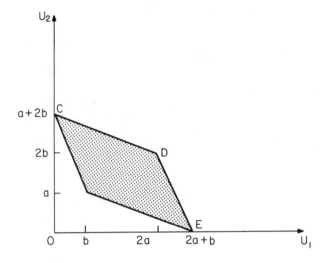

Figure 2.1.

increasing or lowering one's utility zero). Consider the cake division problem discussed earlier (Example 1.3). If the division rule is egalitarian, an agent benefits from pretending to be less hungry than he actually is (by deflating his utility scale). For instance, if brother 1 succeeds in convincing the referee that his utility function is $v_1(x) = u_1(x)/2$ (where u_1 is his true utility), then he will get half of the cake (since both agents will appear to have the same utility), thus increasing his initial share. Similarly, brother 2 receives a bigger share if he can convincingly pretend that his utility is $v_2 = \lambda u_2$, where λ is *any* number smaller than 1. On the contrary, the utilitarian division rule is more favorable to the hungry agent, so this time an agent benefits from inflating his utility scale (e.g., brother 2 pretends to be twice as hungry as he truly is, so as to receive half of the cake).

In Exercise 2.8 we explore systematically the phenomena of profitable inflation (deflation) of individual scales and profitable increase (decrease) of individual zeros. We define them precisely and show in particular that for the leximin SWO it is always profitable to increase one's zero of utility and to deflate one's utility scale, whereas for the utilitarian SWO inflating one's utility scale is always profitable (but changing one's zero of utility has no effect!).

2.3 Independence of common utility pace

The egalitarian CUF and the leximin SWO are independent of common utility pace.

Suppose we wish to compare income distributions. We know the distribution of taxable incomes $(i_1, ..., i_n)$, but we ignore which tax scheme will be used. Do we know enough to draw welfare comparisons about after-tax income distributions? Note that the tax scheme is an increasing function $r = f(i)$ giving after-tax income r as a function of before-tax income i. Most CUFs – notably the utilitarian CUF – will draw different conclusions whether we apply them to before- or after-tax distributions when the tax function f is nonlinear. It is not so with the egalitarian CUF: It prefers u to v because the poorest in u is richer than the poorest in v; after tax deduction, the relative positions of any two incomes remain the same, and hence $f(u)$ is still preferred to $f(v)$.

Definition 2.3.   *The SWO R is independent of the common utility pace (ICP) if, for every increasing bijection f of E into itself, we have*

$$u R v \Leftrightarrow f(u) R f(v) \quad \text{for all } u, v \in E^N$$

where we denote $f(u) = (f(u_1), f(u_2), ..., f(u_n))$. Equivalently, R is ICP if we have, for all u, u^1, v, v^1 in E^N,

$$[\text{for all } i, j \in N, \; u_i \{\substack{\geq \\ \leq}\} v_j \Leftrightarrow u_i' \{\substack{\geq \\ \leq}\} v_j'] \Rightarrow [u R v \Leftrightarrow u' R v'] \quad (4)$$

For a SWO independent of the common utility pace, only the interpersonal comparisons $u_i \{\substack{\geq \\ \leq}\} v_j$ matter, not the (cardinal) intensity of $u_i - v_j$. In this sense the SWO is ordinal.

Examples of SWOs independent of the common utility pace include the leximin SWO, as well as the egalitarian CUF and its generalizations to rank dictatorships that we now define.

Given a utility vector u in E^N, we denote by u_k^* the kth smallest utility level, namely, the kth coordinate of u^* (as defined in Section 2.1). This defines the k-rank dictators CUF W_k:

$$W_k(u) = u_k^*, \quad \text{all } u \in E^N$$

Notice that W_1 is the egalitarian CUF denoted W_e in Chapter 1, whereas $W_n(u) = \max_{1 \leq i \leq n} u_i$, namely, the CUF interested only in the welfare of the happiest agent. Another interesting rank dictator CUF is the *median dictator* corresponding to $k = \frac{1}{2}(n+1)$ (if n is odd) and $k = \frac{1}{2}n$ or $k = \frac{1}{2}n+1$ (if n is even). Here the median of the income distribution is viewed as the representative agent.

Theorem 2.4 (Hammond [1976], d'Aspremont and Gevers [1977]). *The rank k-dictator CUF is ICP for all k, $1 \leq k \leq n$. Conversely, if R is a SWO independent of the common utility pace, there exists an integer k, $1 \leq k \leq n$, such that W_k weakly represents R.*

Proof: That the CUF W_k is ICP is clear. To prove the converse statement, we fix a SWO R satisfying ICP.

For all k, $1 \le k \le n$, define a system of inequalities $A_k(u, v)$:

$$A_k(u, v): \quad v_j^* < u_{j+1}^* \quad \text{for all } j = 1, \dots, n-1$$
$$u_j^* < v_j^* \quad \text{for all } j \ne k$$
$$v_k^* < u_k^*$$

Remember that u^*, v^* is obtained from u, v by reordering the coordinates increasingly. The system $A_k(u, v)$ determines completely all comparisons of v_i^* and u_j^*, for all pairs i, j. Hence, by anonymity and ICP, all pairs u, v satisfying $A_k(u, v)$ are compared in the same way by R. Thus, exactly one of the two following conditions holds:

$$Q_k: \quad \text{for all } u, v, \ A_k(u, v) \Rightarrow u P v$$
$$\text{no } Q_k: \quad \text{for all } u, v, \ A_k(u, v) \Rightarrow v R u$$

The proof now goes in three steps.

Step 1. At least one property Q_k holds true. Indeed, consider the following sequence $u^0, u^1, \dots, u^n$ in E^N:

$$u^0 = (n, 2n, \dots, in, \dots, n^2)$$
$$u^1 = (0, 2n+1, \dots, in+1, \dots, n^2+1)$$
$$u_i^k = (i-1)n+k-1 \quad \text{if } 1 \le i \le k$$
$$u_i^k = in+k \quad\quad\quad \text{if } k+1 \le i \le n$$
$$u^n = (n-1, 2n-1, \dots, in-1, \dots, n^2-1)$$

One checks successively $A_1(u^0, u^1), \dots, A_k(u^{k-1}, u^k), \dots, A_n(u^{n-1}, u^n)$. Thus, if none of the properties Q_k hold, we deduce

$$A_k(u^{k-1}, u^k) \Rightarrow u^k R u^{k-1} \quad \text{all } k = 1, \dots, n$$

By transitivity of R, this gives $u^n R u^0$. Yet u^0 is Pareto superior to u^n, so by unanimity, we have $u^0 P u^n$. This contradiction proves step 1.

Step 2. At most one property Q_k holds true. Suppose, for instance, that Q_2 and Q_5 both hold (the general proof with Q_k and $Q_{k'}$ is identical but uses more cumbersome notation). Then consider three vectors u, v, w such that

$$u^* = (1, 5, 7, 10, 13, 16, \dots) \quad u_i^* = 16+(i-6) \quad \text{for } i \ge 6$$
$$v^* = (2, 4, 8, 11, 15, 17, \dots) \quad v_i^* = 17+(i-6) \quad \text{for } i \ge 6$$
$$w^* = (3, 6, 9, 12, 14, 18, \dots) \quad w_i^* = 18+(i-6) \quad \text{for } i \ge 6$$

Check that $A_2(u, v)$, whence $u P v$ (by Q_2), and that $A_5(v, w)$, whence $v P w$ (by Q_5). On the other hand, w^* is Pareto superior to u^* so by anonymity and unanimity, we must have $w P u$, a contradiction.

Step 3. By steps 1 and 2 exactly one property, say, Q_k, holds true, whereas Q_j does not hold for all $j \neq k$. We prove that the k-rank dictator CUF W_k weakly represents R:

$$v_k^* < u_k^* \Rightarrow u P v \quad \text{for all } u, v$$

The idea is to construct a reference pair u, v such that $u P v$, with $v_k^* < u_k^*$, whereas every other comparison is favorable to v over u:

$$u_1^* \leq \cdots \leq u_{k-1}^* < v_1^* \leq \cdots \leq v_k^* < u_k^* \leq \cdots \leq u_n^* < v_{k+1}^* \leq \cdots \leq v_n^* \tag{5}$$

Once this is achieved, consider any pair u', v' with $u_k'^* > v_k'^*$. We can Pareto improve v' into v'' while Pareto decreasing u' into u'' so as to achieve the configuration (5) between u'' and v''. By ICP and $u P v$ we have $u'' P v''$, and by unanimity we get $u' P u''$ and $v'' P v'$.

It remains to construct the reference pair u, v. For simplicity of notation, we assume $k = 3$, $n = 5$. Consider the sequence

$$u = (3, 5, 14, 16, 17)$$
$$u^1 = (1, 4, 13, 15, 23)$$
$$u^2 = (0, 2, 12, 19, 22)$$
$$u^3 = (1, 3, 11, 21, 23)$$
$$u^4 = (0, 8, 10, 19, 22)$$
$$v = (6, 7, 9, 18, 21)$$

We have $A_5(u^1, u)$ and hence $u R u^1$ by no Q_5. Next is $A_4(u^2, u^1)$ and hence $u^1 R u^2$ by no Q_4. Next is $A_3(u^2, u^3)$ and so $u^2 P u^3$ by Q_3. Next is $A_2(u^4, u^3)$ and hence $u^3 R u^4$ by no Q_2. Finally, $A_1(v, u^4)$ and hence $u^4 R v$ by no Q_1. Thus, $u P v$ and (5) hold, as desired.

The careful reader will easily generalize this construction to arbitrary k and n.   Q.E.D.

Note that Theorem 2.4 is not a characterization of the egalitarian CUF: The ICP axiom buys n distinct CUFs, some of them rather unappealing, such as the n-rank dictatorship W_n. In Section 2.5 we will observe that within the family W_k, $1 \leq k \leq n$, only the egalitarian CUF W_1 is inequality reducing [see property (9)]. This in turn brings a characterization of egalitarianism.

2.4   Separability

Given a society $N = \{1, 2, 3, 4\}$, suppose that some welfare redistribution affects agents 1 and 2 only. Can we make welfare judgments (is society better off after the change?) without knowing the fixed welfare levels of agents 3 and 4?

Under separability, the answer is yes. In other words, welfare comparisons are independent of nonconcerned agents.

Definition 2.4. *Given a society N and a SWO R on E^N, we say that R is separable if for every proper, nonempty subset T of N and for every utility vector u, v, u', v', we have*

$$\{(u_i = u'_i, \ v_i = v'_i \ \text{all} \ i \in T) \ \text{and} \ (u_j = v_j, \ u'_j = v'_j \ \text{all} \ j \in N \backslash T)\}$$
$$\Rightarrow \{u \, R \, v \Leftrightarrow u' \, R \, v'\} \quad (6)$$

A more compact formulation is

$$(u_T u_{N \backslash T}) \, R \, (v_T u_{N \backslash T}) \Leftrightarrow (u_T v_{N \backslash T}) \, R \, (v_T v_{N \backslash T}) \quad \text{for all} \ u, v \quad (7)$$

(where we denote by u_T the T component of u and by $u_{N \backslash T}$ its $N \backslash T$ component).

Separability allows informational decentralization: The SWO can be effectively restricted to any subset of the society. Actually, an equivalent formulation of Definition 2.4 explicitly uses SWOs defined over all subsets of N; see Exercise 2.3.

The main examples of separable SWOs are derived from separably additive CUFs. A *separably additive* CUF is one that can be written as

$$W(u) = \sum_{i=1}^{n} \alpha(u_i)$$

for some increasing real-valued function α. For instance, the SWO represented by the Nash CUF (on E^N_{++}) is separable because it is also represented by the additively separable CUF $W(u) = \sum_{i=1}^{n} \log u_i$. But there are also separable SWOs that cannot be represented (even weakly) by a separably additive CUF:

> *The leximin SWO is separable. Yet the egalitarian CUF does not represent a separable SWO.*

Indeed, denote by R the leximin SWO and suppose $(u_T u_{N \backslash T}) \, R \, (v_T u_{N \backslash T})$. Then u_T^* is lexicographically preferred or indifferent to v_T^*, so $(u_T v_{N \backslash T}) \, R \, (v_T v_{N \backslash T})$ as well. On the other hand, consider the egalitarian CUF. We have $W_e(2, 3, 4) > W_e(3, 3, 4)$, yet $W_e(2, 3, 1) = W_e(3, 3, 1)$, so the corresponding SWO is not separable. (Take $T = \{1\}$.)

The egalitarian CUF does not flagrantly violate separability. Under the premises of property (6) we cannot have $u P v$ and $v' P u'$. To find a clear-cut contradiction of (6), consider the median dictatorship introduced in Section 2.3. Take, for instance, $n = 3$; hence, $W_2(u) = u_2^*$. We have $W(0, 2, 3) > W(0, 1, 4)$, but $W(5, 2, 3) < W(5, 1, 4)$, contradicting (6) with $T = \{2, 3\}$.

Theorem 2.5 (Debreu [1960], Gorman [1968]).   *Suppose $n \geq 3$. Then a separable and continuous SWO is represented by a separably additive and continuous CUF.*

This theorem is a variant of a general theorem on separable preference orderings on E^N (without the anonymity and unanimity assumptions). Its proof is difficult, and we shall not even sketch it. The interested reader can consult Blackorby, Primont, and Russell [1978].

Under some mild additional independence properties, the separability axiom characterizes a small subset of CUFs.

Definition 2.5.   (a) *Consider a SWO R on E^N. We say that R is independent of the common zero of utility if we have, for all $u, v \in E^N$ and all $\lambda \in E$,*

$$u R v \Leftrightarrow (u + \lambda e) R (v + \lambda e)$$

[where $e = (1, 1, \ldots, 1)$ has all its coordinates equal to 1].
   (b) *Consider a SWO R on E_{++}^N. We say that R is independent of the common utility scale if we have, for all $u, v \in E_{++}^N$ and all $\lambda > 0$,*

$$u R v \Leftrightarrow (\lambda u) R (\lambda v)$$

Under independence of the common utility scale, it does not matter whether we measure incomes in dollars or in cents as long as the unit is the same for every income. If a SWO is independent of the common zero of utility, then we can compare indifferently the distributions of income or of the portion of income beyond a common subsistence wage.

Theorem 2.6 (Roberts [1980b]).   *Assume N contains at least three agents.*
   (a) *Let R be a continuous and separable SWO on E^N. Then R is independent of the common zero of utility if and only if it can be represented by one of the following CUFs:*

   (i) $\sum_{i=1}^{n} e^{p u_i}$ *for $p > 0$;*
   (ii) $-\sum_{i=1}^{n} e^{p u_i}$ *for $p < 0$;*
   (iii) $\sum_{i=1}^{n} u_i$.

   (b) *Let R be a continuous and separable SWO on E_{++}^N. Then R is independent of the common utility scale if and only if it can be represented by one of the following CUFs:*

   (i) $\sum_{i=1}^{n} u_i^q$ *for $q > 0$;*
   (ii) $-\sum_{i=1}^{n} u_i^q$ *for $q < 0$;*
   (iii) $\sum_{i=1}^{n} \log u_i$.

Sketch of the proof: Statements (a) and (b) are equivalent, as are Theorems 2.2 and 2.3. We sketch the proof of statement (b). By Theorem 2.5, R is represented by a CUF of the type $W(u) = \sum_{i=1}^{n} \alpha(u_i)$, where α is continuous and increasing on E_{++}.

One shows first that, for *any* number n^1 of agents, the CUF $W^1(u^1) = \sum_{j=1}^{n^1} \alpha(u_i^1)$ defined for a society with size n^1 is independent of the common scale as well.

Next consider five numbers u_1, u_1^1, u_2, u_2^1 and λ, all positive, and suppose

$$u_1 < u_1^1, \quad u_2 > u_2^1 \quad \text{and} \quad \frac{\alpha(\lambda u_1) - \alpha(\lambda u_1^1)}{\alpha(u_1) - \alpha(u_1^1)} \neq \frac{\alpha(\lambda u_2) - \alpha(\lambda u_2^1)}{\alpha(u_2) - \alpha(u_2^1)} \tag{8}$$

Suppose, for instance, that $[\alpha(u_1) - \alpha(u_1^1)]/[\alpha(u_2) - \alpha(u_2^1)] = -\frac{2}{3}$. Then we have $W(u_1, u_1, u_1, u_2, u_2) = W(u_1^1, u_1^1, u_2^1, u_2^1, u_2^1)$. But (8) implies that $W(\lambda u_1, \lambda u_1, \lambda u_1, \lambda u_2, \lambda u_2) \neq W(\lambda u_1^1, \lambda u_1^1, \lambda u_2^1, \lambda u_2^1, \lambda u_2^1)$, contradicting independence of common scale. When $[\alpha(u_1) - \alpha(u_1^1)]/[\alpha(u_2) - \alpha(u_2^1)]$ is an arbitrary negative number, we derive a similar contradiction (by continuity, we can always assume that this quotient is a rational number).

Since (8) implies a contradiction, the following functional equation obtains:

$$\alpha(\lambda u) - \alpha(\lambda v) = \beta(\lambda) \cdot (\alpha(u) - \alpha(v))$$

The continuous solutions of this equation are known (Aczél [1966]) to be

$$\alpha(u) = C \log u + D \quad \text{or} \quad \alpha(u) = C \cdot u^q + D$$

for some real constants C, D, q. This in turn proves statement (b).

Q.E.D.

The two families of CUF described in statements (a) and (b) have only one element in common, namely, the utilitarian CUF, $\sum_{i=1}^{n} u_i$. However, when p or q goes to $-\infty$, the SWOs R_p [represented by (a.ii)] and R^q [represented by (b.ii)] "converge" toward the leximin SWO; see Exercise 2.4.

2.5 Reduction of inequality

The egalitarian program strives to redistribute welfare from the "rich" to the "poor" (at least when there is no equality–efficiency dilemma). The utilitarian program is indifferent to such redistributions. Between these two extremes is a rich class of SWOs, showing some concern for redistributions from the rich to the poor and for increases in the sum of utilities as well.

The Pigou–Dalton principle of transfers states that transferring some utility from one agent to another so as to reduce the difference in their welfare should not reduce social welfare. Formally, consider a SWO R.

We say that R satisfies the Pigou–Dalton principle if for any two agents $i, j \in N$ and any two vectors $u, v \in E^N$, we have

$$\{u_k = v_k \text{ for all } k \neq i, j \text{ and } u_i + u_j = v_i + v_j \text{ and } |v_i - v_j| < |u_i - u_j|\}$$
$$\Rightarrow \{v R u\} \quad (9)$$

The *strict Pigou–Dalton principle* requires that v be strictly preferred to u under the same premises. When a SWO satisfies the Pigou–Dalton (strict Pigou–Dalton) principle, we say that it *does not increase (reduces)* inequality.

For instance, consider a separably additive CUF such as $W(u) = \sum_{i=1}^{n} \alpha(u_i)$. What property of α corresponds to an inequality reducing SWO? The Pigou–Dalton principle writes

$$\{u_i + u_j = v_i + v_j \text{ and } |v_i - v_j| < |u_i - u_j|\} \Rightarrow \{\alpha(u_i) + \alpha(u_j) \leq \alpha(v_i) + \alpha(v_j)\}$$

This is equivalent to

for all $x < y$ and all $\epsilon > 0$: $\quad \alpha(x + \epsilon) - \alpha(x) \geq \alpha(y + \epsilon) - \alpha(y)$

(indeed, set $u_i = x$, $u_j = y + \epsilon$, $v_i = x + \epsilon$ and $v_j = y$). The latter property is simply the concavity of α. Thus, the CUF $\sum_{i=1}^{n} \alpha(u_i)$ does not increase (reduces) inequality if and only if α is concave (strictly concave).

For instance, consider the CUF characterized in Theorem 2.6:

$$W_p(u) = \text{sgn}(p) \sum_{i=1}^{n} e^{pu_i}, \quad \text{with the convention } W_0(u) = \sum_{i=1}^{n} u_i$$

$$W^q(u) = \text{sgn}(q) \cdot \sum_{i=1}^{n} u_i^q, \quad \text{with the convention } W^0(u) = \sum_{i=1}^{n} \log u_i$$

The function $\alpha(x) = \text{sgn}(p)e^{px}$ is concave for $p < 0$ and convex for $p > 0$. Also, the function $\alpha(x) = \text{sgn}(q) \cdot x^q$ is convex for $q > 1$ and concave for $q < 0$ or $0 < q < 1$. Thus, W_p does not increase (reduces) inequality if and only if $-\infty < p \leq 0$ ($-\infty < p < 0$) and W^q does not increase (reduces) inequality if and only if $-\infty < q \leq 1$ ($-\infty < q < 1$). Notice that these two one-dimensional families (W_p for $-\infty < p \leq 0$ and W^q for $-\infty < q \leq 1$) connect the utilitarian CUF at one end (for $p = 0$ and $q = 1$) with the leximin SWO at the other end (when p or q goes to $-\infty$; see Exercise 2.4). One checks easily that the leximin SWO does reduce inequality (and that the egalitarian CUF does not increase it).

Here is another example of the Pigou–Dalton principle. Consider the family of rank dictatorships

$$W_k(u) = u_k^*, \quad k = 1, \dots, n$$

The egalitarian CUF, W_1, does not increase inequality. Every other rank dictator CUF violates the Pigou–Dalton principle.

For instance, W_2 violates the principle. If $n = 2$, $W_2(u) = \max\{u_1, u_2\}$, so a transfer from the rich to the poor always decreases W_2. If $n \geq 3$, consider the utility vector $u = (1, 3, 4, 4, \ldots, 4)$. A transfer from agent 2 to agent 1 changes it to $v = (2, 2, 4, 4, \ldots, 4)$. Meanwhile, W_2 decreases from 3 to 2. The proof that W_k violates the principle for all $k \geq 2$ is similar. On the contrary, W_1 does respect the principle, since an inequality-reducing transfer can never hurt the agent(s) whose welfare level is lowest.

Hence a corollary to Theorem 2.4: If a SWO is independent of the common utility pace and does not increase inequality, it is weakly represented by the egalitarian CUF.

Our next result shows that the Pigou–Dalton principle holds true for many more CUFs than the separably additive ones.

Lemma 2.2. *Suppose the CUF W is differentiable. Then it satisfies the Pigou–Dalton principle if and only if*

$$for\ all\ u \in E^N: \quad u_i \leq u_j \Rightarrow \frac{\partial W}{\partial u_j}(u) \leq \frac{\partial W}{\partial u_i}(u) \tag{10}$$

Proof: Indeed, condition (9) says that for all $u \in E^N$ and all $u, j \in N$

$$\{u_i < u_j, \; \epsilon \leq \tfrac{1}{2}(u_j - u_i)\}$$
$$\Rightarrow \{W(u) \leq W(v) \text{ where } v_i = u_i + \epsilon, \; v_j = u_j - \epsilon, \; v_k = u_k, \text{ all } k \neq i, j\}$$

Since W is differentiable, we compute

$$\frac{d}{d\epsilon}(W(v) - W(u))_{\epsilon = 0} = \frac{\partial W}{\partial u_i}(u) - \frac{\partial W}{\partial u_j}(u)$$

Thus, (9) implies (10). The converse statement is as easy.   Q.E.D.

We now state two general characterizations of the Pigou–Dalton principle. The first relies on a partial ordering of utility distributions that is weaker than the Pareto ordering.

Definition 2.6. *To a utility vector $u \in E^N$, attach its **Lorenz curve**, the vector*

$$L(u) = (u_1^*, u_1^* + u_2^*, \ldots, u_1^* + u_2^* + \cdots + u_n^*) \quad or \quad [L(u)]_k = \sum_{i=1}^{k} u_i^* \; for\ all\ k$$

The Lorenz curve has the lowest utility for the first coordinate, the sum of the two lowest for the second coordinate, and so on. Its nth coordinate is simply the overall sum of utilities (as $\sum_{i=1}^{n} u_i^* = \sum_{i=1}^{n} u_i$). Viewed as a curve, $k \to u_1^* + \cdots + u_k^*$, it is just the aggregate utility of the k poorest agents for all k.

What is the effect of a redistributive transfer of the type described by the Pigou–Dalton principle on the Lorenz curve? Take $i < j$ and suppose $u_i^* < u_j^*$. Next raise u_i^* to $u_i^* + \epsilon$, while lowering u_j^* to $u_j^* - \epsilon$, where ϵ is chosen such that $\epsilon < \frac{1}{2}|u_j^* - u_i^*|$. Here is an example where the redistribution takes away four utilities from u_7^* and gives them to u_2^* (so $i = 2$, $j = 7$, $\epsilon = 4$). We denote by v the vector obtained after redistribution:

$$u^* = (2, 6, 8, 9, 11, 14, 16, 18) \Rightarrow L(u) = (2, 8, 16, 25, 36, 50, 66, 84)$$

$$v = (2, 10, 8, 9, 11, 14, 12, 18) \Rightarrow L(v) = (2, 10, 19, 29, 40, 52, 66, 84)$$

Thus, after redistribution, every coordinate of the Lorenz curve increases or remains constant. This is a general property: Every Pigou–Dalton transfer raises the Lorenz curve. Interestingly, we have also a converse property.

Lemma 2.3. *Say that the vector u **Lorenz dominates** the vector v if its Lorenz curve $L(u)$ is (Pareto) superior to the Lorenz curve $L(v)$:*

$$L(u) < L(v)$$

$$\Leftrightarrow \left\{ \text{for all } k: \sum_{i=1}^{k} u_i^* \geq \sum_{i=1}^{k} v_i^*, \text{ the inequality being strict for at least one } k \right\}$$

If u Pareto dominates v, or if u obtains from v by a Pigou–Dalton transfer, then u Lorenz dominates v. Conversely, if u Lorenz dominates v, then we can find a sequence of Pigou–Dalton transfers and Pareto improvements to transform v into u.

Therefore, a SWO R does not increase (reduces) inequality if and only if it respects Lorenz domination: For all u, v: $L(u) > L(v) \Rightarrow u R v$ ($u P v$). The proof of Lemma 2.3 is the subject of Exercise 2.7.

A consequence of Lemma 2.3 is that a SWO-reducing inequality will pick from any set of feasible utility vectors a Lorenz-optimal element, namely, a vector that no other vector Lorenz dominates. The Lorenz optima are a subset of the Pareto set, often a small subset, as our next two examples show.

Example 2.2. Lorenz optima with only two agents
When $n = 2$, the Lorenz curve is simply

$$L(u_1, u_2) = (\min\{u_1, u_2\}, u_1 + u_2)$$

Hence, a utility vector is Lorenz optimal if and only if one cannot improve upon the utilitarian CUF without hurting the egalitarian CUF (and vice-versa). Figure 2.2 shows the two typical configurations (with and without

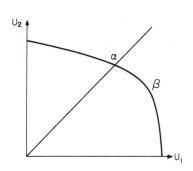
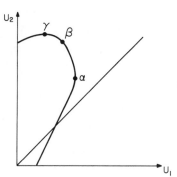

Figure 2.2.

the equality–efficiency dilemma) for a convex feasible set S and the corresponding Lorenz and Pareto optima.

The Lorenz optima are between α (egalitarian outcome) and β (utilitarian outcome). The Pareto optima cover the whole thick line in the left-hand figure and are between γ and α in the right-hand figure.

Example 2.3. Lorenz optima in a location problem
We have five towns located on the interval $[0,1]$ at $0, \frac{1}{4}, \frac{3}{4}, \frac{3}{4}$, and 1. Every location of $[0,1]$ is feasible; they are also Pareto optimal. The egalitarian solution is at $\frac{1}{2}$, whereas the utilitarian one is at $\frac{3}{4}$ (see Exercise 1.1). The Lorenz optima are all locations between $\frac{1}{2}$ and $\frac{3}{4}$ (including these two end points).

Indeed, no location between these two is Lorenz dominated: The egalitarian CUF (the first component of the Lorenz curve) deteriorates when we move (slightly) to the right, and the utilitarian CUF (the last component of the Lorenz curve) deteriorates when we move (slightly) to the left.

On the other hand, every location outside $[\frac{1}{2}, \frac{3}{4}]$ is Lorenz dominated. Actually, any location in $[0, \frac{1}{2}]$ is dominated by $\frac{1}{2}$ and any location in $[\frac{3}{4}, 1]$ is dominated by $\frac{3}{4}$. These claims are routinely checked. For instance, take a location x in $[\frac{1}{4}, \frac{3}{8}]$. The *disutility* vector, reordered in *decreasing* order, is

$$u^*(x) = (1-x, \tfrac{3}{4}-x, \tfrac{3}{4}-x, x, x-\tfrac{1}{4})$$

whence the Lorenz curve is

$$L(x) = (1-x, \tfrac{7}{4}-2x, \tfrac{10}{4}-3x, \tfrac{10}{4}-2x, \tfrac{9}{4}-x)$$

Compare with the location $\frac{1}{2}$:

$$u^*(\tfrac{1}{2}) = (\tfrac{1}{2}, \tfrac{1}{2}, \tfrac{1}{4}, \tfrac{1}{4}, \tfrac{1}{4}), \qquad L(\tfrac{1}{2}) = (\tfrac{1}{2}, 1, \tfrac{5}{4}, \tfrac{3}{2}, \tfrac{7}{4})$$

and check that every component of $L(x)$ is above (sometimes strictly above) the corresponding component of $L(\tfrac{1}{2})$. Of course, since we deal with disutility vectors, a vector is Lorenz optimal if its Lorenz curve cannot be *decreased*. Similarly, for a location x in $[\tfrac{3}{8}, \tfrac{1}{2}]$,

$$u^*(x) = (1-x, x, \tfrac{3}{4}-x, \tfrac{3}{4}-x, x-\tfrac{1}{4})$$
$$L(x) = (1-x, 1, \tfrac{7}{4}-x, \tfrac{10}{4}-2x, \tfrac{9}{4}-x)$$

We leave it to the reader to perform the analogous computations for $[0, \tfrac{1}{8}]$, $[\tfrac{1}{8}, \tfrac{1}{4}]$, $[\tfrac{3}{4}, \tfrac{7}{8}]$, and $[\tfrac{7}{8}, 1]$ successively.

Note that the result of Example 2.3 is not general: For a location problem on $[0,1]$ it is not always the case that Lorenz optima are between the egalitarian and utilitarian solutions; see Exercise 2.5.

The second characterization of the Pigou–Dalton principle is of a technical character. It implies that a convex (strictly convex) SWO does not increase (reduces) inequality. We say that the $n \times n$ matrix $Q = [q_{ij}]$ is doubly stochastic if $q_{ij} \geq 0$, $\sum_i q_{ij} = \sum_j q_{ij} = 1$, for all i, j. A permutation matrix is a doubly stochastic matrix such that $q_{ij} = 0$ or 1 for all i, j.

Theorem 2.7 (Hardy, Littlewood, and Pölya [1934]). *A SWO R does not reduce inequality if and only if it satisfies the following property:*

> *for all $u \in E^N$ and all doubly stochastic $n \times n$ matrices Q, we have $(Qu) R u$*   (11)

Moreover, R reduces inequality if and only if we have $(Qu) P u$ for all u with all its components distinct and for any doubly stochastic matrix Q that is not a permutation matrix.

Corollary. *Say that R is convex (strictly convex) if its upper contour sets $\{v/v R u\}$ are all convex (strictly convex). A convex SWO does not increase inequality. A strictly convex SWO reduces inequality.*

We omit the proof of Theorem 2.7. It consists of showing that for all u, v, $L(v) \geq L(u)$ if and only if $v \geq Qu$ for some doubly stochastic matrix Q. The corollary follows since any doubly stochastic matrix is the convex combination of permutation matrices. A complete proof can be found in Foster [1985]. Application of this mathematical result to distributive justice was proposed first by Kolm [1969] and Atkinson [1970].

A SWO satisfying (11) is also called Shur convex. Figure 2.3 shows the contour of a SWO that is Shur convex but not convex.

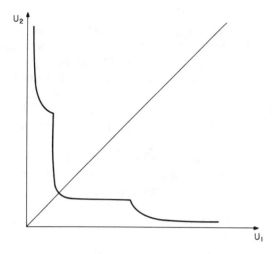

Figure 2.3.

2.6 Inequality indices

An inequality index is a mathematical transformation of a CUF that emphasizes the welfare loss due to the inequality in the utility distribution.

We start with a SWO R reducing inequality. For any positive utility vector u we define the equally distributed equivalent utility $\epsilon(u)$ as follows:

$$(\epsilon(u) \cdot e) I u$$

[recall that e is the vector $(1, 1, ..., 1)$]. Next we define the inequality index J associated with R. Denote by $\bar{u} = (\sum_{i=1}^{n} u_i)/n$ the average utility at u:

$$J(u) = 1 - \frac{\epsilon(u)}{\bar{u}} \quad \text{for all } u \in E_{++}^N \tag{12}$$

Note that J is defined for positive utility distributions only. Because J reduces inequality, the distribution $\bar{u} \cdot e$ is preferred or indifferent to u. Hence,

$$\{(\bar{u} \cdot e) R u, \, u I(\epsilon(u) \cdot e)\} \Rightarrow (\bar{u} \cdot e) R(\epsilon(u) \cdot e) \Rightarrow \bar{u} \geq \epsilon(u)$$

Thus, $J(u)$ is nonnegative for all u. Moreover, $J(u) = 0$ only if $\epsilon(u) = \bar{u}$, which is possible only if u is equally distributed ($u = \bar{u} \cdot e$) since R reduces inequality. Finally, $J(u)$ is bounded above by 1 because $\epsilon(u)$ is nonnegative (the vector u being positive). To summarize,

$$0 \le J(u) \le 1 \quad \text{for all } u, \text{ with } J(u) = 0 \text{ iff } u = \bar{u} \cdot e$$

The theory of inequality indices parallels that of SWOs. Indeed, given an index J we can recover the function ϵ by (12), and ϵ is a CUF representing R. Starting with the pioneer work of Kolm [1969], Atkinson [1970], and Sen [1973], a full-fledged theory of inequality indices has developed. Most of its results can be expressed in the language of SWOs as well. We will not attempt to review systematically this growing literature. The interested reader can consult the recent surveys by Foster [1985] and Shorrocks [1985].

In the rest of this section, we simply define two of the most popular indices, namely, the Atkinson indices and the Gini index. We also discuss a powerful characterization result based upon a separability axiom.

Because an inequality index J represents a SWO-reducing inequality, it will decrease as a result of a Pigou–Dalton transfer [check that when v is obtained from u by a Pigou–Dalton transfer, $\epsilon(v)$ is greater than $\epsilon(u)$]. Lastly, we will assume that our indices are unaffected by a common change of utility scale (this amounts to supposing that the corresponding SWO is independent of the common utility scale). Summarizing, we call *inequality index* a function J defined over E_{++}^N and satisfying

$$0 \le J(u) \le 1 \quad \text{with } J(u) = 0 \text{ iff } u = \bar{u} \cdot e$$

$$J(v) < J(u) \quad \text{if } v \text{ is obtained from } u \text{ by a Pigou–Dalton transfer} \qquad (13)$$

$$J(\lambda u) = J(u) \quad \text{for all positive } \lambda$$

Example 2.4. Atkinson indices
Consider the CUFs characterized in Theorem 2.6(b) by separability and independence of common scale. Restrict attention to those reducing inequality, namely,

$$W_q(u) = \sum_{i=1}^{n} u_i^q, \quad 0 < q < 1$$

$$W_q(u) = -\sum_{i=1}^{n} u_i^q, \quad q < 0$$

$$W_0(u) = \sum_{i=1}^{n} \log u_i$$

The associated inequality measures are straightforwardly computed by (12):

$$J_q(u) = 1 - \left(\frac{1}{n} \sum_{i=1}^{n} \left(\frac{u_i}{\bar{u}} \right)^q \right)^{1/q}, \quad 0 < q < 1 \text{ or } q < 0 \qquad (14)$$

$$J_0(u) = 1 - \left(\prod_{i=n}^{n} \frac{u_i}{\bar{u}} \right)^{1/n}$$

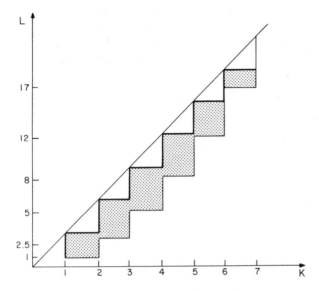

Figure 2.4.

Example 2.5. The Gini inequality index
Consider a utility vector u with associated Lorenz curve $L(u)$. Note that for an equally distributed utility $u = \bar{u} \cdot e$, the Lorenz curve is the straight line $k \to k\bar{u}$, whereas for any other vector the Lorenz curve is bounded above by the straight line

$$\text{for all } k: \quad \sum_{i=1}^{k} u_i^* \le k \cdot \bar{u} \tag{15}$$

To check (15), observe that $u_j^* \ge (1/k) \sum_{i=1}^{k} u_i^*$ for all $j \ge k+1$, whence

$$n\bar{u} \ge \sum_{i=1}^{k} u_i^* + \sum_{j=k+1}^{n} u_j^* \ge \sum_{i=1}^{k} u_i^* + (n-k) \cdot \frac{1}{k} \sum_{i=1}^{k} u_i^*$$

Here is an example:

$$u = (1.5, 4, 1, 5, 2.5, 5, 3)$$
$$L(u) = (1, 2.5, 5, 8, 12, 17, 22)$$

The "straight-line" curve corresponds to the upper stairlike function in Figure 2.4. It looks more and more like a straight line as the number of agents grows. The lower stairlike function represents $L(u)$.

If the distribution is very unequal (say, all agents have zero utility except one), then the Lorenz curve is very far from the straight-line curve.

This suggests taking the *surface* between the straight-line and the Lorenz curve (the shaded area in Figure 2.4) as a measure of inequality. To keep the inequality index below 1, we normalize by dividing the surface by that of the surface below the straight line. This defines the Gini index:

$$G(u) = \sum_{k=1}^{n} (k\bar{u} - L(u)_k) \Big/ \left(\frac{1}{2}n \sum_{i=1}^{n} u_i\right)$$

We compute a more compact formula:

$$G(u) = \frac{2}{n^2\bar{u}} \left(\bar{u} \times \left(\sum_{i=1}^{n} k\right) - \sum_{k=1}^{n}\left(\sum_{i=1}^{k} u_i^*\right)\right)$$

$$= \frac{2}{n^2\bar{u}} \left(\frac{n(n+1)}{2}\bar{u} - \sum_{k=1}^{n} (n-k+1)u_k^*\right)$$

$$\Rightarrow G(u) = 1 - \frac{1}{n^2\bar{u}} \left(\sum_{k=1}^{n} (2(n-k)+1)u_k^*\right) \quad (16)$$

Hence, the Gini index corresponds to the following CUF:

$$W(u) = \frac{1}{n^2} \sum_{k=1}^{n} (2(n-k)+1)\cdot u_k^*$$

Indeed, $W(\lambda \cdot e) = \lambda$ for any positive λ, implying $\epsilon(u) = W(u)$, so the inequality index attached to W by (12) is G.

The CUF W is a variant of classical utilitarianism, where the weight of more fortunate agents decreases linearly as their rank increases.

Another useful formulation of the Gini index is

$$G(u) = \frac{1}{2n^2\bar{u}} \sum_{1 \leq i,j \leq n} |u_i - u_j| \quad (17)$$

The index is, up to normalization, the average of utility differentials across agents. The proof of (17) is the subject of Exercise 2.10.

Despite its appealing interpretation, the Gini index has a serious drawback related to the fact that its associated CUF is not separable. To see it, consider the following utility distribution for five agents:

$$u = (4, 11, 3, 9, 8)$$

Its Gini index is worth [by (16)]

$$G_5(u) = 1 - \frac{1}{5^2 \times 7} (9 \times 3 + 7 \times 4 + 5 \times 8 + 3 \times 9 + 1 \times 11) = \frac{6}{25}$$

Suppose now that a redistribution among the first three agents changes their utilities from $(4, 11, 3)$ to $(7, 10, 1)$. Within the subgroup $\{1, 2, 3\}$ this leaves total utility constant and increases inequality in the Gini sense:

$$G_3(4, 11, 3) = 1 - \frac{1}{3^2 \times 6}(5 \times 3 + 3 \times 4 + 1 \times 11) = \frac{8}{27}$$

$$G_3(7,10,1) = 1 - \frac{1}{3^2 \times 6}(5 \times 1 + 3 \times 7 + 1 \times 10) = \frac{9}{27}$$

Yet the effect on the five-agent society (where the two other agents stay put) is, again in the Gini sense, a decrease of inequality:

$$v = (7, 10, 1, 9, 8),$$

$$G_5(u) = 1 - \frac{1}{5^2 \times 7}(9 \times 1 + 7 \times 7 + 5 \times 8 + 3 \times 9 + 1 \times 10) = \frac{8}{35}$$

and $\frac{8}{35} < \frac{6}{25}$

The property that we need here is the version of separability for inequality indices. We suppose that for each possible size n of the population we are given an inequality index J_n.

Subgroup separability: Given two societies N, T with $T \subset N$, two vectors $u_T, v_T \in E^T_{++}$ such that $\bar{u}_T = \bar{v}_T$, and a vector $u_{N \setminus T} \in E^{N \setminus T}_{++}$, we have

$$J_t(u_T) \geq J_t(v_T) \Leftrightarrow J_n(u_T, u_{N \setminus T}) \geq J_n(v_T, u_{N \setminus T})$$

Clearly, if the CUF W is separable over E^N (Definition 2.4), its restrictions to the subsets of N satisfy subgroup separability. For instance, Atkinson inequality indices (Example 2.4) are all subgroup separable. Actually, there are more separable inequality indices than the Atkinson indices, but not many more, as the following theorem demonstrates.

Theorem 2.8 (Shorrocks [1984]).   *For each n there exists an inequality index J_n that satisfies (13) and is continuous. Assume, moreover, the following replication property:*

$$\text{for all } n \text{ and all } u \in E^N_{++}: \quad J_{2n}(u, u) = J_n(u)$$

*Then J_n, $n = 1, 2, \ldots$, satisfies subgroup separability **if and only if** it takes the following form: For some real number c and some strictly increasing continuous function f with $f(0) = 0$ and $f(x) \leq 1$, all x,*

$$J_n(u) = f\left(\frac{1}{n} \cdot \frac{1}{c(c-1)} \cdot \left(\sum_{i=1}^{n}\left\{\left(\frac{u_i}{\bar{u}}\right)^c - 1\right\}\right)\right) \tag{18}$$

where we make the convention

$$\text{for } c = 0: \quad J_n(u) = f\left(\frac{1}{n} \cdot \sum_{i=1}^{n} \log\left(\frac{\bar{u}}{u_i}\right)\right) \tag{19}$$

$$\text{for } c = 1: \quad J_n(u) = f\left(\frac{1}{n} \sum_{i=1}^{n} \frac{u_i}{\bar{u}} \cdot \log\left(\frac{u_i}{\bar{u}}\right)\right) \tag{20}$$

This family of inequality indices are called entropy measures. Indeed, (19) is a monotonic transformation of the entropy of the vector $(1/\bar{u})\cdot u$.

Theorem 2.8 is similar to Theorem 2.6. If J_n is subgroup separable, any CUF W to which it is attached satisfies a weak form of Definition 2.4, where u_T and v_T have the same average utility. In this sense, Shorrock's theorem is stronger than Theorem 2.6.

Finally, we check that Atkinson indices (Example 2.4) are a particular case of (18). Take $c<0$ or $0<c<1$. Define f as follows:

$$f(x)=1-(c(c-1)x+1)^{1/c}$$

Check that f is increasing and continuous and that formula (18) leads to (14):

$$J(u)=f\left(\frac{1}{n}\frac{1}{c(c-1)}\left(\sum_{i=1}^{n}\left\{\left(\frac{u_i}{\bar{u}}\right)^{c}-1\right\}\right)\right)=1-\left(\frac{1}{n}\sum_{i=1}^{n}\left(\frac{u_i}{\bar{u}}\right)^{c}\right)^{1/c}$$

For the case $c=0$, take $f(x)=1-e^{-x}$ and apply (19):

$$J(u)=f\left(\frac{1}{n}\sum_{i=1}^{n}\log\left(\frac{\bar{u}}{u_i}\right)\right)=1-\left(\prod_{i=1}^{n}\frac{u_i}{\bar{u}}\right)^{1/n}$$

EXERCISES

2.1 **Sharing divisible goods with Nash's CUF.** We generalize the model of Example 2.1 by taking arbitrary linear preferences for the two goods: $u_i=\alpha_i a_i+\beta_i b_i$, $i=1,2$ (where a_i is the amount of good A allocated to agent i). We assume that all coefficients α_i,β_i are positive.

(a) The zero of the utility function u_i is at the zero allocation for agent i. Suppose $\alpha_2/\beta_2<\alpha_1/\beta_1$ and show that the allocation maximizing Nash's CUF is as follows:

if $\alpha_1/\beta_1\le b/a$, then $\begin{cases} a_1=a \\ b_1=\frac{1}{2}[b-(\alpha_1/\beta_1)a] \end{cases}$

if $\alpha_2/\beta_2\le b/a\le\alpha_1/\beta_1$, then $\begin{cases} a_1=a \\ b_1=0 \end{cases}$

if $b/a\le\alpha_2/\beta_2$, then $\begin{cases} a_1=\frac{1}{2}[a+(\beta_2/\alpha_2)b] \\ b_1=0 \end{cases}$

(b) Consider the utility function $\bar{u}_i$ representing the same preferences but with its zero at the physically egalitarian division of the goods:

$$\bar{u}_i=\alpha_i(a_i-\tfrac{1}{2}a)+\beta_i(b_i-\tfrac{1}{2}a)$$

Then show, under the assumption $\alpha_2/\beta_2<\alpha_1/\beta_1$, that Nash's solution is if $\dfrac{1}{2}\left(\dfrac{\alpha_1}{\beta_1}+\dfrac{\alpha_2}{\beta_2}\right)\le\dfrac{b}{a}$, then $\begin{cases} a_1=a \\[2mm] b_1=\dfrac{1}{2}\left(b-\dfrac{1}{2}\left(\dfrac{\alpha_2}{\beta_2}+\dfrac{\alpha_1}{\beta_1}\right)a\right) \end{cases}$

if $\left[\dfrac{1}{2}\left(\dfrac{\beta_1}{\alpha_1}+\dfrac{\beta_2}{\alpha_2}\right)\right]^{-1}\le\dfrac{b}{a}\le\dfrac{1}{2}\left(\dfrac{\alpha_1}{\beta_1}+\dfrac{\alpha_2}{\beta_2}\right)$, then $\begin{cases} a_1=a \\[1mm] b_1=0 \end{cases}$

if $\dfrac{b}{a}\le\left[\dfrac{1}{2}\left(\dfrac{\beta_1}{\alpha_1}+\dfrac{\beta_2}{\alpha_2}\right)\right]^{-1}$, then $\begin{cases} a_1=\dfrac{1}{2}\left(a+\dfrac{1}{2}\left(\dfrac{\beta_1}{\alpha_1}+\dfrac{\beta_2}{\alpha_2}\right)b\right) \\[2mm] b_1=0 \end{cases}$

2.2 The median dictator. Consider a society with an odd number n of agents. Set $n=2n'-1$ so that the median dictator CUF is just the n'th-rank dictatorship, that is,

$$W(u)=u^*_{n'} \quad \text{for all } u$$

The aim of this exercise is to compute the solution recommended by the median dictator in several examples of Chapter 1.

(a) Suppose we have three towns, located in $[0,1]$, respectively, at 0, a, and 1. Show that the best location for the median dictator is at $\frac{1}{2}a$ if $a<\frac{1}{2}$, at $\frac{1}{2}(a+1)$ if $a>\frac{1}{2}$, and at $\frac{1}{4}$ or $\frac{3}{4}$ if $a=\frac{1}{2}$. Compare with the egalitarian location $\frac{1}{2}$ and the utilitarian location a. With five towns located at 0, 0.32, 0.55, 0.74, 1, show that 0.53 is chosen by the median dictator CUF.

(b) What location is chosen on the tree of Exercise 1.1? On the loop of Exercise 1.2?

(c) Consider the cost sharing of a public project (Exercise 1.5). Show that in the numerical example, the median dictator CUF chooses the cost sharing

$$c_1=5, \quad c_2=10, \quad c_3=2, \quad c_4=4, \quad c_5=8$$

Give a method for computing the median dictator optimum for a general cost-sharing problem (with an odd number of agents).

2.3 An equivalent definition of separability (from Blackorby and Donaldson [1984]). Given is a finite *sequence* of SWOs $R_1, R_2, \ldots, R_n$, one for each possible size of the society between 1 and n. For any vectors u, v in E^N and any subset T of N with size t, we suppose

$$\{u_i=v_i=0 \text{ for all } i\in N\setminus T\} \Rightarrow \{u\,R_n\,v \Rightarrow u_T\,R_t\,v_T\}$$

where u_T, v_T denote the projection of u on E^T.

(a) Show that the SWO R_n is separable if and only if all SWOs $R_1, \ldots, R_n$ are.

(b) Show that R_n is separable if and only if, for all integers n_1, n_2 such that $n_1+n_2\le n$ and all vectors $u^1, v^1\in E^{n_1}$, $u^2, v^2\in E^{n_2}$, we have

$$\{u^1 R_{n_1} v^1 \text{ and } u^2 R_{n_2} v^2\} \Rightarrow \{[u^1 u^2] R_{n_1+n_2} [v^1 v^2]\}$$

where $[u^1 u^2]$ is the concatenation of u^1 and u^2 (with dimension n_1+n_2).

2.4   Limits of the CUF from Theorem 2.6. Denote by R_p (R^q) the SWO represented by the CUF of statement (a) [(b)] in Theorem 2.6. Make the convention that R_0 is classical utilitarianism, and R^0 is Nash's SWO. Thus, R_p and R^q are defined for all real numbers p, q.

Denote by R_* the leximin SWO. Show that R_* is the limit of R_p (R^q) as p (q) goes to $-\infty$ in the following sense:

for all $u, v \in E^N$: $\{u R_* v\} \Leftrightarrow \{\exists p_0$ such that for all $p \leq p_0: u R_p v\}$

respectively

for all $u, v \in E_{++}^N$: $\{u R_* v\} \Leftrightarrow \{\exists q_0$ such that for all $q \leq q_0: u R^q v\}$

What is the limit of R_p (R^q) as p (q) goes to $+\infty$?

2.5   Location on an interval. Suppose n towns are located in the interval $[0,1]$. Show that the interval between the egalitarian location and the utilitarian location(s) is made of Lorenz-optimal locations (when n is odd, the utilitarian location is unique; when n is even, it is an interval). Give an example where some Lorenz-optimal location is outside this interval.

2.6   Lorenz-optimal utility vectors. Suppose $n = 2$ and consider a subset S of feasible utility vectors $(S \subseteq E^2)$. Suppose that the egalitarian CUF has a *unique* maximum on S, denoted $u^e = (u_1^e, u_2^e)$, and that the utilitarian CUF has a *unique* maximum on S, denoted $u^0 = (u_1^0, u_2^0)$. Let u be a Lorenz-optimal vector in S. Show

$$u \neq u^e \Rightarrow |u_1^e - u_2^e| < |u_1 - u_2|$$
$$u \neq u^0 \Rightarrow |u_1 - u_2| < |u_1^0 - u_2^0|$$

Thus, the egalitarian (utilitarian) distribution has the smallest (largest) absolute inequality among Lorenz-optimal distributions. Compare with Exercise 1.8.

2.7   Proof of Lemma 2.3. Suppose that u Lorenz dominates v. Without loss of generality, assume $u = u^*$, $v = v^*$. For all $\lambda \geq 0$, consider the system with n equations and unknown $w \in E_{++}^N$:

$$\sum_{i=1}^k w_i = \max\left\{\left(\sum_{i=1}^k u_i\right) - \lambda, \sum_{i=1}^k v_i\right\}, \quad \text{all } k = 1, \ldots, n$$

Show that its unique solution $w(\lambda)$ is such that $w(\lambda) = w^*(\lambda)$ and $L(v) \leq L(w(\lambda)) \leq L(u)$. Show that $w(\lambda)$ is piecewise linear and that each piece corresponds to a Pigou–Dalton transfer or a Pareto improvement.

2.8   Distortion of individual zero and scale. *Notation:* the vector e_i has 1 for the ith coordinate and zero elsewhere. Consider a SWO R on E^N. Say that increasing one's individual zero is profitable under R if

for all $u, v \in E^N$, all $i \in N$, and all $\lambda_i < 0$:

$$\{u R v \text{ and } (v + \lambda_i e_i) R (u + \lambda_i e_i)\} \Rightarrow \{u_i \leq v_i\} \tag{21}$$

Interpretation: Agent i increases his zero by $|\lambda_i|$ while changing u_i to $u_i + \lambda_i$. If this change reverses the comparison $u \, R \, v$ in favor of v, then agent i is better off under v. In particular, fix a feasible set S. After agent i increases his zero by $|\lambda_i|$, the new feasible set is $S + \{\lambda_i e_i\}$ ($\lambda_i < 0$). Thus, (21) implies that maximizing R on S yields a better outcome for agent i after inflation.

Similarly, we say that decreasing the individual zero is profitable under R if property (21) holds for all $\lambda_i > 0$ (instead of for all $\lambda_i < 0$).

(a) Show that for the leximin SWO (but not the egalitarian CUF) increasing the individual zero is profitable.

(b) Consider a separably additive CUF $W(u) = \sum_{i=1}^{n} \alpha(u_i)$. Show that increasing (decreasing) the individual zero is profitable if and only if α is concave (convex). For instance, under the SWO represented by Nash's CUF, increasing one's individual zero is profitable.

(c) If u is a utility factor, λ a positive number, and i an agent, denote by $u(\lambda, i)$ the vector $u(\lambda, i)_i = \lambda u_i$, $u(\lambda, j) = u_j$, all $j \neq i$. Say that inflating (deflating) one's individual scale is profitable if we have

for all $u, v \in E_{++}^N$, all i, and all $\lambda > 1$:

$$\{u \, R \, v \text{ and } v(\lambda, i) \, R \, u(\lambda, i)\} \Rightarrow \{u_i \leq v_i\} \tag{22}$$

(respectively, the same property for all $\lambda < 1$). Show that for the leximin SWO (but not the egalitarian CUF) deflating one's individual scale is profitable.

Consider a separably additive CUF $W(u) = \sum_{i=1}^{n} \beta(u_i)$. Show that deflating (inflating) individual scale is profitable if and only if $\beta(e^x)$ is concave (convex) in x. For instance, under the utilitarian SWO, inflating one's individual scale is profitable.

(d) Show that a profitable increase of the individual zero [property (21)] is equivalent to the following property:

for all $u, v, w \in E^N$:

$$\{u \, R \, v \text{ and } (u_i - v_i) \cdot w_i \leq 0 \text{ for all } i \in N\} \Rightarrow \{(u+w) \, R \, (v+w)\} \tag{23}$$

Property (23) is introduced by Yaari [1978] in a different context. Show that (23) implies the separability of R. Deduce that if R is a continuous SWO, it induces profitable increase (decrease) of individual zero *if and only if* it is represented by a separably additive CUF, $W(u) = \sum_{i=1}^{n} \alpha(u_i)$, with a concave (convex) function α.

Give a similar characterization of a continuous SWO on E_{++}^N inducing profitable inflation (deflation) of individual scale.

2.9 Proof of Theorem 2.1. Let R be a SWO satisfying (2). Define two binary relations P^* and I^* as follows:

$$u \, P^* \, v \Leftrightarrow \exists u' \ll u, v' \gg v : u' \, P \, v'$$

$$u \, I^* \, v \Leftrightarrow \text{no } (u \, P^* \, v) \text{ and no } (v \, P^* \, u)$$

(a)   Check that P^* is transitive and that $u P^* v \Rightarrow u P v$.

(b)   Show that for all $u, v \in E^N$ and all $\zeta \gg 0$, we have

$$v I^* u \Rightarrow (v + \zeta) P u, \qquad v I^* u \Rightarrow u P (v - \zeta)$$

Hint: To establish the first implication, proceed by contradiction. Say $v I^* u$ but $u R (v + \zeta)$. Deduce that for all w, $v \ll w \ll v + \zeta$ and all u', u'', $u' \ll u \ll u''$, we have $u'' P w P u'$; then derive a contradiction by using (2) for u and $v + \frac{1}{2} \zeta$.

(c)   From (b) deduce that I^* is an equivalence relation (symmetrical and transitive).

(d)   Define R^* by

$$u R^* v \Rightarrow u P^* v \text{ or } u I^* v$$

Show that R^* is complete and transitive, and its upper (and lower) contour sets are closed. Hence (by Debreu's theorem) R^* is represented by a continuous CUF.

2.10   Proof of formula (17). The Gini inequality index can be written as

$$G(u) = \frac{1}{2n^2 \bar{u}} \sum_{i=1}^{n} |u_i - u_j|$$

To prove this from (16), use the formula

$$|a - b| = a + b - 2 \min\{a, b\}$$

2.11   Proving Theorem 2.2 without continuity (Kaneko [1984]). Given is a zero-independent (and anonymous) SWO. We show that for all u, v in E^n, we have

$$\sum_i u_i = \sum_i v_i \Rightarrow u I v \tag{24}$$

From the earlier proof, R is weakly represented by the utilitarian CUF; therefore (24) shows that R is indeed the utilitarian CUF.

(a)   Take $n = 2$. Show that for all x, y, λ in E,

$$(x, y) I (y, x) \Rightarrow (x + \lambda, y - \lambda) I (y + \lambda, x - \lambda)$$

Deduce (24) for $n = 2$.

(b)   Show that for all u in E^n and (v_1, v_2) in E^2,

$$u_1 + u_2 = v_1 + v_2 \Rightarrow (u_1, u_2, u_3, \ldots, u_n) I (v_1, v_2, u_3, \ldots, u_n)$$

(c)   Prove (24) using repeatedly the property shown in (b).

CHAPTER 3

Axiomatic bargaining

Overview

Nash [1950] proposed to generalize SWOs to more complex choice rules that we call social choice functions (SCFs). The idea is to take into account the whole feasible set of utility vectors to guide the choice of the most equitable one. Accordingly, any two utility vectors may no longer be compared independently of the context (namely, the actual set of feasible vectors), as was the case with SWOs. To understand how this widens the range of conceivable choice methods, think of relative egalitarianism as opposed to plain egalitarianism. Say that two agents must divide some commodity bundle. The egalitarian program simply chooses the highest feasible equal utility allocation (assuming away the equality–efficiency dilemma) independently of the feasible unequal utility vectors. Relative egalitarianism, on the other hand, computes first the utility $\bar{u}_i$ that each agent would derive from consuming alone the whole bundle; then it chooses this efficient utility vector where the ratio of the actual utility to the highest conceivable utility $\bar{u}_i$ is the same for each agent. In other words, relative egalitarianism equalizes individual ratios of satisfaction (or of frustration) by defining full satisfaction (i.e., zero frustration) in a context-dependent manner. We give a numerical example (Example 1.1), stressing the difference between egalitarianism and relative egalitarianism.

Formally, the key ingredient in Nash's construction is a mapping associating to each conceivable feasible set of utility vectors a Pareto-optimal element of this set. This mapping is called a SCF. Of course, we make some plausible assumptions about the shape of a feasible utility set (see Section 3.1). These assumptions severely limit the domain of SCFs. Even then, a SCF is much more complicated, as a mathematical object, than a SWO. In fact, Nash's model includes one more parameter in the domain of a SCF, namely, a Pareto-inferior utility vector interpreted as a disagreement point. In this chapter, we always take the disgreement point to be the origin of the individual utilities; further, we assume that feasible utility sets contain nonnegative utility vectors only. This is a restriction in two ways. First, we cannot consider axioms evaluating the impact of a change in the disagreement point; such axioms have been introduced very recently in the literature (Peters [1986b], Chun and Thomson [1990]), but the bulk of the existing results can be formulated without loss of generality with a fixed disagreement point. Second, we assume away any influence of a feasible utility vector not bounded below by the disagreement point upon the solution. This is no serious restriction if we interpret the disagreement utility level of an agent as a level that he can guarantee for himself no matter what the other agents may do. If each agent thus has a right to his individual disagreement level, only those feasible vectors bounded below by the disagreement vector are truly feasible, for cooperation can never force an agent to forfeit his rights.

In Section 3.1 we define formally a SCF and discuss the restrictive assumptions on the feasible utility sets constituting its domain. We always assume, as we did in Chapter 2, that a SCF satisfies anonymity and unanimity. In point of fact, all the results presented in this chapter have been extended to the non-anonymous case as well (some of them can also be adapted without unanimity). As usual, we retain these two axioms because it simplifies considerably the proofs without losing their substance.

In Section 3.2 we discuss the seminal result of the theory of axiomatic bargaining, namely, the characterization of Nash's SWO by the two axioms of scale independence and independence of irrelevant alternatives (Theorem 3.1). This result is actually quite similar to the earlier characterization of Nash's SWO (Theorem 2.3). Only the proof technique is original and has inspired many other proofs.

In Sections 3.3 and 3.4 we discuss two genuine characterizations of the egalitarian (and relative egalitarian) solutions. Those two results rely on two different monotonicity axioms. Kalaï's result (Theorem 3.2) uses issue monotonicity: When the set of feasible utility vectors expands, the utility of no agent (as suggested by the SCF) should decrease. This says that everyone should benefit from an improvement of the cooperative opportunities. Surprisingly enough, only the egalitarian solution satisfies the axiom (relative egalitarianism can also be characterized with the help of a weaker version of issue monotonicity; see Remark 3.2). Issue monotonicity is a versatile axiom that will play an important role in the production economies of Chapter 7.

The second characterization of egalitarianism (and relative egalitarianism) is Thomson's Theorem 3.3. It relies on population monotonicity: When the number of agents entitled to a share of the cooperative surplus increases, while no new cooperative opportunity arises, then the utility of the original agents should not increase. In other words, if more guests have to share the same pie, everyone should tighten his belt a bit (see Definition 3.4).

In Section 3.5 we propose a version of the separability axiom adapted to the SCF framework. It is the key ingredient of a powerful result by Lensberg (parallel to Theorem 2.5) characterizing concave and separably additive SWOs.

Finally, Section 3.6 is devoted to a genuine characterization of the (classical) utilitarian SCF by means of the additivity property: The solution commutes with convex combinations of the feasible set. Although it is harder to interpret, Myerson's theorem (Theorem 3.4) provides a mathematically neat complement to our earlier characterizations of classical utilitarianism (see Chapter 2).

Our choice of results covers but a small fraction of the axiomatic bargaining literature while trying to capture the essential ideas. A more complete coverage of this literature is given by the surveys of Roth [1979] and Kalaï [1985] and the very comprehensive book by Thomson (forthcoming).

The axiomatic bargaining model is the most sophisticated tool of the welfarist viewpoint. Its assumptions are numerous and somehow ad hoc (e.g., think of the domain of feasible utility sets; Definition 3.1); its mathematical arguments can be quite involved and may require long lists of assumptions. Yet it is a fascinating intellectual construction encompassing a host of arbitration methods and ethical postulates into a unified framework. We believe that its methodology is potentially applicable to numerous microeconomic problems of distributive justice and will argue this claim throughout Part III. By developing those applications, we can overcome the principal weakness of the welfarist viewpoint (which is also the reason for its appealing simplicity), namely, its systematical ignorance of any aspect of a particular problem that is not conveyed by utility distribution.

3.1   Social choice functions

A SWO (Chapter 2) performs binary comparisons of utility vectors independently of the particular feasible set where these vectors belong. Faced with a given feasible set, the SWO pinpoints the maximal element(s) for society's choice. In the axiomatic bargaining approach we think of society's choice as a mapping that selects an element out of every possible feasible utility set. This mapping is called a social choice function (SCF): It chooses from any feasible utility set $S \subset E_+^N$ (E_+ is the set of nonnegative numbers; $E_+ = [0, +\infty)$) a particular element of S.

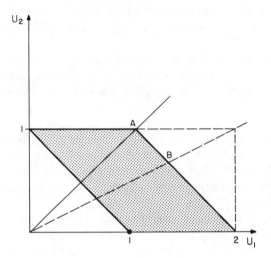

Figure 3.1.

The simplest example of a rule that cannot be derived from maximizing a SWO is *relative egalitarianism*. Given the compact feasible set $S \subset E_+^N$, compute the maximal feasible utility of each agent by taking the vector in S most favorable to agent 1, most favorable to agent 2, and so on. Then equalize *relative* utilities with respect to these maximal utility levels.

Example 3.1. Sharing divisible goods
Two agents receive jointly a gift containing 1 liter of gin and 1 liter of whisky to be shared between them. Agent 2 does not like gin, and agent 1 likes gin or whisky equally. If g_i (w_i) is the amount of gin (whisky) received by agent i, their utilities are

$$u_1 = g_1 + w_1, \quad u_2 = w_2, \quad 0 \le g_1, w_i \le 1, \quad w_1 + w_2 = 1$$

The feasible set S is the shaded area of Figure 3.1. Note that we take the zero of utilities at the no-gift situation. Plain egalitarianism would give all the gin to agent 1 and all the whisky to agent 2, thus achieving the utility vector A. Relative egalitarianism is a bit more subtle. It reckons that agent 2 could never enjoy more than one unit of utility (even if he appropriates the whole gift), whereas agent 1's ceiling is two units. Therefore, it recommends the utility vector B where the relative gains $u_1/2$ and $u_2/1$ coincide. This amounts to solving the system

$$\frac{w_1 + g_1}{2} = \frac{w_2}{1} \quad \text{and} \quad \{w_2 = 1 \text{ or } g_1 = 1\} \quad \text{(Pareto optimality)}$$

with unique solution $w_1 = \frac{1}{3}$, $g_1 = 1$, and $w_2 = \frac{2}{3}$.

Note the implicit bargaining arguments in relative egalitarianism: It would not be fair for agent 2 to enjoy his absolute maximal feasible utility while agent 1 does not.

Before explaining why relative egalitarianism is not derived from a SWO, we need a general definition of SCFs.

Given are society N and a set Σ of subsets of E_+^N. A *social choice function* on (N, Σ) is a mapping φ associating to each set $S \in \Sigma$ a vector $\varphi(S) \in S$.

The choice of the domain Σ is critical. On a very large domain, most axioms are empty. For instance, if Σ contains the finite sets, the anonymity axiom (see what follows) is never satisfied (think of $N = \{1, 2\}$ and $S = \{(1, 2), (2, 1)\}$). Or if Σ contains open sets, its Pareto frontier may be empty, so the unanimity axiom will be empty too.

In this introduction to axiomatic bargaining, we work with a fairly small domain Σ_0. This domain is always contained, often strictly contained, in the various domains used in the literature. The smaller a domain, the more SCFs satisfying given axioms. Thus, we do not lose any interesting choice methods by working with a small domain. We say that a feasible set S is comprehensive if for all $u, v \in E_+^N$, $\{u \in S, v \leq u\} \Rightarrow v \in S$.

Definition 3.1. *The domain Σ_0 consists of all subsets S of E_+^N that are convex, compact, comprehensive, and satisfy the following property, called **minimal transferability**:*

for all $u \in S$, all $i \in N$:

$$\{u_i > 0\} \Rightarrow \{\exists v \in S, v_i < u_i \text{ and } v_j > u_j, \text{ all } j \neq i\} \tag{1}$$

The convexity assumption (called nonpolarization by Yaari [1981]) means that compromises are possible between any two feasible utility vectors. It is a sensible assumption when the set S is derived from some exchange and/or production economy. Its technical importance is considerable.

The compactness assumption is hardly restrictive, and comprehensiveness amounts to free disposal of utility, admittedly a mild assumption.

The three foregoing assumptions are nearly always retained by the literature (with the possible exception of comprehensiveness; see Peters [1986b]). Minimal transferability is less common. It is also less necessary; many of the results that follow (Theorems 3.1 and 3.4) hold true identically on the larger domain of convex, compact, and comprehensive sets, and all can be adapted to this domain. Combined with convexity, minimal transferability eliminates every difference between Pareto-optimal and weakly Pareto-optimal elements of S (defined in Section 1.1). Say that S is convex and satisfies minimal transferability. Then for all $u \in S$

$$\{\exists v \in S, v > u\} \Leftrightarrow \{\exists v \in S, v \gg u\} \tag{2}$$

Hence, a weak Pareto optimum is a Pareto optimum as well.

To prove (2), take $u, v \in S$ such that $v > u$. Then for some agent i, $v_i > u_i$. By (1) there exists $w \in S$ such that $w_i < v_i$ and $w_j > v_j$, all $j \neq i$. By convexity, any convex combination $z = \lambda w + (1 - \lambda) v$ is also in S. For λ small enough, $z \gg u$, and the claim (2) is proved.

An important assumption in Definition 3.1 is that all feasible sets S are subsets of E_+^N. The zero utility vector will play the role of the disagreement utility level (also called status quo utility), the absolute minimum guaranteed to each agent. The agents must unanimously agree to pick one utility distribution in S; any one agent can refuse a proposal and enforce the disagreement point. This interpretation plays a fundamental role in the noncooperative models of bargaining, attempting to develop an explicit game of strategy to describe the agreement process (see Rubinstein [1982]; Binmore, Rubinstein, and Wolinsky [1986]). But for the normative axioms of cooperative justice that concern us, the disagreement point interpretation can be dispensed with.

Our next definition emphasizes two basic axioms already present in Chapters 1 and 2.

Definition 3.2. *Given society N, a social choice function on Σ_0 is a mapping φ from Σ_0 into E_+^N satisfying:*

(i) *Anonymity: For any permutation σ of N and any vector $u \in E_+^N$, write $\sigma(u)$, the vector $\sigma(u)_i = u_{\sigma(i)}$. Then*

   for all $S \in \Sigma_0$: $\varphi(\sigma(S)) = \sigma(\varphi(S))$

(ii) *Unanimity: For all $S \in \Sigma_0$, $\varphi(S)$ is a Pareto-optimal element of S_0.*

The original papers cited after each theorem usually do not make the anonymity assumption. See also Exercises 3.5 and 3.6 for two results that do not assume anonymity and unanimity, respectively.

To illustrate Definition 3.2, we give the mathematical definitions of egalitarianism and relative egalitarianism.

The egalitarian SCF:

$$\text{for all } S \in \Sigma_0: \quad \varphi_e(S) = \lambda e \text{ where } \lambda = \sup\{\lambda \geq 0 / \lambda e \in S\} \tag{3}$$

The relative egalitarian SCF (Kalaï and Smorodinsky [1975]): For all $S \in \Sigma_0$ and all $i \in N$, define $u_i^m(S) = \max\{u_i \mid u \in S\}$. Then

$$\varphi_{\text{re}}(S) = \bar{\mu} u^m(S) \text{ where } \bar{\mu} = \sup\{\mu \geq 0/\mu u^m(S) \in S\} \qquad (4)$$

These two SCFs are well defined by the compactness of S. Check that they are Pareto optimal. If λe were dominated by $v \in S : v \gg \lambda e$, by comprehensiveness of S we could find $\lambda' > \lambda$ with $\lambda' e \in S$, a contradiction. The proof that $\varphi_{\text{re}}(S)$ is Pareto optimal in S is similar. We just proved that the equality–efficiency dilemma does not arise in S.

3.2 Nash's independence of irrelevant alternatives axiom

To a SWO corresponds the SCF picking from every feasible set the utility vector where the SWO is maximal. If there are several such maxima, a tie-breaking rule is necessary. Assume that the SWO R achieves its maximum over S at a unique vector $\varphi(S)$ for every S in Σ_0. Then the corresponding SCF φ satisfies:

Nash's independence of irrelevant alternatives (NIIA):

$$\text{for all } S, S' \in \Sigma_0: \quad \{S \subset S' \text{ and } \varphi(S') \in S\} \Rightarrow \{\varphi(S) = \varphi(S')\} \qquad (5)$$

Indeed, $\varphi(S') = u$ means $u R v$ for all $v \in S'$. A fortiori, $u R v$ for all $v \in S$, and thus $\varphi(S) = u$ as well.

The NIIA axiom is a powerful test for determining whether a SCF can be represented by a SWO. For instance, the egalitarian SCF (3) is represented by the egalitarian SWO (namely, the egalitarian CUF), whereas the relative egalitarian SCF (4) cannot be represented by a CUF. Indeed, consider a society with two agents and the feasible set

$$S' = \{(u_1, u_2) \in E_+^2 \mid u_1 + u_2 \leq 2\} \in \Sigma_0$$

Both agents have the same aspiration level $u_i^m(S')$; hence, relative egalitarianism on S' is plain egalitarianism, $\varphi_{\text{re}}(S') = (1, 1)$. Next shrink S' into the subset S:

$$S = \{(u_1, u_2) \in E_+^2 \mid u_1 + u_2 \leq 2 \text{ and } u_2 \leq 1\}$$

Now $\varphi_{\text{re}}(S) = (\frac{4}{3}, \frac{2}{3})$, as we saw in Example 3.1 (where the feasible set had the same Pareto frontier but lacked comprehensiveness), in contradiction to NIIA since S contains $\varphi_{\text{re}}(S')$. Incidentally, note that *every* SCF φ represented by a SWO must select $\varphi(S) = (1, 1)$ because anonymity forces $\varphi(S') = (1, 1)$.

The NIIA axiom, by itself, does not imply that a SCF can be represented by a SWO. Combined with appropriate continuity assumptions, it does; see Peters and Wakker [1987].

The NIIA axiom is very effective when it is combined with an independence property. The most familiar instance of this is the following seminal result of axiomatic bargaining theory.

Theorem 3.1 (Nash [1950]).   *Given society N, there is exactly one SCF φ on Σ_0 satisfying*

(i)   *Nash's independence of irrelevant alternatives and*
(ii)   *scale independence:*

for all $\lambda \in E_+^N$, all $S \in \Sigma_0$: $\varphi(\lambda \cdot S) = \lambda \cdot \varphi(S)$ (6)

(with $u \cdot v$ as in Definition 2.1, and $v \in \lambda \cdot S$ if and only if there is u in S such that $v = \lambda \cdot u$).

This SCF is represented by Nash's SWO: On every feasible set $S \in \Sigma_0$, it maximizes the product $u_1, \dots, u_n$.

Proof: Check first that Nash's CUF is strictly quasi-concave. Hence, on every convex compact subset of E_+^N, it reaches its maximum at a unique point. Thus, the corresponding SCF satisfies NIIA (see the preceding). Next we know from Theorem 2.3 that Nash's SWO is scale independent (Definition 2.1). Thus, its associated SCF satisfies (6).

We prove the converse statement. Let φ be a SCF satisfying NIIA and (6). For any positive vector a, $a \gg 0$, consider the subset

$$S(a) = \left\{ u \in E_+^N \,\middle|\, \sum_{i=1}^{n} \frac{u_i}{a_i} \le n \right\}$$

Check that $S(a)$ belongs to Σ_0. Then observe that $S(a) = a \cdot S(e)$. By anonymity, $\varphi(S(e)) = e$; hence, by scale independence, $\varphi(S(a)) = a$.

Next consider an arbitrary element S of Σ_0. Denote by a the unique maximum of Nash's CUF, denoted W_N, on S. By quasiconcavity of W_N and convexity of S, the set S and the upper contour W_N at a are separated by a hyperplane. This hyperplane is normal to the gradient of W_N at a, and hence it is normal to $(1/a_1, \dots, 1/a_n)$. Therefore, this hyperplane has equation $\sum_{i=1}^{n}(u_i/a_i) = n$ (remember it contains a). Therefore, the set $S(a)$ contains S (see Figure 3.2). We have $\{\varphi(S(a)) = a, a \in S, S \subset S(a)\}$, implying (by NIIA) $\varphi(S) = a$, as was to be proved.   Q.E.D.

Theorem 3.1, despite its historical importance, does not add much to Theorem 2.3, characterizing Nash's CUF among other SWOs by means of scale independence. In a similar vein, the combination of NIIA with zero independence characterizes classical utilitarianism, a result parallel to Theorem 2.2. Exercise 3.8 gives the details.

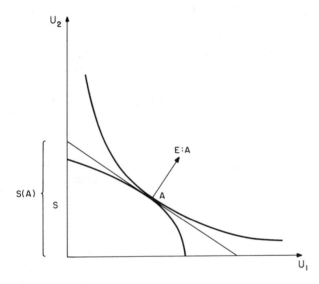

Figure 3.2.

3.3 Issue monotonicity

The contribution of the SCFs to welfarism is twofold: the introduction of new axioms to characterize old choice methods and the exposition of new methods. The next two results illustrate both aspects.

The first original axiom is *issue monotonicity*. Suppose we divide some resources by a welfare egalitarian method (i.e., by measuring utility levels according to some *numéraire*, and equalizing those utilities). If the resources to divide vary but the *numéraire* remains the same, the agents will together benefit or together suffer from the change. It cannot happen that an agent i's utility increases while agent j's decreases. This is so because an egalitarian method picks a utility vector on the diagonal (ignoring the equality–efficiency dilemma), and any two points on the diagonal are compared in the same way by every agent.

This elementary observation has far-reaching consequences. In the current framework, it yields a simple characterization of the egalitarian (and relative egalitarian) SCF. Later on we will also use two variants of issue monotonicity in a nonwelfarist context (see Section 7.6) with similar consequences.

Definition 3.3. *Say that the SCF φ defined on Σ_0 satisfies **issue monotonicity** if we have*

$$for \; all \; S, S' \in \Sigma_0: \quad S \subset S' \Rightarrow \varphi(S) \leq \varphi(S') \tag{7}$$

Check first that issue monotonicity is stronger than NIIA (under Pareto optimality). Indeed, under the premises of (5), issue monotonicity implies $\varphi(S) \leq \varphi(S')$. As $\varphi(S)$ is Pareto optimal in S and $\varphi(S')$ belongs to S, we must have equality.

Both the utilitarian and Nash's SCF satisfy NIIA but violate issue monotonicity (see Exercise 3.1). Hence, the latter is strictly stronger than NIIA.

Theorem 3.2 (Kalaï [1977]).   *Given society N, there is exactly one SCF φ on Σ_0 satisfying issue monotonicity. It is the egalitarian SCF φ_e [given by (3)].*

Proof: The egalitarian SCF satisfies issue monotonicity. Conversely, let a SCF φ satisfy issue monotonicity. Fix a feasible set $S \in \Sigma_0$ and denote $a = \lambda e$, the vector of S selected by the egalitarian SCF (3). If $a = 0$, then $S = \{0\}$ (because a is Pareto optimal), and the desired equality $\varphi(S) = a$ follows. From now on, assume $a \neq 0$, and hence $\lambda > 0$. By (2), for all i we can find $v^i \in S$ such that $v_i^i < \lambda$, $v_j^i > \lambda$, all $j \neq i$. Denote

$$\alpha = \inf_{1 \leq i \neq j \leq n} v_j^i, \quad \alpha > \lambda$$

and define n vectors a^i, $i \in N$, by $a_i^i = 0$, $a_j^i = \alpha$, all $j \neq i$. Since $a^i \leq v^i$, and S is comprehensive, each vector a^i belongs to S.

We define S_0 to be the convex hull of $0, a, a^1, \ldots, a^n$. The careful reader will check that S_0 belongs to Σ_0 and is invariant by any permutation of the coordinates. Thus, by anonymity and unanimity, $\varphi(S_0) = a$. On the other hand, S_0 is a subset of S (S is convex and contains $a, a^1, \ldots, a^n$). Therefore, $a \leq \varphi(S)$ by issue monotonicity. We conclude $\varphi(S) = a$ from the Pareto optimality of a in S.   Q.E.D.

Remark 3.1:   The original proof of Theorem 3.2 in Kalaï [1977] is slightly more complicated because the assumption of minimal transferability (1) is lacking, and Pareto optimality is replaced by weak Pareto optimality.

Remark 3.2:   Kalaï and Smorodinsky [1975] propose a similar characterization of the relative egalitarian SCF under a restricted issue monotonicity axiom *plus* scale independence. This result is the subject of Exercise 3.3.

Thomson and Myerson [1980] study the consequences of issue monotonicity without the anonymity axiom – but with unanimity. They characterize a family of path-monotone methods described in Exercise 3.5.

3.4   Population monotonicity

Monotonicity with respect to variable population is another genuine property of the axiomatic bargaining formulation. Consider two societies N and $N \cup \{\omega\}$, where a new agent ω, $\omega \notin N$, joins. Thomson's population monotonicity axiom says the following: If no new surplus opportunities emerge when ω joins, none of the agents in N should benefit. Intuitively, if a new guest shows up to share the same cake, every other guest should tighten his belt.

The difficulty, of course, is to translate formally the idea that the cake does not expand when agent ω joins. In the axiomatic bargaining framework, the solution is plain. We denote by $\Sigma_0(n)$ the domain of Definition 3.1 for a society of size n. Let $S \in \Sigma_0(n+1)$ be a set of feasible utilities for $N \cup \{\omega\}$, namely, the surplus opportunities of $N \cup \{\omega\}$; removing ω without losing any opportunity is similar to keeping his utility u_ω at its disagreement level $u_\omega = 0$, namely, taking the slice of S at $u_\omega = 0$ or, equivalently, taking the projection $\pi_N(S) \subset E_+^N$ of S over $E^N x\{0\}$ (the slice at $u_\omega = 0$ coincides with the projection over $E_+^N x\{0\}$ because S is comprehensive).

Definition 3.4.   *Given is a sequence φ^n, $n = 1, 2, \ldots$, of SCFs, one for each possible size n of the society N. We say that this sequence is **population monotonic** if for all societies $N \cup \{\omega\}$ with size $n+1$ and all feasible sets $S \in \Sigma_0(n+1)$, we have*

$$\pi_N(\varphi^{n+1}(S)) \leq \varphi^n(\pi_N(S)) \tag{8}$$

Note that population monotonicity bears on a *sequence* of SCFs, not on a single SCF for a fixed society. The separability axiom in the next section is of this kind, too.

Our first task is to illustrate property (8) by showing that the sequence of egalitarian SCFs does satisfy population monotonicity.

Take $N = \{1, 2\}$, $\omega = 3$, and a feasible set $S \in \Sigma_0(3)$. Denote by S_{12} the projection of S on the plane $u_3 = 0$. Next call $x \in E^2$ the egalitarian outcome for S_{12} and $y \in E^3$ that for S; see Figure 3.3.

We must show that the projection of y on $E_+^{\{12\}} x\{0\}$, denoted y_{12}, is below x. Since $y_{12} x\{0\}$ belongs to S (by comprehensiveness), the vector y_{12} belongs to S_{12}. By definition of the egalitarian solution y for S, we have $y_1 = y_2$, and hence y_{12} is on the diagonal of $E_+^{\{1,2\}}$. By definition of x, we have $y_{12} \leq x$, as was to be proved. The proof for N with arbitrary dimension is identical.

Population monotonicity alone does not characterize the egalitarian SCFs. For instance, the relative egalitarian SCFs also satisfy (8). By combining population monotonicity with an independence property, we derive

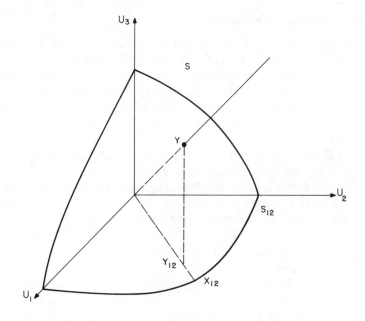

Figure 3.3.

two original characterizations of the egalitarian and relative egalitarian SCF.

Theorem 3.3 (Thomson [1983a, b]).   (a) *There is exactly one sequence of SCFs (one for each size $n = 1, 2, \ldots$, of society) satisfying population monotonicity and NIIA. It is the sequence of egalitarian SCFs.*

(b) *There is exactly one sequence of SCFs satisfying population monotonicity and scale independence. It is the sequence of relative egalitarian SCFs.*

Sketch of the Proof: Statement (a). Given is a sequence φ^n, $n = 1, 2, \ldots$, of SCFs satisfying NIIA for each n and population monotonicity. Consider society $\{1, 2, 3\}$ and a feasible set $S \in \Sigma_0(2)$ for the first two agents ($S \subset E_+^{\{1, 2\}}$). We show that $\varphi^2(S) = \lambda \cdot (1, 1)$, where λ is defined by (3), [i.e., $\varphi^2(s)$ is the egalitarian solution] by constructing a feasible set T in $E_+^{\{1, 2, 3\}}$ of which the projection on $E_+^{\{1, 2\}}$ is S.

Denote $x = (\lambda, \lambda, \lambda)$ and take T as the convex comprehensive hull of x, $(0, 0, 2\lambda)$, and $Sx\{0\}$ (see Figure 3.4). Check that T is in $\Sigma_0(3)$. Next consider the feasible set $H = \{u \in E_+^3 \mid u_1 + u_2 + u_3 \leq 3\lambda\}$. Assume for the moment that T is contained in H. By anonymity, we have $\varphi^3(H) = x$. As

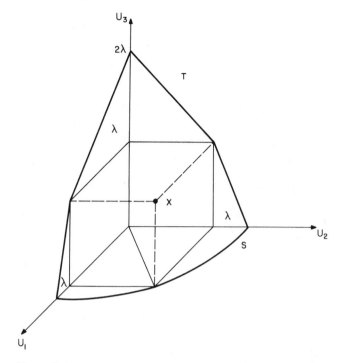

Figure 3.4.

$x \in T$ and $T \subset H$, NIIA implies $\varphi^3(T) = x$. Check next that the projection of T on $E_+^{\{1,2\}}$ is S. Thus, by population monotonicity, we have

$$\pi_{\{12\}}(\varphi^3(T)) = (\lambda, \lambda) \leq \varphi^2(S)$$

Finally Pareto optimality of (λ, λ) forces an equality, as desired.

The preceding argument depends on the assumption that H contains T, equivalent to: H contains $Sx\{0\}$. This is true if S is "not too skewed" in the following sense:

$$u_i^m(S) \leq 2\lambda \quad \text{for } i = 1, 2, \text{ where } u_i^m(S) \text{ is defined in (4)}$$

Indeed, every element $(u_1, u_2, 0)$ of $Sx\{0\}$ satisfies $\{u_1 \leq \lambda \text{ and } u_2 \leq u_2^m(S)\}$ or $\{u_1 \leq u_1^m(S) \text{ and } u_2 \leq \lambda\}$, so it belongs to H as well.

The complete proof of statement (a) (Thomson [1983b]) works by induction on the degree of skewedness of S and extension of the argument to an arbitrary number of agents.

Statement (b). By minimal transferability [property (1)], a feasible set $S \in \Sigma_0(n)$ either is $\{0\}$ or has $u_i^m(S) > 0$ for all i. Thus, if the sequence φ^n,

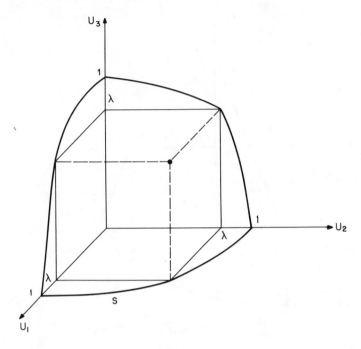

Figure 3.5.

$n = 1, 2, \ldots$, of SCFs satisfies scale independence, it is enough to consider feasible sets $S \in \Sigma_0(n)$ such that $u_i^m(S) = 1$ for all i.

Check that the sequence of relative egalitarian SCFs satisfies population monotonicity. If the feasible set S has $u_i^m(S) = 1$ for all i, relative egalitarianism is just egalitarianism, so there is nothing more to prove.

Conversely, suppose the sequence φ^n, $n = 1, 2, \ldots$, satisfies population monotonicity and scale independence. Fix a society $N = \{1, 2, 3\}$ and consider a feasible set $S \in \Sigma_0(2)$ for the first two agents ($S \subset E_+^{\{1,2\}}$). Assume also $u_i^m(S) = 1$, $i = 1, 2$, and denote by $\lambda(1, 1)$ the egalitarian (and relative egalitarian) outcome of S.

Consider the permutation σ of 1, 2, 3, $\sigma(i) = i + 1$ (with the convention $3 + 1 = 1$), and denote by T the convex comprehensive hull in E_+^3 of $(\lambda, \lambda, \lambda)$, $Sx\{0\}$, $\sigma(Sx\{0\})$, $\sigma^2(Sx\{0\})$; see Figure 3.5. Check first that T is in $\Sigma_0(3)$. Then observe that $(\lambda, \lambda, \lambda)$ is Pareto optimal in T and T is invariant under the permutation σ. Thus, by anonymity, we have $\varphi^3(T) = (\lambda, \lambda, \lambda)$. Next the projection of T on $E_+^{\{1,2\}}$ is S. Thus, population monotonicity implies $(\lambda, \lambda) \leq \varphi^2(S)$ and hence the conclusion by Pareto optimality of (λ, λ) in S. The proof for a feasible set with arbitrary dimension is quite similar; see the details in Thomson [1983b].   Q.E.D.

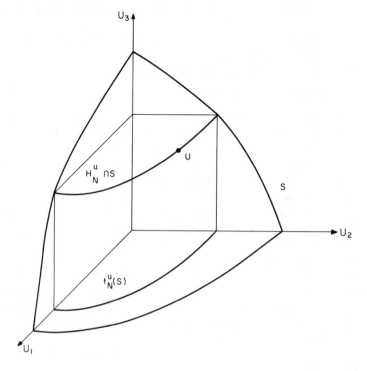

Figure 3.6.

3.5   Separability

For SCFs, separability conveys the same idea as it does for SWOs (see Section 2.4): A decision that concerns a subset of agents can be based on the utilities of those agents only. In the axiomatic bargaining context, the formulation of this axiom is more involved because the restriction to a subset of agents affects their utility possibility frontier.

Notation: Given two societies N, M, with $N \subset M$ and a utility vector $u \in E_+^M$, denote H_N^u the following linear space:

$$H_N^u = \{y \in E_+^M \mid y_j = u_j \text{ for all } j \in M \setminus N\}$$

For all $S \in \Sigma_0(M)$ (a feasible set in E_+^M) and $u \in S$, denote $t_N^u(S) = \pi_N(H_N^u \cap S)$, where π_N is the projection of E^M onto $E^N x\{0\}^{M \setminus N}$.

Thus, u is a feasible vector for society M, $H_N^u \cap S$ contains the feasible vectors of S that give to the agents in $M \setminus N$ the same utilities as u, and $t_N^u(S)$ is the feasible set left within society N after agents of $M \setminus N$ are given what they get in u (see Figure 3.6).

We now define separability, originally introduced by Lensberg [1987] under the name of stability.

Separability: Given is a sequence φ^n, $n = 1, 2, \ldots$, of SCFs, one for each possible size of the society. For any two societies N, M with $N \subset M$ and any feasible set $S \in \Sigma_0(M)$, we require

$$\varphi^m(S) = u \Rightarrow \varphi^n(t_N^u) = \pi_N(u) \tag{9}$$

In words, say the agents in N decide to renegotiate the distribution of their utilities. They give to each agent in $M \setminus N$ whatever utility he gets within society M. This leaves the feasible set t_N^u for society N [where $u = \varphi^m(S)$]. Property (9) says that arbitration in the subgroup N over this restricted feasible set will be entirely consistent with the arbitration in the larger society M over the initial feasible set.

To give an example of a separable sequence of SCFs, just take the egalitarian SCFs for all n. For any feasible set S, we have $\varphi^m(S) = \lambda \cdot e_M$. Note that $\lambda \cdot e_N$ is Pareto optimal in $t_N^{\lambda \cdot e_M}(S)$ because $\lambda \cdot e_M$ is Pareto optimal in S. This in turn implies (9).

A rich family of separable SCFs obtains by choosing an increasing and strictly concave function α of the real variable and maximizing over S the CUF $\sum_{i \in M} \alpha(u_i)$ for all m (where m is the size of M). This function is strictly concave for all n and hence has a unique maximum over any convex feasible set.

We check that the corresponding sequence of SCFs satisfies (9). Fix $S \in \Sigma_0(M)$ and $u = \operatorname{argmax}_S \{\sum_{i \in M} \alpha(u_i)\}$. Pick $N \subset M$ and suppose $\pi_N(u)$ is not the maximum of $\sum_{i \in N} \alpha(w_i)$ over t_N^u:

$$\sum_{i \in N} \alpha(u_i) < \sum_{i \in N} \alpha(v_i) \quad \text{for some } v \in t_N^u$$

Construct a vector w as follows: $w_i = v_i$ for $i \in N$, $w_j = u_j$ for $j \in M \setminus N$. Then w belongs to S (by definition of t_N^u), and $\sum_{i \in M} \alpha(u_i) < \sum_{i \in M} \alpha(w_i)$, a contradiction.

A deep theorem by Lensberg [1987] establishes the converse property: The separability axiom essentially characterizes the sequences of SCFs maximizing some separably additive CUF of the form $\sum_i \alpha(u_i)$ with α strictly concave. One important difference in Lensberg's formulation is that the sequence of egalitarian SCFs (that do not result from maximizing some separably additive CUF) does not qualify as a possible solution for lack of Pareto optimality. Indeed, Lensberg's domain of feasible sets are the compact, convex, comprehensive subsets of E_+^N with nonempty interior. Minimal transferability is not assumed, so that the subset S of E_+^2,

$$S = \{(u_1, u_2) \mid 0 \leq u_1 \leq 1, 0 \leq u_2 \leq 2\}$$

is a perfectly valid feasible set. Yet on S, the egalitarian SCF [defined by (3)] selects $(1, 1)$, not a Pareto optimum (except in the weak sense).

Finally, Lensberg's result uses a continuity axiom for SCFs in addition to separability. This additional requirement also rules out any Pareto-optimal refinement of the egalitarian methods (such as maximization of the leximin SWO) that would otherwise pass the test of separability.

Lensberg's theorem is hard to prove, so we will not even sketch its proof. It shows the profound analogy between the two separability axioms for SWOs (Definition 2.4 and Theorem 2.5) and for SCFs.

3.6   Additivity

We now turn to axioms that focus attention on classical utilitarianism.

We are back into the fixed society framework. Given N, a SCF φ is said to be *utilitarian* if it selects a vector where joint utility is maximal:

$$\text{for all } S \in \Sigma_0: \quad \{\varphi(S) = u\} \Rightarrow \left\{ \sum_{i=1}^{n} u_i \geq \sum_{i=1}^{n} v_i, \text{ for all } v \in S \right\} \tag{10}$$

Note that for certain feasible sets (e.g., the unit simplex of E_+^N) the utilitarian program allows for many winners; condition (10) does not impose a particular tie-breaking rule in this case. For the sake of simplicity, we will in this section restrict even more the domain of feasible sets. Instead of working on Σ_0 (Definition 3.1), we will use the domain Σ_{00} consisting of all compact, *strictly* convex, and comprehensive subsets of E_+^N. We leave it to the reader to check that Σ_{00} is a subset of Σ_0 (strict convexity and comprehensiveness imply minimal transferability). We explain in what follows (Remark 3.3) how the main result can be stated on the domain Σ_0.

On every feasible set $S \in \Sigma_{00}$, the utilitarian CUF has a unique maximum, thus defining an unambiguous utilitarian SCF denoted φ_*. This SCF commutes with the convex combination of feasible sets.

Notation: For a given number λ, $0 \leq \lambda \leq 1$, the convex combination of the two subsets S, S' of E_+^N is denoted $\lambda S + (1-\lambda)S'$:

$$u \in \lambda S + (1-\lambda)S' \Leftrightarrow \exists v \in S, v' \in S': u = \lambda v + (1-\lambda)v'$$

Theorem 3.4 (Myerson [1981]).   *On the domain Σ_{00}, the utilitarian SCF commutes with convex combinations:*

$$\varphi_*(\lambda S + (1-\lambda)S') = \lambda \varphi_*(S) + (1-\lambda)\varphi_*(S'),$$

$$\text{all } S, S' \in \Sigma_{00}, \text{ all } \lambda, \ 0 \leq \lambda \leq 1 \tag{11}$$

Conversely, no other SCF on Σ_{00} satisfies (11).

Myerson [1981] calls (11) the "no-timing-effect" condition. The story he tells has a random feasible set, as when the output of a cooperative venture is uncertain. With probability λ the feasible set will be S, and with probability $1-\lambda$ it will be S'. Condition (11) says that it does not matter whether the arbitration takes place before or after the random event selects the actual feasible set. Doing it ex post, the outcome will be $\varphi(S)$ with probability λ and $\varphi(S')$ with probability $1-\lambda$; doing it ex ante, one faces the feasible set $\lambda S+(1-\lambda)S'$ (since the choices in S and S' are unconstrained).

Proof of Theorem 3.4:   Given are N and a SCF φ on $\Sigma_{00}(N)$. For all S, denote $Q(S)$ the following cone of E_+^N:

$$Q(S)=\left\{p\in E_+^N \,\middle|\, \max_{u\in S}(p\cdot u)>p\cdot\varphi(S)\right\}$$

Suppose there is some $p\in E_+^N$, $p\neq 0$, such that $p\cdot\varphi(S)=\max_{u\in S}(p\cdot u)$, for all $S\in\Sigma_{00}$. Then p must be parallel to e. Consider

$$S=\left\{u\in E_+^N \,\middle|\, \sum_{i=1}^n u_i^2\leq 1\right\}$$

where $p\cdot u$ is maximal at $u=p/\|p\|$; by anonymity we must have $\varphi(S)=(1/\sqrt{n})e$.

Thus, φ is the utilitarian SCF if and only if the sets $Q(S)$, $S\in\Sigma_{00}$, do not cover E_+^N. Suppose they do cover E_+^N; in particular, they cover its unit simplex, a compact set. Since each set $Q(S)$ is open, a finite subset $Q(S_1),\dots,Q(S_K)$ is enough to cover the unit simplex. Set $S=(1/K)\sum_{k=1}^K S_k$ and note that S belongs to Σ_{00} (Σ_{00} is stable by convex combinations). Assumption (11) implies

$$\varphi(S)=\frac{1}{K}\sum_{k=1}^K \varphi(S_k) \tag{12}$$

Since $\varphi(S)$ is Pareto optimal in S, there exists a vector p in the simplex of E_+^N such that

$$p\cdot\varphi(S)=\max_{u\in S} p\cdot u \tag{13}$$

By construction, there exists k_0 such that $p\in Q(S_{k_0})$:

$$p\cdot\varphi(S_{k_0})<\max_{u\in S_{k_0}} p\cdot u \Rightarrow p\cdot\varphi(S_{k_0})<p\cdot u_{k_0}$$

where u_{k_0} is some vector in S_{k_0}.

Consider the vector $u=(1/K)[u_{k_0}+\sum_{k\neq k_0}\varphi(S_k)]\in S$. We have, by (12),

$$p\cdot\varphi(S)=\frac{1}{K}\sum_{k=1}^K p\cdot\varphi(S_k)<\frac{1}{K}\left[p\cdot u_{k_0}+\sum_{k\neq k_0} p\cdot\varphi(S_k)\right]=p\cdot u$$

where u is an element of S, hence a contradiction of (13).   Q.E.D.

Remark 3.3: A variant of Theorem 3.4 holds for SCFs defined on the domain Σ_0 or even on the large domain of compact, convex, and comprehensive subsets of E_+^N. The only difficulty is to extend accurately the definition of the utilitarian SCF to these domains (this can be done in several ways).

Remark 3.4: The utilitarian SCF also commutes with addition of feasible sets:

$$\varphi_*(S+S') = \varphi_*(S) + \varphi_*(S'), \quad \text{all } S, S' \in \Sigma_{00} \tag{14}$$

This property also characterizes the utilitarian SCF, as Exercise 3.8 emphasizes. The interpretation of (14) is "ad hoc": One has to think of two distinct cooperative ventures in which the agents N are engaged. Assuming that the utilities derived from these ventures can be added (an assumption amounting to viewing utilities as transferable payoffs), property (14) says that it does not matter whether we deal with the two bargaining problems separately or aggregate them into a single problem.

Remark 3.5: Despite their relatively poor ethical justification, the additivity [(14)] and affinity [(11)] conditions have received a great deal of attention because of their mathematical tractability. Two prominent variants are superadditivity, $\varphi(S) + \varphi(S') \le \varphi(S+S')$, and superaffinity, $\lambda\varphi(S) + (1-\lambda)\varphi(S') \le \varphi(\lambda S + (1-\lambda)S')$. Both are satisfied by the egalitarian SCF and others. Myerson [1981] utilizes superaffinity to jointly characterize utilitarian and egalitarian SCFs. Maschler and Perles [1981a, b] combine superadditivity with scale independence to characterize an original SCF for $n = 2$ but face an impossibility result for $n \ge 3$.

Another interesting variant is Peters's [1986a] restricted additivity.

EXERCISES

3.1 Some counterexamples.

(a) Consider the two following subsets of $\Sigma_0(2)$:

$$S = \{(u_1, u_2) \in E_+^2 \mid \max\{2u_1 + u_2, u_1 + 2u_2\} \le 3\}$$
$$S' = \{(u_1, u_2) \in E_+^2 \mid \max\{\tfrac{5}{2}u_1 + u_2, \tfrac{10}{7}u_1 + \tfrac{10}{7}u_2\} \le 4\}$$

Compute the solutions on S and S' of the utilitarian and Nash's SCFs. Deduce that neither satisfies issue monotonicity.

(b) Consider the subset S'' of $\Sigma_0(3)$ that is the convex hull of $Sx\{0\}$, $(1.4, 0, 0.8)$ and $(0, 0, 0.9)$. Compute the solution on S'' of the utilitarian SCF and of Nash's SCF. Deduce that neither SCF satisfies population monotonicity.

(c)   Consider the two following subsets of $\Sigma_{00}(2)$:

$$S_1 = \{(u_1, u_2) \in E_+^2 \mid u_1^2 + 8u_1 + u_2^2 \le 9\}$$
$$S_2 = \{(u_1, u_2) \in E_+^2 \mid u_1^2 + 8u_2 + u_2^2 \le 9\}$$

Use these sets to show that the egalitarian and Nash's SCFs do not sat-isfy additivity [(14)] or affinity [(11)].

3.2   Sharing divisible goods. We consider the model of Exercise 2.1. The two agents must share a units of good A and b units of good B, and their utilities are $u_i = \alpha_i a_i + \beta_i b_i$ for $i = 1, 2$. We assume that all coefficients α_i, β_i are positive and that $\alpha_2/\beta_2 < \alpha_1/\beta_1$.

(a)   Show that with those utility functions (having their zero at the zero allo-cation) the relative egalitarian SCF picks the following allocation:

$$\text{if } \left(\frac{\alpha_1}{\beta_1}\right) \cdot \left(\frac{\alpha_2}{\beta_2}\right) \le \frac{b^2}{a^2}, \text{ then } \begin{cases} a_1 = a \\ b_1 = a \cdot \dfrac{b^2/a^2 - \alpha_1/\beta_1 \cdot \alpha_2/\beta_2}{2b/a + \alpha_2/\beta_2 + \alpha_1/\beta_1} \end{cases}$$

$$\text{if } \frac{b^2}{a^2} \le \left(\frac{\alpha_1}{\beta_1}\right) \cdot \left(\frac{\alpha_2}{\beta_2}\right), \text{ then } \begin{cases} a_1 = a - b \left(\dfrac{a^2/b^2 - \beta_1/\alpha_1 \cdot \beta_2/\alpha_2}{2a/b + \beta_2/\alpha_2 + \beta_1/\alpha_1}\right) \\ b_1 = 0 \end{cases}$$

(b)   Compute similarly the relative egalitarian solution when we represent the same preferences by the linear utility functions having their zero at the allocation $a_1 = a/2$, $b_1 = b/2$.

3.3   Risk aversion. Two brothers receive jointly a gift of two lottery tick-ets. Ticket A wins \$200 with probability $\frac{1}{2}$, and ticket B wins \$1000 with probability $\frac{1}{10}$. They must share the tickets, and monetary compensations are not available. Instead, they allocate both tickets at random: agent 1 (agent 2) receives ticket A with probability $\lambda((1-\lambda))$, and he receives ticket B with probability $\mu((1-\mu))$.

Agent 1 is risk neutral. His utility for a package (λ, μ) is just the ex-pected monetary gain:

$$u(\lambda A + \mu B) = 100 \cdot \lambda + 100 \cdot \mu$$

Agent 2, on the other hand, is risk averse. If ticket A is worth 100 units of utility (whatever this unit may be), then ticket B is worth only $100 - r$ of the same units (r is a measure of his risk aversion). His utility for the package $(1-\lambda, 1-\mu)$ is then

$$v((1-\lambda)A + (1-\mu)B) = 100 \cdot (1-\lambda) + (100 - r) \cdot (1-\mu)$$

Compute the ticket allocation recommended by Nash's CUF and by the relative egalitarian SCF.

Use the formulas of Exercises 2.1 and 3.1 and compute according to r, $0 \le r \le 100$, the loss in expected monetary gain to agent 2.

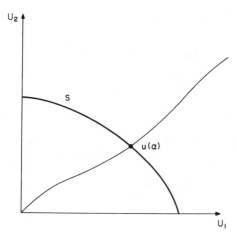

Figure 3.7.

3.4 **Characterization of the relative egalitarian SCF** (Kalaï and Smorodinsky [1975]). Given are a society N and a feasible set $S \in \Sigma_0(N)$. Remember that $u_i^m(S)$ is the highest feasible utility for agent i in S [see (4)]. Consider the following axiom for a SCF φ:

Restricted issue monotonicity: for all $S, S' \in \Sigma_0$:
$$\{u^m(S) = u^m(S') \text{ and } S \subset S'\} \Rightarrow \{\varphi(S) \leq \varphi(S')\}$$

(a) Show that the SCF derived from Nash's CUF and the utilitarian CUF do not satisfy restricted issue monotonicity. Use the following example proposed in Peters [1986b, p. 51]:
$$S = \{(u_1, u_2) \in E_+^2 \mid \max\{\tfrac{1}{3}u_1 + u_2, u_1 + \tfrac{1}{3}u_2\} \leq 1\}$$
$$S' = \{(u_1, u_2) \in E_+^2 \mid \max\{\tfrac{6}{19}u_1 + u_2, u_1 + \tfrac{1}{14}u_2\} \leq 1\}$$

(b) Show that the egalitarian and relative egalitarian SCFs satisfy restricted issue monotonicity.

(c) Show that the relative egalitarian SCF is characterized by scale independence *plus* restricted issue monotonicity.

3.5 **Path-monotone SCFs** (Thomson and Myerson [1980]). In this exercise, a SCF satisfies unanimity but not necessarily anonymity.

Consider an increasing path in E_+^N, namely, a mapping $\alpha \to u(\alpha) = (u_i(\alpha))$ from E_+ into E_+^N, where $u(0) = 0$, u_i is continuous and nondecreasing in α for all i, and $\sum_{i \in N} u_i$ is increasing in α (see Figure 3.7). Then define, for all $S \in \Sigma_0(N)$,

$$\varphi(S) = \sup\{u(\alpha) \mid u(\alpha) \in S\} \tag{15}$$

(a) Show that this defines a (non-anonymous) SCF satisfying issue monotonicity.

(b) Conversely, show that a (non-anonymous) SCF satisfying issue monotonicity can be written as (15) for some increasing path $\alpha \to u(\alpha)$.

Hint: For all α, set $T_\alpha = \{u \in E_+^N \mid \sum_{i \in N} u_i = \alpha\}$ and define $u(\alpha) = \varphi(T_\alpha)$. Then show that $\alpha \to u(\alpha)$ is the desired path.

Peters [1986b] (Proposition 5.14) proposes, in the same spirit, a non-anonymous generalization of relative egalitarianism.

3.6 Another characterization of Nash's SCF (Roth [1979]). In this exercise a SCF satisfies anonymity but not necessarily unanimity.

Consider a SCF satisfying scale independence and NIIA (and anonymity) on Σ_0. Show that it must be Nash's SCF or the dummy SCF: $\varphi(S) = 0$, all $S \in \Sigma_0$. *Hint:* Suppose that, for some feasible set $S \in \Sigma_0$, we have $\varphi(S) \neq 0$ and that $\varphi(S)$ is Pareto inferior in S. Then set $S' = \lambda S$ with λ smaller than 1 and derive a contradiction when λ is close enough to 1.

3.7 Another interpretation of Nash's SCF (Shapley [1969]). Given a society N and a feasible set $S \in \Sigma_0(N)$, let u^* be the vector chosen in S by Nash's SCF.

(a) Show that all coordinates of u^* are positive (unless $S = \{0\}$, in which case $u = 0$). Denote $p = (1/u_1^*, \ldots, 1/u_n^*)$ and show that u^* is a solution of the system:

$$u \in S, \quad p \cdot u \geq p \cdot v, \quad \text{all } v \in S, \quad \text{and} \quad p_i u_i = p_j u_j \text{ all } i, j \qquad (16)$$

This says that, when individual utilities are weighted by $p_1, \ldots, p_n$, respectively, the welfare distribution at u^* is both the utilitarian and the egalitarian solution.

(b) Conversely, fix a vector $p \in E_+^N$, $p \neq 0$, and consider system (16) with unknown u. Show that the system has no solution if p is not parallel to $(1/u_1^*, \ldots, 1/u_n^*)$. In this latter case show that Nash's solution u^* is the unique solution of system (16).

3.8 A variant of Theorem 3.4.

(a) Show that the egalitarian SCF is superadditive:

$$\varphi(S) + \varphi(S') \leq \varphi(S + S'), \quad \text{all } S, S' \in \Sigma_0$$

Show that the relative egalitarian SCF is not superadditive (nor subadditive either).

(b) Show that on domain Σ_{00} (see Section 3.6), the utilitarian SCF is characterized by additivity:

$$\varphi(S) + \varphi(S') = \varphi(S + S'), \quad \text{all } S, S' \in \Sigma_{00}$$

3.9 Another characterization of utilitarianism. In this exercise, the domain $\tilde{\Sigma}$ of feasible sets consists of all subsets S of E^N (instead of E_+^N) with the properties:

S is closed, convex, and comprehensive   and $S \neq E^N$

Given is a SCF φ defined on $\tilde{\Sigma}$ (where it satisfies anonymity and unanimity) satisfying

$$\varphi(S+a) = \varphi(S) + a, \quad \text{for all } S \in \tilde{\Sigma}, \text{ all } a \in E^N$$

where $S+a$ is simply the set S translated by a. Suppose, moreover, that φ satisfies NIIA [defined by (5) on $\tilde{\Sigma}$]. Then show that φ is utilitarian in the sense of property (10).

PART II

Cooperative games

CHAPTER 4

Cost-sharing games and the core

Overview

A cooperative game in society N consists of a feasible utility set for the grand coalition N as well as a utility set for each and every coalition (non-empty subset) of N, including the coalitions containing one agent only. Each of those $2^n - 1$ utility sets is viewed, as in the welfarist models of Part I, as a feasible set of cooperative opportunities: If the agents in a given coalition all agree on it, they can enforce any utility distribution in this set. The game model does not describe the course of action they must take to achieve this utility distribution. This must be made clear by each particular microeconomic model generating a cooperative game.

We view the cooperative game model as an extension of the axiomatic bargaining model (Chapter 3). The latter specifies the feasible utility set for the grand coalition N and for each coalition containing a single agent. Indeed, the disagreement utility of an agent corresponds to his opportunity cost for joining the grand coalition. Thus, the only new ingredients in a cooperative game are the opportunity sets of intermediate coalitions (containing at least two, but not more than $n-1$, agents).

The normative problem raised by a cooperative game is this: Overall cooperation requires an outcome to be picked in the feasible set of the grand coalition N (this actually follows from the unanimity principle in most cases; see what follows). How should the utility sets open to sub-coalitions be used to restrict, possibly determine, this choice? The core idea is to view those coalitional utility sets as the possible opportunity costs of entering into cooperation with the rest of the agents. In the core, one seeks to protect all those rights at once by making sure that no coalition of agents ends up preferring one of its feasible utility vectors to that resulting from overall cooperation.

The core idea has been present for some time in the cost-sharing literature under the name *stand-alone* or *no-subsidy* principle (see Faulhaber

[1975] for an exposition of those principles). The systematical application of the idea to microeconomics was pioneered by Shubik [1962]. Shortly afterward Debreu and Scarf [1963], Scarf [1967], and Foley [1967, 1970] successfully applied the core concept to exchange economies, production economies, and public good economies, respectively, thus establishing its relevance to a wide range of problems. Some of these works are discussed in Part III (Chapters 6 and 7).

The examples discussed in this and the following chapter always give rise to *superadditive* cooperative games. Superadditivity means that whatever two disjoint coalitions can independently do, the union of these two coalitions can do as well. An important consequence is that every Pareto-optimal allocation can be found in the feasible utility set of the grand coalition N; in a superadditive game, the unanimity principle forces overall cooperation. Most economic examples of cooperative games are superadditive.

It is a surprising but simple fact that in a superadditive cooperative game, the core may be empty. Even though the cooperation of all is the only efficient outcome, it may never be compatible with the collection of coalitional rights. In Chapter 4 our main task is to illustrate this possibility and to enounce some mathematical properties that prevent it. The core concept will play a central role in our discussion until Chapter 7 (see also Sections 10.3 and 10.4).

In the first three sections of this chapter (as well as in the whole of Chapter 5) we restrict attention to cooperative games with *transferable utility* (TU) games. This is tantamount to supposing that our agents are endowed with quasi-linear utilities – namely, additively decomposable in money and other goods and linear in money – whereupon utility is fully transferable across agents by means of monetary transfers. In that framework, the classical welfarist analysis (as developed in Part I) is very simple: Pareto optimality is equivalent to maximization of joint utility, whereas side payments (monetary transfers) make any distributive objective, including plain egalitarianism, compatible with Pareto optimality. However, the theory of TU cooperative games is complicated by the data of coalitional opportunity costs.

In Section 4.1 we discuss cost-sharing games and define the corresponding cores. We emphasize that the set of core allocations may be large, small, or even empty. Thus, the core requirement may set loose bounds on the allocation of costs, or it may be impossible to meet altogether. This calls for a more determinist approach to cooperative games whereby we seek to pick a single allocation out of every cooperative game; this is the point of view taken in Chapter 5. In Section 4.2 we characterize the class of TU cooperative games of which the core is nonempty (Theorem

4.1). This useful result is an application of standard linear programming techniques.

All examples of cooperative games in this chapter are about pricing of a natural monopoly. A technology of production is available to society N as well as to any subcoalition S. The technology has the natural monopoly property (subadditivity of costs) that yields superadditive games and makes joint production the only efficient organization. A regulated monopoly (required to just cover its cost) will maximize social welfare. But it lacks guidelines to distribute the surplus among the agents with their various demands (as profit maximization is forbidden). This is where the core enters, as a general principle, for limiting the possible cost sharings. In practice, nonsubsidization is a legal constraint for most public firms. For a detailed discussion, see Baumol, Panzar, and Willig [1982] or Sharkey [1982].

In Section 4.3 we begin a systematical analysis of this pricing problem as a cooperative game (this viewpoint is extended in Chapter 7 by taking demand into account). The core concept is adapted into that of a subsidy-free price vector, and its nonemptyness leads to the notion of a supportable cost function (Theorem 4.2).

Finally, in Section 4.4 we define the most general model of cooperative games, namely, without the transferable utility assumption (NTU games). We quote (without proof) a sufficient condition for the nonemptyness of its core (Theorem 4.3). The NTU model will find some economic applications in Chapter 7 as well as in Chapter 10.

4.1   Stand-alone and subsidy-free principles

Example 4.1. Cost sharing of a facility
Let $N = \{1, 2, ..., n\}$ represent a set of potential customers of a public service or public facility. Each customer will be served or not; the service is indivisible – he will get a telephone or not, hook up to the local water supply or not, and so on (in Section 4.3 we discuss the case where the service is a divisible good or goods).

The cost data are summarized by a joint cost function $c(S)$, where S is any coalition (subset) of agents and $c(S)$ is the least cost of serving the customers in S by the most efficient means. A *cost allocation* is a vector $(x_1, ..., x_n)$ such that $x_1 + \cdots + x_n = c(N)$. In other words, we want to serve all customers and seek to share the corresponding costs.

A typical example from investment planning is that of neighboring municipalities together building a water supply system. Here is a numerical example with three agents. Suppose the cost data for three towns A, B, C are:

Cost of water system for:

town A alone: 120,   town B: 140,   town C: 120

coalition $\{A, B\}$: 170,   coalition $\{B, C\}$: 190

coalition $\{A, C\}$: 160

all three towns: 255

With only two agents involved, the cost-sharing problem has a straight-forward egalitarian solution. Ignore, for instance, town C:

$$c(A) = 120, \quad c(B) = 140 \quad c(AB) = 170$$

The cost saving from joint production is $c(A) + c(B) - c(AB) = 90$. Equally splitting this saving leads to

$$c_A = 120 - \tfrac{1}{2}(90) = 75, \qquad c_B = 140 - \tfrac{1}{2}(90) = 95$$

With three agents involved, it is tempting to use the same method. Compute first the global cost saving,

$$c(A) + c(B) + c(C) - c(ABC) = 125$$

Then share it equally among the three towns:

$$c_A = 120 - \tfrac{1}{3}(125) = 78.3, \quad c_B = 140 - \tfrac{1}{3}(125) = 98.3,$$
$$c_C = 120 - \tfrac{1}{3}(125) = 78.3$$

The problem with this cost allocation is that the total cost imputed to AB exceeds that of serving them independently of town C:

$$c_A + c_B = 176.6 > 170 = c(AB)$$

Thus, the coalition AB would rather stand alone, namely, use its own cooperative opportunity rather than suffering this cost allocation. Alternatively, coalition AB could argue that it unduly subsidizes player C.

Throughout Part II we are given a set N of agents and consider *coalitions* of agents. A coalition is any *nonempty* subset of N. The set N itself is a coalition, called the grand coalition. The set of coalitions is denoted 2^N, with the convention that the empty set is *not* an element of 2^N.

The *stand-alone* principle says that the price charged to a coalition never exceeds the cost incurred by this coalition if it were to provide service by itself:

$$\text{for all } S \subset N: \quad \sum_{i \in S} x_i \leq c(S) \tag{1}$$

The *no-subsidy* principle says that each coalition of customers must be charged at least the incremental cost of serving them (difference between the cost with the coalition and without it):

for all $S \subset N$: $\quad \sum_{i \in S} x_i \geq c(N) - c(N \setminus S)$ \hfill (2)

Since $\sum_{i \in N} x_i = c(N)$, these two principles are equivalent. Indeed, inequality (2) writes

$$\sum_{i \in S} x_i \geq \sum_{i \in N} x_i - c(N \setminus S) \Leftrightarrow c(N \setminus S) \geq \sum_{i \in N \setminus S} x_i$$

Definition 4.1. *Given is a cost-sharing game (N, c), where $N = \{1, 2, \ldots, n\}$ is the set of agents, and c associates to each coalition S of N its cost $c(S) \geq 0$.*

The core of (N, c) is the set of cost allocations x satisfying $\sum_{i=1}^{n} x_i = c(N)$ and property (1).

Let us compute the core cost allocations in our example. Property (1) is the following system when we denote towns A, B, C as agents $1, 2, 3$, respectively:

$$x_1 + x_2 + x_3 = 255, \quad x_1 \leq 120, \quad x_2 \leq 140, \quad x_3 \leq 120$$
$$x_1 + x_2 \leq 170, \quad x_2 + x_3 \leq 190, \quad x_1 + x_3 \leq 160$$

It is easier to visualize the solutions to this system by changing variables. Define agent i's cost saving as $y_i = c(i) - x_i$. Hence, the new system

$$y_1 + y_2 + y_3 = 125, \quad y_i \geq 0, \ i = 1, 2, 3,$$
$$y_1 + y_2 \geq 90, \quad y_2 + y_3 \geq 70, \quad y_1 + y_3 \geq 80$$

In Figure 4.1 we have drawn the simplex $\{y_i \geq 0, \ y_1 + y_2 + y_3 = 125\}$ within which the three additional constraints circumscribe a small subtriangle (shaded area), namely, the core of the cost-saving game. The center of this triangle is easily computed to be

$$y^* = (51.7, 41.7, 31.7)$$

corresponding to the cost allocation

$$x^* = (68.3, 98.3, 88.3)$$

It is a reasonable compromise within the core (actually it corresponds to the nucleolus of this cost-sharing game; see Section 5.4).

The core is our first attempt toward a solution concept for cooperative games. However, it is far from determining a single cost allocation; in Example 4.1, the core is a typical triangle. On the other hand, it may also be the empty set; that is, the system of conditions (1) may have no solution at all. In Example 4.1, suppose we raise the cost of the grand coalition from 255 to 265. The corresponding system (1) has no solution:

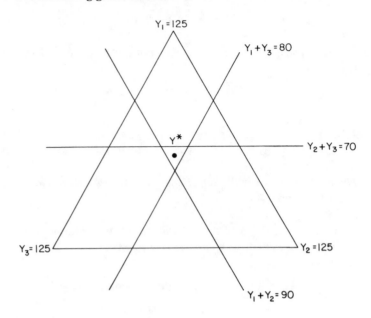

Figure 4.1.

$$\{x_1+x_2 \le 170, x_2+x_3 \le 190, x_1+x_3 \le 160\}$$
$$\Rightarrow 2(x_1+x_2+x_3) \le 170+190+160 = 520$$

contradicting $x_1+x_2+x_3 = 265$.

Notice also that with the higher cost $c(ABC) = 265$, it is still efficient to jointly produce the facility. Indeed, the following inequalities still hold:

$$c(ABC) \le c(A)+c(B)+c(C)$$
$$c(ABC) \le c(A)+c(BC), c(AB)+c(C), c(B)+c(AC)$$

This property is subadditivity of costs: The best organization of production is to produce a joint facility serving all three towns.

In our first example the core was a small, almost deterministic, set of cost-sharing vectors (an agent cost share could not vary by more than 10 units within the core). The next example shows that a very large core is possible, too.

Our second example is a model of cost sharing of a joint facility where the demands of the consumers are taken into account. Thus, a surplus game associating to each coalition the maximal benefit when it cooperates is the accurate description of coalitional opportunities. We still assume quasi-linear utilities of the consumers and production of an indivisible good. These two assumptions will be relaxed in Chapter 7, where existence of the core in production economies will be discussed again (see, in particular, Section 7.3).

Example 4.2. Cost sharing with independent demands
This public utility (water system) serves four consumers, and the cost structure is symmetrical:

cost of serving:		
	one consumer, alone	40
	two consumers	60
	three consumers	70
	all four consumers	80

Benefits to the agents from using the facility are

$$b_1 = 41, \quad b_2 = 24, \quad b_3 = 22, \quad b_4 = 12$$

Quasi-linear utilities mean here that consumer i will buy the facility if and only if he is charged no more than b_i. Independence of the demands means that agent i is indifferent to agent j's consumption of the facility (no externality in consumption).

Note first that the cost function is *subadditive:* For any two disjoint coalitions S, T we have $c(S) + c(T) > c(S \cup T)$. Here is the proof: The per capita cost function $c(S)/|S|$ strictly decreases as the size of S augments, and hence

$$\left. \begin{array}{l} c(S \cup T) < a = \dfrac{|S|+|T|}{|S|} c(S) \\[2ex] c(S \cup T) < b = \dfrac{|S|+|T|}{|T|} c(T) \end{array} \right\} \Rightarrow \begin{array}{l} c(S \cup T) < \dfrac{|S|}{|S|+|T|} a + \dfrac{|T|}{|S|+|T|} b \\[2ex] = c(S) + c(T) \end{array}$$

Under subadditivity of costs it would be inefficient to serve a coalition S by building a facility to serve the disjoint coalition T. Thus, there is some largest set of consumers who will be efficiently served by a single facility. It is not necessarily the case that all consumers are included in this set. In our example, if b_4 were as low as 8, the marginal cost of serving him would never be covered by his benefit, so it would be inefficient to serve him. For another example and a general formula, see Exercise 4.1.

We compute the surplus game describing coalitional opportunities. From serving coalition S, the consumers of S derive the surplus $\sum_{i \in S} b_i - c(S)$. Hence, the maximal available surplus to a given coalition is the largest surplus from serving any of its subcoalitions, including zero surplus if nobody is served. Thus,

$$v(S) = \max_{T \subseteq S} \left\{ \sum_{i \in T} b_i - c(T), 0 \right\}$$

For instance,

$$v(34) = \max\{0, 22-40, 12-40, (22+12)-60\} = 0$$
$$v(12) = \max\{0, 41-40, 24-40, (41+24)-60\} = 5$$
$$v(14) = \max\{0, 41-40, 12-40, (41+12)-60\} = 1$$

Agents 3 and 4 cannot raise any surplus alone or together, as their benefits are too low. By contrast, if agents 1 and 2 cooperate, they raise five units of surplus by producing a facility to serve them both. Finally, if agents 1 and 4 cooperate, agent 4 will actually be of no help, as only agent 1 will be served. Similar computations yield

$$v(1) = 1, \quad v(2) = v(3) = v(4) = 0$$
$$v(12) = 5, \quad v(13) = 3, \quad v(14) = 1, \quad v(23) = v(24) = v(34) = 0$$
$$v(123) = 17, \quad v(124) = 7, \quad v(134) = 5, \quad v(234) = 0$$
$$v(N) = 19$$

Note that the maximal surplus of 19 is achieved with all four consumers served.

For a surplus game, the stand-alone principle says that every coalition should enjoy a surplus not smaller than the surplus it can guarantee by breaking away. Thus, if we give x_i units of surplus to agent i, we require the following conditions on (x_1, x_2, x_3, x_4):

$$x_1+x_2+x_3+x_4 = 19, \quad x_1 \geq 1, \quad x_2, x_3, x_4 \geq 0$$
$$x_1+x_2 \geq 5, \quad x_1+x_3 \geq 3, \quad x_1+x_4 \geq 1$$
$$x_1+x_2+x_3 \geq 17, \quad x_1+x_2+x_4 \geq 7, \quad x_1+x_3+x_4 \geq 5$$

Note that we omitted some redundant inequalities such as $x_2+x_3 \geq 0$ or $x_2+x_3+x_4 \geq 0$.

Check now that the core in this example gives very loose guidelines for allocating costs. In other words, it is a large subset of the simplex $\Sigma_{i=1}^{4} x_i = 19$, $x_1 \geq 1$, $x_2, x_3, x_4 \geq 0$. Since the cooperation of agent 1 is necessary to raise any surplus, this agent could get all the 19 units of surplus: $x' = (19, 0, 0, 0)$ is an allocation in the core. But so is $x'' = (1, 8, 8, 2)$, where all the benefit of agent 1's cooperation goes to the other agents while agent 1 is stuck at his own surplus level. The corresponding cost shares (given by $c_i = b_i - x_i$) are

$$c' = (22, 24, 22, 12) \quad \text{corresponding to } x'$$
$$c'' = (40, 16, 14, 10) \quad \text{corresponding to } x''$$

Definition 4.2 (Gillies [1959]). *A cooperative game with transferable utility (TU game) is a pair* (N, v), *where* N *is the (finite) society and* v

associates to every coalition S its (numerical) surplus $v(S)$. *An allocation is a vector x in* E^N *such that* $\sum_{i \in N} x_i = v(N)$. *The* **core** *of* (N, v) *is the set of allocations x satisfying*

$$\textit{for all } S \subset N: \quad \sum_{i \in S} x_i \geq v(S) \tag{3}$$

This definition views $v(S)$ as the surplus available to coalition S, namely, the net benefit (in monetary forms) that agents of S would cash by cooperating.

Definitions 4.1 and 4.2 are symmetrical. To a cost-sharing game (N, c) we associate a (surplus) TU game (N, v) as follows:

$$v(S) = \sum_{i \in S} c(i) - c(S)$$

To a cost allocation x in (N, c) we associate the allocation y in (N, v) by $y_i = c(i) - x_i$, $i \in N$. Check then that x is a core cost allocation in (N, c) [(1)] if and only if y is a core allocation in (N, v) [(3)].

The surplus game interpretation is more flexible in the applications, so the general discussion will develop in this context.

4.2   Balanced games

The possibility of an empty core is the most serious limitation of the core concept. What good is the stand-alone principle if, no matter how we arrange cost shares, one coalition (or more) would invoke it and object? Far from promoting the consensus, such a principle excludes it. Whence the importance of the core existence problem: Under what conditions does a given cooperative game have a nonempty core? For games with TU this question can be solved entirely by linear programming techniques.

A necessary condition for the core of the game (N, v) to be nonempty is the superadditivity property. Suppose the coalitions $S_1, \ldots, S_K$ partition the grand coalition N (they are pairwise disjoint and their union is N). Then we must have

$$\sum_{k=1}^{K} v(S_k) \leq v(N) \tag{4}$$

Indeed, if (4) fails, add up the inequalities $\sum_{i \in S_k} x_i \geq v(S_k)$ into $\sum_{i \in N} x_i > v(N)$, implying an empty core.

Yet the superadditivity properties (4) (one for each partition of N) are not sufficient to imply a nonempty core, as shown by Example 4.1 [when we raise $c(ABC)$ to 265]. The necessary and sufficient condition for core existence considerably strengthens properties (4). In the next definition we say that a coalition is *proper* if it is different from the grand coalition.

Definition 4.3.   *Given society N, a set of balanced weights is a mapping δ from $2^N \setminus \{N\}$ (the set of all proper coalitions) into $[0,1]$ such that*

$$\sum_{S:i \in S} \delta_S = 1 \quad \text{for all agents } i \tag{5}$$

where the summation bears upon all proper coalitions containing agent i.

Theorem 4.1 (Bondavera [1962]).   *The core of the TU game (N, v) is nonempty if and only if, for all sets of balanced weights δ, we have*

$$\sum_{S \subsetneq N} \delta_S \cdot v(S) \le v(N) \tag{6}$$

Proof: Suppose x is an allocation in the core of (N, v) and δ is a set of balanced weights. Observe that

$$\text{for all } S \subsetneq N: \quad \sum_{i \in N} x_i \ge v(S) \Rightarrow \delta_S \left(\sum_{i \in S} x_i \right) \ge \delta_S \cdot v(S)$$

Summing these inequalities, by (5) we obtain

$$\sum_{S \subsetneq N} \delta_S \cdot v(S) \le \sum_{S \subsetneq N} \delta_S \cdot x(S) = \sum_{i \in N} \sum_{S: i \in S} \delta_S x_i = \sum_{i \in N} x_i = v(N)$$

Conversely, suppose the core of (N, v) is empty. This means that the hyperplane $\sum_{i \in N} x_i = v(N)$ is disjoint from the convex (nonempty) subset of E^N defined by the inequalities

$$\sum_{i \in S} x_i \ge v(S) \quad \text{for all } S \subsetneq N$$

By a standard separation argument (see, e.g., Rockafellar [1970]), this implies the existence for all S of a nonnegative number δ_S such that

$$\text{for all } x \in E^N: \quad \sum_{i \in N} x_i = \sum_{S \subsetneq N} \delta_S \left(\sum_{i \in S} x_i \right) \text{ and } \sum_{S \subsetneq N} \delta_S v(S) > v(N) \tag{7}$$

Property (7) is readily equivalent to (5), so the proof is complete.

Q.E.D.

Remark 4.1:   A cost-sharing game (N, c) has a nonempty core if and only if, for all sets of balanced weights δ, we have

$$\sum_{S \subsetneq N} \delta_S c(S) \ge c(N)$$

Condition (6) is called balancedness of the game (N, v). It is not so easy to interpret because the set of balanced weights is not easy to visualize. At any rate, condition (6) says that coalitional surplus $v(S)$ for proper coalitions are not too large with respect to the surplus $v(N)$ available to the grand coalition.

Notice that inequalities (6) contain the superadditivity property (4) by taking the particular weights

$$\delta_{S_k} = 1 \quad \text{for } k = 1, \dots, K, \qquad \delta_S = 0 \quad \text{for all other coalitions } S \qquad (8)$$

Notice also that balanced weights form a convex, compact polyhedron in E^A, where $A = 2^N \setminus \{N\}$. Thus, it is enough to check property (6) at the extreme points of this polyhedron. Once we have computed those points, the balancedness property can be written as a *finite* system of linear inequalities on v. This is the convenient form for all applications.

A simple illustration is for games with three agents, $N = \{1, 2, 3\}$. The balanced weights form a polyhedron in E^6 with five extreme points and dimension 3. Four of them correspond to the partitions $(1, 2, 3)$, $(12, 3)$, $(1, 23)$, $(2, 13)$ via (8). The fifth one is

$$\delta_S = \tfrac{1}{2} \quad \text{for } |S| = 2, \qquad \delta_S = 0 \quad \text{for } |S| = 1$$

Applying (6) to these five balanced weights we obtain the following corollaries.

Corollary 1 to Theorem 4.1. *The three agents' TU game (N, v) has a nonempty core if and only if*

$$v(1) + v(2) + v(3) \leq v(N)$$
$$v(1) + v(23), \, v(2) + v(13), \, v(3) + v(12) \leq v(N)$$
$$\tfrac{1}{2}[v(12) + v(23) + v(13)] \leq v(N)$$

Next consider games with four agents. This time balanced weights are a polyhedron in E^{14} with 23 extreme points! Therefore, system (6) consists of no less than 23 different inequalities. However, we can drastically reduce the number of inequalities that one needs to check by assuming that the game v is fully superadditive:

for any two disjoint coalitions S, T: $\quad v(S) + v(T) \leq v(S \cup T) \qquad (9)$

Superadditivity is satisfied by all economic games discussed in Parts II and III.

Corollary 2 to Theorem 4.1. *Suppose the four agents' TU game (N, v) is superadditive [property (9)]. Then its core is nonempty if and only if v satisfies seven additional inequalities,*

$$\tfrac{1}{3}[v(123) + v(234) + v(134) + v(124)] \leq v(N) \qquad (10)$$
$$\tfrac{1}{2}[v(123) + v(234) + v(14)] \leq v(N) \qquad (11)$$

and five inequalities similar to (11) *by permuting agents.*

Proof of Corollary 2: With four agents we have only 23 balanced weights δ_S, $S \in 2^N \setminus N$, that cannot be written as a convex combination of two other balanced weights. Those are the 12 vectors δ corresponding to partitions of N (these are characterized by the property that every coordinate δ_S is 0 or 1); the four vectors $\delta_1 = 1$, $\delta_{23} = \delta_{24} = \delta_{34} = \frac{1}{2}$, and $\delta_S = 0$ otherwise; the six vectors $\delta_{123} = \delta_{234} = \delta_{14} = \frac{1}{2}$, $\delta_S = 0$ otherwise; and the vector $\delta_S = \frac{1}{3}$ if $|S| = 3$, $\delta_S = 0$ otherwise. An inequality (6) where δ corresponds to a partition of N is automatically satisfied by superadditivity. Inequality (11) is just (6) when δ is one of the six; similarly, inequality (10) is (6) for the uniform weight over three-person coalitions. It remains to check the four inequalities, such as

$$v(1) + \tfrac{1}{2}[v(23) + v(24) + v(34)] \le v(N) \tag{12}$$

Those follow from superadditivity and (11):

$$\left.\begin{array}{l} (11) \Rightarrow v(124) + v(134) + v(23) \le 2v(N) \\ (9) \Rightarrow v(1) + v(24) \le v(124), \quad v(1) + v(34) \le v(134) \end{array}\right\} \Rightarrow (12) \qquad \text{Q.E.D.}$$

In Chapter 5 we give another sufficient condition for the core existence, called convexity; see Definition 5.2.

4.3   Pricing of a multi-output monopoly

We look now at pricing problems involving divisible goods. We focus on the simple cost-sharing problem, thus ignoring, for the time being, the demand side of the economy (discussed in Chapter 7).

A regulated monopoly produces n goods indexed from 1 to n. The cost of producing the output vector $(q_1, \ldots, q_n)$, where q_i is the quantity of good i, is $C(q_1, \ldots, q_n)$ measured in money. The problem is to find a price system $(p_1, \ldots, p_n)$, where $p_i \ge 0$ is the price of good i, that balances the budget of the monopolist (a regulated firm is not supposed to make positive profit) and is in some sense equitable.

The no-subsidy principle has a simple formulation in this framework:

Definition 4.4.   *Given a cost function $C(q_1, \ldots, q_n)$ and an output level $\bar{q} = (\bar{q}_1, \ldots, \bar{q}_n)$, we say that a price system $p = (p_1, \ldots, p_n)$ is subsidy free if*

$$\sum_{i=1}^{n} p_i \bar{q}_i = C(\bar{q}_1, \ldots, \bar{q}_n) \tag{13}$$

$$\sum_{i=1}^{n} p_i \cdot q_i \le C(q_1, \ldots, q_n) \quad \text{for all } q, \ 0 \le q \le \bar{q} \tag{14}$$

Equation (13) is the budget balance condition; the monopolist exactly covers it costs. Property (14) is the subsidy-freeness condition. Suppose that (14) fails: There exists an output level q, $q \leq \bar{q}$, such that $\sum_{i=1}^n p_i \cdot q_i > C(q)$. The cost imputed to the fraction q of total demand is too high; a subgroup (coalition) of consumers absorbing exactly the output vector q is actually subsidizing the rest of the economy. Note that this interpretation uses a potential coalition in an unspecified society; only after the statement of Theorem 4.2 can we explain precisely the connections with the TU game model.

An alternative interpretation of property (14) is popular in the industrial organization literature (see, e.g., Baumol, Panzar, and Willig [1982]). If (14) fails, a competitor could threaten the monopolist's position by the following hit-and-run strategy. Say $\sum_{i=1}^n p_i q_i > C(q)$; the rival lowers slightly its price relative to the monopolist but serves only the fraction q of the demand. Because of the strict inequality $\sum p_i q_i > C(q)$, the rival has a rebate small enough to preserve some positive profit. The remaining fraction $\bar{q} - q$ of the demand cannot enjoy the rebate and goes back to the monopolist, who no longer covers its cost.

To further illustrate Definition 4.4, consider the single-output case. Then condition (13) reads $p = C(\bar{q})/\bar{q}$, so condition (14) becomes

$$\text{for all } q, \ 0 \leq q \leq \bar{q}: \quad \frac{C(\bar{q})}{\bar{q}} \leq \frac{C(q)}{q} \tag{15}$$

Thus, the average cost is the subsidy-free price if and only if it is not higher than the average cost of any lower output.

Definition 4.5 (Sharkey and Telser [1978]). *A cost function $C(q_1, \ldots, q_n)$ is supportable if and only if there exists a subsidy-free price system at every production level.*

For instance, a single-output cost function $C(q)$ is subsidy free if and only if average costs are nonincreasing (corresponding to nondecreasing returns to scale of production).

Lemma 4.1. *If the cost function C is supportable, then it is subadditive and ray-increasing returns to scale (ray-IRS).*
   C is subadditive:

$$\text{for all } q, q' \in E_+^n: \quad C(q + q') \leq C(q) + C(q') \tag{16}$$

   C is ray-IRS:

$$\text{for all } q \in E_+^n, \text{ all } \lambda \geq 1: \quad C(\lambda q) \leq \lambda C(q) \tag{17}$$

The proof of Lemma 4.1 is the subject of Exercise 4.4.

As expected, supportability makes sense only when the production technology allows for a natural monopoly. Yet subadditivity and ray-IRS together are not sufficient to imply supportability. A counterexample is provided by Sharkey and Telser [1978].

Theorem 4.2. *Given is the continuous cost function $C(q_1, \ldots, q_n)$. Then C is supportable if and only if, for all finite sequences $q^k \in E_+^n$, $k = 1, \ldots, K$, the following cost-sharing game $(\{1, \ldots, K\}, c)$ with K agents has a nonempty core:*

$$\text{for } S \subset \{1, \ldots, K\}: \quad c(S) = C\left(\sum_{k \in S} q^k\right) \tag{18}$$

The given K agents with fixed demands (agent k demands q^k) share the technology C to satisfy their needs. Supportability of C means that we can always share those costs in harmony with the stand-alone principle.

Proof: For "only if". Let C be supportable. Fix $q^1, \ldots, q^K$ and set $\bar{q} = \sum_{k=1}^K q^k$. By Definition 4.5, there is a subsidy-free price p at $\bar{q}$. Property (14) implies, for all coalitions $S \subset \{1, \ldots, K\}$,

$$p \cdot \left(\sum_{k \in S} q^k\right) \leq C\left(\sum_{k \in S} q^k\right) \tag{19}$$

Take a set of balanced weights δ, multiply each inequality (19) by δ_S, and sum:

$$\sum_{\substack{S \subsetneq N}} \delta_S \left\{ p \cdot \left(\sum_{k \in S} q^k\right) \right\} \leq \sum_{\substack{S \subsetneq N}} \delta_S \cdot C\left(\sum_{k \in S} q^k\right) \tag{20}$$

The left-hand term in (20) develops as

$$\sum_{\substack{S \subsetneq N}} \sum_{k \in S} \delta_S (p \cdot q^k) = \sum_{k=1}^K \left(\sum_{S: k \in S} \delta_S\right)(p \cdot q^k) = p \cdot \bar{q}$$

Thus, by (13), inequality (20) reads

$$C(\bar{q}) = p \cdot \bar{q} \leq \sum_S \delta_S \cdot C\left(\sum_{k \in S} q^k\right)$$

This says that the cost-sharing game is balanced, and hence its core is nonempty by Remark 4.1.

For "if" (adapted from Scarf [1986]). Let C be a cost function such that all games such as (18) have a nonempty core. Fix an output vector $\bar{q} = (q_1, \ldots, q_n)$; we must find a subsidy-free price p at $\bar{q}$. Denote $e^i \in E_+^n$ the ith coordinate vector ($e_i^i = 1$, $e_j^i = 0$, all $j \neq i$). For any integer r, we construct a double sequence $q^{i,j}$ of vectors in E_+^n:

$$q^{i,j} = (q_i/2^r) \cdot e^i, \quad \text{where } i = 1, \ldots, n, \ j = 1, \ldots, 2^r$$

Note that $q^{i,j}$ does not vary with j. Consider the cost-sharing game with $K = (n \cdot 2^r)$ agents defined by (18). By assumption, its core is nonempty, so we can find a vector $a = (a^{i,j})$ in $E_+^{n \times 2^r}$ such that

$$\sum_{\substack{1 \le i \le n \\ 1 \le j \le 2^r}} a^{i,j} = C(\bar{q}), \quad \sum_{(i,j) \in S} a^{i,j} \le C\left(\sum_{(i,j) \in S} q^{i,j} \right) \quad \text{for all } S \subset \{1, ..., K\}$$

Denote $\delta_i = \sum_{1 \le j \le 2^r} a^{i,j}$. The preceding formula is equivalently written as

$$\sum_{i=1}^{n} \delta_i = C(\bar{q}), \quad \sum_{i=1}^{n} \frac{k_i}{2^r} \delta_i \le C\left(\frac{k_1}{2^r} q_1, ..., \frac{k_n}{2^r} q_n \right)$$

$$\text{for all } k_1, ..., k_n, \ 0 \le k_i \le 2^r \tag{21}$$

Thus, for each integer r, we have found $(\delta_1, ..., \delta_n)$ in the simplex $\{\delta_i \ge 0, \sum_i \delta_i = C(\bar{q})\}$ satisfying (21). When r grows to infinity, we can take a converging subsequence of vectors $(\delta_1, ..., \delta_n)$. Call $(\delta_1^*, ..., \delta_n^*)$ its limit. By continuity of C, we have

$$\sum_{i=1}^{n} \delta_i^* = C(\bar{q}), \quad \sum_{i=1}^{n} t_i \delta_i^* \le C(t_1 q_1, ..., t_n q_n)$$

$$\text{for all } t_1, ..., t_n, \ 0 \le t_i \le 1 \tag{22}$$

Define $p_i = \delta_i^* / q_i$ if $q_i > 0$ and $p_i = 0$ otherwise. Check that if $q_i = 0$, then $\delta_i = 0$ for all i [by (21)], so $\delta_i^* = 0$ as well. Thus, (22) is equivalent to

$$\sum_{i=1}^{n} p_i \cdot q_i = C(\bar{q}), \quad \sum_{i=1}^{n} p_i \cdot (t_i q_i) \le C((t_1 q_1), ..., (t_n q_n))$$

$$\text{for all } (t_1, ..., t_n) \in [0, 1]^n$$

This says that p is the desired subsidy-free price. Q.E.D.

In addition to Theorem 4.2, some sufficient conditions for the supportability of a cost function are known. One such condition is the *distributivity* of the corresponding production set defined by Scarf [1986]. Another example is given by Sharkey and Telser [1978], who prove that if C is ray-IRS and quasi-convex, it is supportable; see Exercise 4.4. Another sufficient condition is cost complementarity; it is defined in Example 5.5, where it is shown to be equivalent with the convexity of the cost-sharing games (18).

Remark 4.2: A kind of dual model of the multi-output pricing is multi-input surplus sharing. There we have n inputs $r_1, ..., r_n$ used jointly to produce a transferable output – say money – through a production function $F(r_1, ..., r_n)$. The problem is to distribute fairly the output among the inputs. A subsidy-free price at the input level $\bar{r} = (\bar{r}_1, \ldots, r_n)$ is a price $(p_1, \ldots, p_n)$ such that

$$\sum_{i=1}^{n} p_i \bar{r}_i = F(\bar{r}_1, \ldots, \bar{r}_n), \quad \sum_{i=1}^{n} p_i r_i \geq F(r_1, \ldots, r_n) \quad \text{for all } r,\ 0 \leq r \leq \bar{r}$$

Definition 4.5, Lemma 4.1, and Theorem 4.2 apply identically to this model up to a change of sign.

4.4   NTU games

A NTU cooperative game is given by a set of agents (or society) N and by a feasible utility set $v(S)$ for each coalition S of agents, including the grand coalition N. Each feasible set $v(S)$ in E^S summarizes the cooperative opportunities open to coalition S. Each utility vector u_S in $v(S)$ can be achieved by the agents in S through an unspecified cooperative action. Just as in axiomatic bargaining (Chapter 3), the coalitional sets $v(S)$ will typically be convex, comprehensive, and closed. See Theorem 4.3.

The core is defined by the stand-alone principle: A utility distribution $x \in E^N$ is *not* in the core if some coalition could stand alone and improve the welfare of all of its members.

Notation: Given a vector x in E^N and a subset S of N, we write x_S the projection of x on E^s: $(x_S)_i = x_i$ for all $i \in S$.

Definition 4.6.   *Given is a NTU game (N, v), that is, v associates to each nonempty subset S of N the subset $v(S) \subset E^s$ of feasible utility vectors for coalition S. We say that $x \in E^N$ is a core allocation of (N, v) if it belongs to $v(N)$ (it is feasible for coalition N), and there is no nonempty coalition S such that*

$$\text{for some } y_S \in v(S): \quad x_S < y_S \tag{23}$$

(remember $u < v$ means $u_i \leq v_i$ for all i, with at least one strict inequality).

Note that coalition S in (23) could be the grand coalition N. Thus, the core property implies in particular that x is a Pareto-optimal element in $v(N)$.

We check that this definition generalizes Definition 4.2. Indeed, a TU game (N, v_0) can be written as the NTU game (N, v), where

$$v(S) = \left\{ x \in E^S \ \middle|\ \sum_{i \in S} x_i \leq v_0(S) \right\} \tag{24}$$

Comparing (3) and (23) shows that the core of (N, v) and that of (N, v_0) coincide.

The theory of NTU games has much fewer results and is technically more difficult than that of TU games. In this and the following chapter we state or quote its principal results without going into any proofs. In Part III we discuss in some detail the most important microeconomic examples of NTU games: production of a private good by a regulated monopoly (Chapter 7) and provision of a public good (Chapter 6).

As far as core existence is concerned, Theorem 4.1 generalizes into a weaker result, namely, a sufficient condition for a nonempty core.

Definition 4.7. *Given N, a **balanced family of coalitions** is a subset B of the set of proper coalitions $(B \subset 2^N \setminus \{N\})$ such that we can find a weight δ_S, $0 \leq \delta_S \leq 1$, for each $S \in B$ satisfying*

$$\text{for all } i \in N: \quad \sum_{S: i \in S} \delta_S = 1 \tag{25}$$

*We say that the NTU game (N, v) is **balanced** if for all balanced families of coalitions and all utility allocations $x \in E^N$ we have*

$$\{\text{for all } S \in B, \ x_S \in v(S)\} \Rightarrow \{x \in v(N)\}$$

The careful reader will check that a TU game (N, v_0) is balanced [satisfies (6)] if and only if its canonical representation as a NTU game [(24)] is balanced.

Theorem 4.3 (Scarf [1967]). *Given is a NTU game (N, v) where for each coalition S (including the grand coalition), the set $v(S)$ is a closed and comprehensive proper subset of E^S. If the game (N, v) is balanced, then its core is nonempty.*

For a thorough exposition of this result and its applications, an excellent reference is Ichiishi [1983].

EXERCISES

4.1 **Cost sharing with independent demands.** This is a generalization of Example 4.2. There are n agents who will benefit from the facility by the respective amounts $b_1, \ldots, b_n$. Also given is the cost function c (as in Definition 4.1).

   If the subset S of agents is served, the corresponding surplus is $\sum_{i \in S} b_i - c(S)$. It is efficient to serve the subset of agents with the largest surplus (this could be the empty subset if all surpluses are negative).

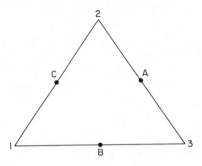

Figure 4.2.

(a) Show that it is efficient to serve all agents if and only if

for all $S \subset N$: $\sum_{i \in S} b_i \geq c(N) - c(N \setminus S)$ (26)

(b) The surplus TU game (N, v) is defined as

$$v(S) = \max_{T \subset S} \left\{ \sum_{i \in T} b_i - c(T), 0 \right\}$$ (27)

Show that v is superadditive if c is subadditive.

(c) Suppose (26), and for a balanced allocation x of (N, v) define y as $y_i = b_i - x_i$, all $i \in N$. Show that x is in the core of (N, v) if and only if y is in the core of the cost-sharing game $(N, \tilde{c})$, where $\tilde{c}$ is defined as

$\tilde{c}(i) = \inf\{c(i), b_i\}$,   all $i \in N$

$\tilde{c}(S) = c(S)$,   all $S \subset N$, $|S| \geq 2$

(d) Using the following example, check that (26) holds, that the cost-sharing game (N, c) has a nonempty core (by Corollary 2 to Theorem 4.1), and that the cost-sharing game $(N, \tilde{c})$ and the surplus game both have an empty core:

$N = \{1, 2, 3, 4\}$

$c(i) = 4$, all i;   for S with $|S| = 2$: $\begin{cases} c(S) = 8 & \text{if } 1 \in S \\ c(S) = 4.5 & \text{if } 1 \notin S \end{cases}$

$c(S) = 8$ for $|S| = 3$, $c(N) = 10$

$b_1 = 2.5$, $b_i = 5$ for $i = 2, 3, 4$

4.2 **An empty core with dependent demands.** Three agents are located at the vertices of a triangle of which the edges represent the three existing streets (see Figure 4.2). They have to share the cost of public street lights, for which possible locations are at any of three midpoints a, b, c. The utilities are as follows:

$u_i = 0$ if there is no light at any of the two nearest locations (e.g., $u_1 = 0$ if there is only one street light located at a or there is no light at all)

$u_i = 30$ if there is exactly one nearby street light

$u_i = 45$ if both nearby locations have a street light

Thus, with one street light at a and one at b we have $(u_1, u_2, u_3) = (30, 30, 45)$.

There are actually three different goods (street light at a, b, or c) and the demand for them is not independent: Agent 1 is less eager to consume a light at c if he is consuming one at b than if he is not. The cost structure has constant returns; any street light costs 40. Compute the TU game describing the surplus game and show that its core is empty.

4.3 Lack of monotonicity of the core. The difficulty uncovered by this example will be generalized in the next chapter (Theorem 5.1).

(a) Consider the following four-agent TU games:

$v(i) = 0$ for $i = 1, \ldots, 4$

$v(12) = v(34) = 0$, $v(13) = v(14) = v(23) = v(24) = 1$

$v(S) = 1$ for $|S| = 3$, $v(N) = 2$

Check that its core is the interval joining $(0, 0, 1, 1)$ to $(1, 1, 0, 0)$. It is thus symmetrical around $(\frac{1}{2}, \frac{1}{2}, \frac{1}{2}, \frac{1}{2})$.

(b) Suppose $v(134)$ raises by 1, thus defining the new TU game v':

$v'(134) = 2$ $v'(S) = v(S)$ for all $S \neq \{134\}$

Show that the core of v' shrinks to a single allocation, and that this reduction can only harm agent 1 if a core allocation is to be chosen in v and in v'. Thus, agent 1's utility goes down even though his cooperative opportunities go up.

4.4 Supportable cost functions (Sharkey and Telser [1978]). Throughout the exercise, a cost function $C(q_1, \ldots, q_n)$ increasing in all its variables is given. Questions (a) and (b) are necessary conditions for the supportability of C (stated earlier as Lemma 4.1). Questions (c) and (d) are sufficient conditions.

(a) If C is supportable, then C is additive [(16)]. Prove this by contradiction. If $C(q_1 + q_2) > C(q_1) + C(q_2)$, pick a subsidy-free price at $q_1 + q_2$ and derive a contradiction.

(b) Show if C is supportable, then C is ray-IRS [(17)].

(c) Say that C is quasi-convex if

$C(\lambda q + (1 - \lambda) q') \leq \sup\{C(q), C(q')\}$ for all $q, q' \geq 0$, all λ, $0 \leq \lambda \leq 1$

Show that if C is ray-IRS and quasi-convex, then C is supportable. Fix an output vector $\bar{q}$ and denote by A the subset $A = \{q \in E_+^n \mid C(q) \leq C(\bar{q})\}$.

Show that $\bar{q}$ is a boundary point of the convex set A and choose a supporting vector p of A at $\bar{q}$. Show that p is subsidy free at $\bar{q}$.

(d) Say that C is CRS (constant returns to scale) if $C(\lambda q) = \lambda C(q)$ for all $\lambda \geq 0$ and $q \in E_+^n$. Show that if C is subadditive and CRS, then C is supportable.

4.5 A production economy with an empty core (Sharkey [1979]). We have four goods and three agents. The first three goods (outputs) are produced from the fourth (input) at a cost:

$$c(x_1, x_2, x_3) = f(x_1) + f(x_2) + f(x_3)$$

where f is the function

$$f(x) = x \quad \text{if } 0 \leq x \leq 1, \qquad f(x) = \tfrac{1}{2}(x+1) \quad \text{if } 1 \leq x$$

Each agent is endowed with 0.6 units of input and has no utility for this good. Here are the utility functions of our three agents:

$$u_1(x) = f(x_1 + x_2), \qquad u_2(x) = f(x_2 + x_3), \qquad u_3(x) = f(x_1 + x_3)$$

(a) Show that C is supportable (use Exercise 4.4) and that the agents' preferences are convex.

(b) Nevertheless, the core of the production game is empty. The general definition of this game is given in Chapter 7 (Section 7.1). For the sake of the exercise, it is enough to show that each agent can guarantee $u_i \geq 0.6$ by himself, that any two agents can guarantee $u_1 + u_2 \geq 1.4$, and that any utility vector feasible for the grand coalition must have $u_1 + u_2 + u_3 \leq 2$.

CHAPTER 5

Values of cooperative games

Overview

The most ambitious task of cooperative game theory is to build a universal solution concept based on widely acceptable equity axioms, picking out of every cooperative game a unique utility distribution, just as the social choice function of Chapter 3 does. Such an object is called a value, or value operator. For more than 30 years, this viewpoint has been tested for TU games. By and large, it proves to be successful. Surely, no *single* solution concept has emerged that would satisfy everyone's sense of equity for all TU games. All the same, no single social choice function is the universal panacea of axiomatic bargaining (see Part I). However, two prominent values have been discovered and prove useful in a wide range of economic models. These are the Shapley value and the nucleolus, to which most of the discussion of this chapter is devoted.

In a nutshell, the nucleolus applies egalitarianism to TU games, whereas the Shapley value follows from a utilitarian principle. Indeed, the nucleolus minimizes the leximin SWO over long utility vectors in which every coordinate corresponds to a different coalition (see Definition 5.4). The Shapley value, on the other hand, renumerates each agent by averaging his marginal contributions to all coalitions containing him; it is utilitarian inasmuch as classical utilitarianism (Chapter 1) is likewise based upon average utility. Accordingly, the nucleolus tends to be harder to compute than the Shapley value (just as maximizing the leximin SWO is a more involved program than maximizing the utilitarian one).

In this chapter we discuss the axiomatic properties and qualitative features of our two values with the help of simple examples: We use a popular cost-sharing model (Example 5.3) and an elementary production economy (Example 5.2) as well as numerical TU games without any specific economic interpretation. More examples appear in Part III (see Chapters 6 and 7).

In Section 5.1 we define the Shapley value and compute it for our simple examples. We find that the Shapley value may fail to be in the core of the game (when the latter is nonempty), its most serious ethical drawback. Therefore, it is especially interesting to find a class of TU games, called convex games, where the Shapley value occupies a central position within the (nonempty) core. Convex games are discussed in Section 5.2. They are defined by the property that the marginal contribution of an agent to a coalition increases as this coalition expands (see Definition 5.2); in other words, cooperation has increasing returns to scale.

In Section 5.3 we present two axiomatic characterizations of the Shapley value. Shapley's original characterization (Theorem 5.2) is based upon an additivity axiom quite similar to the axiom characterizing the utilitarian social choice functions (see Theorem 3.4 and Exercise 3.8). The more recent characterization due to Loehman and Whinston [1974] and Young [1985a] is more subtle. It says that the Shapley value is the only value operator where an agent's value depends only (perhaps in a nonlinear way) upon the vector of his marginal contributions (Theorem 5.1). This simply says that an agent's cooperative productivity is the only thing that should matter in determining his share of the surplus.

In Section 5.4 we define the nucleolus and compute it in the same models for which we computed the Shapley value (a simple production economy in Example 5.2 and a cost-sharing problem in Example 5.3). These computations, quite typically, are much harder than those of the Shapley value. Also, comparing both values on these examples gives some intuition of their general ethical differences.

Section 5.5 starts with a sharp criticism of the nucleolus: When the coalitional opportunities of the grand coalition rise [$v(N)$ increases] while every other coalitional opportunity remains fixed [$v(S)$ is constant for all $S \neq N$], it may happen that some agent suffers a net loss (Lemma 5.2). More generally, a surprising impossibility result (Theorem 5.3) says that every value selecting a core allocation, whenever the core is nonempty, must violate a related monotonicity axiom called coalitional monotonicity (Definition 5.5). Thus, a trade-off exists: A value satisfies at most one property of the stand-alone principle (core selection) and coalitional monotonicity. The nucleolus satisfies the former and the Shapley value the latter.

Section 5.6 is devoted to a difficult axiomatic characterization of the nucleolus due to Sobolev (Theorem 5.4). It rests upon the reduced-game property (Definition 5.7), an axiom of the same inspiration as the separability axioms discussed in Part I (Sections 2.4 and 3.5).

5.1 The Shapley value

A value for TU cooperative games is a mapping associating to any game (N, v) a balanced allocation $x \in E^N$ of $v(N)$, that is, $\sum_{i \in N} x_i = v(N)$.

We start with a cost-sharing game (N, c) for which such a value was invented nearly half a century ago in the accounting literature (see the historical article by Straffin and Heaney [1981]). It is called *equal allocation of nonseparable (EANS) costs*.

We call the quantity $SC_i = c(N) - c(N \setminus i)$ the separable cost of agent i, namely, the marginal cost of serving agent i given that every other agent is already served. After all separable costs have been imputed, the balance is called the nonseparable cost and denoted NSC. It may be positive or negative:

$$NSC = c(N) - \sum_{i \in N} [c(N) - c(N \setminus i)]$$

The EANS cost value imputes SC_i to agent i and divides NSC equally among all agents. This then gives the following cost share to agent i:

$$c_i = SC_i + \frac{1}{n} NSC = \frac{1}{n} \left(c(N) + \sum_{j \in N} c(N \setminus j) \right) - c(N \setminus i) \tag{1}$$

This is our first example of a value since it applies to *all* cost-sharing games and to all TU games (N, v) as well – just replace c by v in formula (1) – in which case it should be called equal sharing of nonseparable surplus.

One obvious defect of the EANS cost value is that it ignores all coalitions except the grand coalition and the coalitions of size $n - 1$. Yet the surplus (or cost) opportunities to smaller coalitions should play some role, as the discussion in Chapter 4 strongly suggests. The first merit of the *Shapley value* is to do just that while preserving the idea that cost shares should be based on marginal contributions (such as the separable costs). Thus, the cost share (surplus share) of agent i is computed as an average of the marginal cost (surplus) inflicted by agent i to each and every coalition of other agents.

To specify the formula, we think of the agents in N randomly ordered as $(i_1, i_2, \ldots, i_n)$, with every ordering equally probable. The Shapley value of agent i is an average of his marginal surpluses $v(S \cup \{i\}) - v(S)$ taken over all coalitions $S \subset N \setminus i$, including the empty set. The weight of coalition S is the probability that the predecessors of agent i in the random ordering $(i_1, \ldots, i_n)$ are exactly the elements of S. It is straightforward to check that this probability is worth $s!(n - s - 1)!/n!$, where s is the size of S. Indeed, there are $s!(n - s - 1)!$ orderings of N of which the s first elements are in S and the $n - s - 1$ last ones are in $N \setminus (S \cup \{i\})$.

Definition 5.1. *Given a TU game (N, v), its Shapley value σ allocates the surplus $v(N)$ of the grand coalition as follows:*

for all agents i:

$$\sigma_i = \sum_{0 \leq s \leq n-1} \frac{s!(n-s-1)!}{n!} \sum_{\substack{S \subset N \setminus i \\ |S| = s}} (v(S \cup \{i\}) - v(S)) \tag{2}$$

with the convention $0! = 1$ and $v(\varnothing) = 0$.

Of course, the Shapley value of a cost-sharing game is given by the same formula where c replaces v.

We claim in Definition 5.1 that the vector $(\sigma_1, ..., \sigma_n)$ is an allocation of $v(N)$. To check that, indeed, $\sum_{i=1}^{n} \sigma_i = v(N)$, we can think of the probabilistic interpretation of the Shapley value given in the preceding. For any given ordering, say $(1, 2, ..., n)$, the vector of marginal contributions x is worth

$$x_1 = v(1); \qquad x_i = v(\{1, ..., i\}) - v(\{1, ..., i-1\}) \quad \text{for } i = 2, ..., n$$

Thus, $\sum_{i=1}^{n} x_i = v(N)$ holds true for each of the marginal contribution vectors of which we take the average, implying $\sum_{i=1}^{n} \sigma_i = v(N)$ as well.

Alternatively, one can check this equality directly in formula (2). Developing $\sum_{i=1}^{n} \sigma_i$, pick any proper coalition S of N and compute its coefficient as

$$s \cdot \left[\frac{(s-1)!(n-(s-1)-1)!}{n!} \right] - (n-s) \cdot \left[\frac{s!(n-s-1)!}{n!} \right] = 0$$

whereas the coefficient of $v(N)$ is $n \cdot [(n-1)! \, 0!/n!] = 1$.

We note first that if the game (N, v) is superadditive, the Shapley value is individually rational; namely, agent i receives at least his opportunity surplus $v(i)$. To prove this claim, observe that superadditivity implies

$$v(S \cup \{i\}) - v(S) \geq v(i) \quad \text{for all } S \subset N \setminus \{i\}$$

In formula (2) the coefficient of $(v(S \cup \{i\}) - v(i))$ is the probability that the predecessors of agent i in the random ordering are exactly the elements of S. Therefore, the sum of these coefficients when S varies in $N \setminus \{i\}$ is 1, implying $\sigma_i \geq v(i)$.

Thus, at the Shapley value, an agent cannot stand alone and object. However, intermediate coalitions may be able to do so, as our first example shows.

Example 5.1. Shapley value of a three-person game
For a three-person game (N, v) with $N = \{1, 2, 3\}$, formula (2) reads

$$\sigma_1 = \tfrac{1}{3}v(1) + \tfrac{1}{6}[(v(12) - v(2)) + (v(13) - v(3))] + \tfrac{1}{3}(v(N) - v(23)) \Leftrightarrow$$

$$\sigma_1 = \tfrac{1}{3}v(N) + \tfrac{1}{6}(v(12) + v(13) - 2v(23)) + \tfrac{1}{6}(2v(1) - v(2) - v(3)) \qquad (3)$$

For instance, in Example 4.1, we find that the cost shares $(\sigma_1, \sigma_2, \sigma_3) =$ $(73.3, 98.3, 83.3)$. This allocation is outside the core (for $\sigma_1 + \sigma_2 > 170$) but not very far from its center $(68.3, 98.3, 88.3)$.

In our next two examples, the Shapley value yields an interesting computation.

Example 5.2. A land corn production economy
We have $n+1$ agents. Agent 0 (the landlord) owns the land and agents $1, 2, \ldots, n$ are n identical workers who own their labor only. The production function shows, for any number i of workers, the amount of corn $f(i)$ they produce by working the (indivisible) land. The function f is nondecreasing, and $f(0) = 0$. The TU game reflects the production possibilities of coalitions: Without agent 0, a coalition is worthless; with him, it can produce an amount depending only upon the number of workers:

$$v(S) = \begin{cases} 0 & \text{if } 0 \notin S \\ f(s) & \text{if } 0 \in S \text{ and } |S| = s+1 \end{cases} \qquad (4)$$

The Shapley value allocates to the landlord $\sigma_0 = [1/(n+1)] \sum_{i=1}^{n} f(i)$ because in a random ordering of $\{0, 1, \ldots, n\}$ his marginal contribution is $f(i)$, where i is the number of workers before him, and the random variable i is uniformly distributed over $0, 1, \ldots, n$. Because all workers are identical, they all receive the same share:

$$\sigma_i = \frac{1}{n}(f(n) - \sigma_0) = \frac{1}{n}\left(f(n) - \frac{1}{n+1} \sum_{i=1}^{n} f(i)\right) \qquad (5)$$

Note that the core of this game is very large and can give as much as all the surplus to the landlord ($x_0 = f(n)$, $x_i = 0$, all $i \geq 1$, is a core allocation) and as little as zero to the landlord if the average product is maximal when all workers are utilized. Indeed, the allocation $x_0 = 0$, $x_i = f(n)/n$, all i, is in the core if and only if

$$\frac{f(s)}{s} \leq \frac{f(n)}{n}, \quad \text{all } s = 1, \ldots, n-1 \qquad (6)$$

When (6) holds true, the Shapley value is a core allocation as well, as the careful reader will easily check.

Example 5.3. User's fee (Littlechild and Owen [1973])
The n airlines share the cost of a runway. To serve the planes of company i, the length of the runway – roughly proportional to its cost – must be c_i. Without loss of generality, we assume

$$c_n \leq c_{n-1} \leq \cdots \leq c_2 \leq c_1$$

This yields the cost-sharing game

$$c(S) = \max_{i \in S}\{c_i\} \quad \text{for all } S \subset \{1, \ldots, n\} \tag{7}$$

Again, the game has a large core (we show in Section 5.2 that it is a convex game) and hence the need for a deterministic allocation. The Shapley value yields an interesting compromise:

$$\sigma_n = \frac{1}{n}c_n, \ \sigma_{n-1} = \frac{1}{n}c_n + \frac{1}{n-1}(c_{n-1}-c_n), \ \ldots, \ \sigma_i = \sum_{j=i}^{n}\frac{1}{j}(c_j - c_{j+1}),$$

$$\text{all } i = 1, \ldots, n \tag{8}$$

with the convention $c_{n+1} = 0$.

To check this formula, use (2), or cut the total cost c_1 into pieces $\delta_n = c_n$, $\delta_i = c_i - c_{i+1}$, $i = 1, \ldots, n-1$. Then observe the following: that in the vector of marginal contributions, for an ordering $(i_1, \ldots, i_n)$ of N,

δ_n is imputed to whoever is first, namely, i_1

δ_{n-1} is imputed to whoever is first among agents $\{1, \ldots, n-1\}$

δ_i is imputed to whoever is first among agents $\{1, \ldots, i\}$

Thus, δ_i is allocated with equal probability $1/i$ to each of the agents $1, \ldots, i$. This in turn yields formula (8).

5.2   Convex games

Example 5.1 shows that the Shapley value does not pass the stand-alone test. There are games with a nonempty core that does not contain the Shapley value.

Convex games are a rich class of games with a nonempty core containing the Shapley value. In fact, the Shapley value occupies a central position within the core of a convex game. Roughly speaking, the game is convex if we have increasing returns to cooperation. In the TU game framework this means that the larger the coalition that agent i joins, the larger his marginal contribution.

Definition 5.2. *A TU cooperative game* (N, v) *is* **convex** *if it satisfies one of the two following equivalent properties:*

for all $i \in N$, *all* $S, T \subset N \setminus \{i\}$:

$$\{S \subset T\} \Rightarrow \{v(S \cup \{i\}) - v(S) \leq v(T \cup \{i\}) - v(T)\} \tag{9}$$

and/or

for all $S, T \subset N$: $\quad v(S) + v(T) \le v(S \cup T) + v(S \cap T)$ $\qquad$ (10)

with the convention $v(\varnothing) = 0$.

To check the claimed equivalence, notice first that (9) is a particular case of (10) for coalitions $S \cup \{i\}$ and T. Conversely, assume (9) and take two coalitions S, T with $S \subset T$. Set $R = N \setminus T$ and a sequence $\{i_1, i_2, \ldots, i_r\}$ covering R. Applying (9) successively, we get

$$v(S \cup i_1) - v(S) \le v(T \cup i_1) - v(T)$$

$$v(S \cup \{i_1, i_2\}) - v(S \cup i_1) \le v(T \cup \{i_1 i_2\}) - v(T \cup i_1)$$

$$v(S \cup \{i_1 \cdots i_k\}) - v(S \cup \{i_1 \cdots i_{k-1}\}) \le v(T \cup \{i_1 \cdots i_k\}) - v(T \cup \{i_1 \cdots i_{k-1}\})$$

Adding these inequalities we find that, for all $R' \subset N \setminus T = R$,

$$v(S \cup R') - v(S) \le v(T \cup R') - v(T) \qquad (11)$$

Fix now two arbitrary coalitions S_0, T_0 (not necessarily included in each other) and apply (11) to $S = S_0 \cap T_0$, $T = T_0$, and $R' = S_0 \setminus T_0$. This yields (10), as desired.

The nice feature of convex games is that for any ordering of N, the corresponding vector of marginal contributions is in the core. Hence, a convex game is balanced. Moreover, the barycenter of the marginal contribution vectors, namely, the Shapley value, is in the core too (since the core is a convex subset of E^N).

Lemma 5.1. *Let (N, v) be a convex TU game and let N be ordered as $\{i_1, i_2, \ldots, i_n\}$. The corresponding vector of marginal contributions*

$$x_{i_k} = v(i_1, \ldots, i_k) - v(i_1, \ldots, i_{k-1})$$

is in the core of the game. Therefore, the Shapley value is in the core, too.

Proof: For simplicity of notation, say that N is ordered as $\{1, \ldots, n\}$ and call x the associated vector of marginal contributions. Pick an arbitrary coalition $S \subset N$ and order its elements as $S = \{i_1, i_2, \ldots, i_s\}$. For every k, $1 \le k \le s$, apply (9) with $S' = \{i_1, \ldots, i_{k-1}\}$, $T' = \{1, 2, \ldots, i_k - 1\}$, and $i = i_k$:

$$v(i_1, \ldots, i_k) - v(i_1, \ldots, i_{k-1}) \le v(1, 2, \ldots, i_k) - v(1, 2, \ldots, i_k - 1) = x_{i_k}$$

Summing these inequalities from $k = 1$ to $k = s - 1$, we get

$$v(i_1, \ldots, i_s) = v(S) \le \sum_{k=1}^{s} x_{i_k} = \sum_{i \in S} x_i$$

the desired inequality. The second statement follows because the core is a convex subset of E^N, and the Shapley value is defined as the uniform average of marginal contribution vectors.   Q.E.D.

Remark 5.1:   Exercise 5.5 proves the converse property, due to Ichiishi [1981]: If all marginal contribution vectors are in the core, then the game is convex.

In a convex game, the Shapley value occupies a central position within the core. Indeed, the marginal contribution vectors are the extreme points (vertices) of the (convex) core; that is, the core is the convex hull of the marginal contribution vectors. This difficult result is proven by Shapley [1971]. It implies that the Shapley value is the barycenter of the core vertices – with the qualification that a vertex is counted twice if it corresponds to the marginal contribution vectors of two different orderings. We illustrate this result for three-person games.

Example 5.4. Convex three-person games
A convex game is (fully) superadditive, as results from (10) when S and T are disjoint. Thus, a normalized convex three-person game takes the form

$$v(i) = 0, \quad \text{all } i = 1, 2, 3; \qquad v(N) = 1;$$
$$0 \le v(ij) \le 1, \quad \text{all } ij, i \ne j \tag{12}$$

Note that formula (10) is trivial when S contains T or vice versa. Thus, convexity of a three-person game amounts to three inequalities, corresponding to (10) when S, T have two elements each and are distinct:

$$v(12) + v(23) \le v(N) + v(2), \ldots$$

In view of the normalization (12), this means

$$v(ij) + v(jk) \le 1, \quad \text{for all } \{ij\}\{jk\} \text{ with } i, j, k \text{ pairwise disjoint}$$

We draw in Figure 5.1 the corresponding core. It is a hexagon (unless some of the preceding inequalities are equalities) and hence a generally large subset of the simplex [although in some extreme cases its surface can be very small, as when $v(12) = 0.98$ and $v(13) = v(23) = 0.01$].

The marginal contribution vectors are at the six intersections of a line $x_i + x_j = v(ij)$ and an edge of the simplex; each line intersects two edges. Consider the two orderings $(1, 2, 3)$ and $(1, 3, 2)$ with associated vectors of marginal contributions $\alpha = (0, v(12), 1 - v(12))$, $\beta = (0, 1 - v(13), v(13))$. From $v(12) + v(13) \le 1$ it follows that α is between β and the vertex $(0, 0, 1)$, whereas β is between α and $(0, 1, 0)$. Figure 5.1 shows results for the numerical values $v(12) = 0.3$, $v(23) = 0.3$, and $v(13) = 0.6$.

Production economy games are often convex when the technology has increasing returns to scale. This is the case for the land corn production

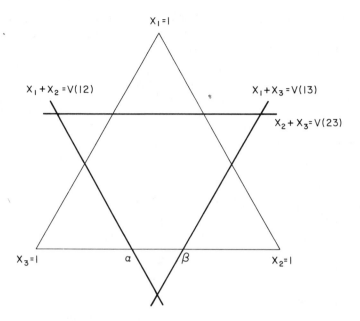

Figure 5.1.

economy of Example 5.2 [see Exercise 5.2, question (a)]. Another important family of convex games are the surplus-sharing games associated with the provision of a public good, to which Chapter 6 is devoted. For the time being, we give two examples of concave cost-sharing games.

Example 5.3. User's fee (continued)
The cost-sharing game of Example 5.3 is a *concave* cost-sharing game:

for all i, all S, T:
$$\{S \subsetneq T \subset N \setminus i\} \Rightarrow c(S \cup \{i\}) - c(S) \geq c(T \cup \{i\}) - c(T) \qquad (13)$$

The marginal cost of including i decreases as the coalition expands. Under concavity of c, the analog of Lemma 5.1 holds: Any vector of marginal costs is in the core, and so is the Shapley value.

To check that user's fee is a concave game, write property (9) with the help of (7):

$$\max_{j \in S \cup \{i\}} \{c_j\} - \max_{j \in S} \{c_j\} \geq \max_{j \in T \cup \{i\}} \{c_j\} - \max_{j \in T} \{c_j\}$$

Denote $\max_S c_j = c_1$ and $\max_T c_j = c_2$. The preceding inequality reads

$$\max(c_1, c_i) - c_1 \geq \max(c_2, c_i) - c_2 \qquad (14)$$

From $S \subseteq T$ follows $c_1 \le c_2$. Distinguish three cases: If $c_i \le c_1$, each member of (14) is zero; if $c_1 \le c_i \le c_2$, (14) reads $c_i - c_1 \ge c_2 - c_2 = 0$; and if $c_2 \le c_i$, (14) reads $c_i - c_1 \ge c_i - c_2$, that is, $c_2 \ge c_1$.

Example 5.5. Pricing a multi-output monopoly
Given is a cost function $C(q_1, ..., q_n)$. To each finite sequence $q^1, ..., q^K \in E^n$, we associate the K-person cost-sharing game given by formula (18) in Chapter 4, where agent k holds the demand q^k. What cost function C guarantees the concavity of each of these cost-sharing games? The desired inequality is the reverse of (10) because we deal with a cost-sharing game:

$$C\left(\sum_S q^k\right) + C\left(\sum_T q^k\right) \ge C\left(\sum_{S \cup T} q^k\right) + C\left(\sum_{S \cap T} q^k\right) \tag{15}$$

Set $a = \sum_{S \cap T} q^k$, $b = \sum_T q^k$, and $x = \sum_{S \setminus T} q^k$. Then (15) reads

$$C(a+x) + C(b) \ge C(b+x) + C(a)$$
$$\Leftrightarrow C(a+x) - C(a) \ge C(b+x) - C(b) \tag{16}$$

This must hold for every $a, b, x \in E_+^n$ with $b \ge a$. Conversely, (16) implies (15) at once. Condition (16) is known as *cost complementarity*. It is equivalently formulated as

$$C(a+b+c) - C(a+b) \le C(a+c) - C(a) \quad \text{for all } a, b, c \in E_+^n$$

When C is twice differentiable, cost complementarity is equivalent to

$$\frac{\partial^2 C}{\partial q_i \, \partial q_j}(q) \le 0 \quad \text{for all } q \in E_+^n$$

Under cost complementarity, all cost-sharing games [equation (18) in Chapter 4] have a nonempty core. Hence (Theorem 4.2) the cost function C is supportable. The analog of the Shapley value in this model is the Aumann–Shapley price, discussed in Section 7.4.

The notion of convex games generalizes to NTU games as well. There are actually two generalizations of convexity, one in the cardinal sense (Sharkey [1981]) and one in the ordinal sense (Vilkov [1977]). Lemma 5.1 generalizes only partially: Every convex game (whether in the ordinal or cardinal sense) has a nonempty core (Vilkov [1977], Peleg [1986]), but only cardinal convexity implies that an appropriate generalization of the Shapley value is in the core (Kern [1985]).

5.3   Characterizations of the Shapley value

The key feature of formula (2) is that the Shapley value allocation σ_i to agent i depends only upon the vector of his marginal contributions

$[v(S \cup \{i\}) - v(S)]$ to all coalitions S in $N \backslash i$. Thus, σ_i depends on 2^{n-1} independent variables, as opposed to $2^n - 1$ for an arbitrary value operator. Another obvious property of the Shapley value is anonymity: The names of the agents do not matter. These two properties together are characteristic.

Definition 5.3. *Given society N, the set of TU games with set of agents N is the vector space E^{2^N}.*

*A **value operator** is a mapping φ from E^{2^N} into E^N associating to any game (N, v) an allocation $\varphi(v)$ of $v(N)$:*

$$\sum_{i \in N} \varphi_i(v) = v(N) \tag{17}$$

Definition 5.4. *Given are society N and a value operator φ on E^{2^N}.*

*We say that φ is **anonymous** if it commutes with permutations of agents. For all bijections τ of N into itself and all $v \in E^{2^N}$,*

$$\tau(\varphi(v)) = \varphi(\tau(v)) \tag{18}$$

where $\tau(v)(S) = v(\tau(S))$ for $S \subset N$, and $\tau(x)_i = x_{\tau(i)}$ for $x \in E^N$.

*We say that φ is **marginalist** if $\varphi_i(v)$ depends only upon the vector $(v(S \cup \{i\}) - v(S))_{S \subset N \backslash \{i\}}$, which means that for all i fixed in N we have for all $v, w \in E^{2^N}$:*

$$\{v(S \cup \{i\}) - v(S) = w(S \cup \{i\}) - w(S) \text{ for all } S \subset N \backslash \{i\}\} \Rightarrow \varphi_i(v) = \varphi_i(w)$$

with the convention $v(\varnothing) = w(\varnothing) = 0$.

Theorem 5.1 (Young [1985a]). *There is only one anonymous and marginalist value operator. It is the Shapley value.*

Proof: We show the proof of Theorem 5.1 in the three-agent case. Young's general proof uses an induction argument.

Check first in (2) that the Shapley value operator σ is marginalist and anonymous. Conversely, suppose the value operator φ shares these two properties. Then define the mapping α from E^{2^N} into E^N as

$$\alpha(v) = \varphi(v) - \sigma(v) \quad \text{for all } v \in E^{2^N}$$

This mapping is anonymous and marginalist. Moreover, $\sum_{i=1}^3 \alpha_i(v) = 0$ for all $v \in E^{2^N}$.

Since $\alpha_1(v)$ is marginalist, it takes the form

$$\alpha_1(v) = \alpha_1(v(N) - v(23), v(12) - v(2), v(13) - v(3), v(1)) \tag{19}$$

Consider the transformation of v into v' as follows:

$$v'(S) = \begin{cases} v(S) + \lambda & \text{if } 1 \in S \\ v(S) & \text{if } 1 \notin S \end{cases}$$

where λ is any given real number. Using a formula similar to (19) for agents 2 and 3, we get

$$\alpha_2(v') = \alpha_2(v); \qquad \alpha_3(v') = \alpha_3(v)$$

By $\sum_{i=1}^{3} \alpha_i(v) = 0$, we deduce $\alpha_1(v') = \alpha_1(v)$, or equivalently,

$$\alpha_1(x+\lambda, y+\lambda, z+\lambda, t+\lambda) = \alpha_1(x, y, z, t)$$

Thus, we can choose $\lambda = -v(1)$ and write $\alpha_1(v)$ in the form

$$\alpha_1(v) = \beta_1(v(N) - v(23) - v(1), v(12) - v(1) - v(2), v(13) - v(3) - v(1))$$

with similar functions β_2, β_3 for α_2, α_3, respectively. By anonymity, $\beta_1 = \beta_2 = \beta_3 = \beta$, and β is a symmetrical function of its last two variables.

Set $v(i) = 0$, all i, and $v(12) = x$, $v(23) = y$, $v(13) = z$, and $v(N) = t$. The assumption $\alpha_1 + \alpha_2 + \alpha_3 = 0$ reads

$$\beta(t-y, x, z) + \beta(t-z, y, x) + \beta(t-x, z, y) = 0 \qquad (20)$$

for all real numbers x, y, z, t.

To solve the functional equation (20), take $x = z$ and define $w = t - x$. We get

$$\beta(w - y + x, x, x) + \beta(w, y, x) + \beta(w, x, y) = 0$$

Since β is symmetrical in its last two variables, we deduce that $\beta(w, y, x)$ depends on $w - y$ only. Similarly, it depends on $w - x$ only, and hence $\beta(x, y, z) = \gamma(x - y - z)$. Reporting this in (20), the desired conclusion $\beta = 0$ follows. Q.E.D.

A weaker version of Theorem 5.1 by Loehman and Whinston [1974] uses a differentiability assumption that is proven unnecessary in Young [1985a]. The latter uses also a weaker symmetry assumption than our anonymity axiom.

A marginalist value operator does not preclude a nonlinear functional dependence of $\varphi_i(v)$ upon the marginal contributions $v(S \cup \{i\}) - v(S)$. Yet Theorem 5.1 says that this dependence is actually linear (under anonymity). The original characterization by Shapley takes the opposite route. Additivity of the value operator w.r.t. the game v is postulated, and marginalism obtains as a consequence of additivity and the dummy axioms.

Additivity:

$$\text{for any } v, w \in E^{2^N}: \quad \varphi(v+w) = \varphi(v) + \varphi(w)$$

Dummy:

for any $i \in N$, any $v \in E^{2^N}$:

$$\{v(S \cup \{i\}) = v(S) \text{ for all } S \subset N \setminus \{i\}\} \Rightarrow \varphi_i(v) = 0$$

Theorem 5.2 (Shapley [1953]). *There is only one value operator satisfying the three axioms anonymity, additivity, and dummy. It is the Shapley value.*

The dummy axiom is a weak form of marginalism. An agent with zero marginal contribution to every other coalition is a dummy. The axiom says that he should be paid zero as well. Under marginalism and anonymity, the value of the null game [$v(S) = 0$ for all S] is the null vector; hence, a dummy of an arbitrary game should get zero.

Without the dummy axiom many value operators are anonymous and additive, for example the EANS costs [formula (1) with v instead of c].

Proof of Theorem 5.2: Let φ be a value operator satisfying all three axioms. For any coalition $S \subset N$, denote by $\delta_S \in E^{2^N}$ the following S-unanimity game:

$$\delta_S(T) = \begin{cases} 1 & \text{if } S \subset T \\ 0 & \text{otherwise} \end{cases}$$

In the game $\lambda \delta_S$, all agents of $N \setminus S$ are dummies so they all get zero. By anonymity, all agents in S receive the same allocation. Thus, by efficiency [condition (17)], the vector $\varphi(\lambda \delta_S)$ is entirely determined. All agents in S get $(\lambda/|S|)$, and all those in $N \setminus S$ get zero.

We show next that the games δ_S, $S \in 2^N$, form a basis of E^{2^N}. It is enough to show that they are linearly independent. Consider a linear combination of those games that sum to zero:

$$\sum_{S \in 2^N} \lambda_S \cdot \delta_S = 0 \tag{21}$$

If the coefficients λ_S are not all zero, there is a coalition S_0 such that $\lambda_{S_0} \neq 0$ and $\lambda_S = 0$ for all $S \subsetneq S_0$. Thus, (21) implies

$$\delta_{S_0} = \sum_S -\frac{\lambda_S}{\lambda_{S_0}} \cdot \delta_S \tag{22}$$

where the sum bears upon coalitions that are not contained in S_0. Taking the value of the right vector at S_0 gives $\delta_{S_0}(S_0) = 0$, a contradiction.

We have proven that the games δ_S, $S \in 2^N$, form a basis of E^{2^N} and that φ is determined on every game $\lambda \cdot \delta_S$. By additivity, there is at most one value operator satisfying our three axioms. Conversely, it is obvious that the Shapley value operator (2) does satisfy these axioms.   Q.E.D.

In Exercise 5.9 we give the explicit formula decomposing any game v in the basis $(\delta_S, \ S \in 2^N)$.

The additivity of the Shapley value has a lot of mathematical appeal. In addition to an explicit formula, it makes sensitivity analysis very tractable: effect of a shift in a coalition's value, impact of merging or splitting of some agents, and so on.

There are a few more characterizations of the Shapley value. One can explicitly decompose an arbitrary game in the basis $(\delta_S, \ S \in 2^N)$ and interpret the alternative formula for the Shapley value as a process of equal sharing of dividends when more and more coalitions add up; see Exercise 5.9 for details. This leads to Myerson's axiomatic characterization of the Shapley value in a model where all coalitions are not necessarily feasible (Myerson [1977]).

Another insight is the reduced-game approach in the variable-population context; see Section 5.6 and the characterization result by Hart and Mas-Colell [1989] described in Exercise 5.12.

The Shapley value is amenable to several generalizations. At least three distinct value operators can be constructed for NTU games that coincide with the Shapley value on the subset of TU games. They have been proposed by Harsanyi [1963] (later axiomatized by Hart [1985]), Shapley [1969] (later axiomatized by Aumann [1985]), and Kalaï and Samet [1985].

Another successful generalization is to games with a continuum of agents (players). The book by Aumann and Shapley [1974] is devoted to this model, in which each agent is an infinitesimal fraction of society. An application is the pricing of a multi-output monopoly.

As in Section 4.3, we have a cost function $C(q_1, \ldots, q_n)$ and a given output level (inelastic demand) $(\bar{q}_1, \ldots, \bar{q}_n)$. The TU game [(18) in Chapter 4] generalizes to a game with a continuum of agents where the global demand is cut into more and more pieces; each agent ultimately represents an infinitesimal fraction of the demand. Analogous to the Shapley value in this context is the *Aumann–Shapley price vector*, given by

$$p_i = \int_0^1 \frac{\partial C}{\partial q_i} (t\bar{q}_1, \ldots, t\bar{q}_n)\, dt, \quad i = 1, \ldots, n$$

Obviously, this price is budget balanced $[\sum_{i=1}^n p_i \cdot \bar{q}_i = C(\bar{q})]$. Mirman, Tauman, and Zang [1985] show that if C exhibits cost complementarity $([\partial^2 C/(\partial q_i\, \partial q_j)](q) \le 0$ for all q and all i, j; raising the level of any output diminishes the marginal cost of every output), then the Aumann–Shapley price is subsidy free (Definition 4.4). This is essentially a generalization of Lemma 5.1.

5.4   The nucleolus

The Shapley value is not a core selection in every balanced game. It makes sense to insist that the value be in the core whenever the latter is non-empty. The most interesting core selection value is called the nucleolus. It is a centrally located element of the core defined by an egalitarian arbitration among coalitions.

Definition 5.5 (Schmeidler [1969]).   *Given is a TU game* (N, v). *Denote by B the set of efficient allocations* $x \in E^N$ $[\sum_{i \in N} x_i = v(N)]$. *To every vector in B, associate the following vector* $e(x) \in E^{2^N \setminus N}$:

$$\text{for all proper coalitions } S \subset N: \quad e(x; S) = \sum_{i \in S} x_i - v(S)$$

There is a unique allocation γ *in B such that for every other* $x \in B$, *the leximin ordering prefers* $e(\gamma)$ *to* $e(x)$. *It is called the nucleolus of the game* (N, v).

The claim of Definition 5.3 results from a property of the leximin ordering proven in Lemma 1.1: When x varies over B, the vector $e(x)$ varies over a closed convex subset A of $E^{2^N \setminus N}$. The set A is not bounded above. Yet to maximize the leximin ordering over A, it is easy to restrict oneself to a compact subset of A, whereafter Lemma 1.1 implies that the leximin ordering has a unique maximum over A (we omit the details). Moreover, the mapping $x \to e(x)$ is one-to-one, so this unique maximum corresponds to a unique allocation, as claimed.

The nucleolus measures the welfare of a coalition S by its excess $e(x, S)$, namely, the extra benefit to coalition S above its own opportunity surplus. It compares the excesses of various coalitions in an egalitarian spirit. Its first concern is with the smallest surplus that it maximizes: The excess vector $e(\gamma)$ maximizes over B the egalitarian CUF, where each coalition's utility is taken to be its excess:

$$\min_{S \subset N} e(\gamma, S) \geq \min_{S \subset N} e(x, S), \text{ all } x \in B$$

$$\Leftrightarrow \min_{S \subset N} \left(\sum_{i \in S} \gamma_i - v(S) \right) = \max_{x \in B} \left\{ \min_{S \subset N} \left(\sum_{i \in S} x_i - v(S) \right) \right\} \quad (23)$$

Then among the solutions of program (23), the nucleolus picks those allocations where the second smallest coalitional surplus is as high as possible, and so on. This process eventually leads to a single allocation, namely, the nucleolus.

Notice that if the core of (N, v) is nonempty, then the solutions of program (23) are all in the core. Indeed, suppose the allocation $x \in B$ is in the core of (N, v), that is, $\min_{S \subset N} e(x, S) \geq 0$. Then every solution of (23) must satisfy the same inequality, which is to say it must be in the core.

Whenever the core is empty, can we at least expect the nucleolus to be individually rational $[\gamma_i \geq v(i)$ for all $i]$? If the game (N, v) is superadditive, the answer is yes (recall that the Shapley value, too, is individually rational in a superadditive game). To show this, denote by γ the nucleolus of (N, v) and by M the set of proper coalitions T of N where the excess $e(\gamma, T)$ is maximal:

$$T \in M \Leftrightarrow e(\gamma, T) = \min_{S \subset N} e(\gamma, S)$$

Suppose $\gamma_1 < v(1)$. We claim that every coalition T in M contains agent 1. Otherwise, we get a contradiction by computing the excess of $T \cup \{1\}$:

$$e(\gamma, T \cup \{1\}) = \gamma_1 + \sum_{i \in T} \gamma_i - v(T \cup \{1\})$$

$$= (\gamma_1 - v(1)) + e(\gamma, T) + (v(1) + v(T) - v(T \cup \{1\}))$$

implying $e(\gamma, T \cup \{1\}) < e(\gamma, T)$ by superadditivity.

Consider next a (small) positive number ϵ and define a new allocation $\gamma' \in B$ as follows:

$$\gamma_1' = \gamma_1 + \epsilon; \qquad \gamma_i' = \gamma_i - \epsilon/(n-1) \quad \text{for all } i \geq 2$$

Since every coalition T in M is proper (smaller than the grand coalition), we have

$$e(\gamma', T) = e(\gamma, T) + \epsilon - \frac{|T| - 1}{n - 1} \epsilon > e(\gamma, T)$$

Thus, for ϵ small enough the vector γ' has a greater minimal excess than γ, a contradiction of (23).

Remark 5.2: Schmeidler's original definition of the nucleolus imposes individual rationality (the set B is replaced by the smaller set B' of efficient and individually rational allocations; the rest of the definition follows as in the preceding). We have just shown that this constraint is superfluous for a superadditive game (virtually all economic examples yield superadditivity). At any rate, our Definition 5.5 (also called quasinucleolus in the literature) proves more suitable for the axiomatic characterization: Theorem 5.4 would not hold under Schmeidler's original definition.

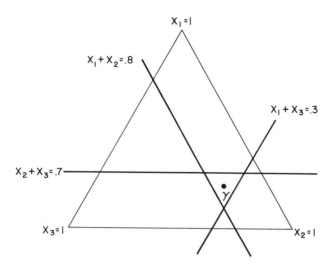

Figure 5.2.

We compute now the nucleolus on a few examples. The first examples are three-person games. They show that the nucleolus occupies a central position within the core.

Example 5.6. Nucleolus of some three-person games
Even for three-person games, it is not easy to give a general formula for the nucleolus. The exhaustive computation for three-person superadditive games is given in Exercise 5.2. Here we merely take three typical cases, all normalized superadditive games: $v(i) = 0$, all i, $v(N) = 1$, $0 \leq v(ij) \leq 1$.

Case 1. Games with small or empty cores: This is a class of games defined by the three inequalities

$$v(ij) + v(jk) \geq 1, \quad \text{all } \{ij\}\{jk\}, \text{ where } i, j, k \text{ are pairwise distinct} \quad (24)$$

In those games, two-person coalitions are quite powerful. Geometrically, the inequalities (24) mean that the three points where the lines $x_i + x_j = v(ij)$ and $x_j + x_k = v(jk)$ intersect, [e.g., the intersection is $x = (1 - v(23), v(12) + v(23) - 1, 1 - v(12))$ if $i = 1, j = 2, k = 3$] are inside the simplex.

Hence we have two possible configurations [depending on the sign of $v(12) + v(23) + v(13) - 2$], one with a nonempty core (see Figure 5.2) and one with an empty core (see Figure 5.3). In both cases the nucleolus is the

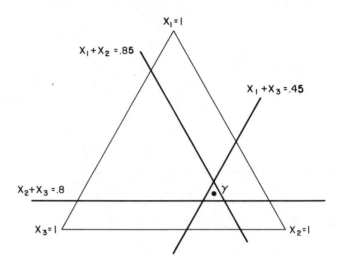

Figure 5.3.

center of the three lines $x_i + x_j = v(ij)$, namely, the center γ of the core if the core is nonempty (see Figure 5.2) or the center of the "shadow core" if the core is empty.

A formal proof of these claims is the subject of Exercise 5.2. Intuitively, since two-person coalitions are strong, only two-person coalitions will matter in the maximin utility program (23):

$$\max_{x \in B} \min_{S \subset N} e(x, S) = \max_{x \in B} \min\{e(x, 12), e(x, 13), e(x, 23)\}$$

Since the sum $\sum e(x, ij)$ is constant on B, the solution γ on the right side is easy to compute:

$$e(\gamma, 12) = e(\gamma, 13) = e(\gamma, 23) \Leftrightarrow \begin{cases} \gamma_1 = \tfrac{1}{3} + \tfrac{1}{3}(v(12) + v(13) - 2v(23)) \\ \gamma_2 = \tfrac{1}{3} + \tfrac{1}{3}(v(12) + v(23) - 2v(13)) \\ \gamma_3 = \tfrac{1}{3} + \tfrac{1}{3}(v(13) + v(23) - 2v(12)) \end{cases}$$

Note that in the games satisfying (24), the Shapley value σ is easily compared with the nucleolus. Indeed, for a normalized game, formula (2) gives

$$\sigma_1 = \tfrac{1}{3} + \tfrac{1}{6}(v(12) + v(13) - 2v(23))$$

and two similar formulas for σ_2, σ_3 by permuting agents. Denote by ω the center of the simplex corresponding to the uniform distribution $\omega = (\tfrac{1}{3}, \tfrac{1}{3}, \tfrac{1}{3})$. The σ is the middle point of ω and γ, $\sigma = \tfrac{1}{2}(\omega + \gamma)$. This says that the nucleolus brings twice as much inequality between surplus shares as the Shapley value.

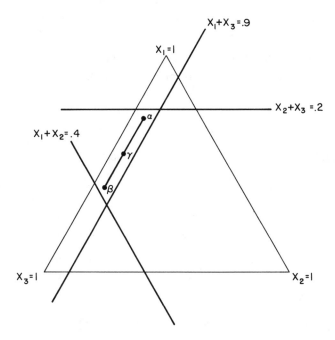

Figure 5.4.

Case 2. Games with very weak two-person coalitions: This class is defined by the inequalities

$$v(ij) \le \tfrac{1}{3}, \quad \text{all } \{ij\}$$

In any two-person coalition, the per capita surplus is at most half of
the per capita surplus in the grand coalition. Consequently, two-person
coalitions play no role in program (23) (the formal proof is again the subject of Exercise 5.2):

$$\max_{x \in B} \min_{S \subset N} e(x, S) = \max_{x \in B} \min\{e(x, 1), e(x, 2), e(x, 3)\}$$

Since the sum $\sum e(x, i)$ is contant over B, the nucleolus is just the center ω of the simplex:

$$e(\gamma, 1) = e(\gamma, 2) = e(\gamma, 3) \Leftrightarrow \gamma = (\tfrac{1}{3}, \tfrac{1}{3}, \tfrac{1}{3})$$

Case 3. $v(12) = 0.4$, $v(23) = 0.2$, $v(13) = 0.9$: This example is typical of an
intermediate situation where two-person coalitions are neither too strong
nor too weak. The nonempty core is depicted in Figure 5.4.

In the maximin program (23) the main constraints are $e(x, 2)$ and $e(x, 13)$. Indeed, we have

$$e(x, 2) + e(x, 13) = (x_2 - v(2)) + (x_1 + x_3 - v(13))$$
$$= v(N) - v(2) - v(13) = 0.1$$

Therefore,

for all $x \in B$: $\min_{S \subset N} e(x, S) \le \min\{e(x, 2), e(x, 13)\} \le 0.05$

The solutions of program (23) are the allocations x such that

$$\min_{S \subset N} e(x, S) = 0.05$$

They cover the interval between

$$\alpha = (0.75, 0.05, 0.2) \quad \text{and} \quad \beta = (0.4, 0.05, 0.55)$$

(see Figure 5.4). This calls for the leximin ordering to break ties; on the interval $[\alpha, \beta]$, the critical excesses are $e(x, 12)$ and $e(x, 23)$:

for all $x \in [\alpha, \beta]$: $e(x, 12) + e(x, 23) = x_2 + v(N) - v(12) - v(23) = 0.45$

The middle point $\gamma = \frac{1}{2}(\alpha + \beta) = (0.575, 0.05, 0.375)$ is the nucleolus of the game.

For a general n-person game, computation of the nucleolus can be quite hard. In this respect, the Shapley value scores much better. The two economic examples 5.2 and 5.3 are a case in point; the nucleolus is much harder to compute than the Shapley value.

Example 5.2. A land corn production economy (continued)
For an arbitrary production function f, the nucleolus of game (4) is not easy to compute. We can give an explicit formula when f has increasing marginal returns and another one with decreasing marginal returns. Assume first decreasing marginal returns:

for all $i = 1, \ldots, n-1$:

$$f(i) - f(i-1) \ge f(i+1) - f(i) \quad \text{with the convention } f(0) = 0 \qquad (25)$$

Note first that the nucleolus gives the same surplus share to every worker (this is the anonymity property; see Theorem 5.4). Therefore, it takes the form

$$\gamma_1 = \cdots = \gamma_n = a; \qquad \gamma_0 = f(n) - na \qquad (26)$$

Next observe that the preceding allocation is in the core if and only if

$$0 \le a \le f(n) - f(n-1) \qquad (27)$$

Indeed, for any coalition S containing the landlord and k workers ($|S| = k+1$), we must check

$$f(n) - na + ka \geq f(k) \Leftrightarrow a \leq \frac{f(n) - f(k)}{n-k}, \quad \text{all } k = 0, \ldots, n-1$$

From assumption (25) it follows easily that

$$f(n) - f(n-1) \leq \frac{f(n) - f(k)}{n-k}, \quad \text{all } k = 0, \ldots, n-1$$

We restrict now the maximin program (23) to allocations of the form (26) and (27). This amounts to finding the solution a of

$$\max_{0 \leq a \leq f(n) - f(n-1)} \quad \min_{k=0,\ldots,n-1} \{(f(n) - na + ka) - f(k), a\} \qquad (28)$$

We claim that for all $k = 0, 1, \ldots, n$,

$$f(n) - f(k) - (n-k)a \geq f(n) - f(n-1) - a \Leftrightarrow a \leq \frac{f(n-1) - f(k)}{(n-1) - k}$$

Indeed, (25) implies

$$f(n) - f(n-1) \leq \frac{f(n-1) - f(k)}{(n-1) - k}$$

Thus, program (28) reduces to

$$\max_{0 \leq a \leq f(n) - f(n-1)} \quad \min\{f(n) - f(n-1) - a, a\}$$

with unique solution $a = \frac{1}{2}(f(n) - f(n-1))$. Summarizing, we have proved that the nucleolus of game (4) under decreasing marginal returns is

$$\gamma_1 = \cdots = \gamma_n = \frac{1}{2}(f(n) - f(n-1)), \quad \gamma_0 = f(n) - \frac{n}{2}(f(n) - f(n-1))$$

This may be compared with the landlord share from the Shapley value: $\sigma_0 = [1/(n+1)] \sum_{i=1}^{n} f(i)$. The nucleolus gives him a bigger share, and the more decreasing are the marginal returns, the bigger the difference:

$$\gamma_0 \geq \sigma_0 \Leftrightarrow \frac{1}{n+1} \sum_{i=1}^{n} f(i) \leq f(n) - \frac{n}{2}(f(n) - f(n-1))$$

To show this inequality, set $g(i) = f(i) - (f(n) - f(n-1)) \cdot i$ and write the corresponding inequality for g. Deduce from (25) that g is nondecreasing and conclude.

Under decreasing marginal returns even the Shapley value gives a bigger share to the landlord than to all workers together. To show this, the careful reader will check the inequality $\sigma_0 \geq f(n)/2$.

The case of increasing marginal returns,

$$\text{for all } i = 1, \ldots, n-1: \quad f(i) - f(i-1) \leq f(i+1) - f(i) \qquad (29)$$

yields dramatically different results. Now the nucleolus gives the *same* share to the landlord and to each worker (at least when marginal returns increase fast enough; see the details in Exercise 5.3):

$$\gamma_0 = \gamma_1 = \cdots = \gamma_n = \frac{f(n)}{n+1} \tag{30}$$

This time the Shapley value gives a (much) bigger share to the landlord, thus tempering the radical egalitarianism of the nucleolus. Hence in both cases (decreasing or increasing marginal returns) the Shapley value proposes a more moderate arbitration: not too favorable to the landlord under decreasing returns, not too favorable to the workers under increasing returns. The proof of (30) is the subject of Exercise 5.3.

Example 5.3. User's fee (continued)
The n costs are ordered as $0 \le c_n \le c_{n-1} \le \cdots \le c_1$ and the cost of serving coalition S is $\max_{i \in S}\{c_i\}$. To compute the Shapley value, we split the maximal cost c_1 into the incremental costs $\delta_i = c_i - c_{i+1}$ (with the convention $c_{n+1} = 0$) so that the total cost to be shared is

$$c_1 = \delta_1 + \delta_2 + \cdots + \delta_n$$

The general computation of the nucleolus is quite hard (see Owen [1982], p. 256). We discuss only the particular case

$$\delta_n \le \delta_{n-1} \le \cdots \le \delta_1$$

where an explicit formula is available.

The Shapley value [formula (8); see also what follows] shares equally δ_i among the agents $1, 2, \ldots, i$ who are "responsible" for it. The nucleolus also splits δ_i among the agents $1, 2, \ldots, i$, but the share of agent i is the largest, and shares decrease at a geometric speed with the index of the agent. More precisely, if $i \ge 2$, then agent i's share is $\frac{1}{2}$, that of agent $i-1$ is $\frac{1}{4}$, and so on, and both agents 2 and 1 pay the share $1/2^{i-1}$. This implies that agents 1 and 2 (with the highest costs) pay less with the nucleolus than with the Shapley value, whereas agent $n-1$ and n (with the lowest costs) pay more. The exact formula (proven in Exercise 5.4) is the following:

$$\gamma_1 = \delta_1 + \frac{\delta_2}{2} + \frac{\delta_3}{4} + \cdots + \frac{\delta_n}{2^{n-1}}$$

$$\gamma_2 = \frac{\delta_2}{2} + \frac{\delta_3}{4} + \cdots + \frac{\delta_n}{2^{n-1}}$$

$$\gamma_i = \sum_{j=i}^{n} \frac{\delta_j}{2^{j-i+1}} \quad \text{for all } i,\ 2 \le i \le n \tag{31}$$

$$\gamma_{n-1} = \frac{\delta_{n-1}}{2} + \frac{\delta_n}{4}$$

$$\gamma_n = \frac{\delta_n}{2}$$

Note the special role of agent 1, to which the general formula of γ_i does not apply. Compare with the Shapley value,

$$\sigma_i = \sum_{j=i}^{n} \frac{\delta_j}{j} \quad \text{for all } i,\ 1 \le i \le n$$

Clearly, $\sigma_1 \ge \gamma_1$, $\sigma_2 \ge \gamma_2$, and $\sigma_{n-1} \le \gamma_{n-1}$, $\sigma_n \le \gamma_n$ (when $n \ge 4$), but the comparison of σ_i with γ_i can go either way for other values of i.

5.5   Core selections

The nucleolus shows an egalitarian concern for excesses of various coalitions without paying attention to the size of the coalition(s) enjoying this surplus (or suffering the loss if the core is empty). One unit of surplus for a simple agent counts as much as one unit for its complement coalition with $n-1$ agents. This is quite arbitrary. Another, perhaps more appealing definition considers the *per capita excess*

$$\bar{e}(x, S) = \frac{1}{|S|} e(x, S)$$

and uses the leximin ordering to compare the vectors $\bar{e}(x)$. This yields the *per capita nucleolus* (unique and well defined, just as in Definition 5.5). It is another core selection. The per capita nucleolus belongs to the core whenever the latter is nonempty. Of course, other variants are possible too. If we wish to give more weight to the surplus of large coalitions, we could take $\bar{e}(x, S) = |S| \cdot e(x, S)$ and derive one more core selection. And so on.

A deeper critique of the nucleolus is that it is not monotonic with respect to the value of the grand coalition. It may happen that the surplus $v(N)$ available to the grand coalition increases, whereas the surplus of every other coalition remains fixed, and yet some agents see their share of the surplus decrease. This is very unappealing since an increase of $v(N)$ presumably requires participation of all agents; if some agents suffer a loss as a result of the improvement, they may withdraw their participation and cancel the raise.

Lemma 5.2 (Meggido [1974]).   *If N contains **nine** agents or more, we can find two games (N, v) and (N, w) such that*

$$v(N) < w(N) \quad \text{and} \quad v(S) = w(S), \quad \text{all } S \subset N \tag{32}$$

and yet if we denote by γ and μ, respectively, their nucleolus allocation, we have

$$\mu_i < \gamma_i \quad \text{for some agent } i$$

Proof: We construct an example with $N = \{1, 2, \ldots, 9\}$. The game v is defined as follows:

$$v(N) = 12$$

$$v(S) = \begin{cases} 6 & \text{if } S \in A = \{123, 14, 24, 34, 15, 25, 35, 789\} \\ 9 & \text{if } S \in B = \{12367, 12368, 12369, 456\} \\ 0 & \text{for any other } S \end{cases}$$

We claim that its nucleolus is $\gamma = (1, 1, 1, 2, 2, 2, 1, 1, 1)$. Indeed, we have

$$e(\gamma, S) = -3 \quad \text{if } S \in A \cup B, \qquad e(\gamma, S) \geq 0 \quad \text{for any other } S \subset N$$

Thus, $\min_S e(\gamma, S) = -3$. On the other hand, fix any other allocation x, $\sum_{i \in N} x_i = 12$, and define $\epsilon_i = x_i - \gamma_i$, all $i \in N$. Consider the balanced set of weights

$$\delta_{456} = \tfrac{1}{2}, \qquad \delta_{789} = \tfrac{5}{6}$$

$$\delta_S = \begin{cases} \tfrac{1}{6} & \text{if } \{S \in A \cup B, S \neq 456, 789\} \\ 0 & \text{if } S \notin A \cup B \end{cases}$$

From $\sum_{i \in N} \epsilon_i = 0$, we deduce

$$\sum_{S \in A \cup B} \delta_S \left(\sum_{i \in S} \epsilon_i \right) = 0 \tag{33}$$

If $\sum_{i \in S} \epsilon_S = 0$ for all $S \in A \cup B$, then $\epsilon = 0$ and $x = \gamma$, as the reader will readily check. Thus for an allocation x other than γ, there is a coalition S in $A \cup B$ with $\sum_{i \in S} \epsilon_i \neq 0$. From (33) and the fact that $\delta_S > 0$ for $S \in A \cup B$, it follows that for some $S \in A \cup B$,

$$\sum_{i \in S} \epsilon_i < 0 \Leftrightarrow e(x, S) < e(\gamma, S) \Rightarrow \min_S e(x, S) < -3$$

This completes the proof of the claim.

Now define a new game (N, w) by $w(N) = 13$, $w(S) = v(S)$ for all $S \subset N$. We claim that its nucleolus is $\mu = (1\tfrac{1}{9}, 1\tfrac{1}{9}, 1\tfrac{1}{9}, 2\tfrac{2}{9}, 2\tfrac{2}{9}, 1\tfrac{8}{9}, 1\tfrac{1}{9}, 1\tfrac{1}{9}, 1\tfrac{1}{9})$, thus showing a loss for agent 6. To prove this new claim, compute

$$e(\mu, S) = -2\tfrac{2}{3} \quad \text{for all } S \in A \cup B, \qquad e(\mu, S) \geq 0 \quad \text{for any other } S$$

Next use the same balanced set of weights to prove similarly that every other allocation x has $e(x, S) < -2\tfrac{2}{3}$ for some S. Q.E.D.

The difficulty raised by Lemma 5.2 is eliminated if we use the per capita nucleolus instead of the nucleolus. In other words, the per capita nucleolus is monotonic with respect to the value of the grand coalition. To prove this, consider two games (N, v), (N, w) such that (32) holds. Denote by $\tilde{\gamma}$ and $\tilde{\mu}$, respectively, their per capita nucleolus. Denote by $\epsilon = w(N) - v(N)$ the increase in the value of the grand coalition. To any balanced allocation x of (N, v), attach the balanced allocation y of (N, w):

$$y_i = x_i + \epsilon/n \quad \text{for all } i \in N$$

Then check the following equality:

$$\tilde{e}_w(y, S) = \tilde{e}_v(x, S) + \epsilon/n \quad \text{for all } S \subset N$$

implying $\tilde{\mu} = \tilde{\gamma} + \epsilon/n$; in other words, the agents share equally the raise of $v(N)$.

Thus we have a strong argument for preferring the per capita nucleolus to the nucleolus. Yet upon looking more carefully, it turns out that the per capita nucleolus violates some related monotonicity properties.

For a given coalition S of agents, what happens when its opportunity surplus $v(S)$ raises while every other $v(T)$ stays put? The natural change would be an increase of the shares of every member of S (or at least for none of them to decrease), thus making the shift desirable for every agent in S.

Definition 5.6. *Given are society N and a value operator φ on E^{2^N}. We say that φ is **coalitionally monotonic** if for all coalitions S and all agents $i \in S$, we have*

$$\text{for all } v, w \in E^{2^N}:$$
$$\{v(S) \leq w(S) \text{ and } v(T) = w(T) \text{ for all } T \neq S\} \Rightarrow \{\varphi_i(v) \leq \varphi_i(w)\}$$

Obviously the Shapley value is coalitionally monotonic, for in formula (2) the coefficient of $v(S)$ is positive if S contains i. But this monotonicity property is never satisfied by a value operator selecting an allocation in the core.

Theorem 5.3 (Young [1985a]). *Suppose N contains five agents or more, and let φ be a value operator. It cannot be both a core selection [$\varphi(v)$ belongs to the core of (N, v) when the latter is nonempty] and coalitionally monotonic.*

For instance, the per capita nucleolus is not coalitionally monotonic. The bottom line of Theorem 5.3 is a criticism of the core property itself.

Proof of Theorem 5.3: The proof, again, is by a simple example. Consider the society $N = \{1, 2, 3, 4, 5\}$ and the game v:

$$v(123) = v(35) = 3, \qquad v(134) = v(245) = v(1245) = 9$$
$$v(N) = 11, \qquad v(S) = 0 \quad \text{for any other coalition } S$$

We claim that the core of v contains the single allocation $\gamma = (0, 1, 2, 7, 1)$. Indeed, write some of the core conditions for an allocation x:

$$x_1 + x_2 + x_3 \geq 3, \qquad x_3 + x_5 \geq 3, \qquad x_1 + x_3 + x_4 \geq 9$$
$$x_2 + x_4 + x_5 \geq 9, \qquad x_1 + x_2 + x_4 + x_5 \geq 9 \tag{34}$$

Adding these inequalities gives $3(\sum_{i=1}^{5} x_i) \geq 33$. Taking efficiency into account ($\sum_{i=1}^{5} x_i = 11$), we deduce that all inequalities (34) are equalities; this is a system of five independent equations with a unique solution γ.

Next we raise $v(1245)$ and $v(N)$ to obtain the game (N, w):

$$w(1245) = w(N) = 12$$
$$w(S) = v(S) \quad \text{for any coalition } S \neq \{1245\}, N$$

Its core contains the single allocation $\mu = (3, 0, 0, 6, 3)$. This follows from a similar argument: Write the system of core conditions for the same coalitions as in (34) and add them to $3(\sum_{i=1}^{5} x_i) \geq 36$; thus there exists an equality by efficiency. The rest follows as before.

If the value operator φ is a core selection, then $\varphi(v) = \gamma$ and $\varphi(w) = \mu$. If it is coalitionally monotonic, then $\varphi_i(v) \leq \varphi_i(w)$ for $i = 1, 2, 4, 5$. The contradiction thus follows from $\mu_2 < \gamma_2$ and $\mu_4 < \gamma_4$. $\qquad$ Q.E.D.

Remark 5.3: In the proofs of Lemma 5.2 and Theorem 5.3 we used some TU games lacking superadditivity. This is by no means essential; the same proof carries over when we replace v (or w) by their *superadditive cover,* namely, the smallest superadditive game dominating them.

5.6   Characterization of the nucleolus

The characterization of the nucleolus develops in the context of variable population as in Section 3.4. The central axiom is akin to the separability property for axiomatic bargaining (Section 3.5). It is called the reduced-game property.

As population is variable, we work with value operators φ defined over the pairs (N, v), where N is an arbitrary finite society and $v \in E^{2^N}$ is a TU cooperative game for this society.

For a two-person game the simple egalitarian idea of equally dividing the cooperative surplus $[v(12) - v(1) - v(2)]$ – even if this number is negative – is very compelling. Indeed, it is the only value operator anonymous and independent of individual zeros.

Definition 5.7. *A value operator φ is said to be zero independent if for all N, all $u, v \in E^{2^N}$, and all $\beta \in E^N$, we have*

$$\left\{ w(s) = v(S) + \sum_{i \in S} \beta_i \text{ for all } S \right\} \Rightarrow \{\varphi(N, w) = \varphi(N, v) + \beta\} \tag{35}$$

If the zero of agent i's utility shifts downward by β_i for all i, the TU game v changes into w as in the premises of (35). Zero independence then says that the solution for w is the same as for v up to the translation of individual zeros.

Lemma 5.3. *If φ is a value operator that is anonymous and zero independent, then for a two-person TU game, φ divides equally the cooperative surplus:*

$$\text{if } |N|=2, \quad \varphi_i(N, v) = v(i) + \tfrac{1}{2}(v(N)-v(1)-v(2))$$
$$= \tfrac{1}{2}(v(N)+v(i)-v(j)) \tag{36}$$

We omit the obvious proof.

As we now have our value for two-person games, we try to derive the solution for three-person games by a separability argument. Let $N = \{1, 2, 3\}$ and a game (N, v) be fixed. By zero independence, we can assume $v(i) = 0$ for all i without loss of generality. Denote $\varphi(N, v) = (x_1, x_2, x_3)$ the allocation selected by our value operator. Suppose agents 1 and 2 reconsider the allocation of the joint utility $x_1 + x_2$. What is their opportunity surplus in the reduced two-person game to share $x_1 + x_2$? Agent 1, for instance, could stand alone and get $v(i) = 0$, or he could buy agent 3's cooperation in coalition $\{13\}$ at price x_3, namely, agent 3's price as set by the value itself. This suggests a definition of the reduced game $(\{1, 2\}, \bar{v})$ as follows:

$$\bar{v}(12) = x_1 + x_2$$
$$\bar{v}(1) = \max(0, v(13) - x_3), \qquad \bar{v}(2) = \max(0, v(23) - x_3)$$

The reduced-game property says that in the reduced two-person game, the value suggests precisely the shares (x_1, x_2): The shares of agents 1 and 2 are fair even with respect to pairwise comparisons. In view of Lemma 5.3, this means

$$x_1 = \tfrac{1}{2}(\bar{v}(12) + \bar{v}(1) - \bar{v}(2))$$
$$= \tfrac{1}{2}(x_1 + x_2 + \max(0, v(13) - x_3) - \max(0, v(23) - x_3))$$

that is,

$$x_1 - (v(13) - x_3)^+ = x_2 - (v(23) - x_3)^+ \tag{37}$$

with the notation $\max(0, y) = y^+$. The preceding argument applies to the other two-person coalitions $\{23\}$ and $\{13\}$, yielding two similar formulas:

$$x_2 - (v(12) - x_1)^+ = x_3 - (v(13) - x_1)^+$$
$$x_1 - (v(12) - x_2)^+ = x_3 - (v(23) - x_2)^+ \tag{38}$$

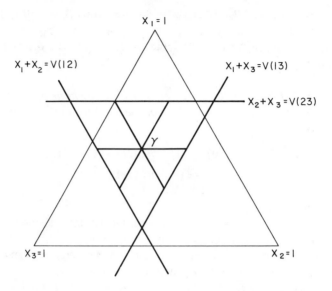

Figure 5.5.

To interpret these formulas, we assume, for simplicity, that the game (N, v) has a nonempty core. Then (37) and (38) say that x is the center of the core in the following sense. Fix x_3 and consider the allocations (y_1, y_2, x_3) near (x_1, x_2, x_3) and still in the core. This is the case if and only if (y_1, y_2) satisfies the following system:

$$y_1 + y_2 = x_1 + x_2$$
$$\{y_1 \geq 0,\ y_1 + x_3 \geq v(13)\} \Leftrightarrow y_1 \geq (v(13) - x_3)^+$$
$$\{y_2 \geq 0,\ y_2 + x_3 \geq v(23)\} \Leftrightarrow y_2 \geq (v(23) - x_3)^+$$

Thus equation (37) means that (x_1, x_2) is the middle point of the intersection of the core with the straight line $y_1 + y_2 = x_1 + x_2$, namely, the interval between

$$((v(13) - x_3)^+, x_1 + x_2 - (v(13) - x_3)^+) \quad \text{and}$$
$$(x_1 + x_2 - (v(23) - x_3)^+, (v(23) - x_3)^+)$$

Hence formulas (37) and (38) say that x is the middle point of any slice of the core through x that is parallel to an edge of the simplex; see Figure 5.5.

It turns out that formulas (37) and (38) characterize the nucleolus of any three-person game whether or not its core is nonempty. This result will be proved in Exercise 5.2 after we compute explicitly the nucleolus of all (superadditive) three-person games.

Amazingly enough, the result generalizes into a characterization of the nucleolus of all TU games with an arbitrary number of agents.

Definition 5.8 (Peleg [1986]).   *Given a TU game (N, v), an efficient allocation x ($\sum_{i \in N} x_i = v(N)$), and a proper coalition $S \subset N$, the **reduced game** on S at x is the following game (S, v_x^S):*

$$v_x^S(S) = \sum_{i \in S} x_i$$

$$\text{for all } T \subset S: \quad v_x^S(T) = \max_{\varnothing \subset R \subset N \setminus S} \left\{ v(T \cup R) - \sum_{i \in R} x_i \right\} \tag{39}$$

*Consider a value operator φ defined for the TU games of all sizes. We say that φ satisfies the **reduced-game property** if for any game (N, v) and any proper coalition $S \subset N$, we have*

$$x = \varphi(N, v) \Rightarrow \varphi(S, v_x^S) = \pi_S(x) \tag{40}$$

where π_S is the projection of E^N onto E^S.

In the reduced game v_x^S, any proper coalition of S can buy the cooperation of any subset of $N \setminus S$ at the price set by x. The reduced-game property says that if within a proper coalition the agents compute their sub-coalitional opportunities by the reduced-game formula (39), they will agree that the value allocation is fair even within the limits of their own subgroup.

Theorem 5.4 (Sobolev [1975]).   *There is exactly one value operator satisfying anonymity, zero independence, and the reduced-game property. It is the nucleolus.*

The proof for an arbitrary number of agents is difficult.

The reduced-game property can also be adapted to multivalued value operators, that is, where $\varphi(N, v)$ is a subset of allocations of $v(N)$ instead of a single allocation. It is then the key ingredient of an axiomatic characterization of the core; see Peleg [1986] (for TU games) and Peleg [1985] (for NTU games).

Of course, the reduced-game property is a sophisticated axiom with a delicate interpretation. The computation of opportunity surpluses within the separating coalition depends critically on the ability to buy out *any* subset of agents in $N \setminus S$ at the price set by the value for the grand game. Other definitions of these opportunity surpluses are possible and bring very different results. One of them has the coalition T always cooperating with the agents of $N \setminus S$ and paying them their value within the restriction of the game to $T \cup (N \setminus S)$ – instead of their value in the grand game. This definition is fairly arbitrary mainly because the agents in T are forced to call the cooperation of $N \backslash S$ in computing their own coalitional opportunities. Nevertheless it brings about a genuine characterization of the Shapley value, due to Hart and Mas-Colell [1985] and explained in Exercise 5.12.

EXERCISES

5.1 **The gloves market** (Aumann [1985]).

(a) Two agents (call them 1 and 2) own a right-hand glove each, and two other agents (call them 3 and 4) own a left-hand glove each. The market value of a single glove is zero and that of any pair (with one right-handed and one left-handed) is $10. The situation is described by the following TU game (N, v):

$$v(13) = v(14) = v(23) = v(24) = 1$$
$$v(S) = 1 \quad \text{if } |S| = 3$$
$$v(N) = 2$$
$$v(S) = 0 \quad \text{for every other coalition}$$

Show that any anonymous value operator picks the allocation $\omega = (\frac{1}{2}, \frac{1}{2}, \frac{1}{2}, \frac{1}{2})$ for this game.

(b) Suppose next that agent 1 owns *two* right-hand gloves, whereas the endowment of every other agent remains the same. This yields the following game (N, v'):

$$v'(134) = 2, \qquad v'(S) = v(S) \quad \text{for all } S \neq \{134\}$$

Justify this definition and then compute the nucleolus and the Shapley value of (N, v'). (*Hint:* for the nucleolus, use Exercise 4.3.) Observe that the nucleolus penalizes agents 1 and 2 while going from v to v', whereas the Shapley value penalizes agent 2 only.

(c) Consider a *five*-person game where three agents (call them agents 0, 1, and 2) own one right-hand glove each whereas two agents own one left-hand glove each. Define the TU cooperative game describing this situation. Show that its nucleolus is essentially the same as in question (b) (the left-glove owners share the whole surplus). Compute the Shapley value and show that it treats the left-glove owners a little better than in question (b).

5.2 **Nucleolus of three-person superadditive games** (Legros [1981]). Given is a superadditive three-person game. By zero independence we can assume without loss $v(i) = 0$ for all i. Up to a permutation of the agents we can also assume

$$0 \leq v(23) \leq v(13) \leq v(12) \leq v(N)$$

We define five classes of games, and in each class we give the explicit formula for the nucleolus. You must prove these formulas.

(a) *Class 1:* $v(12) \le \frac{1}{3}v(N)$. Then $\gamma = (\frac{1}{3}v(N), \frac{1}{3}v(N), \frac{1}{3}v(N))$. *Hint:* Prove that $\min_{S \subset N} e(\gamma, S) = \frac{1}{3}v(N)$ and show that γ is the only solution of the maximin program (23).

(b) *Class 2:* $\frac{2}{3}v(13) + \frac{1}{3}v(12) \le \frac{1}{3}v(N) \le v(12)$. Then

$$\gamma_1 = \gamma_2 = \frac{1}{4}(v(N) + v(12)), \qquad \gamma_3 = \frac{1}{2}(v(N) - v(12))$$

Hint: Check $e(\gamma, 3) = e(\gamma, 12) \le e(\gamma, 1) = e(\gamma, 2) \le e(\gamma, S)$ for $S = \{23\}$ or $\{13\}$. If x is another allocation such that $e(x)$ is leximin superior to $e(\gamma)$, show that $x_3 = \gamma_3$ [because $e(x, 3) + e(x, 12) = e(\gamma, 3) + e(\gamma, 12)$] and next that $x_1 = \gamma_1$ [because $e(x, 1) + e(x, 2) = e(\gamma, 1) + e(\gamma, 2)$].

(c) *Class 3:* $\frac{2}{3}v(23) + \frac{1}{3}v(12) \le \frac{1}{3}v(N) \le \frac{2}{3}v(13) + \frac{1}{3}v(12)$. Then

$$\gamma = (\frac{1}{2}(v(12) + v(13)), \frac{1}{2}(v(N) - v(13)), \frac{1}{2}(v(N) - v(12)))$$

Hint: Check $e(\gamma, 3) = e(\gamma, 12) \le e(\gamma, 2) = e(\gamma, 13) \le e(\gamma, S)$ for $S = \{1\}$ or $\{23\}$. Then use the same trick as in question (b).

(d) *Class 4:* $\frac{2}{3}(v(13) + v(23)) - \frac{1}{3}v(12) \le \frac{1}{3}v(N) \le \frac{2}{3}v(23) + \frac{1}{3}v(12)$. Then

$$\gamma = (\frac{1}{4}(v(N) + v(12)) + \frac{1}{2}(v(13) - v(23)),$$
$$\frac{1}{4}(v(N) + v(12)) + \frac{1}{2}(v(23) - v(13)), \frac{1}{2}(v(N) - v(12)))$$

Hint: Check $e(\gamma, 3) = e(\gamma, 12) \le e(\gamma, 13) = e(\gamma, 23) \le e(\gamma, S)$ for $S = \{2\}$ or $\{1\}$. Then proceed as in question (b).

(e) *Class 5:* $\frac{1}{3}v(N) \le \frac{2}{3}(v(13) + v(23)) - \frac{1}{3}v(12)$. Then

$$\gamma = (\frac{1}{3}(v(N) + v(12) + v(13) - 2v(23)),$$
$$\frac{1}{3}(v(N) + v(12) + v(23) - 2v(13)), \frac{1}{3}(v(N) + v(13) + v(23) - 2v(12)))$$

Hint: Prove that $\min_{S \subset N} e(\gamma, S) = \frac{1}{3}(2v(N) - v(12) - v(23) - v(13))$ and proceed as in question (a).

(f) Show that in classes 1–4, the core of the game is nonempty.

(g) Check that in every class, the nucleolus satisfies the reduced-game property [formulas (37) and (38)].

5.3 Nucleolus of the land corn production economy (continued). This is the model of Example 5.2 in which we assume increasing marginal returns,

for all $i = 1, \ldots, n-1$: $f(i) - f(i-1) \le f(i+1) - f(i)$ (41)

with the convention $f(0) = 0$.

(a) Show that the game (4) is convex if and only if the marginal returns are increasing.

(b) Show that an allocation such as (26) is in the core if and only if $0 \le a \le f(n)/n$. Thus the maximin program (23) reduces to

$$\max_{0 \le a \le f(n)/n} \min \left\{ a, \min_{k=0, \ldots, n-1} \{f(n) - f(k) - (n-k)a\} \right\}$$ (42)

(c) Show that the unique solution of program (42) (hence the nucleolus of our game) equals

$$a^* = \min\left\{\frac{1}{n+1}f(n), \frac{1}{2}(f(n)-f(n-1))\right\}$$

Thus if $[1/(n+1)]f(n) \le \frac{1}{2}(f(n)-f(n-1))$, the nucleolus is strictly egalitarian among the $n+1$ agents.

Hint: Use assumption (41) to show that only the values $k=0$ and $k=n-1$ matter in (42).

5.4 Nucleolus of user's fee (continued). We consider the model of Example 5.3 with the assumptions

$$0 \le c_n \le c_{n-1} \le \cdots \le c_1$$

$$\delta_i = c_i - c_{i+1}, \quad \text{with the convention } c_{n+1} = 0$$

We wish to prove formula (31). This is a cost-sharing game, so instead of maximizing the vector of excesses $\sum_{i \in S} x_i - v(S)$, we minimize the vector of excess costs $\sum_{i \in S} x_i - c(S)$. In particular, the maximin program (23) turns into the minimax program:

$$\min_{x \in B}\left\{\max_{S \subset N}\left(\sum_{i \in S} x_i - c(S)\right)\right\} = \min_{x \in B} \epsilon(x) \tag{43}$$

(a) Consider the allocation $\gamma \in B$ given by (31). Show that $\epsilon(\gamma) = -\frac{1}{2}\delta_n$ if and only if

$$\text{for all } i = 1, \dots, n: \quad \sum_{j=i}^{n} \frac{\delta_j}{2^{j-i+1}} \ge \frac{\delta_n}{2} \tag{44}$$

By considering coalitions $S = \{n\}$ and $S = \{1, \dots, n-1\}$, show that if (44) holds true, then any solution x of program (43) has $x_n = \frac{1}{2}\delta_n$.

(b) Assume (44). Show that an allocation $(x_1, \dots, x_n)$ is the nucleolus of game (N, c) if and only if $\{x_n = \frac{1}{2}c_n$ and $(x_1, \dots, x_{n-1})$ is the nucleolus of the game $(N \setminus \{n\}, c')\}$, where

$$c_i' = c_i - \frac{1}{2}c_n \text{ for all } i = 1, \dots, n-1 \iff$$
$$\delta_i' = \delta_i \text{ for } i = 1, \dots, n-2 \text{ and } \delta_{n-1}' = \delta_{n-1} + \frac{1}{2}\delta_n$$

(c) Assume $\delta_n \le \delta_{n-1} \le \cdots \le \delta_1$. Use an induction argument to show that the nucleolus of (N, c) is given by (31).

5.5 Shapley value and nucleolus of some quota games (Aumann [1976]). Given the society $N = \{1, \dots, n\}$, the quota game $\{q; p_1, \dots, p_n\}$ is the following TU game (N, v):

$$v(S) = \begin{cases} 1 & \text{if } \sum_{i \in S} p_i \ge q \\ 0 & \text{if } \sum_{i \in S} p_i < q \end{cases}$$

We assume that the weights $p_1, \dots, p_n$ form a positive convex combination ($p_i > 0$, $\sum_{i=1}^{n} p_i = 1$) and that the quota q is greater than $\frac{1}{2}$ and smaller than 1.

A coalition wins $[v(S) = 1]$ if its total weight reaches the quota and loses $[v(S) = 0]$ otherwise. A value operator proposes a compromise (akin to the distribution of portfolios among the parties represented in a parliament) by allocating shares $(x_1, \dots, x_n)$, $\sum_{i=1}^{n} x_i = 1$, which may deviate significantly from the relative weight $(p_i / \sum_{j=1}^{n} p_j)$.

(a) Show that the core of the quota game is empty if and only if $p_i \leq 1 - q$ for all i.

(b) Consider the quota game with seven agents:

$$q = \tfrac{5}{9}, \qquad p_1 = p_2 = \tfrac{2}{9}, \qquad p_3 = \cdots = p_7 = \tfrac{1}{9}$$

A coalition wins if it contains all five small agents, or one big agent and three small ones, or two big agents and one small agent.

Show that the nucleolus allocates to each agent its weight $(\gamma_i = p_i)$, whereas the Shapley value gives $\tfrac{5}{21}$ to each big agent and only $\tfrac{11}{105}$ to each small one. *Hint:* For the nucleolus, solve the maximin program by taking into account only the winning coalitions minimal w.r.t. inclusion. For the Shapley value, compute the probability for a big agent of being pivotal when agents enter randomly (the pivot is the agent whose entry makes the current coalition win).

(c) Consider the quota game with $n+1$ persons:

$$q = \frac{1}{2}, \qquad p_0 = \frac{1}{3}, \qquad p_1 = \cdots = p_n = \frac{2}{3n}$$

Show that when n grows large, its nucleolus is, again, near the vector of weights, whereas the Shapley value gives nearly $\tfrac{1}{2}$ to the big agent (while distributing uniformly the rest among the small agents).

(d) Consider the quota game with $n+2$ persons:

$$q = \frac{1}{2}, \qquad p_1 = p_2 = \frac{1}{3}, \qquad p_3 = \cdots = p_{n+2} = \frac{1}{3n}$$

Show that for large n, the nucleolus and the Shapley value coincide, and give only $\tfrac{1}{4}$ to each big agent.

Thus in the game of question (d), big agents are penalized (relative to their weight) by the Shapley value, whereas they get a bonus in the games of questions (b) and (c).

5.6 The separable cost-remaining benefit method. This value operator for cost-sharing games is frequently used (see the survey by Young [1985b]). It consists of dividing $c(N)$ in proportion to the separable costs SC_i:

$$c_i = \frac{SC_i}{\sum_{j=1}^{n} SC_j} \cdot c(N), \qquad \text{where } SC_i = c(N) - c(N \setminus i)$$

Of course, we assume that all SC_i are nonnegative and at least one is positive. Show that this value satisfies anonymity, the dummy axiom, and scale independence but not zero independence.

Show that it is not monotonic w.r.t. to the grand coalition; c_i may decrease as a result of an increase in $c(N)$, ceteris paribus.

5.7   Convex games and the EANS cost value. Give an example of a three-person convex game (you can take it normalized as in Example 5.6) where the EANS cost value [given by formula (1) with v instead of c] is not in the core. *Hint:* Find the geometric construction of the EANS cost value on the simplex representation of the game.

5.8   Shapley value and population monotonicity. Consider a *convex* game (N, v) and, for every coalition $S \subset N$, denote by $\sigma(S, v)$ the Shapley value of the game $(S, \bar{v})$, where $\bar{v}$ is the restriction of v to S [thus $\bar{v}$ is obtained from v by simply deleting $v(T)$ for all coalitions T not contained in S]. Show that the Shapley value of a given agent increases as society expands:

$$\{i \in S \subset T\} \Rightarrow \{\sigma_i(S, v) \le \sigma_i(T, v)\} \quad \text{for all } S, T, i$$

Show that this inequality may fail if the game v is superadditive but not convex.

5.9   A characterization of convex games (Ichiishi [1981]). A game (N, v) is convex if and only if the vectors of marginal contributions (for all possible orderings of N) are in the core. The "only if" statement was proven in Lemma 5.1. Prove the "if" statement. *Hint:* Pick any two coalitions $S, T \subset N$ and order the agents of N so as to exhaust first $S \cap T$, next $T \setminus S$, next $S \setminus T$, and finally $N \setminus (S \cup T)$. Then apply the core inequality to the corresponding vector of marginal contributions and coalition S.

5.10   Another formula of the Shapley value

(a)   The proof of Theorem 5.2 shows that the system $(\delta_S, S \subset N)$ forms a basis of the vector space E^{2^N} of the TU games over N. Show now that an arbitrary game $v \in E^{2^N}$ has the following coordinates in this basis:

$$v = \sum_{S \subset N} \alpha_S \cdot \delta_S, \quad \text{where } \alpha_S = \sum_{T \subset S} (-1)^{s-t} v(T)$$

with the convention $s = |S|$, $t = |T|$. *Hint:* Fix a coalition S_0 and compute

$$\sum_{S \subset N} \alpha_S \cdot \delta_S(S_0) = \sum_{S \subset S_0} \alpha_S = \sum_{S \subset S_0} \sum_{T \subset S} (-1)^{s-t} v(T)$$

In the right term of this formula, compute the coefficient of $v(T)$ for all $T \subset S_0$.

(b)   Show that the Shapley value operator σ can be written as

$$\sigma(v) = \sum_{S: i \in S} \frac{\alpha_S}{s}$$

Interpret this formula as the successive payments of dividends to agent i. Here α_S is the dividend of coalition S divided equally between all members of S. For more details and generalizations to NTU games, see Harsanyi [1963] and Kalaï and Samet [1985].

5.11   Another look at the Shapley value for three-person games. Consider a value operator φ for two- and three-person games. For two-person games it is given by (36). For three-person games it gives equal benefit (or loss) from merging to every two-person coalition. We state formally this last property.

Let (N, v) be a three-person game. If agents 1 and 2 merge, we are left with a two-person game with agents 12 and 3 and cooperative opportunities computed as before from v. Denote by δ_{ij} the difference between the overall allocation to coalition ij before and after they merge. We want $\delta_{12} = \delta_{13} = \delta_{23}$.

Show that this property forces the Shapley value.

5.12 **Other reduced-game properties** (Hart and Mas-Colell [in press]). Throughout the exercise, φ is a value operator defined for all games (N, v) with arbitrary finite societies.

(a) Define the reduced game on S at x as

$$v_x^S(S) = \sum_{i \in S} x_i$$

for all $T \subset S$: $v_x^S(T) = v(T \cup (N \setminus S)) - \sum_{i \in N \setminus S} x_i$

Show that EANS costs [formula (1) with the value v in place of the costs] satisfies the corresponding reduced-game property. Show that EANS costs are characterized by anonymity, zero independence, and this reduced-game property. *Hint:* Use Lemma 5.3 and apply (40) for coalitions S with two agents.

(b) Define the reduced game on S, given φ, as follows:

for all $T \subset S$: $v^S(T) = \sum_{i \in T} \varphi_i(T \cup (N \setminus S), v)$ (45)

In the expression $\varphi(T \cup (N \setminus S), v)$, the game v is the ordinary restriction of (N, v) to $T \cup (N \setminus S)$.

Note that this definition of the reduced game depends upon the value operator itself, not upon an arbitrary allocation x. In the corresponding reduced-game property [(40)], simply replace v_x^S by v^S.

The Shapley value is characterized by the corresponding reduced-game property, anonymity, and zero independence (Hart and Mas-Colell [1985]). To prove this, define the "potential" function P as follows:

for all TU games (N, v): $P(N, v) = \sum_{S \subset N} \dfrac{(s-1)!(n-s)!}{n!} v(S)$

w¹ ·e s is the size of S. Check that the Shapley value operator σ is given by

$$\sigma_i(N, v) = P(N, v) - P(N \setminus \{i\}, v)$$

Consider the coalition $S = N \setminus 1$ and the associated reduced game (45) on S given σ, denoted v^{-1}:

$$v^{-1}(T) = \sum_{i \in T} \sigma_i(T \cup \{1\}, v)$$
$$= \sum_{i \in T} P(T \cup \{1\}, v) - P(T \cup \{1\} \setminus \{i\}, v)   \quad \text{for all } T \subset N \setminus \{1\}$$

Show that for all $T \subset N \setminus \{1\}$ we have $P(T, v^{-1}) = P(T \cup \{1\}, v)$, and deduce that

$$\sigma_j(N \setminus \{1\}, v^{-1}) = \sigma_j(N, v) \quad \text{for all } j \in N \setminus \{1\}$$

which is just the desired reduced-game property for $S = N \setminus 1$. Then use an induction argument to show that σ satisfies the reduced-game property for all $S \subset N$.

Conversely, show by induction on $|N|$ that a value operator φ that (i) satisfies the reduced-game property and (ii) is given by (36) for two-person games must be the Shapley value operator.

(c)   Define the reduced game on S given φ as follows:

$$v^S(S) = \sum_{i \in S} \varphi_i(N, v)$$

for all $T \subset S$: $$v^S(T) = \max_{R \subset N \setminus S} \sum_{i \in T} \varphi_i(T \cup R, v) \tag{46}$$

Show that a value operator φ given by (36) for two-person games and satisfying the reduced-game property associated with (46) for three-person games must be the following modified Shapley value:

$$\varphi_1(N, v) = \tfrac{1}{3} v(N) + \tfrac{1}{6} [(v(12) - v(1) - v(2))^+ + (v(13) - v(1) - v(3))^+$$
$$- 2(v(23) - v(2) - v(3))^+]$$
$$+ \tfrac{1}{3} (2v(1) - v(2) - v(3))$$

Note that this is the ordinary Shapley value for superadditive games. Show that it is impossible to extend this value operator to four-person games while respecting the reduced-game property associated with (46).

Public decision mechanisms

CHAPTER 6

Equal versus proportional sharing

Overview

In Part III we apply the tools forged in Parts I and II to specific microeconomic surplus-sharing problems. The two problems discussed in this chapter are the simplest models of surplus and cost sharing, in which the distributive issue has no obvious answer.

The cost-sharing problem is best thought of as the provision of an indivisible public good, say, a bridge or any such public facility. The issue is how to share the cost of the facility. The only available data are the total cost of building the bridge and the benefits that each agent derives from the facility (a single dollar figure per agent since we assume quasi-linear utilities). Another interpretation of the same formal model is the settlement of a bankruptcy. Here the agents are creditors of the bankrupt firm; each agent holds a monetary claim over its estate, but the total value of the estate falls short of the sum of the claims. The problem is to share the estate among its creditors.

The surplus-sharing problem is that of dividing the proceeds of an indivisible cooperative venture among several partners. Think of an orchestra giving a single performance. The receipts must be shared among the musicians; the sharing rule must be based upon the estimated "market value" of each musician, again, a single number per agent representing his opportunity cost of joining the orchestra. Assuming that the receipts exceed the sum of the opportunity costs, how should it be divided among the agents?

The common feature in these two problems is the extreme simplicity of the available data and hence their wide applicability. Think of any business partnership gathering professionals with different qualifications. Assume that the only estimation of their opportunity cost to join the partnership is a dollar figure and that we have no other measure (such as effort) of their relative contributions to the cooperative venture. If the net income of the partnership exceeds (falls short of) the sum of opportunity costs, we have a surplus-sharing model (a cost-sharing model).

Simple problems call for simple solutions. Indeed, the two simple ideas of equal or proportional divisions of the benefits (or the costs) yield the most common answers to our problems. In this chapter we compare systematically these two ideas and justify axiomatically their paramount importance. Some of the arguments (in particular the axioms in Sections 6.5 and 6.6 and the mathematics of the characterization results) are far from obvious. Moreover, we shall uncover some nontrivial alternative mechanisms (see Section 6.4). Our problems, after all, are not so simple.

In the surplus-sharing problem (Section 6.1) the proportional solution divides total revenue in proportion to individual opportunity costs; the egalitarian solution, on the other hand, reimburses first opportunity costs and divides equally the surplus left above and over. In the cost-sharing problem (Section 6.2) the proportional solution is defined just as easily (agents are taxed in proportion to their benefits), but the picture is a bit more complicated for egalitarianism. First, we have two egalitarian ideas, namely, to equalize costs or to equalize benefits net of costs. Second, we must ensure that the vector of cost shares passes the stand-alone test: The cost imputed to a coalition of agents should exceed neither the total cost of the good (otherwise the coalition prefers to produce the good independently) nor the joint benefit of that coalition (otherwise it prefers to produce no public good whatsoever). In Section 6.3 we adjust the two egalitarian ideas so as to pass this test. The resulting solutions are called, respectively, the head tax and leveling tax (Definition 6.1).

Section 6.4 discusses two more mechanisms for sharing the cost of our indivisible public good. They correspond to the nucleolus and Shapley value of the TU cooperative game derived from the stand-alone test. These two methods are hard to compute but prove surprisingly relevant, especially in the bankruptcy interpretation (see Example 6.4).

The last two sections are devoted to axiomatic results. We discuss two powerful independence axioms. One of them is a variant of the separability conditions analyzed earlier. The new axiom (Section 6.5) is called decentralizability: The cost share (surplus share) of an agent should depend only upon total cost, his own benefit from the good, and the joint benefit to all agents taken together (respectively, total revenue, his own opportunity cost, and the sum of opportunity costs). In the cost-sharing problem this axiom is essentially enough to characterize the proportional solution (Theorem 6.1). Not so in the surplus-sharing problem, where it is satisfied by the proportional and egalitarian solutions and by many others. In Section 6.6 we introduce a powerful separability axiom (akin to the separability axiom of Chapter 3 and to the reduced-game property of Chapter 5). It says that the cost shares (or surplus shares) within a coalition should depend only upon the total cost imputed to that coalition and its members' benefits (or upon the total surplus allocated to the coalition and its members' opportunity costs). The separability axiom characterizes an infinite family of solutions called parametric solutions and containing all but one solution introduced in the preceding. In the surplus-sharing problem the combination of decentralizability and separability characterizes a one-dimensional family of solutions containing the equal and proportional solutions as its two extreme points. This in turn yields a genuine characterization of the *pair* containing our two focal solutions (Exercise 6.6).

6.1 The surplus-sharing model

The surplus-sharing problem. The n agents' cooperation yields a total return $r > 0$. Agent i's opportunity cost is worth $c_i > 0$. We assume that cooperation brings a surplus, namely $\sum_{i=1}^{n} c_i \le r$. How should it be divided?

The first principle in allocating the return r is individual rationality: Every agent should get at least his opportunity cost for otherwise he would rather not cooperate. Once those priority payments are made, we are left with the surplus $s = r - \sum_{i=1}^{n} c_i$. Since we have no way to attribute this surplus to the effort of a particular agent (or coalition of agents), why not divide it equally? The principle is clear: Since cooperation of all agents is necessary to generate any surplus, they all have an equal right to it. Thus the *egalitarian* solution: Agent i's share is $s/n + c_i$.

The preceding argument can be stated in the language of cooperative games: Our problem is just a TU game where the value of the grand coalition is $v(N) = r$ and that of a single-agent coalition is $v(i) = c_i$. As we know nothing of the value $v(S)$ of an intermediate coalition, we postulate that S is not capable of bringing any cooperative surplus $[v(S) = \sum_{i \in S} c_i]$. Now any value operator satisfying zero independence (Definition 5.7) and anonymity will divide $v(N)$ as the egalitarian solution does. (Exercise: Why?)

Surely an agent with above-average opportunity cost may disagree with this argument. He would argue that the postulate of inessential intermediate coalitions $[v(S) = \sum_{i \in S} c_i]$ is not warranted. Opportunity costs should instead be viewed as the inputs in a production process of which the return is the output. In first approximation, this process has constant returns to scale and transforms x units of input into $r/\sum_{i=1}^{n} c_i \cdot x$ units of output. So each agent should receive whatever output he produces, namely, agent i receives $r \cdot (c_i / \sum_{j=1}^{n} c_j)$. This is the *proportional* solution.

Table 6.1.

Distribution		Number of respondents	
John	Peter	Variant (a)	Variant (b)
90,000	0	0	0
60,000	30,000	1	5
50,000	40,000	33	15
45,000	45,000	6	21
40,000	50,000	0	0
30,000	60,000	0	0
0	90,000	0	0
	N	40	41

The principle, again, is clear: The reward per unit of individual investment is the same for all.

Our first example provides some experimental evidence that the egalitarian and proportional solutions are the two focal solutions of the surplus-sharing problem.

Example 6.1. An experiment (Schokkaert and Overlaet [1986])
In this experiment, the participants must suggest a just division of a surplus; they were confronted with one of the two following stories: variant (a) or (b). Forty subjects were told variant (a) and 41 were told variant (b). The answers are strikingly concentrated upon the egalitarian and proportional sharing rules, gathering together 97 percent of the answers in variant (a) and 87 percent in variant (b). (See Table 6.1.)

John and Peter are glassblowers and set up a business together. (a) John works five days a week and Peter only four; (b) John is artistically more gifted than Peter and could therefore earn elsewhere a higher income. Their work is complementary, and they both are absolutely indispensable. John has a net income of 500,000 BF a year and Peter earns 400,000 BF. After a year, they have a sales revenue of 990,000 BF, so after deduction of their wages they have realized a profit of 90,000 BF. What would you consider to be a just division of this profit?

6.2   The cost-sharing model

The provision of an indivisible public good problem. This public facility (bridge) costs $c > 0$ and brings a benefit $b_i \geq 0$ to each of its users $i = 1, \ldots, n$. It is a pure public good: Agent i derives b_i utils from consuming it no matter how many are derived by other agents. We assume that it is efficient to build the facility: $\sum_{i=1}^{n} b_i \geq c$. How should we share its cost?

The model is formally symmetrical to the surplus-sharing model if we interpret b_i as agent i's opportunity cost and $\sum_{i=1}^{n} b_i - c$ as the total return. We come back to this interpretation in Section 6.4 (see Example 6.4).

The *proportional* solution imputes costs in proportion to benefits, so that agent i pays $x_i = c \cdot (b_i / \sum_{j=1}^{n} b_j)$. Note that the cost share x_i is nonnegative (no one is subsidized to consume the good) and bounded above by b_i (no one pays more than his full benefit).

The egalitarian idea can be applied in two ways, by equalizing either cost shares or benefits net of costs. The *uniform cost-sharing* solution imputes $x_i = c/n$ to every agent, whereas the *equal-surpluses* solution imputes $x_i = b_i - (\sum_{j=1}^{n} b_j - c)/n$ to agent i (so that $b_i - x_i = b_j - x_j$ for all i, j). An obvious problem with uniform cost sharing is that an agent may have to pay more than his full benefit (if b_i is below c/n); with equal surpluses, on the other hand, he may end up subsidized for consuming the good (if b_i is below $(\sum_{j=1}^{n} b_j - c)/n$), a situation that the $n-1$ other agents would not be very happy with. In the next section we will modify these two solutions so as to eliminate those difficulties.

The necessity of the (lower and upper) bounds to the cost shares corresponds to the core property in the TU cooperative game describing coalitional opportunity costs. In the provision of a public good problem, a coalition may be able to generate some surplus by building the facility and covering its full cost. In other words, a coalition S achieves the following surplus:

$$v(S) = \left(\sum_{i \in S} b_i - c \right)^+ \quad \text{with the notation } z^+ = \max(z, 0) \qquad (1)$$

Notice that this cooperative game is a particular case of the cost allocation games with independent demands (see Exercise 4.1). Here the cost of serving any coalition is the same: $c(S) = c$ for all coalitions S.

Assume $\sum_{i=1}^{n} b_i > c$. A vector $(x_1, \ldots, x_n)$ of cost shares passes the standalone test if and only if the corresponding vector of surpluses $(b_1 - x_1, \ldots, b_n - x_n)$ is in the core of game (1), namely,

$$\sum_{i=1}^{n} x_i = c \quad \text{and} \quad \text{for all } S \subset N:$$

$$\sum_{i \in S} (b_i - x_i) \geq \left(\sum_{i \in S} b_i - c \right)^+ \Leftrightarrow \sum_{i \in S} x_i \leq \min \left\{ c, \sum_{i \in S} b_i \right\}$$

These inequalities imply, in particular, that $x_i \leq b_i$ [take $S = \{i\}$]: No one has to pay more than the (gross) benefit he derives from the public good.

Another consequence is that $x_i \geq 0$ (take $S = N\setminus\{i\}$ and write $\sum_{N\setminus\{i\}} x_j = c - x_i$): No one receives money to consume the public good. Conversely, these bounds on individual cost shares and the budget balance equation together imply the core property:

> The vector of cost shares $(x_1, \ldots, x_n)$ is in the core of (1) (1)
> *if and only if* $\sum_{i=1}^{n} x_i = c$ and $0 \leq x_i \leq b_i$ for all i.   (2)

(Note the abuse of language: It is truly the vector $b - x$ that belongs to the core.) The obvious proof is omitted. Thus, the core sets fairly loose bounds on the cost shares. Actually the cooperative game (1) is convex (Definition 5.2. Exercise: Prove this claim). As noticed earlier, the proportional cost shares are in the core. In the next two sections we construct four more core selections for the cost-sharing problem.

6.3   The leveling tax and head tax

We construct two core selections inspired by equal surpluses and uniform cost sharing. We noticed earlier that the former may be outside the core for failing to meet the constraint $0 \leq x_i$ and the latter for failing to meet $x_i \leq b_i$. To avoid this problem, we impose the inequalities $0 \leq x_i \leq b_i$ as constraints. This brings two solutions in the core called the leveling tax and the head tax.

Definition 6.1.   *Given is a cost-sharing problem with $\sum_{i=1}^{n} b_i \geq c$. The leveling tax is the (unique) cost-sharing $(x_1, \ldots, x_n)$ solution of the program*

$$(x_1, \ldots, x_n) \in A = \left\{ (y_1, \ldots, y_n) \;\middle|\; \sum_{i=1}^{n} y_i = c \text{ and } 0 \leq y_i \leq b_i \text{ for all } i \right\}$$

$$(b_1 - x_1, \ldots, b_n - x_n) R_* (b_1 - y_1, \ldots, b_n - y_n) \quad \textit{for all } y \in A$$

where R_* is the leximin ordering of E^n.

   The head tax is the (unique) cost-sharing $(x_1, \ldots, x_n)$ solution of the program

$$(x_1, \ldots, x_n) \in A$$
$$(x_1, \ldots, x_n) R_* (y_1, \ldots, y_n) \quad \textit{for all } y \in A$$

The leveling tax equalizes surpluses (net benefits) within the bounds $0 \leq x_i \leq b_i$, whereas the head tax equalizes costs within those bounds. If the equal-surplus cost shares (uniform cost shares) happen to meet those bounds, then it coincides with the leveling tax (head tax). The uniqueness of these two solutions always holds because we are maximizing the leximin ordering over a convex compact subset of E^n (Lemma 1.1).

The "tax" terminology follows Young [1987], who interprets the indivisible public good as the services provided by the tax collector. Agent i's before-tax income is b_i, and his after-tax income is $b_i - x_i$. Thus, c is the total amount of tax needed (the collector's budget).

Both the leveling and head taxes can be computed explicitly. See formulas (5) and (6) in Exercise 1.6 for the leveling tax; analogous formulas for the head tax are easily derived [the change of variable $x_i^1 = b_i - x_i$ transforms the head tax of problem $(b_1, \ldots, b_n; c)$ into the leveling tax of problem $(b_1, \ldots, b_n; c^1)$ with $c^1 = \sum_{i=1}^{n} b_i - c$].

An alternative parametric representation is more illuminating.

Lemma 6.1. *Given a problem $(b_1, \ldots, b_n; c)$, its head tax is computed by solving the following equation with unknown $\lambda \geq 0$:*

$$\sum_{i=1}^{n} \min\{\lambda, b_i\} = c \Rightarrow x_i = \min\{\lambda, b_i\} \tag{3}$$

The leveling tax is computed by solving the following equations with unknown $\lambda \geq 0$:

$$\sum_{i=1}^{n} \min\{\lambda, b_i\} = \sum_{i=1}^{n} b_i - c \Rightarrow x_i = b_i - \min\{\lambda, b_i\} \tag{4}$$

The proof of formulas (3) and (4) is the subject of Exercise 6.1. We illustrate them by two examples.

Example 6.2. Cost-sharing among two agents
Equation (3) for $n = 2$ reads

$$\min\{\lambda, b_1\} + \min\{\lambda, b_2\} = c, \qquad x_i = \min\{\lambda, b_i\}$$

Assuming $b_1 < b_2$, the explicit solution is

$$\begin{aligned} \lambda = \tfrac{1}{2}c \text{ and } x_1 = x_2 = \tfrac{1}{2}c & \qquad \text{if } 0 \leq c \leq 2b_1 \\ \lambda = c - b_1 \text{ and } x_1 = b_1, \ x_2 = c - b_1 & \qquad \text{if } 2b_1 \leq c \leq b_1 + b_2 \end{aligned} \tag{5}$$

Similarly, equation (4) reads

$$\min\{\lambda, b_1\} + \min\{\lambda, b_2\} = (b_1 + b_2 - c), \qquad x_i = b_i - \min\{\lambda, b_i\}$$

with the following solution when $b_1 < b_2$:

$$\begin{aligned} \lambda = b_2 - c \text{ and } x_1 = 0, \ x_2 = c & \quad \text{if } 0 \leq c \leq b_2 - b_1 \\ \lambda = \tfrac{1}{2}(b_1 + b_2 - c) \text{ and } b_1 - x_1 = b_2 - x_2 = \tfrac{1}{2}(b_1 + b_2 - c) & \\ & \text{if } b_2 - b_1 \leq c \leq b_1 + b_2 \end{aligned} \tag{6}$$

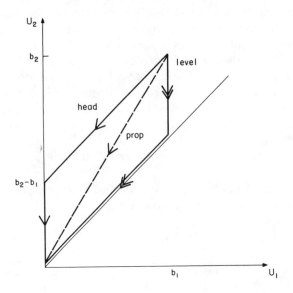

Figure 6.1.

In Figure 6.1 we have drawn the three curves traced by the surplus vector $(b_1 - x_1, b_2 - x_2)$ when the cost c raises from zero to $b_1 + b_2$ for the proportional tax, head tax, and leveling tax.

From formulas (5) and (6) we see that the head tax coincides with uniform cost sharing for small values of c, and the leveling tax coincides with equal surpluses for large values of c. This feature still holds for arbitrary n. If each b_i is positive and $c/n \leq \min\{b_j\}$, the solution of (3) is $\lambda = x_i = c/n$, whereas if $\sum_j b_j - n \cdot \min(b_j) \leq c \leq \sum_j b_j$, the solution of (4) is $\lambda = b_i - x_i = (1/n)(\sum_j b_j - c)$.

Example 6.3. A numerical example
We have five agents with benefits

$$b_1 = 4, \quad b_2 = 12, \quad b_3 = 20, \quad b_4 = 24, \quad \text{and} \quad b_5 = 30$$

Total benefit is $\sum_{i=1}^{n} b_i = 90$. Consider first (as in Exercise 1.3) a fairly low cost $c = 30$. It is not low enough to have the head tax coincide with uniform cost sharing ($x_i = 6$ for all i). Agent 1 can only pay $x_1 = 4$, after which the last four agents equally share the remaining cost. By contrast, the leveling tax is very sweet on agents 1 and 2, who pay nothing, whereas every other agent enjoys $14\frac{2}{3}$ units of surplus:

Benefits	4	12	20	24	30	Total cost
Head tax	4	$6\frac{1}{2}$	$6\frac{1}{2}$	$6\frac{1}{2}$	$6\frac{1}{2}$	30
Proportional tax	$1\frac{1}{3}$	4	$6\frac{2}{3}$	8	10	30
Leveling tax	0	0	$5\frac{1}{3}$	$9\frac{1}{3}$	$15\frac{1}{3}$	30

Next we pick a fairly high cost $c = 66$. With the leveling tax all agents but agent 1 enjoy five units of surplus. In the head tax the first two agents make no surplus at all, and the remaining three pay $16\frac{2}{3}$ each:

Benefits	4	12	20	24	30	Total cost
Head tax	4	12	$16\frac{2}{3}$	$16\frac{2}{3}$	$16\frac{2}{3}$	66
Proportional tax	2.9	8.8	14.7	17.6	22	66
Leveling tax	0	7	15	19	25	66

Notice in these two examples that the proportional tax is typically, but not always, between the head tax and the leveling tax.

Each of our three core selections (i.e., proportional, head, and leveling taxes) can be defended by a specific axiomatic argument. The proportional cost sharing admits a genuine characterization, explained in Section 6.5 (Theorem 6.1). The head tax (leveling tax) is the core selection that minimizes inequality in cost distribution (surplus distribution); see Exercise 6.2. These three methods also have a long tradition in empirical allocation. This contrasts with the two somewhat exotic solutions uncovered in the next section by application of our two favorite value operators for TU games.

6.4 The Shapley value and nucleolus cost sharing

We construct two more solutions of the cost-sharing model based on the Shapley value and the nucleolus of the TU game (1).

First observe that if the cost of the public good is so small that any single agent would like to produce it at his own expense, namely $0 \le c \le \min_j b_j$, the game (1) writes

$$v(S) = \sum_{i \in S} b_i - c \quad \text{for all } S \subseteq N$$

In this case its value corresponds to uniform cost sharing $x_i = c/n$, all i; this is also the head tax for any value satisfying zero independence and anonymity (in particular, the Shapley value and the nucleolus). Indeed, by zero independence the value is worth $(b_1 + y_1, \ldots, b_n + y_n)$, where $(y_1, \ldots, y_n)$ is the value of the game w, $w(S) = -c$ for all S. By anonymity, the value of w is $y_i = -c/n$ for all i.

Next suppose that the cost c is so high that it is efficient to produce the public good only if all agents can consume it, namely,

$$\text{for all } i: \quad \sum_{j \neq i} b_j \leq c \leq \sum_{i=1}^{n} b_i$$

Then the TU game (1) writes $v(S) = 0$ for all $S \subset N$, $v(N) = \sum_N b_i - c$. Thus, any anonymous value operator will equally share the surplus $v(N)$, corresponding to the equal-surplus method $b_i - x_i = b_j - x_j$ for all i, j; this is also the leveling tax.

These two limit behaviors – uniform cost sharing if the cost is small enough and equal surpluses if it is high enough – make good sense, especially in the bankruptcy interpretation of our problem discussed by Aumann and Maschler [1985]. In this story b_i is the claim of creditor i on some estate that is worth only e, $e < \sum_{i=1}^{n} b_i$. The deficit $c = \sum_{i=1}^{n} b_i - e$ is the cost that the creditors must agree to share before they liquidate the estate. If the deficit is very small (relative to each claim), everyone knows that his own claim will be almost fulfilled, and attention focuses on the deficit, which in turn equalizes cost shares. On the other hand, if the value of the estate is very small (say smaller than any of the claims), the portion of a claim above e becomes pointless, which puts all agents on the same footing, suggesting uniform sharing of e, namely, equal surpluses.

We consider now a two-agent problem. All zero-independent and anonymous values agree in this case (Lemma 5.3) and suggest the following cost sharing.

Lemma 6.2.   *Given is a two-person cost-sharing problem (b_1, b_2, c) with $b_1 \leq b_2$. A zero-independent anonymous value operator suggests the following cost shares for the surplus-sharing game (1):*

$$
\begin{aligned}
x_1 = x_2 = \tfrac{1}{2}c & \qquad \text{if } 0 \leq c \leq b_1 \\
x_1 = \tfrac{1}{2}b_1, \ x_2 = c - \tfrac{1}{2}b_1 & \qquad \text{if } b_1 \leq c \leq b_2 \qquad\qquad (7) \\
b_1 - x_1 = b_2 - x_2 = \tfrac{1}{2}(b_1 + b_2 - c) & \qquad \text{if } b_2 \leq c \leq b_1 + b_2
\end{aligned}
$$

Proof: In view of Lemma 5.3, the surplus vector $(b_1 - x_1, b_2 - x_2)$ is given by formula (36) in Chapter 5. Given our definition of the game (1), this reads

$$b_1 - x_1 = \tfrac{1}{2}((b_1 + b_2 - c) + (b_1 - c)^+ - (b_2 - c)^+)$$
$$b_2 - x_2 = \tfrac{1}{2}((b_1 + b_2 - c) + (b_2 - c)^+ - (b_1 - c)^+)$$

The relative position of c w.r.t. b_1 and b_2 yields formula (7).   Q.E.D.

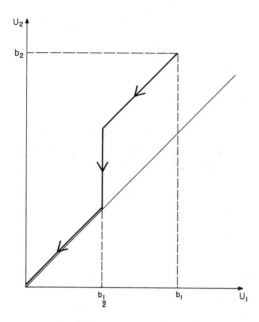

Figure 6.2.

As in Figure 6.1, we can draw the downward path of surplus vectors $(b_1 - x_1, b_2 - x_2)$ when the cost rises from 0 to $b_1 + b_2$ (see Figure 6.2).

For three agents or more, an explicit formula for the nucleolus is available. Two regions are distinguished. If $c \leq \frac{1}{2} \sum_1^n b_i$, cost is relatively low, and cost shares are equalized under the constraint $x_i \leq \frac{1}{2} b_i$. On the other hand, if $\frac{1}{2} \sum_1^n b_i \leq c$, surplus is relatively low, and surpluses are equalized under the constraint $b_i - x_i \leq \frac{1}{2} b_i$.

Lemma 6.3 (Aumann and Maschler [1985]). *The nucleolus of game* (1) *corresponds to the following cost shares:*

if $c \leq \dfrac{1}{2} \displaystyle\sum_1^n b_i$:

$$\left\{ \sum_{i=1}^n \min\left\{\lambda, \frac{b_i}{2}\right\} = c \right\} \Rightarrow \left\{ x_i = \min\left\{\lambda, \frac{b_i}{2}\right\} \text{ for all } i \right\} \tag{8}$$

if $\dfrac{1}{2} \displaystyle\sum_1^n b_i \leq c$:

$$\left\{ \sum_{i=1}^n \min\left\{\lambda, \frac{b_i}{2}\right\} = \sum_{i=1}^n b_i - c \right\} \Rightarrow x_i = b_i - \min\left\{\lambda, \frac{b_i}{2}\right\} \text{ for all } i \tag{9}$$

We omit the proof. Exercise 6.3 gives more explicit formulas for this cost sharing.

Aumann and Maschler emphasize that the nucleolus solves an intriguing puzzle from the Talmudic literature.

Example 6.4. A bankruptcy problem from the Mishna
(Aumann and Maschler [1985])
A man dies, leaving three wives with respective claims 100, 200, and 300 on their husband's estate. The Talmud recommends the following shares when the total estate is worth 100, 200, or 300.

Claim	100	200	300	Total estate
Shares	$33\frac{1}{3}$	$33\frac{1}{3}$	$33\frac{1}{3}$	100
Shares	50	75	75	200
Shares	50	100	150	300

What logical method underlies the solution of the rabbis? The shares for dividing 100 correspond to equal surpluses, but in the two other cases the proposed surplus sharing differs from the leveling tax (that gives 66.66 to each widow if the estate is worth 200) and from the head tax and proportional tax.

The nucleolus solves the puzzle. As the total cost $c = b_1 + b_2 + b_3 - e$ is never below $\frac{1}{2}(b_1 + b_2 + b_3) = 300$, we use formula (9). When the value $e = 600 - c$ of the estate rises from 0 to 300, surpluses $b_i - x_i$ remain equal until $e = 150$, at which point agent 1's surplus hits $50 = \frac{1}{2}b_1$ and stays put thereafter. From $e = 150$ to $e = 250$, agents 2 and 3 get the same surplus, up to 100 each for $e = 250$. From $e = 250$ to $e = 300$, agent 3 pockets all the additional surplus. Past $e = 300$ formula (8) gives symmetrical variations for the cost shares: For $e = 400$ the cost shares are $(50, 75, 75)$ [hence, estate shares are $(50, 125, 225)$], and for $e = 500$ the cost shares are $(33\frac{1}{3}, 33\frac{1}{3}, 33\frac{1}{3})$. The symmetry around $c = \frac{1}{2}\sum_1^n b_i$ is detailed in Exercise 6.3.

The Shapley value of game (1) does not give an easy formula such as the nucleolus. However, its usual interpretation as the average of marginal contributions leads to the following story. The agents run away from the tax collector, who catches them one by one in a random ordering (every ordering is equiprobable). The agents successively caught pay up to the full extent of their benefit until the cost is entirely covered. Suppose the ordering is $(1, \ldots, n)$ and that the cost is covered only after agent $i + 1$ is caught:

$$\sum_{j=1}^{i} b_j < c \le \sum_{j=1}^{i+1} b_j \tag{10}$$

Then the first i agents pay b_i, agent $i+1$ pays $c - \sum_{j=1}^{i} b_j$, and the remaining $n - i$ agents pay nothing.

In the bankruptcy interpretation, we have a symmetrical story (O'Neill [1982]). The agents run to the bank and receive up to the full amount of their claim – on a first-come-first-served basis – until the estate is completely exhausted. In the Talmudic example, the Shapley value coincides with the nucleolus if the estate is worth 100 or 300 but differs if the estate is 200. We check this last claim. Suppose $e = 200$. Hence, $c = 400$. Then agent 1 will pay his full benefit if he is caught first or second and nothing if he is last. Hence, his cost share is $66\frac{2}{3}$. Next agent 2 must pay 200 if caught first, 100 or 200 with equal probability if caught second, and nothing if caught last; hence his cost share is $116\frac{2}{3}$. Thus, the estate is divided into $(33\frac{1}{3}, 83\frac{1}{3}, 83\frac{1}{3})$. As an easy exercise, the reader can detail the Shapley value when the claims are 100, 200, and 300 and the value e of the estate varies from 0 to 600.

6.5   Decentralizability

The cost-sharing and surplus-sharing models have been considered in the axiomatic angle by several authors (Banker [1981], O'Neill [1982], Aumann and Maschler [1985], Young [1985a, 1987], Moulin [1985d, 1987a], Chun [1987]). We review some typical results in this and the next section.

Definition 6.2.   *Given society* $\{1, \dots, n\}$, *a cost-sharing mechanism is a mapping x associating to each problem* $(b_1, \dots, b_n; c)$ *such that* $\sum_{i=1}^{n} b_i \geq c$ *a vector of cost shares* $x(b; c) = (x_i(b_1, \dots, b_n; c))$ *such that* $\sum_{i=1}^{n} x_i(b; c) = c$. *A surplus-sharing mechanism is a mapping y associating to each problem* $(c_1, \dots, c_n; r)$ *such that* $\sum_{i=1}^{n} c_i \leq r$ *a vector of shares* $y(c; r) = (y_i(c_1, \dots, c_n; r))$ *such that* $\sum_{i=1}^{n} y_i(c; r) = r$.

Definition 6.3 (Moulin [1985b, 1987a]).   *We say that the cost-sharing mechanism x (surplus-sharing mechanism y) is decentralizable if agent i's share* $x_i(b; c)$ *depends only upon the cost c, his own benefit* b_i, *and the aggregate benefit* $\sum_{j=1}^{n} b_j$:

$$x_i(b; c) = t_i(b_i; \textstyle\sum_j b_j; c) \tag{11}$$

[*respectively, if* $y_i(c; r)$ *depends only upon the revenue r, his own opportunity cost* c_i, *and the aggregate opportunity cost* $\sum_j c_j$:

$$y_i(c; r) = t_i(c_i; \textstyle\sum_j c_j; r)]$$

Decentralizability is an independence condition to compute an agent's share, and the agent need not know the details of the benefit distribution across his fellow agents. Only the aggregate (or average) benefit is needed. When n is very large, this is eminently convenient for it allows a a decentralized computation of cost shares (or surplus shares).

A consequence of decentralizability is that the joint cost share of any coalition can be computed from the total cost and the joint benefits to this coalition and to its complement. For all S, $\varnothing \neq S \subset N$, there exists a function r_S such that

$$\sum_{i \in S} x_i(b;c) = r_S\left(\sum_S b_i; \sum_{N \setminus S} b_j; c\right) \tag{12}$$

For an arbitrary coalition S, (11) implies that $\sum_S x_i$ depends only upon $\sum_{N \setminus S} b_j$. By exchanging the role of S and $N \setminus S$, we see that $\sum_{N \setminus S} x_j$ depends only upon $\sum_S b_i$. Since $\sum_S x_i = c - \sum_{N \setminus S} x_j$, formula (12) obtains. Of course, a decentralizable surplus-sharing method satisfies a formula similar to (12). Moulin [1985b] gives a strategic interpretation to decentralizability in which he rules out profitable side payments inside a coalition.

In the surplus-sharing problem, both the proportional and the egalitarian mechanisms are decentralizable. In the cost-sharing problem, however, neither the leveling tax nor the head tax yield a decentralizable mechanism. Consider, for instance, the problem of Example 6.3. Change the benefits of the agents 1 and 2 from $b_1 = 4$, $b_2 = 12$ to $b_1' = b_2' = 8$. Decentralizability would imply that the cost shares of agents 3, 4, and 5 are unaffected by this change. Yet if the total cost is 30, the head tax becomes $c_i' = 6$ for all i (thus, agents 3, 4, and 5 pay less), and if the total cost is 66, the leveling tax becomes $(c_1', c_2', c_3', c_4', c_5') = (3.2, 3.2, 15.2, 19.2, 25.2)$ (thus, agents 3, 4, and 5 pay more).

Theorem 6.1 (from Moulin [1985b]).   *Suppose that a society contains three agents or more. There is exactly one cost-sharing mechanism satisfying decentralizability and the core property. It is the proportional tax.*

Core property: $0 \leq x_i(b;c) \leq b_i$ for all b, c and all i.

Proof: The proportional tax $x_i = (b_i / \sum_N b_j) \cdot c$ is obviously decentralizable. Conversely, consider an anonymous mechanism x given by formula (11). We fix $S = \{1, 2\}$ and apply (12) to S:

$$x_1(b;c) + x_2(b;c) = r_{12}\left(b_1 + b_2; \sum_{i \geq 3} b_i; c\right) \tag{13}$$

By formula (11) we have $x_1(b;c) = t_1(b_1; \sum_N b_j; c)$, and so on. Set $b_0 = \sum_{j \in N} b_j$. Then property (13) yields

$$t_1(b_1; b_0; c) + t_2(b_2; b_0; c) = r_{12}(b_1 + b_2, b_0 - (b_1 + b_2); c)$$

Thus, for any given b_0 and c, the sum $t_1(b_1) + t_2(b_2)$ depends only on $b_1 + b_2$ as long as $b_1 + b_2$ is below b_0. This is a popular functional equation known as Jensen's equation (see Aczél [1966]). Its solutions (up to a topological detail) take the form

$$t_1(b_1; b_0; c) = h_1(b_0; c) + b_1 \cdot k_1(b_0; c) \qquad (14)$$

Invoke now the core property to completely determine the function h_1:

$$\{b_1 = 0 \Rightarrow x_1 = 0 \Rightarrow t_1(0; b_0; c) = 0\} \Rightarrow h_1 = 0$$

Thus, $t_1(b_1; b_0; c) = b_1 \cdot k_1(b_0; c)$. By budget balance and the core property again we have

$$t_1(b_0; b_0; c) = c$$

This in turn shows $k_1(b_0; c) = c/b_0$. As the choice of agent 1 was arbitrary, the proof is complete. Q.E.D.

In Theorem 6.1 the core property cannot be dispensed with. Indeed, both the uniform cost-sharing ($x_i = c/n$) and the equal-surplus ($b_i - x_i = b_j - x_j$, all i, j) mechanisms are decentralizable.

The proportional cost sharing satisfies an even stronger property than decentralizability. Say that our population N is partitioned as

$$N = S_1 \cup \cdots \cup S_K$$

Then we can compute the (proportional) cost shares over N in two steps. First we compute the (proportional) cost shares in the K-person problem $(\Sigma_{S_1} b_i, \ldots, \Sigma_{S_K} b_i; c)$, say, $c_1, \ldots, c_K$. Next we compute the final cost shares within each coalition S_k as the solution of the problem $(b_i, i \in S_k; c_k)$. Banker [1981] and O'Neill [1982] use this property to characterize the proportional cost sharing. Their argument can be adapted to characterize the proportional mechanism in the surplus-sharing problem.

6.6   Separability

Definition 6.4 (Young [1987]).   *Given is a cost-sharing mechanism $x(b, c)$ [surplus-sharing mechanism $y(c; r)$] over society $\{1, \ldots, n\}$. We say that it is separable if for every proper coalition $S \subsetneq N$ and every b, b', c, c' we have*

$$\left\{ b_i = b_i' \text{ for all } i \in S \text{ and } \sum_{i \in S} x_i(b; c) = \sum_{i \in S} x_i(b'; c') \right\}$$

$$\Rightarrow \{x_i(b; c) = x_i(b'; c') \text{ for all } i \in S\} \qquad (15)$$

and if for every c, c', r, r' we have

$$\left\{ c_i = c_i' \text{ for all } i \in S \text{ and } \sum_{i \in S} y_i(c;r) = \sum_{i \in S} y_i(c';r') \right\}$$

$$\Rightarrow \{ y_i(c;r) = y_i(c';r') \text{ for all } i \in S \} \quad (16)$$

In words, the distribution of costs shares (surplus shares) within coalition S depends upon the benefits (opportunity costs) of S's members and the joint cost (joint surplus) of S.

Separability is already a familiar idea (see Chapters 2 and 3 and the reduced-game property in Chapter 5). The distributive issue can be reduced to an arbitrary subgroup of agents. Note the complementarity of decentralizability and separability. The former simplifies the computation of the joint shares (cost or surplus) of a coalition [see formula (12)], and by the latter the shares within a coalition are determined completely by the coalition's joint share (and the utility parameters of the coalition members).

Separability has other possible formulations. Young [1987] proposes a *consistency* axiom mimicking Definition 6.4 in the variable-population context. Another equivalent property is the following *agreement* axiom that we state in the surplus-sharing case. For any two agents i, j and every c, c', r, r',

$$\{ c_i = c_i' \text{ and } c_j = c_j' \} \Rightarrow \{ (y_i(c;r) - y_i(c';r')) \cdot (y_j(c;r) - y_j(c';r')) \geq 0 \}$$

$$(17)$$

In words, consider any two agents whose opportunity costs are kept fixed while everything else (revenue, other agents' opportunity costs) changes. Then the change will be beneficial for both or harmful for both. The equivalence of agreement and separability is the subject of Exercise 6.4.

Most of the cost-sharing (or surplus-sharing) methods introduced in the preceding satisfy separability. The only exception is the Shapley value cost-sharing mechanism (see Exercise 6.4).

The class of separable cost-sharing (or surplus-sharing) mechanisms admits an analytical representation. We explain this result in the cost-sharing case first.

Definition 6.5 (Young [1987]).   *Consider a real-valued function $h(\lambda, b)$ defined for all $b \geq 0$ and all λ, $0 \leq \lambda \leq \bar{\lambda}$, where $\bar{\lambda}$ is a fixed positive number (possibly $+\infty$). Suppose h is nondecreasing and continuous in λ - for fixed b - and that, moreover,*

$$h(0, b) = 0, \quad h(\bar{\lambda}, b) = b \quad \text{for all } b \geq 0$$

*To such a function h, associate the following **parametric** cost-sharing mechanism. Given the problem $(b_1, \ldots, b_n; c)$, find the essentially unique solution λ^* of the equation*

$$\sum_{i=1}^{n} h(\lambda, b_i) = c \tag{18}$$

Then take $x_i = h(\lambda^*, b_i)$.

As λ rises from 0 to $\bar{\lambda}$, the function $\sum_{i=1}^{n} h(\lambda, b_i)$ continuously increases (or is constant) from 0 to $\sum_{i=1}^{n} b_i$. Therefore, equation (18) has a solution if and only if it is efficient to produce the public good. It may have several solutions if all functions $h(\lambda, b_i)$ are flat in λ at the same time, but the vector of cost shares $(x_1, \dots, x_n)$ is always unique.

A parametric method always picks a cost sharing in the core since by construction of h, we have $0 \leq h(\lambda, b_i) \leq b_i$ [see property (2)].

From Lemma 6.2 it is apparent that the head tax and leveling tax are two parametric methods with the following functions h:

$$h(\lambda, b) = \min\{\lambda, b\}, \qquad \bar{\lambda} = +\infty \quad \text{(head tax)}$$

$$h(\lambda, b) = b - \min\{1/\lambda, b\}, \qquad \bar{\lambda} = +\infty \quad \text{(leveling tax)}$$

Evidently, the proportional tax corresponds to the function

$$h(\lambda, b) = \lambda \cdot b, \qquad \bar{\lambda} = 1 \quad \text{(proportional tax)}$$

Finally, the nucleolus of game (1) is another parametric method as one can guess from Lemma 6.4: Formulas (8) and (9) are similar to two pieces of a parametric representation. An exact representation of the nucleolus as in Definition 6.5 is given in Exercise 6.3, question (c).

Clearly, a parametric cost-sharing method is separable. Consider a coalition $S \subsetneq N$ and two cost-sharing problems $(b; c)$ and $(b'; c')$ with associated parameters λ and λ'. Suppose $b_i = b_i'$ for all $i \in S$:

$$\sum_{i \in S} x_i(b; c) = \sum_{i \in S} x_i(b'; c') \Leftrightarrow \sum_{i \in S} h(\lambda, b_i) = \sum_{i \in S} h(\lambda', b_i)$$

$$\Rightarrow h(\lambda, b_i) = h(\lambda', b_i) \quad \text{for all } i \in S$$

The results of Young [1987] imply that the family of parametric cost-sharing methods (Definition 6.5) is *characterized* by the four properties of anonymity, core bounds (agent i's cost shares are between 0 and b_i), continuity (cost shares vary continuously with c), and consistency.

In the surplus-sharing problem, parametric mechanisms are defined similarly. Pick a real-valued function $k(\mu, c)$ defined for all $c \geq 0$ and $\mu \geq 0$. Suppose k is nondecreasing and continuous in μ and that, moreover,

$$k(0, c) = c, \qquad k(+\infty, c) = +\infty$$

For every problem $(c_1, \dots, c_n; r)$, find the (essentially unique) solution μ^* of the equation

$$\sum_{i=1}^{n} k(\mu, c_i) = r$$

Setting $y_i = k(\mu^*, c_i)$ defines the parametric surplus-sharing mechanism corresponding to the function k.

Parametric surplus-sharing mechanisms are, again, characterized by separability, continuity, and anonymity (Young [1987]).

The egalitarian and proportional surplus-sharing mechanisms thus satisfy our two informational axioms. Actually, the combination of separability and decentralizability characterizes a one-dimensional family of mechanisms containing the proportional and egalitarian mechanisms as its two extreme points (Moulin [1987a]). In order to pin down axiomatically our two focal mechanisms, one more axiom is needed. It is an additivity property of individual shares w.r.t. total revenue, called path independence (see Exercise 6.6). Together, the three axioms decentralizability, separability, and path independence characterize the *pair* egalitarian and proportional mechanisms; see Moulin [1987a] for a precise statement and some variants of this result.

EXERCISES

6.1 Proof of Lemma 6.1.

(a) Consider a cost-sharing problem $(b_1, \ldots, b_n, c)$ and denote by λ^* the solution of equation (3). Show that it is unique because $\sum_{i=1}^{n} b_i > c$. Denote $x_i^* = \min\{\lambda^*, b_i\}$ and show that x^* is a solution of the program

$$\max_{x \in A} \left(\min_{i=1, \ldots, n} \{x_i\} \right)$$

Hint: Distinguish two cases: (a) $\lambda^* \leq b_i$ for all i and (b) $\lambda^* \geq b_i$ for some i. To prove that x^* is the head tax, denote by i_0 an agent such that $x_{i_0} \leq x_i^*$, all i. Consider the $(n-1)$-agent problem $(b_i, \text{ all } i \neq i_0; c - x_{i_0}^*)$ and use an induction argument.

(b) Use the change of variable $y_i = b_i - x_i$ to prove the second statement as a corollary of the first.

6.2 Two more characterizations of the head tax and the leveling tax. Consider the cost-sharing problem $(b_1, \ldots, b_n; c)$ for an indivisible good, and denote by x^h (x^e) the head tax (leveling tax). We denote by A, as in Definition 6.1, the set of cost-sharing vectors where an agent is not subsidized and gets a nonnegative surplus.

(a) Show that x^h Lorenz dominates (Section 2.5) any cost sharing x in A, $x \neq x^h$. Show that $b - x^e$ Lorenz dominates any surplus vector $b - x$, where x is in A, $x \neq x^e$.

(b) Denote by D the following subset of A:

$$x \in D \Leftrightarrow \{x \in A \text{ and } (b_i \le b_j \Rightarrow 0 \le x_j - x_i \le b_j - b_i, \text{ all } i, j\}$$

This says that if agent 1 benefits more from the good than agent 2, then agent 1 does not pay less and does not get a smaller surplus than agent 2.

Show that any cost sharing x in D, $x \in x^e$, Lorenz dominates x^e. Show that any surplus vector $b - x$, where $x \in D$, $x \ne x^h$, Lorenz dominates $b - x^h$.

6.3 The nucleolus of the cost-sharing game (1). Given is a cost-sharing problem $(b_1, \ldots, b_n; c)$, where we assume, without loss of generality,

$$b_1 \le b_2 \le \cdots \le b_n$$

(a) Say that a cost-sharing method is symmetrical when it satisfies:

If $(x_1, \ldots, x_n)$ is the cost sharing for problem $(b_1, \ldots, b_n; c)$, then $(b_1 - x_1, \ldots, b_n - x_n)$ is the cost sharing for $(b_1, \ldots, b_n; \sum_{i=1}^{n} b_i - c)$.

Show that the nucleolus (Lemma 6.4) and the Shapley value of game (1) yield symmetrical cost-sharing methods.

(b) Define the following numbers:

$$\alpha_0 = 0, \qquad \alpha_k = \frac{1}{2}\left[\sum_{1}^{k-1} b_i + (n-k+1)b_k\right] \quad \text{for all } k = 1, \ldots, n$$

$$\beta_0 = \sum_{i=1}^{n} b_i, \qquad \beta_k = \frac{1}{2}\sum_{1}^{k-1} b_i - \left(\frac{n-k-1}{2}\right)b_k + \sum_{k+1}^{n} b_i$$

$$\text{for all } k = 1, \ldots, n$$

(with the convention $\sum_{1}^{0} = \sum_{n+1}^{n} = 0$). Note that

$$0 = \alpha_0 \le \cdots \le \alpha_n = \frac{1}{2}\sum_{1}^{n} b_i = \beta_n \le \beta_{n-1} \le \cdots \le \beta_0 = \sum_{1}^{n} b_i$$

Prove that the nucleolus cost sharing [defined by (8) and (9)] is equivalently given by the following formula: If $\alpha_k \le c \le \alpha_{k+1}$ (for some $k = 0, 1, \ldots, n-1$), then

$$x_i = \frac{1}{2}b_i \quad \text{if } 1 \le i \le k$$

$$x_j = \frac{1}{n-k}\left[c - \frac{1}{2}\sum_{1}^{k} b_i\right] \quad \text{if } k+1 \le j \le n$$

If $\beta_{k+1} \le c \le \beta_k$ (for some $k = 0, 1, \ldots, n-1$), then

$$x_i = \frac{1}{2}b_i \quad \text{if } 1 \le i \le k$$

$$x_j = b_j - \frac{1}{n-k}\left[\frac{1}{2}\sum_{1}^{k} b_i + \sum_{k+1}^{n} b_j - c\right] \quad \text{if } k+1 \le j \le n$$

(c) Show that the nucleolus is a parametric cost-sharing mechanism (Definition 6.5). *Hint:* Consider the function $h(\mu, b)$, where the parameter μ varies over the whole E (from $-\infty$ to $+\infty$):

$$h(\mu, b) = \min\left(-\frac{1}{\mu}, \frac{b}{2}\right) \quad \text{if } \mu \le 0$$

$$= \max\left(b - \frac{1}{\mu}, \frac{b}{2}\right) \quad \text{if } \mu \ge 0$$

Show that h represents the nucleolus cost sharing. Then use a change of variable to get an equivalent parametric representation where the parameter remains nonnegative.

6.4 More on separability.

(a) Show that the Shapley value cost-sharing method (Section 6.4) is *not* separable. Use the numerical example given at the end of Section 6.4, namely, the problem $(100, 200, 300; 400)$. Consider the other problem $(100, 200, 0; 116\frac{2}{3})$ and deduce a contradiction of (15) for $S = \{1, 2\}$.

(b) Show that for a surplus-sharing mechanism, agreement [property (17)] implies separability [formula (16)]. Conversely, suppose y is a separable mechanism. Assume also that each function y_i is nondecreasing in r. Show that the mechanism satisfies agreement. *Hint:* Fix $i = 1$ and $j = 2$, and define two functions S_i, $i = 1, 2$, as follows:

$$\delta_i(c_1, c_2; \sigma) = d_i(c_1, c_2, c_2, \ldots, c_2; r)$$

where r is the unique solution of $(d_1 + d_2)(c_1, c_2, c_2, \ldots, c_2; r) = \sigma$. Check that δ_i is nondecreasing in σ. Observe that for an arbitrary problem $(c; r)$ we have

$$d_i(c; r) = \delta_i(c_1, c_2; d_1(c; r) + d_2(c; r))$$

6.5 Decentralizable surplus-sharing mechanisms (Moulin [1987a]).

(a) Consider an arbitrary function $\mathcal{L}$ defined over E_+^2 and define a surplus-sharing mechanism as follows:

$$y_i(c; r) = \frac{r}{n} + \left(c_i - \frac{1}{n} \sum_{j=1}^{n} c_j\right) \cdot \mathcal{L}\left(r, \sum_{j=1}^{n} c_j\right)$$

Check that this mechanism is anonymous (by permuting two agents' opportunity costs we exchange their shares and leave other agents' shares constant) and decentralizable.

(b) Conversely, show that an anonymous and decentralizable mechanism takes the form of (a). *Hint:* Mimic the proof of Theorem 6.1. Invoke anonymity only after establishing the analogs of formula (14).

6.6 Decentralizable and separable surplus sharing (Moulin [1987a]).

(a) Fix a real number λ, $1 \le \lambda \le +\infty$, and define the surplus-sharing mechanism y^λ as follows:

$$y_i^\lambda(c;r) = r \cdot \left(c_i \Big/ \sum_{j=1}^n c_j \right) \qquad \text{if } r \le \lambda \cdot \left(\sum_{j=1}^n c_j \right)$$

$$y_i^\lambda(c;r) = \lambda \cdot c_i + \frac{1}{n} \left(r - \lambda \sum_{j=1}^n c_j \right) \quad \text{if } r \ge \lambda \cdot \left(\sum_{j=1}^n c_j \right)$$

Check that y^1 is the egalitarian mechanism and $y^{+\infty}$ the proportional one. Show that every mechanism y^λ is decentralizable and separable. Conversely, Theorem 1 in Moulin [1987a] shows that these two axioms essentially characterize the family y^λ, $1 \le \lambda \le +\infty$.

(b) Consider the path independence axiom defined as follows. Given any vector c of opportunity costs and revenues r, r',

$$y(c, r + r') = y(c + y(c, r); r')$$

Interpret this property and show that in the family y^λ, only the egalitarian and the proportional mechanisms satisfy path independence. Thus, decentralizability, separability, and path independence together characterize the pair made up of the proportional and egalitarian mechanisms. Moulin [1987a] proposes three more characterizations of this pair.

6.7 **A core selection with arbitrary preferences.** Individual preferences are no longer assumed to be quasi-linear. The public project can be undertaken ($\epsilon = 1$) or not ($\epsilon = 0$). Agent i's preferences over (ϵ, x_i) (where x_i is net disbursement – possibly negative if agent i receives some money) are strictly decreasing in x_i and nondecreasing in ϵ.

Agent i's maximal willingness to pay for the project is $\bar{x}_i$ such that he is indifferent between $(\epsilon = 1, \bar{x}_i)$ and $(\epsilon = 0, 0)$. Further, there is a monetary compensation $\underline{x}_i$ that is equivalent to the free public good: Agent i is indifferent between $(\epsilon = 1, 0)$ and $(\epsilon = 0, -\underline{x}_i)$. But the two numbers $\bar{x}_i, \underline{x}_i$ cannot be systematically ordered (in the quasi-linear case $\bar{x}_i = \underline{x}_i$).

(a) Show that the (initial) allocation "no project" ($\epsilon = 0$, $x_i = 0$, for all i) is Pareto inferior if and only if

$$\sum_{i=1}^n \bar{x}_i > c \tag{19}$$

(b) Assume (19) and that individual preferences are continuous. Show the existence of a unique cost sharing x^* such that for some positive number λ, $\sum_1^n x_i^* = c$ and agent i is indifferent between $(1, x_i^*)$ and $(0, -\lambda \cdot x_i^*)$ for all i. What cost sharing do we obtain if preferences are quasi-linear?

(c) Show that the allocation $(1, x_1^*, \ldots, x_n^*)$ is in the core of the NTU surplus game of our cost-sharing problem (the definition of the NTU game of a public good economy is given in Section 7.2).

CHAPTER 7

Regulated monopoly

Overview

The economic behavior of a public firm is among the oldest problems of welfare economics. The two main instances where a public firm is called for are the provision of a public good and that of a private good of which the production technology has increasing returns to scale (IRS). Those are cases of natural monopoly. On the economic theory of natural monopolies see Baumol, Panzar, and Willig [1982]; on the optimal provision of a public good see the historical review by Musgrave and Peacock [1958] and the theoretical survey of Milleron [1972]. In both cases, the only efficient organization of production utilizes a single production unit, yet it would be socially wasteful to let this unit be operated by a profit-maximizing monopolist. Thus, there exist the need for a regulated public firm and the compelling normative question of its pricing policy.

Even under decreasing returns to scale (DRS), the case for joint production frequently arises. The workers of a cooperative jointly own its machines, and the partners of a law firm share its patrons. They must choose an equitable scheme to share the fruits of their cooperation. Thus, the general discussion of a public firm involves an arbitrary technology; if it has decreasing returns, we mean that it is operated jointly by the agents with no possibility of duplication (there is a large implicit fixed cost to open a new production unit).

The traditional answers to the regulated monopoly problem mimic the competitive market equilibrium. In the public good case this leads to the personalized Lindahl prices: Each agent forces a different price for the public good; at these prices all demands coincide. In the private good case this yields marginal pricing rules. The difficult task is to justify such proposals when the usual competitive stories do not apply. How could I take my personalized price as an exogenous signal unless the public firm has coercive power? Is it fair to charge also a lump-sum fee to cover the firm's deficit?

166

The recent and successful application of the cooperative game model to public pricing hinges upon the core idea. The stand-alone test follows from letting each coalition utilize the technology at will (free access to technology). It will lead the discussion in this chapter.

In the light of cooperative games, we discuss two kinds of solutions for the regulated monopoly problem. The first category contains marginal utility pricing methods: Lindahl's equilibrium and its extension as ratio equilibrium (RE) in the public good model as well as competitive equilibrium where each agent owns an equal share of the public firm in the private good model. The second category contains two welfare egalitarian solutions sharing a very compact axiomatic characterization. Those solutions are described in what follows.

In this chapter (Sections 7.1–7.7) we restrict ourselves to the one input–one output model, for the multi-output and/or multi-input case (see Remark 7.2) is tremendously more complex. The input is a private good and the output may be a private or a public good. We discuss both models in parallel. The concerned agents are described by ordinal preferences over input × output and some endowment of input. The data of the production function complete the description of a full-fledged production economy with nontransferable utility (NTU).

A surplus-sharing mechanism (Section 7.1) must select an efficient allocation, specifying each agent's input contribution and output share (or simply output level in the public good case). We are looking for fully efficient (first-best) mechanisms, selecting a Pareto-optimal allocation in every economy.

Sections 7.2 and 7.3 define the NTU cooperative game where each coalition has free access to the technology and its core. In the public good model, this game is convex (in a NTU sense), and its core is always nonempty. In the private good model (Section 7.3) the situation is a bit more involved. Consider first the case where the production function happens to have constant returns to scale (CRS) (so many units of output per unit of input). This implies that joint utilization of the transformation process creates no externalities, positive or negative, between the agents: Each agent can freely exchange input for output (at the constant technical rate of substitution) without altering the exchange opportunities of any other agent. The core then contains essentially a unique outcome: Each agent independently decides just how much output to produce while paying the corresponding amount of input.

In the general model where output is a private good, we expect the core to be nonempty when production has increasing returns to scale (IRS), because the utilization of the production unit by an agent creates positive externalities. When production has decreasing returns to scale (DRS), those externalities are negative, and the core is typically empty. We can then use the coalitional opportunity sets to place upper bounds on the agents' utilities (these sets give lower bounds in the core property). This yields the concept of anticore (discussed in Section 7.3; see also Exercise 7.7). The anticore is typically nonempty under DRS.

In Section 7.4 we develop the marginal pricing (MP) idea for the public good model. The notion of Lindahl equilibrium conveys adequately this idea if the production has CRS. It is then a core allocation (Theorem 7.1). For an arbitrary production function the correct generalization of Lindahl allocation is Kaneko's ratio equilibrium; when it exists, it is a core allocation, and it exists when returns to scale are decreasing.

Section 7.5 shows that MP solutions are not so satisfactory in the private good model. The MP equilibrium is defined in much the same way as the competitive equilibrium of an Arrow–Debreu economy where each agent owns an identical share of the firm (the only difference is that the firm may not be maximizing its profit). In the increasing-returns case, the agents share the firm's deficit, and the MP equilibrium may result in a net loss of utility for some agents; in particular, it may not be a core allocation. In the decreasing-returns case, the agents share the firm's surplus, and the MP equilibrium may not be an anticore allocation.

We construct in Section 7.6 two surplus-sharing mechanisms (for the public and private good economy) based on the egalitarian principle. The idea is to represent preferences by the "right" utility function. In the public good case, the trick is to take the public good itself as a *numéraire* to represent the agents' preferences. Thus, my utility for five units of public good at the cost (to me) of $10 will be 3 if I am indifferent between three units of public good for free and five units at $10. Using this cardinal representation of preferences, there is always an efficient outcome bringing equal utility for every agent. This outcome defines the egalitarian equivalent (EE) allocation. It is a surprising fact that this allocation belongs to the core without any restrictive assumption on preferences (Theorem 7.2).

In the private good case, a similar construction brings a core (or anticore) selection. Here the *numéraire* chosen to evaluate an allocation (input × output) is the price p of output relative to input such than an agent is indifferent between this allocation and the possibility of buying any amount of output he wishes at price p. By equalizing individual utilities measured in this way, the constant-returns equivalent (CRE) allocation obtains. Under increasing returns, this allocation is in the core (Theorem 7.3). Under decreasing returns (and convex preferences), it is in the anticore (Exercise 7.7).

Finally, we briefly review in Section 7.7 a characterization result of the EE and CRE mechanisms based upon the technological monotonicity

(TM) axiom. This axiom says that the utility of no agent should decrease as a result of an improvement of the technology (reduction of the production costs at all output levels). We conclude by comparing the MP versus the welfare egalitarian mechanisms from an axiomatic standpoint.

7.1 Two production economies

Model 1. Provision of a public good
The economy has two goods, one pure public good and one private good (money). The cost of producing y units of public good is $c(y)$ units of money. The function c is nondecreasing and $c(0) = 0$.

We have n agents. Initially, agent i is endowed with ω_i units of money, and no public good is produced ($y = 0$). At the final allocation each agent contributes some money, say, agent i contributes x_i, to produce y units of public good. The feasibility constraint is

$$\sum_{i=1}^{n} x_i = c(y) \tag{1}$$

Agent i's preferences are described by a utility function $u_i(\omega_i - x_i, y)$ over money $\times$ public good.

Model 2. Production of a private good
The economy has two private goods: Labor is used as input to produce corn (the output). The production of y units of corn requires $x = c(y)$ units of labor.

We have n agents. Initially, agent i is endowed with ω_i units of leisure (leisure can be consumed or used up as labor) and no corn. At the final allocation, he uses a fraction of his leisure, say, x_i, as labor and consumes y_i units of corn. His preferences are described by a utility function $u_i(\omega_i - x_i, y_i)$ over leisure $\times$ corn. An allocation $(x, y) = (x_1, \ldots, x_n; y_1, \ldots, y_n)$ is thus feasible if (and only if)

$$0 \le x_i \le \omega_i, \ 0 \le y_i \quad \text{for all } i \text{ and } \sum_{i=1}^{n} x_i = c\left(\sum_{i=1}^{n} y_i\right) \tag{2}$$

Despite the use of a cardinal utility function to represent preferences, the whole analysis of Chapter 7 is purely ordinal.

Note that in the public good model, agents can freely transfer the input (money): A feasible allocation $(x_1, \ldots, x_n; y)$ may have $x_i < 0$ (agent i receives a cash payment of $|x_i|$ dollars) or $x_i > \omega_i$ (his cost share exceeds his initial wealth). The core property defined in Section 7.2 will rule out these eventualities.

By contrast, in the private good model inputs are not transferable across agents: Agent i cannot end up with more leisure than he initially has, nor can he borrow someone else's leisure.

What allocations are Pareto optimal in these two economies? Assuming differentiability of the utility function, it is a simple exercise to show that an allocation is Pareto optimal in the public good model only if it satisfies

$$\sum_{i=1}^{n} \frac{u_{iy}}{u_{ix}} (\omega_i - x_i, y) = c'(y) \tag{3}$$

where u_{iy} (u_{ix}) is the partial derivative of u_i w.r.t. the public (private) good. Condition (3) is known as Samuelson's condition.

Similarly, in the private good model consider an interior allocation ($0 < x_i < w_i$, $0 < y_i$). It is Pareto optimal only if it satisfies

$$\frac{u_{iy}}{u_{ix}} (\omega_i - x_i, y_i) = c'\left(\sum_{j=1}^{n} y_j \right) \quad \text{for all } i = 1, \dots, n \tag{4}$$

Conversely, if preferences are convex (u_i is a quasi-concave function) and the cost function c is convex, those conditions are also sufficient.

Example 7.1. The case of quasi-linear utilities
Assume that all preferences are additively separable in the input and output goods and linear in the output. Thus, in the public good model,

$$u_i(\omega_i - x_i, y) = b_i(y) + (\omega_i - x_i)$$

where $b_i(y)$ is the monetary equivalent of y units of public good: Agent i is indifferent between receiving a payment of $b_i(y)$ dollars or consuming y units of public good for free.

Under quasilinearity of utilities, Samuelson's condition (3) simplifies to

$$\sum_{i=1}^{n} b_i'(y) = c'(y)$$

namely, the sum of marginal benefits equals the marginal cost of the public good. Note that the input levels x_i disappeared from the formula. Pareto optimality forces the level of public good to produce but places no constraint on its cost sharing. This useful feature of the quasi-linear model will be exploited in many of the examples that follow. In fact, in a quasi-linear public good model, Pareto optimality is *equivalent* to maximization of the surplus,

$$\sum_{i=1}^{n} u_i(-x_i, y) = \sum_{i=1}^{n} b_i(y) - c(y)$$

This is a very general fact that requires no differentiability or convexity assumption. Check first that if $(x_1, \ldots, x_n, y)$ is Pareto superior to $(x_1', \ldots, x_n', y')$ then $(\sum_{i=1}^{n} b_i - c)(y)$ is greater than $(\sum_{i=1}^{n} b_i - c)(y')$. Conversely, if y does not maximize $\sum_{i=1}^{n} b_i - c$, any feasible allocation $(x_1, \ldots, x_n, y)$ is Pareto inferior: There exist y' and $\epsilon > 0$ such that

$$\left(\sum_i b_i - c \right)(y') = \left(\sum_i b_i - c \right)(y) + \epsilon$$

Hence, the allocation $(x_1', \ldots, x_n', y')$ is feasible and Pareto superior to our allocation, where

$$x_i' = x_i + b_i(y') - b_i(y) - \epsilon/n \quad \text{for all } i$$

In the private good model quasi-linear utilities take the form

$$u_i(\omega_i - x_i, y_i) = b_i(y_i) + (\omega_i - x_i)$$

where $b_i(y_i)$ measures the input equivalent of y_i units of output. The first-order Pareto-optimal conditions (4) become

$$b_i'(y_i) = c'\left(\sum_{j=1}^{n} y_j \right) \quad \text{all } i = 1, \ldots, n \tag{5}$$

These conditions are the first-order conditions for maximizing the surplus,

$$\sum_{i=1}^{n} u_i(-x_i, y_i) = \sum_{i=1}^{n} b_i(y_i) - c\left(\sum_{i=1}^{n} y_i \right)$$

Indeed, any allocation where $(y_1, \ldots, y_n)$ maximizes the surplus $\sum_i b_i(y_i) - c(\sum_i y_i)$ is Pareto optimal. Conversely, an interior Pareto-optimal allocation maximizes the surplus (the argument is similar to that of the public good case). Note once more that Pareto optimality imposes no restriction on the input vector $(x_1, \ldots, x_n)$ (the cost shares) but forces the output levels. Indeed, if the benefit functions are concave and c is a convex function, the solution of system (5) is essentially unique.

7.2 The core of the public good economy

Suppose in model 1 that the technology for transforming private into public good is jointly owned by the agents. Then one way of materializing joint ownership is to let each and every coalition use the technology as it pleases. Any coalition of agents can decide to produce any level of public good provided it fully covers its cost. This places lower bounds on the utility levels of the various coalitions that in turn limit the admissible cost sharings. Those lower bounds are described by the following NTU game (Definition 4.6).

Definition 7.1. NTU game of the public good economy. *Given a coalition $S \subset \{1, \ldots, n\}$, a utility vector $\bar{u}_S$ is feasible for S $[u_S \in v(S)]$ if and only if there exist $y \geq 0$ and x_i for all $i \in S$ such that*

$$\sum_{i \in S} x_i = c(y) \quad and \quad \bar{u}_i \leq u_i(\omega_i - x_i, y) \quad for\ all\ i \in S$$

The core of this NTU game expresses, as usual, a stand-alone test: If an allocation $(x_1, \ldots, x_n, y)$ is in the core, no coalition can stand alone and improve the welfare of its members.

As a first example, the uniform cost-sharing mechanisms do *not* pass the stand-alone test. These mechanisms pick some Pareto-optimal allocations where all agents pay the same share of the cost: $x_i = (1/n) \cdot c(y)$ for all i. In the case of quasi-linear preferences (Example 7.1), one simply chooses an efficient level of production of the public good and divides its cost uniformly. To see that this may not yield a core allocation, think of an agent who derives almost no utility from the public good: If the efficient level y^* is large enough, we will have

$$u_i\left(\omega_i - \frac{1}{n} \cdot c(y^*), y^*\right) < u_i(\omega_i, 0)$$

In this event, agent i would rather stand alone and produce no public good at all.

A second consequence of the core property is that no agent is ever subsidized to consume the public good ($x_i \geq 0$ for all i). Suppose that $(x_1, \ldots, x_n, y)$ is a core allocation such that $x_1 < 0$. Then coalition $N \setminus \{1\}$ would rather stand alone to produce y, which economizes $|x_1|$ dollars.

It turns out that the NTU game of a public good economy always has a nonempty core under very mild assumptions on preferences and costs. All we need is a continuous nondecreasing cost function, continuous and monotonic preferences, and some assumption guaranteeing that the agents do not want to produce an infinite amount of public good; a precise statement is given in Section 7.6 (Theorem 7.2), where a particular core allocation is explicitly constructed. In fact, the NTU game in question has a large core because it is convex (Demange [1987]). In order to fully understand this statement, one needs first to generalize the notion of convex games (Definition 5.2) to NTU games. Yet the intuition is clear: When an agent joins an existing coalition, he adds his cost share to the pot, thereby raising the utility of all coalition members. The larger is the existing coalition, the larger the welfare increment when he joins. We give now another intuition of the claim by looking at the quasi-linear case.

Example 7.2. Public good economy with quasi-linear preferences
Consider a public good economy where agent i's utility if he pays x_i to

consume y units of public good is $b_i(y) - x_i$ (we omit the initial endowment of money that plays no role).

Just as the Pareto-optimal allocations obtain by maximizing total surplus $\sum_i b_i - c$, a coalition standing alone will produce this level y maximizing $\sum_{i \in S} b_i - c$. It can then use the cost shares to allocate at will this surplus across agents. In other words, free access to the technology for all coalitions can be modeled as the following *transferable utility* (TU) cooperative game:

$$\text{for all } S \subset \{1, \dots, n\}: \quad v(S) = \max_{y \geq 0} \left\{ \sum_{i \in S} b_i(y) - c(y) \right\} \tag{6}$$

A feasible allocation $(x_1, \dots, x_n, y)$ is then in the core of our TU public good economy if and only if

$$\sum_{i \in S} (b_i(y) - x_i) \geq v(S) \quad \text{for all } S \subset N \tag{7}$$

Note that inequality (7) for $S = N$ means precisely that the level y is efficient (i.e., maximizes total surplus $\sum_{i \in N} b_i - c$).

We check now that the TU game (6) is convex (Definition 5.2), implying that its core is large (Lemma 5.1).

Pick two coalitions S, T with $S \subset T$ and an agent i outside T. We prove inequality (9) in Chapter 5:

$$v(S \cup \{i\}) + v(T) \leq v(S) + v(T \cup \{i\})$$

It is enough to prove, for all $y \geq 0$ and all $z \geq 0$,

$$\left[\left(\sum_S b_j(y) \right) + b_i(y) - c(y) \right] + \left[\left(\sum_T b_j(z) \right) - c(z) \right] \leq v(S) + v(T \cup \{i\})$$

Distinguish two cases. If $y \leq z$, then switch $b_i(y)$ from the left bracket to the right one and use $b_i(y) \leq b_i(z)$. On the other hand, if $z \leq y$, the left term in the preceding inequality is bounded above by

$$\left[\sum_S b_j(y) + b_i(y) - c(y) \right] + \left[\sum_{T \setminus S} b_j(y) + \sum_S b_j(z) - c(z) \right]$$

$$= \left[\sum_{T \cup \{i\}} b_j(y) - c(y) \right] + \left[\sum_S b_j(z) - c(z) \right] \leq v(T \cup \{i\}) + v(S)$$

Example 7.3. A numerical example

The technology has CRS: $c(y) = \frac{3}{2}y$ for all y. There are two agents with quasi-linear preferences:

$$b_1(y) = \log(1 + y), \qquad b_2(y) = 2\sqrt{y}$$

As the surplus function $b_1 + b_2 - c$ is strictly concave, its unique maximum y^* is computed by solving Samuelson's condition (3):

$$\frac{1}{1+y} + \frac{1}{\sqrt{y}} = \frac{3}{2} \Rightarrow y^* = 1$$

The corresponding surplus is

$$v(12) = (b_1 + b_2 - c)(y^*) = 1.19$$

Now compute the surplus that single-agent coalitions can achieve:

$$v(1) = \max_{y \geq 0} \log(1+y) - \frac{3}{2}y = 0, \qquad v(2) = \max_{y \geq 0} 2\sqrt{y} - \frac{3}{2}y = 0.67$$

The core allocations divide arbitrarily the cooperative surplus $v(12) - v(1) - v(2) = 0.53$ between the two agents. At one extreme, agent 1 keeps all the cooperative surplus, implying the following cost shares x_1, x_2:

$$b_1(y^*) - x_1 = 0.53 \Rightarrow x_1 = 0.17$$
$$b_2(y^*) - x_2 = 0.67 \Rightarrow x_2 = 1.33$$

At the other extreme, agent 2 keeps the cooperative surplus, and hence the cost shares (x_1', x_2'):

$$b_1(y^*) - x_1' = 0 \Rightarrow x_1' = 0.69$$
$$b_2(y^*) - x_2' = 1.19 \Rightarrow x_2' = 0.81$$

7.3   The core of the private good economy

In the private good economy (model 2) the definition of the NTU game where all coalitions have free access to the technology is formally identical to Definition 7.1.

Definition 7.2. NTU game of the private good economy.   *Given a coalition $S \subset \{1, \ldots, n\}$, a utility vector $(\bar{u}_i)_{i \in S}$ is feasible for S $[\bar{u}_S \in v(S)]$ if and only if there exist $y_i \geq 0$ and x_i for all $i \in S$ such that*

$$0 \leq x_i \leq \omega_i \text{ for all } i \in S, \quad \sum_{i \in S} x_i = c\left(\sum_{i \in S} y_i\right), \quad \text{and} \quad \bar{u}_i \leq u_i(\omega_i - x_i, y_i)$$

The nonemptyness of the core of this game depends critically upon the returns to scale of the technology.

Consider first the case where the production function has CRS: $c(y) = c \cdot y$, where the fixed number c is the price of 1 bushel of corn in hours of labor. Each agent can then utilize the production process without altering the production opportunities offered to the other agents. The obviously equitable outcome consists of choosing the best production plan for each agent. This amounts to solving n decentralized programs:

$$\max_{0 \le x_i \le \omega_i} u_i\left(\omega_i - x_i, \frac{x_i}{c}\right) \tag{8}$$

Let us denote by x_i^* an optimal solution of program (8) (assume it exists) and by $\gamma_i(c)$ its optimal value [thus, $\gamma_i(c) = u_i(\omega_i - x_i^*, x_i^*/c)$]. The allocation $(x_i^*, y_i^* = x_i^*/c)_{i=1,\dots,n}$ can be called the *noncooperative outcome* because cooperation is pointless in the CRS case. It is a Pareto-optimal allocation (assuming u_i is nondecreasing in leisure and in corn and strictly increasing in at least one).

Example 7.4. Two agents with different productivities
We go back to the model of Example 1.4 and Exercise 1.7 with two agents and a CRS technology transforming 1 hour of standard labor into 1 bushel of corn. The two agents have identical preferences over leisure × corn, identical endowment ω of leisure, but different productivities: Agent i transforms x_i' unit of his labor into $\pi_i x_i'$ units of standard labor, so that a feasible utility vector takes the form

$$(u(\omega - x_1', y_1), u(\omega - x_2', y_2)), \quad \text{where } y_1 + y_2 = \pi_1 x_1' + \pi_2 x_2'$$

This economy is readily transformed into our general model. Simply replace leisure by standard labor $x_i = \pi_i x_i'$ so that the two agents now have different endowments ($\pi_i \omega$ for agent i) and different utility functions:

$$u_i(\pi_i \omega - x_i, y_i) = u((\pi_i \omega - x_i)/\pi_i, y_i)$$

The noncooperative outcome takes equitably into account the differences in productivity: The more productive agent ends up with a higher utility level,

$$\pi_1 \ge \pi_2 \Rightarrow \gamma_1(c) \ge \gamma_2(c)$$

Indeed, denote by x_2^* the optimal amount of standard labor for agent 2:

$$\gamma_2(c) = u_2\left(\pi_2 \cdot \omega - \frac{x_2^*}{c}\right) = u\left(\omega - \frac{x_2^*}{\pi_2}, \frac{x_2^*}{c}\right)$$

If agent 1 supplies x_2^*, he enjoys a higher utility than agent 2; hence,

$$\gamma_2(c) = u\left(\omega - \frac{x_2^*}{\pi_2}, \frac{x_2^*}{c}\right) \le u\left(\omega - \frac{x_2^*}{\pi_1}, \frac{x_2^*}{c}\right) \le \gamma_1(c)$$

This is in contrast with the outcome selected by the classical utilitarian program, where the more productive agent ends up with a lower utility level (see Exercise 1.7). Exercise 7.9 gives more details about the model of Example 7.4. In particular, the two main mechanisms (MP and CRE) are discussed.

Consider the case where the technology for producing the output has IRS: The average cost $c(y)/y$ is decreasing in y. This is the natural monopoly assumption: Joint operation of the technology brings positive externalities, and the core is indeed nonempty under very general circumstances (see Theorem 7.3). As in the public good model, the NTU game is convex (Moulin [1987c]) so that the core is large. We show that the core is nonempty by constructing a particular core allocation (Theorem 7.3).

Example 7.5. An IRS production economy with Cobb–Douglas preferences
We have two agents endowed with one unit of leisure each and with the following utility functions:

$$u_1(1-x_1, y_1) = (1-x_1) \cdot y_1$$
$$u_2(1-x_2, y_2) = (1-x_2) \cdot (y_2)^{1/2}$$

Note that agent 2's marginal rate of substitution for corn relative to leisure $(u_{2y}/u_{2\ell})$ is half that of agent 1. The cost function is $c(y) = \sqrt{y}$. We compute the NTU game attached to this economy. First we assume that a single agent has free access to the technology:

$$\gamma_1(c) = v(1) = \max_{0 \le y_1 \le 1} (1 - \sqrt{y_1}) \cdot y_1 = 0.148$$
$$\gamma_2(c) = v(2) = \max_{0 \le y_2 \le 1} (1 - \sqrt{y_2}) \cdot y_2^{1/2} = 0.25$$

The set $v(12)$ is the utility possibility frontier or the image of the Pareto-optimal allocations. The first-order conditions for efficiency [system (4)] give here

$$\frac{1-x_1}{y_1} = \frac{1-x_2}{2y_2} = \frac{1}{2\sqrt{y}}, \quad \text{where } y = y_1 + y_2 \tag{9}$$

Taking into account $x_1 + x_2 = \sqrt{y}$ implies

$$(1-x_1) + (1-x_2) = 2 - \sqrt{y} \Rightarrow y_1 + 2y_2 = 4\sqrt{y} - 2y$$

Thus, we can express all coordinates of a Pareto-optimal allocation in terms of total output y:

$$y_1 = 4y - 4\sqrt{y}, \qquad y_2 = 4\sqrt{y} - 3y$$
$$1 - x_1 = 2\sqrt{y} - 2, \qquad 1 - x_2 = 4 - 3\sqrt{y} \tag{10}$$

The constraints $y_i \ge 0$, $0 \le x_i \le 1$, limit the range of the parameter $\lambda = \sqrt{y}$:

$$1 \le \lambda \le \tfrac{4}{3} \Leftrightarrow 1 \le y \le \tfrac{16}{9}$$

Thus, the parametric equations of the Pareto-optimal utility vectors are

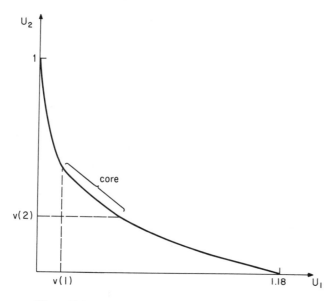

Figure 7.1.

$$u_1 = 8\lambda(\lambda-1)^2, \quad u_2 = \sqrt{\lambda}\cdot(4-3\lambda)^{3/2}, \quad 1 \le \lambda \le \tfrac{4}{3} \tag{11}$$

This curve is drawn in Figure 7.1 along with the utility levels $v(i)$, $i = 1, 2$. Notice that the vector $(v(1), v(2))$ is below the Pareto frontier. The core utility vectors correspond to the parameter values $1.13 \le \lambda \le 1.21$, cutting a large chunk in the Pareto frontier.

We now turn to the case where the technology has DRS $[c(y)/y$ increases with $y]$. This implies that joint operation of the production process brings negative externalities; hence, the free-access-to-technology assumption cannot be sustained because the core is typically *empty*. To see this, consider the utility reached by agent i if he has access, alone, to the technology:

$$\gamma_i(c) = \max u_i(\omega_i - c(y_i), y_i)$$

where the maximum bears upon all $y_i \ge 0$ such that $c(y_i) \le \omega_i$. Decreasing returns to scale generally preclude the vector $(\gamma_1(c), \ldots, \gamma_n(c))$ from being feasible by the grand coalition, as illustrated by our next numerical example.

Example 7.6. A DRS production economy with Cobb–Douglas preferences

We have the same agents as in Example 7.5 but a different cost function: $c(y) = y^2$. Compute first the numbers $v(i)$:

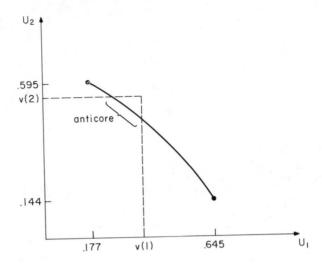

Figure 7.2.

$$\gamma_1(c) = v(1) = \max_{0 \le y_1 \le 1} (1-y_1^2) \cdot y_1 = 3.85$$

$$\gamma_2(c) = v(2) = \max_{0 \le y_1 \le 1} (1-y_2^2) \cdot y_2^{1/2} = 0.535$$

Then proceed as in Example 7.5 to find a parametric representation of the Pareto frontier. The first-order system (9) is

$$\frac{1-x_1}{y_1} = \frac{1-x_2}{2y_2} = 2y$$

and

$$(1-x_1)+(1-x_2) = 2-y^2 \Rightarrow y_1+2y_2 = \frac{1}{y} - \frac{y}{2}$$

Thus,

$$y_1 = \frac{5}{2} - \frac{1}{y}, \quad y_2 = \frac{1}{y} - \frac{3}{2}y, \quad 1-x_i = 5y^2-2, \quad 1-x_2 = 4-6y^2$$

Hence, the equations of the Pareto frontier in terms of the parameter $\lambda = y$ are

$$u_1 = \frac{(5\lambda^2-2)^2}{2\lambda}, \quad u_2 = \left\{ \frac{2}{\lambda} \cdot (2-3\lambda^2)^3 \right\}^{1/2}, \quad 0.707 \le \lambda \le 0.775 \tag{12}$$

Figure 7.2 shows the set $v(12)$ and the vector $(v(1), v(2))$ outside this set.

Thus, in the DRS case, the NTU game of Definition 7.2 is not even superadditive: If each individual agent has free access to the technology, they have no incentive to cooperate. Since we assume that they must operate jointly a single production process, cooperation can be perceived as a burden to share, in the vein of the deficit-sharing problems of the previous chapter (see Example 6.4). In this interpretation, the coalitional utility sets of Definition 7.2 can be used as *upper* bounds to coalitional utility vectors: We look for a Pareto-optimal utility vector such that every subcoalition can achieve the corresponding utility levels (and more) if it is given free access to the technology. This means that each coalition contributes something to cover the loss imposed by monopolistic production. In a two-person economy this corresponds to Pareto-optimal utility vectors where each agent gets no more than his payoff $v(i)$. Figure 7.2 shows this region for the numerical Example 7.6.

The concept of *anticore* introduced in Moulin [1987c] provides a rigorous formulation of this idea; it yields a nonempty subset of efficient allocation if the technology has DRS and agents' preferences are convex (see Exercise 7.7).

7.4   Marginal pricing in the public good economy

We start with the public good model. The analog of a competitive pricing system in a public good production economy is the system of personalized prices for the public good called Lindahl prices. Each agent i faces a different price p_i for the public good; the "market clears" if (i) each agent purchases the same level of public good and (ii) the sum of individual payments exactly covers the cost of producing this level. We illustrate these conditions on our previous numerical example.

Example 7.3 (continued)
In the numerical Example 7.3 we pick a pair of nonnegative prices p_1, p_2 and compute the corresponding demands of public good. Agent 1 solves the following program:

$$\max_{y \geq 0} \log(1+y) - p_1 y \Rightarrow y = \frac{1}{p_1} - 1$$

Agent 2 solves

$$\max_{y \geq 0} 2\sqrt{y} - p_2 y \Rightarrow y = \frac{1}{p_2^2}$$

Therefore, the two conditions stated in the preceding (equal demands and budget balance) amount to

$$\frac{1}{p_1} - 1 = \frac{1}{p_2^2} \quad \text{and} \quad p_1 + p_2 = \frac{3}{2}$$

with unique nonnegative solution $p_1 = \frac{1}{2}$, $p_2 = 1$. The corresponding cost shares are $x_1 = 0.5$, $x_2 = 1$, with associated utility vector

$$b_1(y^*) - x_1 = 0.20, \qquad b_2(y^*) - x_2 = 1$$

Thus, agent 1 keeps 38 percent of the cooperative surplus, and agent 2 gets the remaining 62 percent.

The general definition of a Lindahl price system is easily stated if the technology has CRS $[c(y) = c \cdot y$ for all $y]$. Then we call $(p_1, \ldots, p_n; y^*)$ a Lindahl equilibrium if the following conditions hold:

$$\text{for all } i = 1, \ldots, n: \quad u_i(\omega_i - p_i \cdot y^*, y^*) = \max_{y \geq 0} u_i(\omega_i - p_i y, y)$$

$$\text{and } \sum_{i=1}^{n} p_i = c$$

The first condition says that all agents demand the same amount of public good and the second condition that its cost is exactly covered. With an arbitrary technology we adapt this definition into that of a ratio equilibrium (RE) (Kaneko [1977]). Each agent is assigned a fixed proportion of the actual cost of producing the good (his ratio). Thus, if agent i's ratio is $r_i \geq 0$, he must pay $r_i c(y)$ for the level y of the public good. A RE is a $(n+1)$-tuple $(r_1, \ldots, r_n; y^*)$ such that (i) every agent demands the same level y^* given his ratio and (ii) the ratios add to 1:

$$\text{for all } i = 1, \ldots, n: \quad u_i(\omega_i - r_i \cdot c(y^*), y^*) = \max_{y \geq 0} u_i(\omega_i - r_i c(y), y) \qquad (13)$$

$$r_i \geq 0 \quad \text{for all } i \quad \text{and} \quad \sum_{i=1}^{n} r_i = 1 \qquad (14)$$

Theorem 7.1 (Foley [1970], Kaneko [1977]). *Given is a public good economy* $(u_1, \ldots, u_n, \omega_1, \ldots, \omega_n, c)$. *Suppose that the agents' preferences are strictly increasing in the private good. Then a ratio equilibrium* $(r_1, \ldots, r_n;$ $y^*)$ *yields an allocation* $[x_i = r_i - c(y^*)$ *for all* $i]$ *in the core of the NTU game (Definition 7.1).*

Proof: Suppose, to the contrary, that a coalition S, $S \subset N$, can object against the RE $(r_1, \ldots, r_n; y^*)$. For some $y \geq 0$ and some $x_i \geq 0$, $i \in S$, we have

$$u_i(\omega_i - x_i, y) \geq u_i(\omega_i - r_i \cdot c(y^*), y^*) \quad \text{for all } i \in S$$

with at least one strict inequality and $\sum_{i \in S} x_i = c(y)$. From (13) we deduce

$$u_i(\omega_i - x_i, y) \geq u_i(\omega_i - r_i \cdot c(y), y) \quad \text{for all } i \in S \qquad (15)$$

One of these inequalities must be strict, say, for $i = 1$, implying $x_1 < r_1 \cdot c(y)$. Taking (14) into account, we get

$$\sum_{i \in S} r_i \cdot c(y) \leq c(y) = \sum_{i \in S} x_i \quad \text{and} \quad x_1 < r_1 \cdot c(y)$$

Thus, for some $j \in S$ we have $r_j \cdot c(y) < x_j$, and hence a contradiction of (15) since u_i is strictly increasing in the private good.   Q.E.D.

The RE passes the stand-alone test. Its existence is guaranteed when the cost function is convex (implying DRS) and the agents' preferences are convex (the utility functions are quasi-concave); see Kaneko [1977]. In this case the first-order optimality conditions of the programs (13) read

$$\frac{u_{iy}}{u_{ix}} = r_i \cdot c'(y^*) \quad \text{for all } i = 1, \ldots, n \tag{16}$$

Therefore, the vector of ratios is parallel to the vector of marginal rates of substitution between private and public goods. Note that by summing the preceding equations, we get Samuelson's condition (3).

Viewed as a mechanism to share the cost of a public good, the RE has a lot of appeal. It relies on a meaningful proportionality rule [system (16)] and yields a core allocation. Its main defect is that it may fail to exist when returns to scale are increasing and/or individual preferences are not convex. Exercise 7.3 gives an example.

Remark 7.1: The RE is not the only concept generalizing Lindahl equilibrium to arbitrary cost functions. Another familiar possibility is to use a two-part tariff; all agents get a fixed (positive or negative) monetary transfer (the same for every agent); each agent also pays a personalized price p_i per unit of the public good. An equilibrium occurs if they all demand the same quantity of public good, and the total revenue from the agent covers the cost of production. We give the precise definition in Exercise 7.5, where we show also that this equilibrium may not pass the stand-alone test (we give a DRS example *and* an IRS example). The idea of two-part tariffs is the key to the MP equilibrium of the private good regulated monopoly.

7.5   Marginal pricing in the private good economy

For a CRS technology the noncooperative outcome (see Section 7.3) results by quoting the true price of production. In the case of an arbitrary technology, MP seeks to imitate the CRS case by quoting a single well-chosen price (the same for every agent) generating an efficient allocation. This generally leaves the "firm" with some surplus or deficit (the revenues from the agents do not balance the cost of production). To obviate this problem, we distribute uniformly this surplus or deficit as a lump-sum transfer of private good. Thus, we look for a two-part tariff at which the individual demands sum to an efficient allocation.

Definition 7.3.   *In the corn labor economy $E = (u_1, \ldots, u_n, \omega_1, \ldots, \omega_n; c)$ consider a pair (p, t), where p is the (nonnegative) unit price of corn relative to labor and t is a fixed quantity of corn (positive or negative).*

*We say that the allocation (x^*, y^*) is a **marginal pricing equilibrium** at (p, t) if it satisfies two properties:*

(a)   *It is feasible [(2)] and Pareto optimal in the economy E.*
(b)   *For all agents $i = 1, \ldots, n$ we have $x_i^* = p \cdot (y_i^* - t)$ and*

$$u_i(\omega_i - x_i^*, y_i^*) = \max_{\substack{0 \le x_i \le \omega_i, \, 0 \le y_i \\ x_i = p \cdot (y_i - t)}} u_i(\omega_i - x_i, y_i) \tag{17}$$

This definition resembles that of an Arrow–Debreu competitive equilibrium in a production economy where each agent owns an equal share of the firm. The difference is that the firm does not necessarily maximize its profit. Thus, we must impose the efficiency condition *a*.

Still, the MP equilibrium shares the basic decentralizability property of the competitive equilibrium: Each agent chooses his allocation independently from the (two-part) price signal. We illustrate Definition 7.3 for our two earlier numerical examples.

Example 7.5. An IRS production economy with Cobb–Douglas preferences (continued)
The first-order optimality conditions of program (17) read $u_{iy}/u_{ix} = p$; hence, in this numerical example

$$\frac{1 - x_1}{y_1} = \frac{1 - x_2}{2y_2} = p \tag{18}$$

Comparing this with the efficiency conditions (9), we get $p = \frac{1}{2}\sqrt{y}$. Finally, the MP equilibrium satisfies

$$(1 - x_1) + py_1 = (1 - x_2) + py_2$$

In this last equation all variables can now be expressed in terms of y [by (10)]:

$$(2\sqrt{y} - 2) + \frac{1}{2\sqrt{y}}(4y - 4\sqrt{y}) = 4 - 3\sqrt{y} + \frac{1}{2\sqrt{y}}(4\sqrt{y} - 3y)$$

This yields $\sqrt{y} = \frac{20}{17}$, or $y = 1.38$, and the following MP equilibrium:

$$y_1 = 0.83, \quad y_2 = 0.55, \quad 1 - x_1 = 0.35, \quad 1 - x_2 = 0.47$$
$$u_1 = 0.293, \quad u_2 = 0.35$$

Note that this allocation is in the core of the economy (but this is not a general property, as illustrated by Example 7.7). Notice also that the transfer $t = y_i - x_i/p$ is negative ($t = -0.70$) so each agent must buy the right to exchange labor for corn at the advantageous price $p = 0.425$.

*Example 7.6. A DRS productive economy with Cobb–Douglas
preferences* (continued)
As in the previous example, a straightforward computation yields the MP
equilibrium

$$\frac{1-x_1}{y_1} = \frac{1-x_2}{2y_2} = p = 2y \quad \text{and} \quad (1-x_1)+py_1=(1-x_2)+py_2$$
$$\Rightarrow y = 0.725$$

so that

$$y_1 = 0.43, \quad y_2 = 0.295, \quad 1-x_1 = 0.63, \quad 1-x_2 = 0.85$$
$$u_1 = 0.272, \quad u_2 = 0.457$$

This time the lump-sum transfer $t = y_i - x_i/p$ is positive ($t = 0.30$). Each
agent is subsidized but has to purchase corn from labor at the high price
$p = 2.9$.

   In fact, the MP equilibrium may fail the stand-alone test even when
the core is nonempty. This can be viewed on a simple two-person economy with an IRS technology.

Example 7.7. Where the MP equilibrium is outside the core
The two agents have the same Cobb–Douglas preferences and differ by
their endowment of labor,

$$\omega_1 = 6, \quad \omega_2 = 2, \quad u_i(\omega_i - x_i, y_i) = (\omega_i - x_i) \cdot y_i$$

The cost function is

$$c(y) = \begin{cases} 2y & \text{if } 0 \le y \le 2 \\ y+2 & \text{if } 2 \le y \end{cases}$$

Thus, average costs are nonincreasing. Consider the budget constraint
$x_i = y_i + 1$ (each agent pays one unit of labor and exchanges one-to-one additional labor for corn). The corresponding demands of the agents solve
the programs (s.t. = subject to):

$$\max_{\text{s.t. } x_1 = y_1+1, 0 \le x_1 \le 6} (6-x_1) \cdot y_1 \Rightarrow (\bar{x}_1, \bar{y}_1) = (3.5, 2.5)$$

$$\max_{\text{s.t. } x_2 = y_2+1, 0 \le x_2 \le 2} (2-x_2) \cdot y_2 \Rightarrow (\bar{x}_2, \bar{y}_2) = (1.5, 0.5)$$

Note that the corresponding allocation is efficient since $x_1+x_2 = c(y_1+y_2)$,
and the marginal rates of substitution are both equal to marginal cost.
Therefore, it is a MP equilibrium. The careful reader will check that there
is no other such equilibrium.

Check next that this allocation is not in the core. If he runs the technology alone, agent 2 reaches the utility level 0.5 (by producing 0.5 unit of corn),

$$\max_{\text{s.t. } x_2 = c(y_2)} u_2(\omega_2 - x_2, y_2) = \max_{0 \le y_2 \le 1} (2 - 2y_2) \cdot y_2 = 0.5$$

Thus, agent 2 prefers standing alone to the MP since $u_2(\omega_2 - \bar{x}_2, \bar{y}_2) = 0.25$.

In the case of a DRS technology, it can similarly be shown that the MP equilibrium may be outside the anticore: Some agents end up doing better than they would by having free access to the technology (see Exercise 7.7).

In the next section we discuss a fairly different mechanism of an egalitarian inspiration that invariably picks an allocation in the core (case of an IRS technology) or in the anticore (case of a DRS technology) of the private good economy.

7.6   Two welfare egalitarian core selections

We start with a public good economy (model 1). The idea behind the egalitarian equivalent (EE) mechanism is to pick a particular utility function to represent these preferences and to equalize utilities across agents.

Specifically, we use the public good as a *numéraire* to measure utilities. Thus, the utility of agent i for the allocation $(\omega_i - x_i, y)$ is the level of the public good w_i such that he is indifferent between this allocation and (ω_i, w_i) (i.e., consuming w_i units of public good for free). Formally, we define the function $w_i(\cdot, \cdot)$ as follows:

$$w_i(\omega_i - x_i, y) = \alpha \Leftrightarrow u_i(\omega_i - x_i, y) = u_i(\omega_i, \alpha)$$

This property defines w_i if u_i is continuous and strictly increasing in the public good and if $u_i(\omega_i - x_i, y_i) \ge u_i(\omega_i, 0)$. An *egalitarian equivalent* allocation is an efficient allocation equalizing the utilities w_i. Formally, denote by $v(N)$ the set of feasible utility vectors of the public good economy (Definition 7.1). Then we define the EE level $\bar{y}$ of public good as the highest level of public good such that consuming this amount of public good at no cost (an unfeasible allocation) yields nevertheless a feasible utility vector

$$\bar{y} = \sup\{y \ge 0 \mid (u_i(\omega_i, y))_{i=1,\dots,n} \in v(N)\}$$

An EE allocation is any feasible allocation achieving the utility vector $(u_i(\omega_i, \bar{y}))_{i=1,\dots,n}$.

Of course, some topological assumptions on preferences and the cost function are necessary to guarantee the existence of this allocation. It is essentially enough that preferences be monotonic in both goods and continuous, and that the cost function be monotonic and continuous (see Moulin [1987b] for details).

Consider the case where agents have quasi-linear preferences, as in Example 7.1. Call y^* the efficient level of public good, maximizing the surplus $[\sum_{i=1}^{n} b_i(y) - c(y)]$ (suppose, for simplicity, that y^* is unique). Then the utility vector $(u_i(\omega_i, y))_i$ is feasible if and only if

$$\sum_{i=1}^{n} b_i(y) \le \sum_{i=1}^{n} b_i(y^*) - c(y^*)$$

Thus, the EE level $\bar{y}$ solves the equation

$$\sum_{i=1}^{n} b_i(\bar{y}) = \sum_{i=1}^{n} b_i(y^*) - c(y^*) \tag{19}$$

Next the EE cost sharing of y^* is defined as

$$b_i(y^*) - x_i = b_i(\bar{y}) \Rightarrow x_i = b_i(y^*) - b_i(\bar{y}) \quad \text{for all } i \tag{20}$$

We illustrate these formulas by an example.

Example 7.3 (continued)
In the numerical example, the efficient level of public good is $y^* = 1$. We find the EE level by solving (19):

$$\log(1+\bar{y}) + 2\sqrt{\bar{y}} = \log 2 + 2 - \tfrac{3}{2} = 1.19 \Rightarrow \bar{y} = 0.24$$

and hence the cost shares are

$$x_1 = \log 2 - \log(1.24) = 0.48, \qquad x_2 = 2\sqrt{1} - 2\sqrt{0.24} = 1.02$$

whereby player 1 keeps 42 percent of the surplus (measured with the private good for *numéraire*) and player 2 keeps 58 percent. Compare with the Lindahl allocation (see Section 7.4) giving 38 percent of the surplus to player 1. The difference is fairly small!

Theorem 7.2 (Mas-Colell [1980], Moulin [1987b]). *Suppose that the agents' preferences are strictly increasing in the private good. Then an EE allocation is in the core of the public good economy.*

Proof: The proof starts by showing that if $(x_1, \ldots, x_n, y)$ is an EE allocation and $\bar{y}$ is the EE level of public good, we have

$$u_i(\omega_i - x_i, y) = u_i(\omega_i, \bar{y}) \quad \text{for all } i$$

This implies in particular that all EE allocations yield the same utility vector and that all are Pareto optimal. Next suppose that our EE allocation is not in the core: Some coalition T can find $(x_i', i \in T; y')$ such that

$$c(y') = \sum_{i \in T} x_i' \quad \text{and} \quad u_i(\omega_i - x_i, y) \le u_i(\omega_i - x_i', y') \quad \text{for all } i \in T \quad (21)$$

with at least one strict inequality.

Consider the feasible allocation $(x_1', \dots, x_n'; y')$, where $x_i' = 0$ for all $i \in N \setminus T$. Note that the inequality $\bar{y} \le y'$ implies

$$u_i(\omega_i - x_i, y) = u_i(\omega_i, \bar{y}) \le u_i(\omega_i - x_i', y') \quad \text{for all } i \in N \setminus T$$

whereas

$$u_i(\omega_i - x_i, y) \le u_i(\omega_i - x_i', y') \quad \text{for all } i \in T$$

Since at least one of the latter inequalities is strict, we derive a contradiction from the Pareto optimality of $(x_1, \dots, x_n; y)$. Thus, we must have $y' < \bar{y}$, and the inequalities (21) imply

$$u_i(\omega_i, \bar{y}) = u_i(\omega_i - x_i, y) \le u_i(\omega_i - x_i', y') \le u_i(\omega_i - x_i', \bar{y}) \quad \text{for all } i \in T$$

This in turn implies $x_i' \le 0$ for all $i \in T$ so that feasibility (21) requires $x_i' = 0$ for all $i \in T$. Hence,

$$u_i(\omega_i - x_i', y') = u_i(\omega_i, y') \le u_i(\omega_i, \bar{y}) = u_i(\omega_i - x_i, y)$$

and all inequalities in (21) are actually equalities, which is the desired contradiction.   Q.E.D.

Together, Theorems 7.1 and 7.2 provide two systematical core selections for the public good economy, namely, the RE and the EE allocation. The latter even admits a compact axiomatic characterization discussed in Section 7.7. A few numerical tests will convince the reader that these two mechanisms are often close to each other, as in Example 7.3 (see also Exercise 7.2).

We turn now to the welfare egalitarian core selection of the private good economy. The trick, again, is to choose a clever *numéraire* to represent the agents' preferences.

For a given positive price p consider the CRS technology $c(y) = p \cdot y$ and denote by $\gamma_i(p)$ the utility achieved by agent i in the corresponding noncooperative outcome (see Section 7.3):

$$\gamma_i(p) = \max_{0 \le x_i \le \omega_i} u_i\left(\omega_i - x_i, \frac{x_i}{p}\right)$$

The function γ_i depends upon agent i's utility function only, so the utility path $\gamma(p) = (\gamma_1(p), \dots, \gamma_n(p))$ depends on the utility profile only. Moreover, $\gamma_i(p)$ is decreasing in p for all i, and for large p it converges toward $u_i(\omega_i, 0)$.

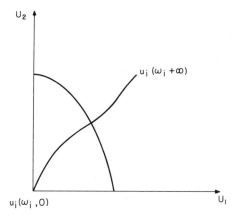

Figure 7.3.

For a given arbitrary cost function c we look for the highest feasible utility vector along this path. Such a vector exists because for $p = 0$ the vector $\gamma(0) = (u_i(\omega_i, +\infty))_i$ is unfeasible, whereas for $p = +\infty$ the vector $\gamma(+\infty) = (u_i(\omega_i, 0))_i$ is feasible. The highest feasible utility vector on this path is thus Pareto optimal; see Figure 7.3 or Moulin [1987c] for details.

As in the public good case, denote by $v(N)$ the set of feasible utility vectors in the public good economy. The *constant-returns equivalent price* is the lowest price such that $\gamma(p)$ is feasible:

$$\bar{p} = \inf\{p \geq 0 \mid \gamma(p) \in v(N)\}$$

A *CRE allocation* is any feasible allocation achieving the utility vector $\gamma(\bar{p})$. The CRE mechanism amounts to equalizing utilities if we choose to represent preferences by the following *disutility* function w_i:

$$w_i(\omega_i - x_i, y_i) = p \Leftrightarrow \gamma_i(p) = u_i(\omega_i - x_i, y_i)$$

In words, agent i derives p units of disutility from an allocation if he is indifferent between this allocation and the opportunity to buy corn at price p (relative to labor).

As discussed earlier, a CRE allocation is indeed Pareto optimal (under the assumptions of Theorem 7.3).

Examples 7.5 and 7.6 (continued)
We compute the CRE price and allocation for the two economies of Example 7.5 (IRS case) and 7.6 (DRS case). Compute first the functions $\gamma_i(p)$, $i = 1, 2$,

$$\gamma_1(p) = \max_{0 \le x_1 \le 1} (1-x_1) \cdot \frac{x_1}{p} = \frac{1}{4p}$$

$$\gamma_2(p) = \max_{0 \le x_2 \le 1} (1-x_2) \cdot \left(\frac{x_2}{p}\right)^{1/2} = \frac{2\sqrt{3}}{9} \cdot \frac{1}{(p)^{1/2}}$$

A utility vector on the path $\gamma(p)$ satisfies

$$4\gamma_1 = \tfrac{27}{4}\gamma_2^2 \tag{22}$$

The IRS Case: Using the parametric representation of the Pareto-optimal utility vectors [(11)], we get the equation

$$4 \cdot 8\lambda(\lambda-1)^2 = \frac{27}{4} \cdot \lambda(4-3\lambda)^3 \Leftrightarrow \frac{(4-3\lambda)^3}{(\lambda-1)^2} = 4.74$$

where the unknown is $\lambda = \sqrt{y}$. The solution of this equation is $\lambda = 1.165$ or $y = 1.36$ with corresponding allocation

$$y_1 = 0.77, \quad y_2 = 0.59, \quad 1-x_1 = 0.33, \quad 1-x_2 = 0.505$$
$$u_1 = 0.254, \quad u_2 = 0.387$$

This is fairly close to the MP equilibrium (less than 10 percent variation in any variable).

The DRS Case: This time the parametric representation of the Pareto utility vectors is given by (12). Its intersection with the curve (22) brings the equation

$$4 \cdot \frac{(5\lambda^2-2)^2}{2\lambda} = \frac{27}{4} \cdot \frac{2}{\lambda}(2-3\lambda^2)^3 \Leftrightarrow \frac{(2-3\lambda^2)^3}{(5\lambda^2-2)^2} = 0.148$$

with solution $\lambda^2 = 0.532$ or $\lambda = y = 0.729$. The corresponding allocation is

$$y_1 = 0.450, \quad y_2 = 0.279, \quad 1-x_1 = 0.657, \quad 1-x_2 = 0.811$$
$$u_1 = 0.296, \quad u_2 = 0.428$$

Again, this comes close to the MP equilibrium (the allocation varies by less than 5 percent).

Despite the fact that CRE and MP allocations are often numerically close, there is an important conceptual difference. As we saw earlier, the latter may fail to be in the core of the economy when returns to scale are increasing (see Example 7.7), but the former always lies in the core.

Theorem 7.3 (Mas-Colell [1980], Moulin [1987c]).   *Suppose that preferences are continuous, strictly increasing in labor, and nonincreasing in corn. Suppose that the cost function is continuous and nondecreasing and* *that the average cost $c(y)/y$ is nonincreasing in y (IRS). Then a CRE allocation belongs to the core of the economy. In particular, the core is nonempty.*

The proof of Theorem 7.3 is outlined in Exercise 7.8.

Remark 7.2:   The preceding result is the simplest result of nonemptyness of the core in a production economy with increasing returns. The two restrictive assumptions here are (1) that inputs cannot be transferred among agents and (2) that a single input is transformed into a single output. Neither of these two assumptions is easily relaxed. Scarf [1986] shows that with transferable inputs, nonconstant returns to scale can always bring about an empty core. In the case of multiple outputs (and a single nontransferable input), supportability of the cost function (Definition 5.4) is not sufficient for a nonempty core, even with convex preferences (see Exercise 4.5). Sharkey [1979] provides some fairly strong sufficient conditions for nonemptyness, such as convexity of preferences *plus* quasiconvexity of costs *plus* ray-increasing returns to scale (ray-IRS).

7.7   Technological monotonicity

An appealing property of the two core selections discussed in Section 7.6 is that they do respond monotonically to changes in cost conditions. The *technological monotonicity* axiom says that all agents should benefit as a result of an improvement in the production function (expansion of the production set). In other words, technical progress should be unanimously desired.

We view the TM axiom as a normative consequence of public ownership of the technology. If we own jointly some asset, then none of us should suffer a utility loss if this asset becomes objectively more valuable. The TM axiom is very similar to the issue monotonicity axiom of axiomatic bargaining (Definition 3.3). In fact, both the EE mechanism (public good case) and the CRE mechanism (private good case) are special instances of path-monotone social choice functions (Exercise 3.4) and therefore satisfy the TM axiom. Each mechanism works by drawing a utility path depending upon the utility profile only. For any choice of the cost function, the intersection of the feasible utility set with the fixed utility path determines the final utility vector. When the cost function decreases from c_1 to c_2 [in the sense $c_2(y) \le c_1(y)$ for all y], the feasible utility set expands from $v_1(N)$ to $v_2(N)$ and hence the final utility of every agent increases too (see Figure 7.4).

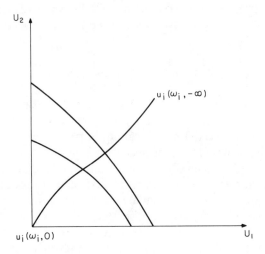

Figure 7.4.

We check now that other mechanisms such as Kaneko's RE (public good case) or the MP equilibrium (private good case) do *not* satisfy TM. We construct an explicit example in a two-person public good economy with the following quasi-linear preferences:

$$b_1(y) = 2\sqrt{y}, \qquad b_2(y) = \min\{18 \cdot \sqrt{y}, (0.1)y + 18\}$$

The idea is to pick a cost function c_1 such that the efficient level of public good is $y_1^* = 1$, whereas the smaller cost function c_2 yields the efficient level of public good $y_2^* = 1.23$. The RE shares cost proportionally to $b_1'(y), b_2'(y)$. At $y_1^* = 1$, this means 10 percent of the cost to agent 1 [since $b_2(y) = 18 \cdot \sqrt{y}$ in the neighborhood of $y = 1$], but at $y_2^* = 1.23$, agent 1 must pay 90 percent of the cost [since $b_2(y) = (0.1)y + 18$ in the neighborhood of $y = \frac{100}{81}$]. The net result is a utility loss for agent 1. Specifically, consider the following cost functions:

$$c_1(y) = \max\{y, 10y - 8\} \geq c_2(y) = y \quad \text{for all } y$$

Check that $y_1^* = 1$ is the efficient level in the economy (b_1, b_2, c_1) with corresponding RE:

$$\frac{b_1'(1)}{b_2'(1)} = \frac{1}{9}, \quad c_1(1) = 2 \;\Rightarrow\; x_1 = 0.2 \text{ and } u_1 = b_1(y_1^*) - x_1 = 1.8$$

Next $y_2^* = \frac{100}{81} = 1.23$ is the efficient level in the economy (b_1, b_2, c_2) with corresponding RE:

$$\frac{b_1'(1.23)}{b_2'(1.23)} = 9, \quad c_2(1.23) = 1.23 \quad \Rightarrow \quad x_1' = 1.11 \text{ and } u_2 = b_1(y_2^*) - x_1' = 1.11$$

Thus, agent 1's utility decreases as a result of a technological improvement, so the RE violates TM, as was to be proved.

A similar example can be constructed to show that the MP mechanism violates TM as well.

The TM axiom is the key to the axiomatic characterization of the EE and CRE mechanisms. The general characterization of issue monotonicity in the axiomatic bargaining context can be adapted to production economies: Any Pareto-optimal mechanism satisfying TM works by seeking the highest feasible utility vector along a fixed monotone utility path (Moulin [1987c]). In other words, it equalizes some cardinal utilities representing the agents' preferences.

If we combine TM with the core property in a public good economy (with fixed preference profile and variable cost functions), the EE mechanism is uniquely characterized (Moulin [1987b]). If we combine TM with the core property in a private good economy with IRS (fixed preference profile; cost function varying in the IRS domain), the CRE mechanism uniquely emerges (Moulin [1987c]).

To conclude, the EE and CRE mechanisms do share better global properties than the RE and MP equilibria, respectively. First, EE and CRE are always defined, whereas RE and MP may not exist under nonconvex preferences. Second, EE and CRE invariably pass the stand-alone test, whereas RE and MP may not. Finally, EE and CRE are technologically monotonic, contrary to RE and MP.

On the other hand, the RE and MP allocations can be computed using marginal data only, whereas EE and CRE require global knowledge of preferences and costs. Equivalently, RE and MP decentralize the allocation problem into n individual utility maximization problems.

EXERCISES

The first five exercises bear on the public good model, the last four on the private good model.

7.1 Some numerical examples of the public good model. These are public good economies with quasi-linear preferences (Examples 7.1 and 7.2).

(a) In our first example the technology for producing the public good has CRS: $c(y) = 2y$. There are two agents who derive the following benefits from consuming the public good:

$$b_1(y) = y, \qquad b_2(y) = 2\sqrt{y}$$

Compute the TU cooperative game (6) and deduce the set of core utility vectors.

Compute the Lindahl equilibrium (note that the demand function of agent 1 is discontinuous at $p_1 = 1$). What are the corresponding shares of the cooperative surplus $v(12) - v(1) - v(2)$? Compute the EE level of public good and the EE allocation. Check that it is more advantageous to agent 1 than the Lindahl equilibrium.

(b)   In our second example we have three agents deriving the following benefits from the public good:

$$b_1(y) = \tfrac{12}{5} \log(1+y), \qquad b_2(y) = b_3(y) = \tfrac{6}{5} y$$

The technology has DRS:

$$c(y) = \tfrac{1}{2} y^2 \quad \text{for all } y \geq 0$$

Compute the TU game (16) and its symmetrical core allocations where agent 2 and 3 pay the same cost share. Compute the cost share corresponding to the Shapley value and to the nucleolus of game (6). Compute the EE and the RE cost shares. Locate the four cost-sharing vectors in the interval comprising the symmetrical core allocations.

7.2   Proportional benefit functions. Consider a public good economy where all agents have quasi-linear preferences and moreover their benefit functions are proportional; there is some nonnegative function $b(y)$ and positive coefficients $\beta_i > 0$, $i = 1, \ldots, n$, such that

$$b_i(y) = \beta_i \cdot b(y) \quad \text{for all } i = 1, \ldots, n \text{ and all } y \geq 0$$

Assume that there is a unique efficient level y^* of the public good.

Show that there is a unique RE and that it coincides with the EE allocation. Compute explicitly the corresponding cost-sharing vector.

7.3   Where no RE exists. Consider the IRS technology $c(y) = \tfrac{3}{2} \cdot \sqrt{y}$ and two quasi-linear preferences

$$b_1(y) = \min\{y, 1\}, \qquad b_2(y) = \min\{y, 2\}$$

Check that the efficient level of public good is $y^* = 2$ and that the only ratio at which agent 1 demands y^* is $r_1 = 0$. Deduce that no RE exists.

7.4   Value and technological monotonicity. In a public good economy with quasi-linear preferences, we can represent coalitional opportunities by the TU game (6). Applying a value operator such as the Shapley value or the nucleolus to this game yields an allocation in the core [since the game (6) is convex]. A numerical example is given in Exercise 7.1, question (b). We will show that both of these two mechanisms violate TM.

Consider the two-person economy

$$b_1(y) = \tfrac{3}{2} y, \quad b_2(y) = \min\{y, 1\}, \quad c(y) = 0 \text{ if } y \leq 1, \quad c(y) = (y-1)^2 \text{ if } y \geq 1$$

Both value operators split equally the cooperative surplus. Compute the corresponding utility vector.

Next suppose the cost function increases to $c'(y) = \max\{y/2, c(x)\}$. Compute the new value allocation and check that TM is violated.

7.5 Lindahl prices with lump-sum transfers. This exercise elaborates on Remark 7.1. Consider a public good economy (model 1) with an arbitrary cost function. We look for a two-part tariff where each agent faces a personalized price p_i and receives a lump-sum transfer t of private good (the same for every agent). Thus, each agent solves the program

$$\max_{y \geq 0} u_i(\omega_i - p_i \cdot y + t, y)$$

A (generalized) Lindahl equilibrium is an $(n+1)$-tuple $(p_1, \ldots, p_n; t)$ such that (i) each agent demands the same level y^* of public good, (ii) the payments exactly cover the cost $[\sum_i p_i y^* - nt = c(y^*)]$, and (iii) the firm's profit $\sum_i p_i y - nt - c(y)$ is maximal at y^*.

(a) Check that this definition brings an efficient allocation.
(b) Compute the generalized Lindahl equilibrium in the two following two-agent economies with quasi-linear preferences:

DRS example: $b_1(y) = (0.8)y$, $b_2(y) = (0.2)y$, $c(y) = \frac{1}{2}y^2$

IRS example: $b_1(y) = \min\{9y, 36\}$, $b_2(y) = \min\{y, 4\}$, $c(y) = 10\sqrt{y}$

In the IRS example, note that at the optimal level 4, there is a continuum of Lindahl price vectors (p_1, p_2, t), all solutions of the system

$$0 \leq p_1 \leq 9, \quad 0 \leq p_2 \leq 1, \quad p_1 + p_2 = \frac{5}{2}, \quad t = 2(p_1 + p_2) - 10$$

Hence, we have a continuum of generalized Lindahl equilibria.

(c) In each of the preceding examples, show that the generalized Lindahl allocation is *not* in the core of the economy. In the IRS example, this means that one agent prefers standing alone to any of the Lindahl equilibrium allocations.

7.6 Private good economy with identical Cobb–Douglas preferences. In this corn labor economy, all agents have the same preferences:

$$u_i(\omega_i - x_i, y_i) = (\omega_i - x_i) \cdot y_i \quad \text{for all } i$$

They differ in endowments only. The technology has DRS: $c(y) = y^2$.

(a) Check that the MP equilibrium yields the following allocation:

$$x_i = \frac{\omega_i}{2} - \frac{1}{6n} \cdot \omega_N, \quad y_i = \frac{\sqrt{3}}{4}\left(\frac{\omega_i}{\sqrt{\omega_N}} + \frac{1}{3n}\sqrt{\omega_N}\right)$$

where we denote $\omega_N = \sum_{i=1}^{n} \omega_i$.

(b) Check that the CRE allocation is

$$x_i = \frac{1}{3}\omega_i, \quad y_i = \frac{\omega_i}{\sqrt{3\omega_N}}$$

7.7 The anticore (Moulin [1987c]). In the private good economy (model 2) we say that a feasible allocation is in the *anticore* if (i) it is Pareto optimal and (ii) its utility vector $(u_1, \ldots, u_n)$ is such that for every proper coalition $S \subsetneqq N$, there is a utility vector $(\bar{u}_i)_{i \in S}$ feasible for S (Definition 7.2) such that $u_i \le \bar{u}_i$ for all $i \in S$.

(a) When the technology has (strictly) IRS, show that the anticore is empty (use the fact that the cost function is strictly subadditive).

(b) When the technology has DRS, the anticore is typically nonempty (see what follows). Yet the MP equilibrium may not be in the anticore. To show this, use the numerical example of Exercise 7.6 with $n = 2$, $\omega_1 = 1$, $\omega_2 = 9$, and $S = \{1\}$.

(c) In the example of Exercise 7.6, check that the CRE allocation is in the anticore. In general, if preferences are convex and the technology is DRS. the CRE allocation belongs to the anticore (Moulin [1987c]). The proof is similar to that of Theorem 7.3, outlined in the next exercise.

7.8 Proof of Theorem 7.3. We denote by $\bar{p}$ the CRE price associated with a given economy $(u_1, \ldots, u_n; \omega_1, \ldots, \omega_n, c)$. Take a proper coalition S and suppose that the vector $(\gamma_i(\bar{p}))_{i \in S}$ is feasible for S. There exist $(x_i, y_i)_{i \in S}$ such that

$$\sum_{i \in S} x_i = c\left(\sum_{i \in S} y_i\right) \quad \text{and} \quad u_i(\omega_i - x_i, y_i) \ge \gamma_i(\bar{p}) \quad \text{for all } i \in S$$

If S can object against the CRE allocation, at least one of the preceding inequalities must be strict. Show the existence of an S allocation $(x_i', y_i')_{i \in S}$ such that

$$\sum_{i \in S} x_i' > c\left(\sum_{i \in S} y_i'\right) \quad \text{and} \quad u_i(\omega_i - x_i', y_i') \ge \gamma_i(\bar{p}) \quad \text{for all } i \in S$$

Denote $x = \sum_{i \in S} x_i'$, $y = \sum_{i \in S} y_i'$. Show that the inequality $x \le \bar{p} \cdot y$ must hold. For any agent j *outside* coalition S, denote

$$U_j = \{(x_j, y_j) \mid u_j(\omega_j - x_j, y_j) \ge \gamma_i(\bar{p})\}$$

Check that U_j intersects the line $x_j = \bar{p} \cdot y_j$ (drawing a picture is useful at this point) and deduce the existence of $\lambda_j \ge 0$ such that $(\lambda_j x, \lambda_j y)$ belongs to U_j.

Next invoke the subadditivity of the cost function [a consequence of IRS and $c(0) = 0$] to prove that the allocation $(x_i', y_i')_{i = 1, \ldots, n}$ [where $(x_j', y_j') = \lambda_j(x, y)$ for all $j \in N \setminus S$] satisfies

$$\sum_{i=1}^{n} x_i' > c\left(\sum_{i=1}^{n} y_i'\right)$$

Deduce a contradiction of the definition of $\bar{p}$.

7.9 Agents with different productivities. We consider the economy of Example 7.4, with an arbitrary technology and agents differing only in their productivities. In other words, there is a common utility function u and a common initial endowment of leisure ω such that agent i derives utility $u(\omega - x_i/\pi_i, y_i)$ from consuming y_i units of output and supplying x_i units of input. The parameter $\pi_i > 0$ is productivity. Finally, the feasibility condition is

$$\sum_i x_i = c\left(\sum_i y_i\right)$$

(a) Show that at a MP equilibrium and at the CRE allocation, the more skilled an agent, the higher his final utility:

$$\pi_i > \pi_j \Rightarrow u_i\left(\omega_i - \frac{x_i}{\pi_i}, y_i\right) \geq u_j\left(\omega - \frac{x_j}{\pi_j}, y_j\right)$$

(b) Suppose the utility function u is concave and the second derivative u_{xy} is nonnegative (no inferior good).

Show that at a MP equilibrium *and* at the CRE allocation, the more skilled an agent, the more input he supplies and the more output he consumes:

$$\pi_i > \pi_j \Rightarrow x_i > x_j \text{ and } y_i > y_j$$

Yet this does not mean that the more skilled is an agent, the harder he works. Under $\pi_i > \pi_j$, both $x_i/\pi_i > x_j/\pi_j$ and $x_i/\pi_i < x_j/\pi_j$ are possible.

(c) Under the same assumptions as in question (b), suppose the economy has only two agents and production has IRS. Show that the MP equilibrium is more favorable to the more skilled agent than the CRE allocation. *Hint:* Let p be the price supporting the MP equilibrium (x_1, y_1, x_2, y_2). If agent 2 is the less skilled agent, denote by p' the price such that $\gamma_2(p') = u(\omega - x_2/\pi_2, y_2)$. Show successively that $p' \leq p$ and then that $u(\omega - x_1/\pi_1, y_1) \geq \gamma_1(p')$. Deduce that the CRE price $\bar{p} \geq p'$ and conclude.

CHAPTER 8

Strategyproof mechanisms

Overview

Suppose the public decision maker (hereafter called the planner) faces a specific cost- or surplus-sharing problem and has made up his mind about the just outcome (e.g., he adopts one of the five paramount methods for sharing the cost of a public good discussed in Chapter 6). He still has one difficulty to solve before his favorite solution is implemented, namely, he must elicit from individual agents a report of their preferences (in this particular example, he must find out about the individual benefits from consuming the public good).

Information about individual preferences is fundamentally private to the agent himself. Even if I have clear evidence that you prefer wine over beer, I cannot deny your right of pretending to the contrary.

Thus, in a legal and practical sense, all information about preferences must emanate from the concerned agents themselves. This implies that an agent can influence the outcome of the mechanism by falsifying his preferences (e.g., by understating or overstating the benefit he derives from the public good). Of course, he will manipulate in such fashion only when it is in his interest to do so.

The issue of strategic manipulation of decision mechanisms has received considerable attention in the last two decades. The seminal problem is the search for a strategyproof mechanism, that is, a mechanism whereby every agent, no matter what his preferences are, has every noncooperative incentive to reveal it sincerely to the decision maker. This question has received fairly complete answers in two particularly simple models, namely, public decision making with money (analyzed in this chapter) and voting (discussed in Sections 10.1 and 10.2). Here we describe in some detail the class of strategyproof public decision mechanisms (the so-called Groves mechanisms) and its most prominent representative, the pivotal mechanism. But we also touch upon the more general and much more difficult question of strategic manipulations by noncooperative agents.

If, indeed, most familiar mechanisms are not strategyproof, then we expect the agents to manipulate their report (i.e., to send a biased description of their preferences). But can we at least measure the impact of these manipulations by comparing the predicted noncooperative equilibrium outcome (when each agent manipulates and takes into account the other agents' manipulations as well) with the outcome resulting from the truthful, unbiased messages? This deeper question is also harder to answer because game theory does not provide a straightforward noncooperative prediction in most game situations. As a matter of fact, very little is known about the comparative strategies of even the most common public decision mechanisms.

In Section 8.1 we give several examples of noncooperative manipulations in various mechanisms. Those include proportional cost sharing of a public good (Chapter 6) and voluntary subscription of input in a regulated monopoly (Chapter 7). No systematical conclusion is reached. Our goal is merely to illustrate the versatility of such manipulations in the pure-compensation problem, where a costless public decision must be selected and monetary transfers can be used to induce the proper incentives. The pivotal mechanism is strategyproof and selects an efficient (surplus-maximizing) public decision. Its main drawback is that the planner accumulates a budget surplus that he does not redistribute among the agents. Section 8.3 applies several variants of the pivotal mechanism to cost-sharing problems.

Starting with Section 8.4, we present some more abstract characterization results. First, we analyze the strategyproof (also called demand-revealing) mechanisms in the general compensation problem. We find that all such mechanisms resemble the pivotal one provided they pick an efficient decision at every profile. It follows that no strategyproof mechanism is fully efficient at every preference profile (Theorem 8.2). In Section 8.5 we explain axiomatically the prominent role of the pivotal mechanism within the demand-revealing class. Although its anonymity and neutrality do not suffice to single it out, we give some alternative axioms that do.

8.1   Noncooperative manipulations

We illustrate the consequences of noncooperative behavior in a few typical mechanisms from the last two chapters. Our goal in this section is to demonstrate that such manipulations affect the outcome of various mechanisms in many different ways.

Example 8.1. Proportional cost sharing of a public good

This is the cost sharing of an indivisible public good (Section 6.2), with cost $c = 1$, and two agents. The mechanism asks each agent to report his benefit b_i, $i = 1, 2$, and next produces the public good if and only if $b_1 + b_2 \geq 1$ and shares its cost proportionally: $x_i = b_i/(b_1 + b_2)$.

Suppose the true benefits are $b_1 = 2$ and $b_2 = 0.4$. Surely reporting their true benefits is not a noncooperative equilibrium of the manipulation game. Indeed, if agent 1 reports truthfully, agent 2 cancels his cost share by reporting $a_2 = 0$, whereupon the public good is still produced. Similarly, if agent 2 is sincere, agent 1 can report a benefit as low as $a_1 = 0.6$ and preserve the efficient decision while reducing his own cost share to $0.6/(0.4 + 0.6) = 0.6 \leq b_1/(b_1 + b_2) = 0.83$.

What pairs of reports (a_1, a_2) are a possible noncooperative outcome (Nash equilibrium) of the report game?

One such pair is $a_1 = 0.8$, $a_2 = 0.2$. The public good is produced, and the agents pay 0.8 and 0.2, respectively, resulting in net utilities $u_1 = 2 - 0.8 = 1.2$, $u_2 = 0.6 - 0.2 = 0.4$. No agent can profit from lowering his reported benefit since this would stop the production of the good and nullify his gain. On the other hand, by raising his report, an agent increases his own cost share.

The same argument applies to every pair a_1, a_2 of nonnegative reports such that $a_1 + a_2 = 1$ as long as each agent's net utility remains nonnegative:

$$2 - \frac{a_1}{a_1 + a_2} \geq 0, \quad 0.4 - \frac{a_2}{a_1 + a_2} \geq 0 \Leftrightarrow a_2 \leq 0.4$$

Indeed, each agent guarantees a nonnegative net utility by reporting the truth; therefore, a Nash equilibrium cannot yield a negative net utility.

Thus, every pair (a_1, a_2) with $a_1 + a_2 = 1$, $a_1 \geq 0.6$, $a_2 \geq 0$, is a Nash equilibrium of the report game. The corresponding cost sharings are all (x_1, x_2) such that $x_1 + x_2 = 1$, $x_1 \leq 1$, $x_2 \leq 0.4$, namely, all cost sharings that satisfy the individual rationality constraint $x_i \leq \min\{b_i, c\}$.

In this example the Nash equilibrium behavior is highly undetermined, and its predictive power is virtually nil (none of the refinements of the Nash concept would help to further reduce the equilibrium set). If both agents know each other's benefits, the situation is one of "competition for the first move" (Moulin [1986a], Chapter 2), where each player tries to commit himself first to his most favorable equilibrium strategy: Agent 1 wants to commit to $a_1 = 0.61$ so as to force agent 2 to announce $a_2 = 0.39$, whereby agent 1 reaps almost all the surplus (1.39). Similarly, agent 2 tries to commit to $a_2 = 0$ and free ride on the public good produced by agent 1.

The conclusions of Example 8.1 can be considerably generalized. Consider any provision of a public good mechanism selecting a cost sharing in the core. In the game of demand revelation (where each agent reports his benefit), all core cost sharings result from a Nash equilibrium message; see Exercise 8.1, where this result and two similar results for the surplus-sharing and pure-compensation problems are explained.

Example 8.2. Pure compensation
A (finite) set A of public decisions is given, and the n concerned agents can costlessly pick one decision. Preferences are quasi-linear over decisions and money; the monetary transfers are used to compensate the "losers," namely, the agents who do not like the efficient decision.

The pure-compensation model plays an important role in this chapter. Our first numerical example involves two possible locations of a public service. Among the four towns involved, the first two would benefit if location a is chosen and suffer a loss if location b is chosen; the last two have opposite preferences:

Name of town	1	2	3	4	
Location a	+20	+15	−10	0	(1)
Location b	−10	−5	+12	+4	

The table gives the utilities of the four agents for the two locations. Given the quasi-linear preferences, what matters is the difference in utility between the two locations: Agent 1 would pay up to \$30 to switch from decision 2 to decision 1, whereas agent 4 would pay \$4 to switch from decision a to decision b. Without loss of generality, we can choose arbitrarily the zero of individual utilities. It is convenient to choose it so that $u_i(a) + u_i(b) = 0$. In our example the preference profile now reads:

Town	1	2	3	4
a	+15	+10	−11	−2
b	−15	−10	+11	+2

This normalization allows a clear partition of N between supporters of a versus supporters of b. The utility zero is taken at $\frac{1}{2}(u_i(a) + u_i(b))$, corresponding to the virtual status quo where a decision is selected at random with equal probability (this interpretation requires, however, risk-neutral, expected utility maximizer agents).

The efficient decision maximizes joint utility. In our example $\sum_i u_i(a) = 12 > -12 = \sum_i u_i(b)$. Consider the laissez-faire mechanism that picks the efficient decision and performs no transfer whatsoever (except when *both* decisions are efficient, in which case the mechanism brings everyone's final utility to zero). This is by far the simplest efficient mechanism for solving the pure-compensation problem. Yet it is highly manipulable. Call agent i a loser if his preferred decision is not the efficient one; in our example the losers are agents 3 and 4. A loser profitability misreports by exaggerating his dislike of the efficient decision [in the example, agent 3 might report $v_3(a) - v_3(b) = -50$]. Actually reporting his true preferences is not rational for any agent. *Some* inflation of one's message is absolutely safe. In game-theoretical parlance, the truthful message is *dominated* by an inflated one. See Exercise 8.1 for details.

When the agents inflate their message, the resulting decision could very well be the inefficient one, whereupon manipulation entails a social loss. By contrast, consider the *egalitarian* mechanism where the joint surplus above the zero utility level is distributed uniformly among the agents. In our example the surplus is $\sum_i u_i(a) = 12$, so each agent ends up with the utility level $+3$ by means of the transfers

$$t_1 = -12, \quad t_2 = -7, \quad t_3 = +14, \quad t_4 = +5$$

The manipulations of the egalitarian mechanism resemble closely those of Example 8.1. An agent minimizes his preferences for the efficient decision without making it look inefficient. In our example, if agents 2, 3, and 4 report truthfully, agent 1 can reduce his transfer by almost 9 while reporting $v_i(a) = 3 + \epsilon$, $v_i(b) = -3 - \epsilon$, thus making decision a appear barely efficient. The same kind of strategy will be used by any manipulating player, so that noncooperative manipulations of the egalitarian mechanism bear no social cost. Exercise 8.1 states precisely this property.

Remark 8.1: In the pure-compensation problem, the laissez-faire and egalitarian solutions are amenable to axiomatic characterization in their own right; see Moulin [1985b] for an application of decentralizability and Moulin [1987d] for a systematical comparison of these two solutions.

Our next example concerns the production of divisible goods, namely, regulated monopolies producing either a private or a public good (Chapter 7). The simplest mechanisms rely on individual contributions of input.

Example 8.3. Voluntary subscription in a regulated monopoly
In a public good economy (model 1 in Section 7.1), suppose each agent makes a voluntary contribution x_i to the provision of the public good. The sum of these contributions is then utilized as input to produce the public good. If the agents behave noncooperatively, this mechanism induces a vastly suboptimal level of production. This holds true for very general preferences and production functions. We give the intuition of this fact in the simple case where the agents have concave quasi-linear preferences and the production function is concave.

Define α_i to be the contribution made by agent i if he were alone in the economy. So α_i solves the following program:

$$\max_{x_i \geq 0} b_i(f(x_i)) - x_i \tag{2}$$

where f is the production function (i.e., the inverse of the cost function). Suppose, without loss of generality, that agent 1 would produce the highest amount of public good: $\alpha_1 \geq \alpha_i$ for all i. Then, in any Nash equilibrium of the voluntary subscription game, the public good level is typically $f(\alpha_1)$. Indeed, consider any vector of contributions $(\bar{x}_1, \ldots, \bar{x}_n)$ such that $\sum_i \bar{x}_i < \alpha_1$: Agent 1 is better off by increasing his contribution because the solution of the program

$$\max_{x_1} b_1\left(f\left(x_1 + \sum_{j \neq 1} \bar{x}_j\right)\right) - x_1$$

is $x_1 = \alpha_1 - \sum_{j \neq 1} \bar{x}_j$. Next, if the vector $(\bar{x}_1, \ldots, \bar{x}_n)$ is such that $\sum_i \bar{x}_i > \alpha_1$, one checks similarly that any agent who makes a positive contribution is better off by reducing it.

It should be clear that the level of public good $y_0 = f(\alpha_1)$ is much below the optimal level y^*. Indeed, at the level y_0 the marginal utility of agent 1 *alone* equals marginal cost $[b_1'(y_0) = c'(y_0)]$, whereas at the level y^* the *sum* of individual marginal utilities equals marginal costs [Samuelson's condition (3) in Chapter 7].

We turn next to the regulated monopoly producing a private good (model 2 in Section 7.2). Suppose the output (corn) is divided proportionally into input (labor) contributions, so that if agent i supplies the quantity x_i of labor, $i = 1, \ldots, n$, his final utility is

$$u_i\left(\omega_i - x_i, \frac{x_i}{x_N} f(x_N)\right), \quad \text{where } x_N = \sum_{j=1}^n x_j$$

In the game of voluntary subscription of input the Nash equilibrium outcome is Pareto optimal only if production has CRS. If returns to scale are decreasing, the production is excessive, and it is insufficient if returns to scale are increasing. (Exercise: Why?)

8.2 Strategyproofness and the pivotal mechanism

A public decision-making mechanism is strategyproof if, for all conceivable preferences, each agent possesses a message that is his best noncooperative message no matter what messages are sent by the other agents. In game-theoretic terms, each agent has a dominant strategy for each of his possible preferences.

A direct mechanism is one where each agent must report his individual preferences. A direct mechanism is strategyproof if sending the truthful message is a dominant strategy for each agent and for any individual preferences. It can be shown that restricting attention to direct mechanisms entails no loss of generality as far as strategyproofness is concerned (this fact is known as the "revelation principle"). Therefore, in the rest of this chapter we discuss direct mechanisms only and shall indifferently speak of strategyproof, truth-telling, or even demand-revealing mechanisms.

We now introduce the pivotal mechanism in the pure-compensation problem. Recall that we have a finite set of public decisions A and n agents with quasi-linear preferences over decisions $\times$ money. Consider the numerical Example 8.2. Since it involves only two decisions a, b and decision a is efficient, we identify the winners as those agents preferring a over b. The pivotal mechanism picks the efficient decision and does *not* compensate the losers; on the other hand, *some* winners will be taxed, namely, those who prefer a over b so much that if they were removed, the efficient decision would be b instead. Since some winners are taxed and the losers are not compensated, the pivotal mechanism may generate a budget surplus that is not redistributed. This is its principal weakness, discussed in what follows.

Say that agent i is *pivotal* if the efficient decision for the agents in $N \setminus \{i\}$ differs from the overall efficient decision. In our example, agent 1 is pivotal; among $\{2, 3, 4\}$ location b is efficient. No other agent is pivotal: For the coalitions $\{1, 2, 4\}$, $\{1, 2, 3\}$, and $\{1, 3, 4\}$ location a is uniquely efficient. Agent 1 is taxed by the pivotal mechanism the exact loss in joint utility incurred by $\{2, 3, 4\}$ when switching from decision b to decision a:

$$x_1 = (-10 + 11 + 2) - (10 - 11 - 2) = 6$$

A nonpivotal agent is not taxed: $x_2 = x_3 = x_4 = 0$.

To see why this tax system induces truthful revelation of preferences, consider agent 1 first. Any report that does not change the efficient decision (location a) is neither profitable nor harmful since his tax does not change; any report that makes location b look like the efficient decision cancels this tax but induces a utility loss of 30. Next consider agent 3. If he exaggerates his distaste for location a [say, by reporting $v_3(a) = -25$, $v_3(b) = 25$], then location b will look efficient, but he will be taxed the exact loss in joint utility incurred by $\{1, 2, 4\}$ when switching from decision a to decision b:

$$x_3 = (15 + 10 - 2) - (-15 - 10 + 2) = 46$$

Such a large tax offsets the benefit of consuming decision b (namely, $+22$). A similar argument applies for agents 2 and 4.

In order to define rigorously the pivotal mechanism, we need some definitions.

Definition 8.1. *A quasi-linear compensation problem is given by a set N of n individual agents who jointly pick up a **public decision** a within the finite set A. Decision a is public since no individual agent can be excluded from its consumption (although his opinion could be ignored in the choice process); it is also costless. Thus, an **outcome** is a pair (a, t), where $a \in A$ and $t = (t_i)_{i \in N}$ is a vector of monetary transfers.*

Agents' preferences are additively separable in the public decision and in money, and linear in money. Thus, agent i's preferences are described by a vector u_i in E^A such that his utility for outcome (a, t) is $u_i(a) + t_i$.

Denote by 1 the vector in E^A with all components equal to 1. Then two vectors u_i, v_i in E^A such that $v_i = u_i + a \cdot 1$ for some real number a represent the same preferences over the outcome set and should therefore be identified. Property (3) in the following definition takes care of this by stating that the zero of the agent's utility function plays no role.

Definition 8.2. *Given (N, A) both finite, a **mechanism** is a mapping associating to every utility profile $u = (u_i)_{i \in N}$, $u_i \in E^A$, an outcome $(a(u), t(u))$ such that this mapping is independent of the individual zero of utility:*

For all $i \in N$, all profiles u, v such that $v_i = u_i + a \cdot 1$ for
some real number a and $v_j = u_j$ for all $j \neq i$: $a(u) = a(v)$,   (3)
$t(u) = t(v)$.

*The mechanism is **efficient** if it selects an efficient public decision at all profiles:*

$a(u)$ *is an efficient public decision:* $\sum_{i \in N} u_i(a) = \max_{b \in A} \left\{ \sum_{i \in N} u_i(b) \right\}$

*The mechanism is **feasible** if $t(u)$ exhibits no deficit at any profile:*

$$\sum_{i \in N} t_i(u) \leq 0$$

Notice that an efficient and feasible mechanism may still generate a budget surplus and may thus lack first-best Pareto optimality. From the point of view of the agents, the budget surplus is the price they must pay for incentive compatibility (see Theorem 8.2).

Definition 8.3. *The mechanism $(a(\cdot), t(\cdot))$ is **strategyproof** if for each profile $u = (u_j)_{j \in N}$, each agent i and each utility fuction $v_i \in E^A$, agent i cannot benefit from reporting v_i whenever his true utility function is u_i:*

$$u_i(a(u)) + t_i(u) \geq u_i(a(v_i, u_{-i})) + t_i(v_i, u_{-i})$$ (4)

The pivotal mechanism was invented in the early 1970s by Clarke [1971] and Groves [1973] and raised considerable interest in the public economics literature; see Green, Kohlberg, and Laffont [1976]; Tideman and Tullock [1976]; and the monograph by Green and Laffont [1979]. We present first the mechanism in a costless public decision problem.

In the pivotal mechanism, each agent reports his utility, next an efficient decision (maximizing joint utility) is selected, and finally each agent is taxed the exact cost that his presence imposes upon the rest of the agents, that is, the difference in their joint utility between the selected decision and the decision they would select if his preferences were simply ignored.

Lemma 8.1. *A pivotal mechanism is a mechanism such that, for each profile u, $a(u)$ is an efficient public decision and*

$$t_i(u) = \sum_{j \neq i} u_j(a(u)) - \max_{b \in A} \left\{ \sum_{j \neq i} u_j(b) \right\} = u_{N \setminus i}(a(u)) - \max_A u_{N \setminus i} \tag{5}$$

It is efficient, feasible, and strategyproof.

At profiles u where several efficient public decisions coexist, several outcomes (a, t) satisfying (4) can be chosen. They all yield the same final utility to each and every agent:

$$S_i^*(u) = \max_A \left\{ \sum_{j=1}^{n} u_j \right\} - \max_A \left\{ \sum_{j \neq i} u_j \right\} = \max_A u_N - \max_A u_{N \setminus i} \tag{6}$$

Proof: To check feasibility, it is enough to show that for each profile u

$$\sum_{i=1}^{n} S_i^*(u) \leq \max_A u_N$$

Given (5), this amounts to

$$(n-1) \max_A u_N \leq \sum_{i=1}^{n} \max_A u_{N \setminus i}$$

Pick an efficient decision $a(u)$ (maximizing u_N); then

$$(n-1) \max_A u_N = (n-1) u_N(a) = \sum_{i=1}^{n} u_{N \setminus i}(a) \leq \sum_{i=1}^{n} \max_A u_{N \setminus i}$$

To check strategyproofness, fix a profile u, an agent i, and a message $v_i \in E^A$. Denote $a(u) = a$, $a(v_i, u_{-i}) = b$. In view of (5), inequality (4) reads

$$u_i(a) + u_{N \setminus i}(a) - \max_A u_{N \setminus i} \geq u_i(b) + u_{N \setminus i}(b) - \max_A u_{N-i} \qquad \text{Q.E.D.}$$

The main drawback of the pivotal mechanism is the budget surplus that it generates at all profiles where at least one agent is pivotal. However, when all $(n-1)$-agent coalitions agree on one efficient decision (i.e., there is some decision that every $n-1$ coalition views as efficient), then nobody is pivotal, and the mechanism yields a fully efficient outcome. With a large number of agents this configuration is likely to happen; see Green and Laffont [1979] and Rob [1982].

It is interesting to compare the pivotal mechanism with the egalitarian surplus sharing proposed by Dubins [1977] and illustrated in Example 8.2.

Definition 8.4. *An egalitarian mechanism picks for every profile an efficient decision $a(u)$ and the following transfers:*

$$t_i(u) = -u_i(a(u)) + \frac{1}{n}\sigma \qquad (7)$$

where σ is the joint surplus above and beyond the "average" utility:

$$\sigma = \max_A u_N - \frac{1}{|A|}\sum_{a\in A} u_N(a) \qquad (8)$$

As we noticed in Example 8.2, this mechanism is not strategyproof. Its Nash equilibrium outcomes yield all efficient utility vectors where each agent gets at least his average utility $(1/|A|)\sum_{a\in A} u_i(a)$ (see Exercise 8.1). Thus, when the surplus σ is very small, the egalitarian mechanism resists manipulations very well. Actually, when σ is zero, the truthful messages are the deterministic outcomes of the game (in the very strong sense that the game is inessential; see Moulin [1986a], Chapter 2). On the other hand, if σ is very small, then every agent is likely to be pivotal, and hence the pivotal mechanism is very wasteful.

By contrast, think of a situation where all individual agents agree on the best decision so that the pivotal mechanism is fully efficient. Then the surplus σ is likely to be large so that the manipulations of the egalitarian mechanism yield a fairly undetermined outcome.

Another comparison of our two mechanisms is by way of their *secure utility level,* namely, the utility level that an agent is guaranteed upon participating in a given mechanism. In the egalitarian mechanism, the secure utility level of agent i is precisely $(1/|A|)\sum_{a\in A} u_i(a)$. In the pivotal mechanism, it is only $\min_{a\in A} u_i(a)$; see Lemma 8.2.

8.3 Strategyproof cost sharing

We discuss first the provision of an indivisible public good problem (Section 6.2) to which the pivotal mechanism is easily adapted.

Example 8.4. Cost sharing of an indivisible public good
Consider an indivisible public good with cost $c > 0$ and benefits $b_1, \ldots, b_n$ to individual agents. We view this as a compensation problem (Definition

8.1) with two decisions: Decision $a = 0$ is the status quo (the good is not produced) and decision $a = 1$ means that the good is produced and its costs are uniformly shared among the n agents. The pivotal mechanism reads as follows:

Each agent reports his benefit b_i:

(i) if $\sum_{i \in N} b_i \leq c$, the good is not produced. Agent i pays nothing

if $\sum_{j \neq i} b_j \leq \dfrac{n-1}{n} c$; otherwise he pays $|t_i| = \sum_{j \neq i} b_j - \dfrac{n-1}{n} c$

$$(9)$$

(ii) if $\sum_{i \in N} b_i > c$, the good is produced. Agent i pays $\dfrac{c}{n}$ if

$\sum_{j \neq i} b_j \geq \dfrac{n-1}{n} c$, otherwise he pays $|t_i| = \dfrac{c}{n} + \left(\dfrac{n-1}{n} c - \sum_{j \neq i} b_j \right)$

This is just formula (5) where $u_i(0) = 0$ and $u_i(1) = b_i - c/n$:

(i) $b_N \leq c \Rightarrow a(u) = 0, \quad t_i(u) = 0 - \max\left\{ b_{N \setminus i} - \dfrac{n-1}{n} c, 0 \right\}$

(ii) $b_N > c \Rightarrow a(u) = 1,$

$$(10)$$

$$t_i(u) = b_{N \setminus i} - \dfrac{n-1}{n} c - \max\left\{ b_{N \setminus i} - \dfrac{n-1}{n} c, 0 \right\}$$

$$= -\max\left\{ \dfrac{n-1}{n} c - b_{N \setminus i}, 0 \right\}$$

Notice that the pivotal mechanism does not propose an original cost sharing. It simply assumes some fixed (in our case, uniform) cost shares and charges an additional tax on every pivotal agent, namely, every agent such that the decision chosen would be different in his absence. The surtax on a pivotal agent is heavy. Indeed, it is the full amount of the loss in joint utility that he inflicts on the rest of the agents (but his tax is not used to compensate them).

The budget surplus measures the lack of (first-best) Pareto optimality of our mechanism. When only few agents are involved, it can be large. In fact, with only two agents the budget surplus can exceed the total cooperative surplus from undertaking the project. For instance, suppose $c = 4$, $b_1 = 1$, and $b_2 = 3.5$. Then the efficient decision is to produce the good, bringing $1 + 3.5 - 4 = 0.5$ dollar of surplus. However, agent 2 is pivotal (since $b_1 < c/2$), whence he has to pay an additional $c/2 - b_1 = 1$ dollar. Thus, the net balance is a loss of 50 cents from the initial (inefficient) decision!

The pivotal mechanism can be similarly adapted to any public decision problem where a cost is attached to every public decision; see Exercise 8.3.

Example 8.4 illustrates the main drawback of the pivotal mechanism: Although it does pick the efficient decision, its transfers are not budget balanced. In the next section, Theorem 8.2 demonstrates that this lack of budget balance is very general; a fully efficient mechanism cannot be strategyproof.

In a second-best perspective, we could allow the mechanism to pick an inefficient decision while insisting on budget balance. Many easy mechanisms then emerge. For instance, in the context of Example 8.4 consider the direct mechanism where agents report their benefit b_i, after which

(i)   If $b_i \geq c/n$ for all $i \in N$, the public good is produced and each agent pays c/n.

(ii) If $b_i < c/n$ for at least one agent i, the good is not produced and nobody is charged.

Other examples of inefficient strategyproof mechanisms are discussed in Exercise 8.5 and in Example 10.2 for the provision of a divisible public good problem.

Our next example is an economy with quasi-linear preferences where a divisible public good is produced.

Example 8.5. Cost sharing of a divisible public good
We have a CRS production technology $c(y) = y$ (the price of the public good is 1) and n agents endowed with proportional benefit functions $b_i(y) = \beta_i \sqrt{y}$, $i = 1, ..., n$.

The efficient level of a public good is $y^* = \frac{1}{4}\beta_N^2$, where we denote $\beta_N = \sum_{i=1}^{n} \beta_i$. Marginal pricing and the egalitarian equivalent solution both recommend the same cost shares $c_i = \frac{1}{4}\beta_i \cdot \beta_N$. The direct mechanism where each agent reports β_i and the corresponding outcome $(y^*, c_1, ..., c_n)$ is enforced is *not* strategyproof. Agents have an incentive to underreport their taste for the public good, and at the unique Nash equilibrium message, the public good supplied is much below the socially optimal level (Exercise 8.2 gives the details). To avoid misrepresentation, Groves and Loeb [1975] have proposed the following mechanism.

The Groves–Loeb mechanism: Each agent reports his parameter β_i. Then $y^* = \frac{1}{4}\beta_N^2$ is produced, and the cost share imputed to agent i is

$$x_i = \frac{1}{4}\beta_i^2 + \frac{1}{2(n-2)} \sum_{\substack{j,k \neq i \\ j<k}} \beta_j \cdot \beta_k \tag{11}$$

Check first that the cost shares (11) exactly cover the cost of y^*:

$$\sum_i x_i = \frac{1}{4}\left(\sum_i \beta_i^2\right) + \frac{1}{2}\sum_{j<k}\beta_j\cdot\beta_k = \frac{1}{4}\left(\sum_i \beta_i\right)^2 = c(y^*)$$

Next we prove that agent i never has an incentive to report anything but the truth. Suppose the messages of the other agents are α_j, all $j \neq i$. Then agent i's report α_i yields the level $y(\alpha_i, \alpha_{-i}) = \frac{1}{4}(\alpha_N)^2$ and the cost share $x_i(\alpha_i, \alpha_{-i})$ given by (11) (with each β_j replaced by α_j). Thus, his utility maximization program is

$$\max_{\alpha_i \geq 0}\{\beta_i\cdot\sqrt{y(\alpha_i, \alpha_{-i})} - x_i(\alpha_i, \alpha_{-i})\} = \max_{\alpha_i \geq 0}\{\tfrac{1}{2}\beta_i\cdot\alpha_N - \tfrac{1}{4}\alpha_i^2 - \theta\} \qquad (12)$$

where the residual term θ does not depend on α_i [because $2(n-2)\theta = \sum_{j,k \neq i,\, j<k}\beta_j\cdot\beta_k$]. The solution of problem (12) is that of

$$\max_{\alpha_i \geq 0}\{\beta_i\cdot(\alpha_i + \alpha_{N\setminus i}) - \tfrac{1}{2}\alpha_i^2\}$$

namely, $\alpha_i = \beta_i$, as was to be proved.

Mechanism (12) is truly remarkable. Simultaneously it makes the truthful report a dominating strategy for each agent for each value of the parameters (strategyproofness), it produces the efficient level of public good, and it exactly covers its cost (budget balance). Actually, for the particular economy of this example, this mechanism is uniquely characterized by strategyproofness plus Pareto optimality (efficient level of the public good plus budget balance) and anonymity. See Exercise 8.4.

On the other hand, the Groves–Loeb mechanism fails to guarantee a bounded minimal utility level to individual agents. Indeed, consider the final utility level of agent i when the agents truthfully report $(\beta_1, ..., \beta_n)$:

$$u_i(\beta_1, ..., \beta_n) = \frac{1}{2}\beta_i\cdot\beta_N - \frac{1}{4}\beta_i^2 - \frac{1}{2(n-2)}\sum_{\substack{j<k \\ k,j \neq i}}\beta_j\cdot\beta_k$$

Clearly, for fixed β_i, this utility can become negative and even arbitrarily small. For instance, take $\beta_j = \lambda$ for all $j \neq i$ and compute

$$u_i(\lambda, ..., \lambda, \beta_i, \lambda, ..., \lambda) = \tfrac{1}{4}\beta_i^2 + \tfrac{1}{2}(n-1)\beta_i\cdot\lambda - \tfrac{1}{4}(n-1)\lambda^2$$

When λ is worth $3\beta_i$, this utility is already negative [$u_i = -\tfrac{1}{2}(n-1)\beta_i^2$], and when λ grows large, u_i goes to $-\infty$.

Thus, upon entering the Groves–Loeb mechanism, an agent is not guaranteed of his initial zero utility level when no public good is produced and no monetary transfers occur. Worse, if he suspects that he likes the public good much less than the other agents, he can expect to be taxed very heavily, and there is no upper bound on the amount he may have to pay! This lack of *individual rationality* is a serious drawback of the Groves–

Loeb mechanism: Does the incentive to report preferences truthfully justify giving to the social planner a right to unlimited coercive taxes?

In the preceding example the existence of a strategyproof and fully efficient mechanism is quite miraculous. We show (Remark 8.3) that for a different choice of the cost function (or benefit functions), such a mechanism would typically not exist. But we need first to characterize in full generality the class of strategyproof mechanisms.

8.4   The class of demand-revealing mechanisms

The class of strategyproof and efficient mechanisms – for the pure-compensation problem – is a simple generalization of the pivotal one.

Theorem 8.1 (Green and Laffont [1979]).   *For all $i \in N$, denote by $h_i(u_{-i})$ an arbitrary numerical function defined for all $u_{-i} \in (E^A)^{N \setminus \{i\}}$. Then consider a mechanism $(a(\cdot), t(\cdot))$ such that*

$a(u)$ *is an efficient decision for each profile u*
$$t_i(u) = u_{N \setminus i}(a(u)) - h_i(u_{-i}) \text{ for each profile } u \text{ and all } i \in N \qquad (13)$$

This mechanism is strategyproof. Conversely, any strategyproof and efficient mechanism is of this form.

Proof: That mechanism (13) is strategyproof is proven in the same way as for the pivotal mechanism (Lemma 8.1). We prove now the converse statement. Let $(a(\cdot), t(\cdot))$ be a strategyproof and efficient mechanism. Define

$$k_i(u) = u_{N \setminus i}(a(u)) - t_i(u) \quad \text{for all } u, \text{ all } i \in N$$

We want to show that k_i actually is independent of $u_i \in E^A$.

Fix u_{-i} and apply the strategyproofness inequality (4) to the profile (u_i, u_{-i}) and (mis)report v_i:

$$u_i(a(u_i)) + t_i(u_i) = u_N(a(u_i)) - k_i(u_i)$$
$$\geq u_N(a(v_i)) - k_i(v_i) = u_i(a(v_i)) + t_i(v_i)$$

Notice that, for simplicity, we have omitted u_{-i} in $a(u_i, u_{-i})$, $t_i(v_i, u_{-i})$, and so on. The preceding inequality reads

$$u_N(a(u_i)) - u_N(a(v_i)) \geq k_i(u_i) - k_i(v_i) \qquad (14)$$

Suppose now that $a(u_i) = a(v_i)$. From (14) and a symmetrical inequality where the roles of u_i and v_i are exchanged, we derive $k_i(u_i) = k_i(v_i)$. Thus, for all $b \in A$, let us denote by $k_i(b)$ the common value of $k_i(u_i)$ for all u_i such that $a(u_i) = b$ (u_{-i} remains fixed throughout).

Next choose two decisions b, b' and construct a utility function u_i such that

$$u_N(b) = u_N(b') \geq u_N(c) + 1 \quad \text{for all } c \neq b, b'$$

Then define $v_i^\epsilon, w_i^\epsilon$ as

$$v_i^\epsilon(b) = u_i(b) + \epsilon, \quad v_i^\epsilon(c) = u_i(c) \quad \text{for all } c \neq b$$

$$w_i^\epsilon(b') = u_i(b') + \epsilon, \quad w_i^\epsilon(c) = u_i(c) \quad \text{for all } c \neq b'$$

For all positive ϵ, the unique efficient decision at (v_i^ϵ, u_{-i}) $[(w_i^\epsilon, u_{-i})]$ is b (b'), and hence by efficiency of our mechanism, $a(v_i^\epsilon) = b$ $[a(w_i^\epsilon) = b']$. Applying (14) to the profile (v_i^ϵ, u_{-i}) and (mis)reporting w_i^ϵ, we get

$$(v_i^\epsilon + u_{N\setminus i})(b) + (v_i^\epsilon + u_{N\setminus i})(b') \geq k_i(b) - k_i(b')$$

Allowing ϵ to approach zero and taking into account $u_N(b) = u_N(b')$ gives $k_i(b) - k_i(b') \leq 0$. Exchanging the roles of b and b' gives the symmetrical inequality, and therefore $k_i(b) = k_i(b')$, concluding the proof that k_i does not depend on u_i.   Q.E.D.

Remark 8.2:   A more general result by K. Roberts [1979] characterizes all strategyproof mechanisms, whether they are efficient or not. Every such mechanism picks a decision maximizing some weighted average of the individual utilities (unless it picks an imposed decision at all profiles). In the quasi-linear framework, this is not at all appealing. Exercise 8.9 describes the class of Roberts mechanisms.

We prove next that in the class of strategyproof and efficient mechanisms, none is budget balanced. Therefore, first-best Pareto optimality is not compatible with the strategyproofness requirement.

Theorem 8.2 (Green and Laffont [1979]).   *There is no strategyproof, efficient, and budget-balanced mechanism.*

Proof: Fix a strategyproof and efficient mechanism $(a(\cdot), t(\cdot))$ where the transfers take the form (13) for some functions h_i, $i \in N$. Budget balance reads

$$\sum_{i \in N} t_i(u) = 0 \Leftrightarrow \sum_{i \in N} h_i(u_{-i}) = \sum_{i \in N} u_{N\setminus i}(a(u)) = (n-1) \max_A u_N$$

Set $\theta(u) = \sum_{i \in N} h_i(u_{-i})$. This function satisfies the following difference equation.

Denote by $T = \{1, 2\}^N$ the set of mappings σ from N into $\{1, 2\}$. Define also $\epsilon(\sigma) = \Sigma_{i \in N} \sigma(i)$. Next pick two profiles u^1, u^2 in $(E^A)^N$ and denote by u^σ the profile

$$u_i^\sigma = u_i^{\sigma(i)} \quad \text{for all } i \in N$$

Here is the difference equation characterizing all functions $\theta(u)$ decomposable into n functions depending only upon $n-1$ variables:

$$\sum_{\sigma \in S} (-1)^{\epsilon(\sigma)} \theta(u^\sigma) = 0 \tag{15}$$

This equation holds for any choice of u^1, u^2. We need to check that the function $\lambda(u) = \max_A u_N$ does not satisfy (15). This is easy to check for $n = 2, 3$. For an arbitrary n, construct a pair u^1, u^2 as follows. Fix two decisions a, b and define

$$u_i^1(a) = 1, \quad u_i^1(b) = 1 + \frac{1}{n}, \quad u_i^1(c) = 0 \quad \text{for all } i \in N, \text{ all } c \neq a, b$$

$$u_i^2(a) = 1, \qquad u_i^2(b) = u_i^2(c) = 0$$

Given an element σ of S, compute

$$\max_A u_N^1 = u_N(b) = n + 1, \qquad \max_A u_N^\sigma = u_N^\sigma(a) = n \quad \text{for every other } \sigma$$

Thus,

$$\sum_{\sigma \in S} (-1)^{\epsilon(\sigma)} \theta(u^\sigma) = \sum_{k=0}^{n} (-1)^k \binom{n}{k} \left(\max_A u_N^\sigma \right)$$

$$= n \sum_{k=0}^{n-1} (-1)^k \binom{n}{k} + (-1)^n (n+1) = (-1)^n \neq 0$$

Q.E.D.

Remark 8.3: Given Theorem 8.2, why did we discover in Example 8.5 a strategyproof, efficient, and budget-balanced mechanism? This is because we picked a miraculous configuration of (i) a restricted class of utility functions with a single unknown parameter and (ii) a well-chosen cost function.

Laffont and Maskin [1980] give general necessary conditions for the existence of such Pareto-optimal and strategyproof mechanisms. We describe their approach in the simple Example 8.5.

Consider the same benefit functions $b_i(y) = \beta_i \sqrt{y}$ and a convex, increasing cost function $c(y)$. We will characterize the cost functions for which a strategyproof, efficient, and budget-balanced mechanism exists. We already know that $c(y) = y$ is one of them and want to know what other functions are allowed.

Let $(a(\cdot), t(\cdot))$ be strategyproof, efficient, and budget balanced. The efficient decision at profile $(\beta_1, \ldots, \beta_n)$ maximizes the concave function $\beta_N \cdot \sqrt{y} - c(y)$. Thus, ignoring boundary cases, it is the solution of

$$\sqrt{y} \cdot c'(y) = \frac{\beta_N}{2} \tag{16}$$

Denote by α the inverse function of $\sqrt{y} \cdot c'(y)$:

$$\sqrt{y} \cdot c'(y) = x \Leftrightarrow y = \alpha(x) \tag{17}$$

Thus, our mechanism takes the decision $a(\beta_1, \ldots, \beta_n) = \alpha(\beta_N/2)$. Next the strategyproofness condition reads

$$\beta_i \cdot \sqrt{\alpha\left(\frac{\beta_N}{2}\right)} + t_i(\beta) \geq \beta_i \sqrt{\alpha\left(\alpha_i + \frac{\beta_{N \setminus i}}{2}\right)} + t_i(\alpha_i, \beta_{-i})$$

Viewed as a function of $\alpha_i \geq 0$, the right side reaches its maximum at $\alpha_i = \beta_i$.

Assuming that t_i is differentiable with respect to β_i (this assumption can be relaxed without changing the result), this implies

$$\frac{1}{4}\beta_i \frac{\alpha'(\beta_N/2)}{\sqrt{\alpha(\beta_N/2)}} + \frac{\partial t_i}{\partial \beta_i}(\beta) = 0 \tag{18}$$

Denote by Γ a primitive of the function $\sqrt{\alpha(x/2)}$ of the variable x. Then the function

$$\bar{t}_i(\beta) = \Gamma(\beta_N) - \beta_i \sqrt{\alpha\left(\frac{\beta_N}{2}\right)}$$

is one solution of equation (18). Any other solution takes the form

$$t_i(\beta) = \bar{t}_i(\beta) + h_i(\beta_{-i})$$

This completes the characterization of efficient and strategyproof mechanisms. It remains to determine whether budget balance is possible. This amounts to finding n functions h_i such that

$$\sum_{i=1}^{n} (\bar{t}_i(\beta) + h_i(\beta_{-i})) + c\left(\alpha\left(\frac{\beta_N}{2}\right)\right) = 0$$

or equivalently,

$$n\Gamma(\beta_N) - \beta_N \cdot \sqrt{\alpha\left(\frac{\beta_N}{2}\right)} + c\left(\alpha\left(\frac{\beta_N}{2}\right)\right) = -\sum_{i=1}^{n} h_i(\beta_{-i}) \tag{19}$$

In this formula, the left side is a function of $(\beta_1 + \cdots + \beta_n)$ only. The function on the right side is additively decomposed into functions of $n-1$ variables only. Assuming differentiability again, its cross derivative of order n

must be zero:

$$\frac{\partial^n}{\partial \beta_1, \dots, \partial \beta_n}\left(\sum_{i=1}^n h_i(\beta_{-i})\right) = 0 \tag{20}$$

For a function such as $f(\beta_1 + \cdots + \beta_n)$, the cross derivative of order n is just the nth derivative $f^{(n)}(\beta_1 + \cdots + \beta_n)$. Thus, (19) and (20) together imply that the function

$$f(x) = n \cdot \Gamma(x) - x \cdot \sqrt{\alpha\left(\frac{x}{2}\right)} + c\left(\alpha\left(\frac{x}{2}\right)\right)$$

has $f^{(n)}(x)$ identically zero. Therefore, f is a polynomial of degree at most $n-1$, and its derivative f' is a polynomial of degree at most $n-2$. Compute f' by taking (17) into account:

$$f'(x) = (n-1)\sqrt{\alpha\left(\frac{x}{2}\right)} - \frac{x}{4}\frac{\alpha'(x/2)}{\sqrt{\alpha(x/2)}} + \frac{1}{2}c'\left(\alpha\left(\frac{x}{2}\right)\right) \cdot \alpha'\left(\frac{x}{2}\right)$$

$$= (n-1)\sqrt{\alpha\left(\frac{x}{2}\right)} - \frac{1}{2}\alpha'\left(\frac{x}{2}\right) \cdot \left\{c'\left(\alpha\left(\frac{x}{2}\right)\right) - \frac{x}{2\sqrt{\alpha(x/2)}}\right\}$$

$$\Leftrightarrow f'(x) = (n-1)\sqrt{\alpha\left(\frac{x}{2}\right)}$$

We conclude that $\sqrt{\alpha(x)}$ must be a polynomial of degree at most $n-2$. This restricts considerably the class of allowed cost functions. For instance, if $n = 3$, there exist some fixed parameters λ, μ, γ such that

$$\alpha(x) = (\lambda x + \mu)^2 \Rightarrow \sqrt{y} \cdot c'(y) = \frac{1}{\lambda}(\sqrt{y} - \mu) \Rightarrow c(y) = \frac{1}{\lambda}y - 2\frac{\mu}{\lambda}\sqrt{y} + \gamma$$

namely, a three-parameter family. With n agents the class of allowed cost functions has n independent parameters.

Thus, for the provision of a public good problem, fully efficient and strategyproof mechanisms do not exist in general. However, one can construct mechanisms similar to the one described in Example 8.5 of which the sole Nash equilibrium message yields a fully efficient outcome; see Groves and Ledyard [1977], Hurwicz [1979], and Kim [1986].

8.5 Characterizations of the pivotal mechanism

Within the class of mechanisms uncovered by Theorem 8.1 – the so-called Groves mechanisms (see Groves [1973]) – what makes the pivotal one so prominent?

One possible answer is that the pivotal mechanism guarantees the best minimal utility level.

Lemma 8.2 (Moulin [1986b]).   *Let $S_i^*(u)$ be the final utility of agent i at profile u in the pivotal mechanism [given by (6)]. Fix an agent i and his utility function u_i. Then we have*

$$\min_{u_{-i}} S_i^*(u_i, u_{-i}) = \min_A u_i \tag{21}$$

Conversely, let $S_i(u)$ be the final utility of agent i at profile u in some strategyproof, feasible, and efficient mechanism. If we have

$$S_i(u) \geq \min_A u_i \quad \text{for each profile u and agent i} \tag{22}$$

then the mechanism is the pivotal one.

Proof: Given an agent i and a utility function u_i, choose u_{-i} such that $u_{N\setminus i} = -u_i$. Then

$$S_i^*(u_i, u_{-i}) = \max_A u_N - \max_A u_{N\setminus i} = 0 - \max_A(-u_i) = \min_A u_i \tag{23}$$

Moreover, for an arbitrary pair of vectors z, w in E^A, we have

$$\max_A(z+w) \geq \max_A z + \min_A w$$

Applying this to $z = u_{N\setminus i}$ and $w = u_i$ for an arbitrary profile gives

$$S_i^*(u) = \max_A u_N - \max_A u_{N\setminus i} \geq \min_A u_i \tag{24}$$

Together, (23) and (24) prove (21). We prove the converse statement. Let $S_i(u)$ be as in the statement of the lemma. By Theorem 8.1, S_i takes the form

$$S_i(u) = \max_A u_N - h_i(u_{-i})$$

By assumption (22), we have

$$h_i(u_{-i}) \leq \max_A u_N - \min_A u_i$$

Fixing u_{-i} and choosing $u_i = -u_{N\setminus i}$ yields

$$h_i(u_{-i}) \leq -\min_A(-u_{N\setminus i}) = \max_A u_{N\setminus i} \tag{25}$$

Therefore, $S_i(u) \geq S_i^*(u)$ at each profile u and for each agent i. It remains to show that these inequalities are all equalities. This will follow from the feasibility of S.

We need to show that (25) is actually an equality. Fix an $n-1$ profile u_{-i} and call b a decision where $u_{N\setminus i}$ is maximal. Then construct a utility u_i such that $u_{N\setminus j}$ is maximal at b for all $j \in N$ [this is possible by taking $u_i(c) = 0$ for all $c \neq b$ and $u_i(b)$ large enough]. Then at profile (u_i, u_{-i}), no agent is pivotal and the utility vector $(S_i^*(u), i \in N)$ is Pareto optimal. By feasibility of $(S_i(u), i \in N)$, it follows that $S_i(u) = S_i^*(u)$:

$$u_N(b) - h_i(u_{-i}) = S_i(u) = S_i^*(u) = u_i(b)$$

Hence, $h_i(u_{-i}) = u_{N \setminus i}(b) = \max_A u_{N \setminus i}$, as was to be proved.   Q.E.D.

Exercise 8.7 presents an alternative characterization of the pivotal mechanism where the upper bound on an agent's utility is used in lieu of the lower bound (as in Lemma 8.2).

Another desirable property of the pivotal mechanism is that it treats symmetrically agents (anonymity) and public decisions (neutrality).

Definition 8.5. *Let $(a(\cdot), t(\cdot))$ be a mechanism (Definition 8.2), and denote by S_i, $i \in N$, the final utility to agent i:*

$$S_i(u) = u_i(a(u)) + t_i(u)$$

*Say that the mechanism is **anonymous** if $S = (S_i)_{i \in N}$ is a symmetrical mapping of u_i, $i \in N$: If v is obtained from u by exchanging u_i and u_j, then $S_i(u) = S_j(v)$ and $S_k(u) = S_k(v)$ for all $k \neq i, j$. Say that the mechanism is **neutral** if for each bijection σ of A we have*

$$S_i(u) = S_i(u^\sigma)$$

where u_j^σ is defined as $u_j^\sigma(a) = u_j(\sigma(a))$.

It is straightforward to check that the pivotal mechanism is anonymous and neutral. Now consider the class of strategyproof and efficient mechanisms (the Groves mechanisms) characterized in Theorem 8.1. In this class, the additional requirements of anonymity and neutrality limit the choice of the transfers functions (13). Indeed, they take the form

$$t_i(u) = u_{N \setminus i}(a(u)) - h(u_{-i})$$

where the function h is symmetrical in all its variables and neutral.

Question: If such a mechanism must in addition be feasible, are we driven to the pivotal one? The case of two agents $(n = 2)$ suggests a positive answer. Indeed, feasibility reads

$$t_1(u) + t_2(u) = (u_2(a(u)) - h(u_2)) + (u_1(a(u)) - h(u_1)) \le 0$$

$$\Leftrightarrow \max_A \{u_1 + u_2\} \le h(u_1) + h(u_2)$$

The latter inequality is equivalent to $\max_A u_i \le h(u_i)$ (make $u_1 = u_2$), which in turn amounts to

$$t_1(u) = u_2(a(u)) - h(u_2) \le u_2(a(u)) - \max_A u_2 = t_1^*(u)$$

where $t_1^*(u)$ is the transfer required by the pivotal mechanism itself. Hence, our mechanism is actually Pareto inferior to (or coincides with) the pivotal one: It selects an efficient decision as well but taxes each agent more heavily. Even if there are several efficient decisions, each agent is always better off with the pivotal mechanism:

$$S_1(u) = \max_A(u_1+u_2) - h(u_2) \le \max_A(u_1+u_2) - \max_A(u_2) = S_1^*(u)$$

Thus, for two-agent problems where anonymity and neutrality are desirable, the pivotal mechanism has no serious rivals. This conclusion, however, does not carry over to three agents and more.

Lemma 8.3 (Moulin [1986b]).

(i)   *If there are only two agents then any strategyproof, efficient, feasible, and anonymous mechanism is Pareto inferior to (or coincides with) the pivotal mechanism.*

(ii) *If there are three agents or more then there exist strategyproof, efficient, feasible, anonymous, and neutral mechanisms that at some profiles generate a lower budget surplus than the pivotal:*

$$\sum_{i \in N} S_i^*(u) < \sum_{i \in N} S_i(u) \le \max_A \left(\sum_{i \in N} u_i \right) \quad \text{for some profile } u$$

The proof of statement (i) is explained in the preceding: note that the neutrality assumption is not necessary. The proof of statement (ii) is detailed in Exercise 8.7 by means of an example.

Finally, the pivotal mechanism can be characterized within the class of Groves mechanisms by a single axiom pertaining to a variable population. Decision a is selected as a pure public good from the consumption of which no agent can be excluded. Then an agent might consider withdrawing from the mechanism and *free riding* on the decision selected by the others. Sure enough, he loses any influence on the choice of a decision but he cannot be taxed anymore. The second effect may offset the first, and our agent might be better off free riding than participating.

With the pivotal mechanism, free riding is never profitable. Indeed, fix a profile u and an agent i. For *every* decision a efficient in the restricted society $N \setminus i$, we check that

$$u_i(a) \le S_i^*(u) = \max_A u_N - \max_A u_{N \setminus i}$$

Since $\max_A u_{N \setminus i} = u_{N \setminus i}(a)$, the preceding inequality is obvious.

Moulin [1986b] proves the converse statement: Within the class of Groves mechanisms (strategyproof, efficient, and feasible), only the pivotal mechanism generates no incentive to free ride. The proof is outlined in Exercise 8.7.

EXERCISES

8.1 Nash equilibrium messages in binary decisions

(a) Consider the cost sharing of an indivisible public good as in Example 8.1. Consider a direct mechanism whereby each agent reports his benefit a_i. The cost c of the public good is known to the planner. If $\sum_i a_i < c$, the good is not produced, and nobody pays anything. If $\sum_i a_i \geq c$, the good is produced, and agent i's cost share is $x_i(a, c)$ such that

$$0 \leq x_i(a, c) \leq \min\{a_i, c\}$$

Show that any cost sharing in the core of the *true* problem $(b_1, \ldots, b_n, c)$ is a Nash equilibrium outcome. Show that the only other Nash equilibria are messages where the good is not produced.

(b) Consider a surplus-sharing mechanism as in Section 6.1 where each agent reports his opportunity cost γ_i (the true opportunity cost is c_i). The overall return of cooperation is r. The mechanism does not undertake the cooperative venture if $\sum_i \gamma_i > r$. If $\sum_i \gamma_i \leq r$, on the other hand, cooperation takes place, and agent i receives the share $y_i(\gamma; r)$:

$$\sum_i y_i(\gamma, r) = r, \quad y_i(\gamma; r) \geq \gamma_i \quad \text{for all } i$$

Compute the Nash equilibrium messages when the true problem is $(c_1, \ldots, c_n; r)$ with $\sum_i c_i \leq r$.

(c) Consider a quasi-linear compensation problem as in Definition 8.1 but with two decisions a, b only, as in Example 8.2. Check that in the laissez-faire mechanism, if agent i's true utility is $u_i(a) = u_i$ [and $u_i(b) = -u_i$], the message $2u_i$ [i.e., $v_i(a) = 2u_i$, $v_i(b) = -2u_i$] dominates the truthful report.

(d) In the same problem as question (c), consider an efficient direct mechanism that guarantees the zero utility level to each agent (assuming that his reported message is the truth). Show that the Nash equilibrium utility vectors are all the efficient utility distributions where each agent gets a (true) nonnegative utility.

(e) Generalize the results of questions (c) and (d) to a quasi-linear compensation problem with an arbitrary number of public decisions.

8.2 Manipulations of the proportional cost sharing in Example 8.5. Consider the direct mechanism where each agent reports α_i (his true parameter is β_i), and the resulting outcome is

public good level: $y = \frac{1}{4}\alpha_N^2$

cost shares: $c_i = \frac{1}{4}\alpha_i \cdot \alpha_N$

Show that the vector of messages $(\alpha_1, \ldots, \alpha_n)$ is a Nash equilibrium when the true parameters are $(\beta_1, \ldots, \beta_n)$ if and only if:

$$\text{for all } i: \quad \alpha_i = \begin{cases} \beta_i - \frac{1}{2}\alpha_{N\setminus i} & \text{if } \beta_i \geq \frac{1}{2}\alpha_{N\setminus i} \\ 0 & \text{if } \beta_i < \frac{1}{2}\alpha_{N\setminus i} \end{cases}$$

Show that when all β_i are nearly equal (in a sense made precise in what follows), the Nash equilibrium level of public good is $\{(n+1)^2/4\}$ times smaller than the efficient level.

We now describe in full generality the unique solution of the preceding system. Assume that the agents are ranked in such a way that $\beta_1 \geq \beta_2 \geq \cdots \geq \beta_n$. Show the existence of a unique integer t, $1 \leq t \leq n$, such that

$$\beta_{t+1} \leq \frac{1}{t+1} \cdot \left(\sum_{i=1}^{t} \beta_i \right) < \beta_t$$

Then show that the unique solution of our system is given by

$$\alpha_i = \begin{cases} 2\left(\beta_i - \frac{1}{t+1}\left\{ \sum_{j=1}^{t} \beta_j \right\} \right) & \text{for } i = 1, \ldots, t \\ 0 & \text{for } i \geq t+1 \end{cases}$$

Deduce that the Nash equilibrium production of public good is always suboptimal if at least two agents have positive parameters β_i.

8.3   Pivotal mechanism with costs. There are n agents and a finite set A of public decisions. To each decision a is attached a cost $c(a)$. Utilities are quasi-linear as usual. The budget-balanced condition and the feasibility constraint are

$$\sum_{i=1}^{n} t_i + c(a) = 0, \qquad \sum_{i=1}^{n} t_i + c(a) \leq 0$$

Define as follows the pivotal mechanism:

decision $a(u)$ maximizes $\left(\sum_{i=1}^{n} u_i - c \right)$ over A

transfer to agent i: $t_i = \sum_{j \neq i} u_j(a(u)) - c(a(u)) - \max_{a \in A}\left\{ \left(\sum_{j \neq i} u_j \right) - \frac{n-1}{n}c \right\}$

Check that this is a feasible, strategyproof mechanism. Check that it coincides with the pivotal mechanism whenever $c = 0$. For what profiles is the mechanism budget balanced?

Compute the outcome of this mechanism in the following example:

	u_1	u_2	u_3	c
a	0	8	-5	0
b	-4	0	$+10$	$+5$
d	0	12	0	$+9$
e	3	-7	$+15$	$+15$

8.4 Comparing the pivotal and Groves–Loeb mechanism in Example 8.5.
Consider a strategyproof and efficient mechanism for the relevation of the parameters β_i. Thus, each agent reveals β_i. Then the public good is produced at the level $\frac{1}{4}\beta_N^2$, and the agents must pay the cost shares $x_i(\beta_1, \ldots, \beta_n)$, $i = 1, \ldots, n$.

(a) Show that the functions x_i take the form

$$x_i(\beta_1, \ldots, \beta_n) = \tfrac{1}{4}\beta_i^2 + h_i(\beta_{-i})$$

(you can use Theorem 8.1 by making sure that a decision means a level of public good *and* uniform cost shares to finance it; you can also make a direct argument).

(b) Suppose that our mechanism is anonymous (Definition 8.5) and budget balanced. Show that it is equal to the Groves–Loeb mechanism (11).

(c) Show that the pivotal mechanism with costs (see Exercise 8.3) corresponds to the following taxes (covering the cost of the public good and sometimes leaving a surplus):

$$x_i(\beta_1, \ldots, \beta_n) = \frac{1}{4}\left(\beta_i^2 + \frac{1}{n-1} \cdot \{\beta_{N\setminus i}\}^2 \right)$$

Check that when all agents but i have the same parameter $\beta_j = \lambda$, the tax on agent i is the same in the pivotal and in the Groves–Loeb mechanism. Thus, the pivotal mechanism does not offer a better guaranteed utility level than the Groves–Loeb.

8.5 A budget-balanced but inefficient mechanism (Champsaur and Rochet [1983]). We have two agents who must choose a public good level y, $0 \le y \le 1$. The cost is $c(y) = y$, and the benefit functions are linear:

$$b_i(y) = b_i \cdot y, \quad \text{all } y, \, 0 \le y \le 1$$

Assume $0 \le b_i \le 1$, $i = 1, 2$, and consider the following mechanism:
  Each agent reports his marginal utility b_i.
  If $b_1 + b_2 < 1$, no public good is produced: $y = 0$ and $x_1 = x_2 = 0$.
  If $b_1 + b_2 \ge 1$, the quantity $y = b_1 + b_2 - 1$ is produced and its cost shared as

$$x_1 = \tfrac{1}{2}(b_1^2 - (b_2 - 1)^2), \qquad x_2 = \tfrac{1}{2}(b_2^2 - (b_1 - 1)^2)$$

(a) Show that this mechanism is strategyproof, budget balanced, anonymous, and individually rational (agent i's utility is never below that of the initial position $y = 0$, $x_i = 0$). Show that it is, however, inefficient.

(b) Compute at each profile (b_1, b_2) the surplus wasted by the mechanism (loss in aggregate utility from the first-best outcomes). Compare this surplus loss function with that of the pivotal mechanism (adapted to take costs into account; see Exercise 8.3).

8.6 Strategyproof mechanisms with a status quo decision. Given are A, N as in Theorem 8.1 and a particular decision a_0 in A. Consider a strategyproof and efficient mechanism $(a(\cdot), t(\cdot))$ guaranteeing the utility level of the decision a_0 (interpreted as a status quo) to each agent:

$$u_i(a(u)) + t_i(u) \geq u_i(a_0) \quad \text{for all } i \in N, \text{ each profile } u$$

Show that this mechanism is not feasible and that its budget deficit is at least $n-1$ times the cooperative surplus above a_0:

$$\sum_{i \in N} t_i(u) \geq (n-1)\left(\max_A(u_N) - u_N(a_0)\right)$$

8.7 **Two more characterizations of the pivotal mechanism** (Moulin [1986b]). Notation is the same as in Lemma 8.2.

(a) Show that the maximal utility level of agent i in the pivotal mechanism corresponds to enjoying his favorite decision at no cost:

$$\max_{u_{-i}} S_i^*(u_i, u_{-i}) = \max_A u_i$$

(b) Consider a feasible, efficient, and strategyproof mechanism satisfying the following inequality:

$$S_i(u) \leq \max_A u_i \quad \text{for all } i, \text{ all } u$$

[where $S_i(u)$ is the final utility of agent i at profile u]. Show that our mechanism is Pareto dominated by – or equal to – the pivotal mechanism:

$$S_i(u) \leq S_i^*(u) \quad \text{for all } i, \text{ all } u$$

(c) *The no-free-ride axiom.* Given is a mechanism $(a^N(\cdot), t^N(\cdot))$ for each possible society N. The no-free-ride axiom is stated as follows:

for all N, all $i \in N$, each profile $u \in (E^A)^N$:

$$u_i(a^N(u)) + t_i^N(u) \geq u_i(a^{N\backslash i}(u_{-i}))$$

This says that agent i is better off participating in the mechanism rather than free riding on the decision taken by the remaining agents in his absence. We have noticed that the pivotal mechanism satisfies no free ride (see the end of Section 8.5). Conversely, show that if a mechanism is strategyproof, efficient, feasible, and satisfies no free ride, it must be a pivotal mechanism.

Hint: By Theorem 8.1, the mechanism takes the form (13). Use no free ride with $u_i = 0$ to derive $h_i(u_{-i}) \leq \max_A \{u_{N\backslash i}\}$. To prove the converse inequality, fix an arbitrary profile u_{-i} on $N\backslash i$ and construct u_i such that all $u_{N\backslash j}, j \in N$, have a common efficient decision.

8.8 **Proof of Lemma 8.3** (Moulin [1986b]). We have *two* decisions $A = \{a, b\}$ and three agents. Consider a mechanism given by (13) with the following functions $h_i(u_{-i})$:

$$h_i = h \quad \text{for } i = 1, 2, 3, \qquad h(u_2, u_3) = \max_A \{u_2 + u_3\} + k(u_2, u_3)$$

where

$$k(u_2, u_3) = \begin{cases} -\min\{|\delta_2|, |\delta_3|\} & \text{if } \delta_2 \cdot \delta_3 \leq 0 \\ 2\min\{|\delta_2|, |\delta_3|\} & \text{if } \delta_2 \cdot \delta_3 \geq 0 \end{cases}$$

and

$$\delta_i = u_i(a) - u_i(b)$$

In words, an agent is more heavily taxed than by the pivotal mechanism if the other two agree in comparing a and b. If they disagree, he is less taxed than by the pivotal mechanism (and may even be subsidized).

(a) Check that the mechanism is anonymous and neutral.
(b) Denote by $BS(u)$ the budget surplus of our mechanism:

$$BS(u) = \max_A u_N - \sum_{i=1}^{3} S_i(u) = \sum_{i=1}^{3} h(u_{-i}) - 2\max_A u_N$$

Then check that $BS(u)$ is nonnegative at all profiles (feasibility). Find some profiles where $BS(u) = 0$, whereas $BS^*(u) > 0$ (the budget surplus of the pivotal mechanism). Find some profiles where $BS^*(u) = 0$, whereas $BS(u) > 0$.

Hint: Assume, without loss, $\delta_1 \geq \delta_2 \geq \delta_3$ and distinguish the three cases (1) $\delta_i \geq 0$, all i; (2) $\delta_1, \delta_2 \geq 0$, $\delta_3 \leq 0$; and (3) $\delta_1 \geq 0$, $\delta_2, \delta_3 \leq 0$. In case (2), distinguish three subcases according to the sign of $\delta_1 + \delta_3$ and $\delta_2 + \delta_3$.

8.9 The Roberts mechanisms (K. Roberts [1979]). Notation is as in Definition 8.2. Given are A, N, a fixed utility function $u_0 \in E^A$, and a positive vector of weights $\lambda \in E_+^N$, $\lambda_i > 0$, for all $i \in N$. Consider a mechanism $(a(\cdot), t(\cdot))$ defined as follows:

for each profile u: $a(u)$ maximizes $u_0 + \sum_{i \in N} \lambda_i u_i$ over A

for all u and all i: $t_i(u) = \dfrac{1}{\lambda_i}\left[u_0(a(u)) + \sum_{j \neq i} \lambda_j u_j(a(u))\right] - h_i(u_{-i})$

Show that this mechanism is strategyproof. Conversely, K. Roberts [1979] shows that when A contains three decisions or more, this class contains essentially all strategyproof mechanisms.

Voting and social choice

CHAPTER 9

Majority voting and scoring methods

Overview

"Democracy uses, as a method of governing, social summaries of citizens'
decisions in elections and legislators' decisions in representative bodies"
(Riker [1982], p. 21). Indeed, most public allocative decisions (such as
taxes and public expenses) are made by voting. Elections are also used
to fill many public offices. These are important examples of pure public
goods (all citizens of a given town consume their mayor, with no possibility of exclusion) chosen by voting and precluding side payments.

Ever since the political philosophy of the Enlightenment, the choice of
a voting rule has been a major ethical question with far-reaching implications on the behavior of most political institutions. The debate about
fairness of various voting methods has been with us since the contributions of de Borda [1781] and Condorcet [1785]. In 1952, Arrow proposed
the formal model that framed for three decades a voluminous mathematically oriented literature known as social choice (see Arrow [1963]). It
studies the properties of various voting rules from an axiomatic angle.
The object of Part IV is to discuss the most important contributions of
the social choice approach.

Formally, a voting rule solves the collective decision problem where
several individual agents (voters) must jointly choose one among several
outcomes (also called candidates), about which their opinions conflict. In
this chapter we assume that a finite set N of voters must pick one candidate within a finite set A (we discuss other options in Chapter 10). For
simplicity we assume that individual opinions (or preferences) display no
ties; they are arbitrary linear orders of A (i.e., complete, transitive, and
asymmetric binary relations). This assumption entails no serious loss of
generality.

A voting rule achieves a systematic decision without precluding any
pattern of individual opinions. Denoting by $L(A)$ the set of linear orders

of A, a voting rule is thus a mapping from $L(A)^N$ into A. That the voting rule may be defined for any conceivable configuration of preferences expresses a fundamental freedom of opinion: Every voter is entitled to rank the candidates in any crazy way it pleases him. Nevertheless, in some voting models involving economic variables or uncertain outcomes, one may safely assume that voters' preferences follow some common patterns. This is especially relevant to the analysis of strategic voting and preference aggregation (see Sections 10.3 and 11.6).

A voting rule selects a candidate on the basis of the reported ordinal preferences, and of those preferences only. This contrasts with the models discussed in Parts I–III, where money and other divisible goods allow for arbitrarily small compensations among agents. Voting does not permit compromising between two candidates, except perhaps through a third candidate.

In this chapter we discuss actual voting rules, postponing until the last chapter the discussion of Arrow's famous impossibility theorem. The latter, as we shall see, pinpoints some axiomatic difficulties shared by *all* voting rules. More realistically, we seek here practical voting rules that can be recommended on *some* theoretical grounds.

When only two candidates are at stake, the ordinary majority voting is unambiguously the fairest method. This majority principle is the benchmark of democratic decision processes and was clearly enounced two centuries ago, although its origin is much more ancient (see the historical survey by Leo Moulin [1953]). The axiomatic formulation of the majority principle is due to May [1952]. May's theorem (Theorem 11.1) says that majority voting is the only method that is anonymous (equal treatment of all voters), neutral (equal treatment of the candidates), and monotonic (more support for a candidate does not jeopardize its election).

Consider voting among three candidates or more. What voting rule would properly extend majority voting among pairs? Plurality voting comes to mind first: Each voter writes the name of (exactly) one candidate on his ballot, and the candidate receiving most votes wins. This is by far the most popular voting rule, and its two celebrated critiques generated most of the modern scholarly research on voting rules. Both Borda and Condorcet noticed that plurality voting may elect a poor candidate, namely, one that would lose in pairwise majority comparisons to *every* other candidate. An example is discussed in Section 9.1.

To solve this difficulty, Condorcet and Borda proposed abandoning altogether plurality voting, and each came up with a different rule to replace it. That plurality voting is still widely used gives an idea of the speed at which those theories find their way into the real world.

Condorcet suggested electing the candidate defeating every other candidate in pairwise comparisons – if such a *Condorcet winner* exists. Borda assigned points to each candidate, linearly increasing with his ranking in a voter's opinion; he then proposed electing the candidate collecting the highest total score over all voters. These two ideas yield the two most important families of voting rules, namely, the Condorcet consistent methods (those rules must elect the Condorcet winner when there is one, with no further restrictions when there is none) and the scoring methods (where the system of points varies arbitrarily with rank). Chapter 9 compares critically the two families.

In Sections 9.1 and 9.2 we show how different their outcomes may be and check their basic efficiency and equity properties. One such property is the monotonicity axiom (Section 9.2). A voting rule is monotonic if a candidate *remains* elected when his support increases (i.e., when the relative position of this candidate improves in somebody's preferences while the relative position of the other candidates is unaffected). All scoring methods are monotonic, but some familiar methods derived from scoring are not. Examples are the (popular) plurality with runoff and the alternative-vote method.

In Section 9.3 we introduce two axioms that lead to a criticism of Condorcet consistent rules (because such rules must violate these two axioms) on the one hand and a characterization of scoring methods on the other. The axioms compare the candidate elected by different electorates; they are called reinforcement and participation. Reinforcement says that when two disjoint electorates (e.g., the Senate and the House) agree to elect candidate *a*, then the reunion of these two bodies confirms the election of *a*. Participation says that a voter never benefits by abstaining from voting rather than showing up at the polls to report sincerely his preferences. It is a surprising fact that *any* Condorcet consistent rule must violate both axioms (Theorems 9.2 and 9.3). By contrast, scoring rules are essentially characterized by reinforcement (Young's Theorem 9.4), and they do satisfy participation. Young's theorem is the most convincing argument to date in support of the scoring methods and, in particular, of the Borda points system.

Despite the criticisms of Section 9.3, Condorcet consistent voting rules are extremely popular, in part because of the simplicity of the pairwise majority comparisons argument. A prominent class of Condorcet consistent methods work by successive majority comparisons. A bill and its various amendments in the U.S. Congress are voted upon in this way. We observe that the familiar method of successive elimination may violate Pareto optimality. Other binary trees of majority comparisons violate the monotonicity axiom. The simplest pattern of successive comparisons meeting both Pareto optimality and monotonicity is called the multistage elimination method. It works by performing an elimination algorithm involving fewer pairwise comparisons than other conceptually simpler methods such as the Copeland rule. The latter elects whoever wins most majority duels. Thus, voting by successive majority comparisons can fulfill our most important axiomatic requirements but only if we choose the sequence accurately.

9.1   Condorcet versus Borda

When more than two candidates are at stake, the most popular voting method is plurality.

> *Plurality rule:* Each voter casts a vote for his or her favorite candidate. Elect the candidate who is named most often (ties are possible, but it is not necessary at this point to specify how they are broken).

On the face of it, this rule respects the will of the majority, for if a majority of voters have the same top candidate, he wins. Closer inspection, however, reveals that plurality may contradict the majority opinion. Here is Condorcet's argument. Consider a situation with 21 voters, 4 candidates, and the following preference *profile:*

$$
\begin{array}{cccc}
3 & 5 & 7 & 6 \\
a & a & b & c \\
b & c & d & b \\
c & b & c & d \\
d & d & a & a
\end{array}
\tag{1}
$$

This table reads: Three voters have the ordering $a > b > c > d$, five have $a > c > b > d$, and so on. According to plurality, a wins (with 8 votes) but, says Condorcet, a is actually the *worst* candidate for a clear majority of voters (13). This majority prefers any candidate to a. Furthermore, another majority (of 14 voters) prefers c to d, and a third majority (of only 11 voters) prefers c to b. Thus, argues Condorcet, c should actually be elected if we abide by the majority opinion.

Discussing the same profile (1), Borda agrees with Condorcet that a would be a poor candidate to elect, but he proposes a different winner – namely, b. He wants to take into account the ranking of each candidate in the voters' opinions. If I rank some candidate first, this should help him more than if I rank him second.

Compare b and c in (1). Then b is ranked first by 7 voters (against 6 for c); b is ranked first or second by 16 voters (against 11 for c), and b is ranked first, second, or third by all voters (as is c). Thus, b should have precedence over c. Borda actually proposes a specific way of taking ranks into account by scoring points linearly decreasing with the rank.

Definition 9.1: The Borda rule. *Each voter reports his preferences by ranking the p candidates from top to bottom (ties are not allowed). A candidate receives no points for being ranked last, one point for being ranked next to last, and so on, up to $p-1$ points for being ranked first. A candidate with highest **total** score, called a **Borda winner**, wins.*

Again, we do not specify how possible ties are broken. We define next Condorcet consistency.

Definition 9.2. *Given a preference profile, a **Condorcet winner** is a candidate a (necessarily unique) who defeats every other candidate in majority comparisons:*

for all $b \neq a$ more voters prefer a to b than b to a

A Condorcet consistent voting rule is one that elects a Condorcet winner when it exists.

Of course, we call a Borda loser (Condorcet loser) a candidate with the lowest Borda score (a candidate defeated by every other candidate in majority comparisons).

Note first that Borda's rule is truly a voting rule (once a tie-breaking device is chosen, it selects one candidate at every profile), whereas Condorcet consistency determines the elected candidate at a fraction of the profiles only, namely, at those profiles where a Condorcet winner exists. When a Condorcet winner does not exist, we have a configuration sometimes called a Condorcet paradox, where majority comparisons yield a cycle. A typical example is the following profile:

$$
\begin{array}{ccc}
8 & 7 & 6 \\
a & b & c \\
b & c & a \\
c & a & b
\end{array}
\tag{2}
$$

where 14 agents (of 21) prefer a to b, 15 prefer b to c, and 13 prefer c to a.

The absence of a Condorcet winner is the celebrated "voting paradox." In point of fact, there is nothing paradoxical in a cycle of majority

Table 9.1. *Probability of no Condorcet winner*

Number of candidates	Number of voters					
	3	5	7	9	11	Limit
3	.056	.069	.075	.078	.080 ...	.088
4	.111	.139	.150	.156	.160 ...	.176
5	.160	.200	.215	.230	.251 ...	.251
6	.202	.255[a]	.258[a]	.284[a]	.294[a] ...	.315
7	.239	.299[a]	.305[a]	.342[a]	.343[a] ...	.369
⋮	⋮	⋮	⋮	⋮	⋮	⋮
Limit	1	1	1	1	1	1

[a] Estimates.
Source: Fishburn [1973], p. 95.

preferences since a different majority may decide for each different pair of the cycle (as in the example just given). Immediately after proposing his notion of a winner, Condorcet recognizes the possibility of cycles and gives a similar example.

How often does the voting paradox happen? Political scientists generally agree that is is a rare phenomenon, although several historical instances are known where the paradox did occur and influenced the course of events; see the excellent book by Riker [1982], in particular Chapters 7 and 9. From a mathematical standpoint, one can estimate the probability of the paradox under the "impartial culture" assumption. Fix the number of voters, say, three, and of candidates, say, three. Draw at random a preference for each voter. Each voter is assigned one of the six possible orderings of candidates a, b, c with equal probability; further, the preferences of the three voters are mutually independent (no one is influenced by someone else's opinion). Under these premises, the probability that a Condorcet winner does *not* exist is only 0.056. To check this, fix the preferences of voter 1, say, $a > b > c$. Then the paradox arises if and only if the preferences of voters 2 and 3 are $b > c > a$ and $c > a > b$ in some order. This happens with probability $\frac{1}{18}$.

In general, the probability $\pi(p, n)$ that a Condorcet winner does not exist with p candidates and n voters appears to be increasing with p as well as when the number of voters rises from n to $n+2$. This has been tested by estimating $\pi(n, p)$ for small values of n and p, but the general statement remains an unproven conjecture (see Kelly [1986]). The probability of the paradox grows fairly rapidly when p grows larger, as shown in Table 9.1.

Thus, the voting paradox is almost a sure thing when the number of candidates becomes arbitrarily large for fixed n. When the number of voters becomes very large, for fixed p, the limit probability $\pi(p)$ has been estimated by Fishburn [1984]:

$$\pi(p) = \frac{p+0.2}{p+9.53} - (0.63)^{(p-3)/2}$$

which is accurate to within one half of a percent for $p \leq 50$. Of course, the impartial culture assumption is fairly unrealistic for large n (in a mass election, voters' opinions do influence each other) and for large p (because indifferences among some outcomes do emerge if there are too many outcomes).

A Condorcet consistent voting rule chooses a way to live with the paradox: When a Condorcet winner does not exist, it picks a reasonable substitute for it. This can be done in several ways; see the Copeland and Simpson rules in Section 9.2 and the sequential majority comparisons in Section 9.4. At this point we emphasize that Condorcet consistency is in fundamental disagreement with any method of point scoring where points are given according to ranks.

Definition 9.3: Scoring voting rules. *Fix a nondecreasing sequence of real numbers*

$$s_0 \leq s_1 \leq \cdots \leq s_{p-1} \quad \text{with} \quad s_0 < s_{p-1}$$

Voters rank the candidates, thus giving s_0 points to the one ranked last, s_1 to the one ranked next to last, and so on. A candidate with a maximal total score is elected.

The Borda and plurality rules are two examples of scoring rules (for plurality take $s_0 = s_1 = \cdots = s_{p-2} < s_{p-1}$). Another example is the anti-plurality rule, in which voters are asked to name the candidate they like least, and the candidate with the fewest votes wins.

Theorem 9.1 (Fishburn [1973]). *There are profiles where the Condorcet winner is never elected by any scoring method.*

Proof: Consider the following profile with seven voters and three candidates (Fishburn [1984]):

No. of voters:	3	2	1	1
s_2	c	a	a	b
s_1	a	b	c	c
s_0	b	c	b	a

Here c is the Condorcet winner. Yet if a scoring method has strictly increasing points ($s_0 < s_1 < s_2$), it must elect a instead:

$$\text{score of } a = 3s_2 + 3s_1 + s_0 > 3s_2 + 2s_1 + 2s_0 = \text{score of } c$$

The theorem holds also for arbitrary scoring methods where the sequence of points is not *strictly* increasing, as in plurality voting. The smallest example to show this involves no less than 17 voters (and 3 candidates):

No. of voters:	6	3	4	4
s_2	a	c	b	b
s_1	b	a	a	c
s_0	c	b	c	a

Here a is the Condorcet winner. Yet b wins in any scoring method. To see this, assume, without loss of generality, that $s_0 = 0$ so that $0 \leq s_1 \leq s_2$ and $s_2 > 0$. Compare total scores for a and b:

$$\text{score of } a = 6s_2 + 7s_1$$
$$\text{score of } b = 8s_2 + 6s_1$$

Observe that $8s_2 + 6s_1 = 8(s_2 - s_1) + 14s_1 > 6(s_2 - s_1) + 13s_1 = 6s_2 + 7s_1$, the inequality being strict since both $s_2 - s_1$ and s_1 are nonnegative and at least one is strictly positive. Q.E.D.

Interestingly, the set of candidates that can be elected by *some* scoring methods is easy to describe. Given a profile and a candidate a, construct a vector $r(a)$ in E^p as follows:

$$r_1(a) = \text{number of voters who rank } a \text{ first}$$
$$r_2(a) = \text{number of voters who rank } a \text{ first or second} \qquad (3)$$
$$r_k(a) = \text{number of voters who rank } a \ k\text{th or less}$$
$$\text{for } k = 1, \ldots, p-1, \text{ where } p \text{ is number of candidates}$$

Then candidate a will never be a winner in any scoring method if the vector $r(a)$ is Pareto inferior (in each coordinate) to the vector $r(b)$ for some other candidate b. This essentially determines the set of possible outcomes from scoring rules. See Exercise 9.3 for details.

Notice also that the plurality winner may be a Condorcet loser [as in profile (1)], but a Borda winner cannot be a Condorcet loser. Indeed, a Borda winner is a candidate who has *on average* the highest ranking or, equivalently, has on average the largest number of supporters in binary duels against other candidates. For a formal proof see Exercise 9.3.

9.2 Equity and monotonicity properties

We wish to compare scoring voting rules and Condorcet consistent rules by means of their normative properties. For that purpose we need to define explicitly some Condorcet consistent rule. The two most natural extensions of the Condorcet winner are defined as follows.

Definition 9.4: The Copeland rule. *Compare candidate a with every other candidate x. Score +1 if a majority prefers a to x, −1 if a majority prefers x to a, and 0 if it is a tie. Summing up those scores over all x, x ≠ a, yields the Copeland score of a. A candidate with the highest such score, called a* **Copeland winner,** *is elected.*

Definition 9.5: The Simpson rule. *Consider candidate a, and for every other candidate x, compute the number $N(a, x)$ of voters preferring a to x. The Simpson score of a is the minimum of $N(a, x)$ over all x, x ≠ a. A candidate with the highest such score, called a* **Simpson winner,** *is elected.*

To win with the Copeland rule, you must defeat as many other candidates as possible, even by a tiny margin. To win with the Simpson rule, you must make sure that no other candidate rallies a huge majority against you.

These two rules are Condorcet consistent. Indeed, a Condorcet winner uniquely achieves the highest Copeland score $p - 1$ (if p is the number of candidates) as well as a Simpson score above $\frac{1}{2}n$ (if n is the number of voters). Just as for the Borda rule or any scoring rule (Definitions 9.1 and 9.3), the Copeland and Simpson rules pick from each profile a subset of winners that may contain several tied candidates.

Here are the three basic normative properties of a voting rule:

Pareto optimality. If candidate a is unanimously preferred to candidate b, then b should not be elected.

Anonymity. The name of voters does not matter: If two voters exchange their votes, the outcome of the election is not affected.

Neutrality. The name of candidates does not matter: If we exchange two candidates a and b in the ordering of every voter, then the outcome of the election changes accordingly (if a was previously elected then b now is, and vice-versa; if some x different from a and b was elected, it still is).

Anonymity and neutrality must be imposed if we want to treat equitably voters as well as candidates. Pareto optimality is the familar efficiency requirement.

The Copeland rule and the Simpson rule are both Pareto optimal, anonymous, and neutral when we view them as correspondences, associating a subset of winners to every preference profile. Anonymity and neutrality are obvious. Checking that the set of Borda (Copeland, Simpson) winners contains only Pareto-optimal candidates is easy. For instance, the Simpson score of a Pareto-dominated candidate is zero, whereas that of a Pareto-optimal candidate is positive.

The Borda rule is Pareto optimal, anonymous, and neutral; so is any scoring voting rule in which the scores are all distinct ($s_k < s_{k+1}$; see Definition 9.3). But some scoring voting rules are not Pareto optimal, for instance, the anti-plurality rule ($s_0 = 0 < 1 = s_1 = \cdots = s_{p-1}$, with $p \geq 3$). Indeed, if all voters share the same opinion, all candidates but the bottom one will be elected, although only the top one is Pareto optimal.

What if we need to break ties to pick a single winner (in the Copeland, Simpson, or scoring case)? In general, we cannot do so without violating either anonymity or neutrality. This should be obvious when we have three voters, three candidates, and a symmetrical preference profile such as

$$
\begin{array}{ccc}
u_1 & u_2 & u_3 \\
a & c & b \\
b & a & c \\
c & b & a
\end{array}
\tag{4}
$$

If an anonymous, neutral, and deterministic voting rule elects, say, b, then by neutrality it should elect c at the profile obtained by permuting a into b, b into c, and c into a:

$$
\begin{array}{ccc}
u'_1 & u'_2 & u'_3 \\
b & a & c \\
c & b & a \\
a & c & b
\end{array}
\tag{5}
$$

But anonymity implies that profiles (4) and (5) elect the same outcome.

Thus, for most choices of n (number of voters) and p (number of candidates), there is no deterministic voting rule satisfying our three basic requirements. The only case in which such a rule exists is when n has no prime factor less than or equal to p; see Exercise 9.9 for details.

In practice, we will be happy with voting correspondences (such as the set of Borda winners or of Copeland winners) that respect the three principles and do not tie too frequently. If a deterministic election is called for, we will use either a non-anonymous tie-breaking rule (choose among tied candidates the one that agent 1 likes best) or a nonneutral one (among tied candidates, choose the first in alphabetical order).

Our next criterion is a monotonicity property. It says that more support for a candidate should not diminish its chances of being elected. This property is sometimes called positive responsiveness.

> *Monotonicity:* Suppose a is elected (is among the winners) at a given profile and that the profile changes only inasmuch as the ranking of a improves, the relative comparison of any other pair of candidates by any voter being unaffected. Then a is still elected (is still among the winners) at the new profile.

Not surprisingly, all scoring rules as well as the Copeland and Simpson rules are monotonic, whether we view them as correspondences or as deterministic choice rules (breaking ties by one of the two methods described). Indeed, when the profile changes by pushing candidate a up without affecting the restriction of the profile to the remaining candidates, the scores of a (its Copeland, Simpson, or Borda scores) cannot decrease, whereas the scores of any other candidate cannot increase.

The monotonicity requirement eliminates all sorts of foolish voting methods, such as the one electing Borda *losers.* That rule would be ruled out by Pareto optimality anyway, but consider the following rule: Among Pareto optimal candidates, choose one with lowest Borda scores.

A more serious consequence of monotonicity concerns plurality with runoff (widely used in France).

> *Plurality with runoff:* In the first round each voter casts a vote for one candidate. If a candidate wins a strict majority of votes, he is elected. Otherwise, a runoff by majority voting is called between the two candidates winning most votes in the first round.

Supporters of this method argue that it is almost as simple as plurality (a voter need not report a complete ordering of candidates) and avoids wasted votes. Under ordinary plurality, if I vote for a candidate receiving little support, my vote will be wasted. If there is a runoff, however, I have one more chance to influence the outcome. However, this method is *not* monotonic, as the two following profiles with 17 voters demonstrate:

No. of voters:	Profile A				No. of voters:	Profile B			
	6	5	4	2		6	5	4	2
	a	c	b	b		a	c	b	a
	b	a	c	a		b	a	c	b
	c	b	a	c		c	b	a	c

With profile A, a and b go for a runoff, won by a (11 votes to 6). Profile B is identical, except that the two voters with preferences $b > a > c$

now prefer a to b, $a > b > c$. Then a and c go for a runoff won by c (9 votes to 8). Thus, the push-up to a results in his defeat!

In the same vein as plurality with runoff, we have:

> *The alternative-vote method:* Eliminate first the plurality losers. Compute plurality scores among the remaining candidates, and eliminate, again, the losers. Repeat the operation until a single candidate (or a set of tied candidates) is left.

Here, great care is taken to waste no votes and give a chance to everyone to support the candidate he likes best. The idea is to repeatedly use scoring methods to eliminate the losing candidates.

This seems to make sense, as we take certainly less risk by eliminating a Borda loser than by electing a Borda winner (if we replace plurality by the Borda rule in each elimination round, we even get a Condorcet consistent method; see Exercise 9.4). Alas, *any* rule based on successive elimination by scoring methods must violate monotonicity at some profiles. The proof is a 27-voter example due to Fishburn [1982]:

$$
\begin{array}{ccccccc}
\text{No. of voters:} & 6 & 4 & 6 & 2 & 6 & 3 \\
 & a & b & b & c & c & a \\
 & b & a & c & b & a & c \\
 & c & c & a & a & b & b
\end{array}
\tag{6}
$$

Say that we eliminate first according to a vector of scores $s_0 = 0 \le s_1 \le s_2$ (where $0 < s_2$) and next according to majority voting. First c is eliminated, since $9s_1 + 8s_2 < \min\{10s_1 + 9s_2, 8s_1 + 10s_2\}$; next b loses in the second round.

Suppose next that five agents (three among the four with $b > a > c$ and the two with $c > b > a$) give a little push-up to a, who now beats b. The new profile is

$$
\begin{array}{cccccc}
\text{No. of voters:} & 9 & 1 & 6 & 8 & 3 \\
 & a & b & b & c & a \\
 & b & a & c & a & c \\
 & c & c & a & b & b
\end{array}
$$

In the first round, b is now eliminated ($9s_1 + 7s_2 < \min\{9s_1 + 12s_2, 9s_1 + 8s_2\}$) so in the second round c knocks a down 14 to 13.

9.3   Reinforcement and participation

In the debate between Condorcet consistent and scoring methods, the followers of Condorcet argue for the very simplicity of their principle; the notion of majority comparisons is easy to grasp and seems closer to the people's opinion than scores. Many will feel that the addition of elaborate scores grinds any single vote through a mathematical formula, whereas a succession of majority duels gives reliable information about the group's preferences. This line of argument leads to the voting methods by successive majority comparisons, to which Section 9.4 is devoted. It also justifies Arrow's independence of irrelevant alternatives, which is the central axiom of Chapter 11.

Yet Borda's supporters also have very strong arguments to support scoring methods against Condorcet consistency.

The two most compelling arguments express consistency properties of the election outcomes from different bodies of voters. These axioms are formulated in the variable-population context (as in Sections 3.4, 3.5, and 5.6). The first property was introduced by Smith [1973] and Young [1974] and is known as Young's reinforcement axiom.

> *Reinforcement (deterministic voting rules):* Two disjoint groups of voters N_1, N_2 face the same set A of candidates. Say that electorate N_1 and N_2 both elect candidate a. Then the electorate $N_1 \cup N_2$ should elect a as well within A.

This property is very reasonable when the overall voting body is likely to split into many subsets, as for regional assemblies or subcommittees. Suppose A is the set of formulations of a bill, and the relevant committees in the House of Representatives and Senate each vote separately to recommend the same alternative $a \in A$. The reinforcement axiom says that in joint session they should still select a.

The axiom can also be stated for voting correspondences, selecting a subset of tied winners from every preference profile. This is useful when we insist on the anonymity and neutrality requirements (see Theorem 9.4).

> *Reinforcement (voting correspondences):* Two disjoint groups of voters N_1, N_2 face the same set A of candidates. Say the electorate N_i selects subset B_i of A for each $i = 1, 2$. If B_1 and B_2 intersect, then electorate $N_1 \cup N_2$ should select $B_1 \cap B_2$ as the set of equally best outcomes.

Theorem 9.2 (Young [1975]).   (a) *All scoring voting correspondences (choosing the subset of candidates with highest total score) satisfy reinforcement. If ties are broken according to a fixed ordering of A, the corresponding scoring voting rules satisfy reinforcement as well.*

(b) *There is no Condorcet consistent voting rule (or voting correspondence) satisfying reinforcement.*

Proof: Statement (a). If a receives a total score t_1 from the voters in N_1 and t_2 from those in N_2, he will get $t_1 + t_2$ from $N_1 \cup N_2$. Hence, scoring voting correspondences satisfy reinforcement. When the tie-breaking rule is by a fixed ordering of A, the axiom still holds: If a is highest in B_1 and B_2 for this ordering, it is highest in $B_1 \cap B_2$ as well.

Statement (b). Note that if voting is restricted to profiles in which at least one Condorcet winner exists, then selecting the Condorcet winners does satisfy the reinforcement axiom. Indeed, if a majority in N_1 and a majority in N_2 prefer a to x, then a majority in $N_1 \cup N_2$ prefers a to x. Thus, the violation of reinforcement is due to majority cycles.

Take any number $n_1 \geq 3$ of agents and any preference profile u where no Condorcet winner exists. Suppose our Condorcet consistent method selects some candidate a (among others). Since a is not a Condorcet winner, there is another candidate b such that m agents, $\frac{1}{2}n_1 < m \leq n_1$, prefer b to a. Now set $n_2 = 2m + n_1$ and consider the following profile on $2N_1 \cup N_2$:

No. of voters:	n_1	n_1	$2m$	n_1
			a	b
			b	a
	u	u	c	c
			$\vdots$	$\vdots$
	$\underbrace{}_{N_1}$	$\underbrace{}_{N_1}$	$\underbrace{}_{N_2}$	

Since a is elected by N_1, it must also be elected by $2N_1$ if reinforcement holds true. Since a is the unique Condorcet winner on N_2, it must be elected (uniquely) by N_2. But in $2N_1 \cup N_2$, b is the unique Condorcet winner, so reinforcement cannot hold after all.   Q.E.D.

Next to reinforcement we have a related monotonicity axiom called participation. We give the intuition of this axiom by showing first why a typical Condorcet consistent method, the Simpson voting correspondence, violates it.

Consider an election with 4 candidates and 15 voters with the following preferences:

No. of voters:	3	3	5	4
	a	a	d	b
	d	d	b	c
	c	b	c	a
	b	c	a	d

The Simpson scores are

$$S(a) = N(a,c) = N(a,b) = 6$$
$$S(b) = N(b,d) = 4$$

$$S(c) = N(c, b) = 3$$
$$S(d) = N(d, a) = 5$$

Thus, a is the unambiguous Simpson winner (although it is not a Condorcet winner). Next suppose that four additional voters with identical preferences $c > a > b > d$ show up at the polls. We compute the new scores:

$$S(a) = N(a, c) = 6$$
$$S(b) = N(b, d) = 8$$
$$S(c) = N(c, b) = 7$$
$$S(d) = N(d, a) = 5$$

Now b wins. Therefore, the four new voters had rather stayed home, making a win, than participated! This is the *no-show paradox* (Brams and Fishburn [1983]). It may happen that adding my own ballot to the urn results in a utility loss for me. To avoid this perverse phenomenon – akin to, but different from, the violation of monotonicity – we formulate the following axiom:

> *Participation:* Say that candidate a is elected from the set A by the electorate N. Next consider a voter i outside N. Then the electorate $N \cup \{i\}$ should elect a or some candidate whom agent i strictly prefers to a.

This says that if an additional vote succeeds in changing the outcome of the election, it can only be to the benefit of this "pivotal" voter.

Theorem 9.3 (Moulin [1986c]).   (a) *All scoring voting rules – where ties are broken according to a fixed ordering of A – satisfy participation.*
    (b) *If A contains four candidates or more, there is no Condorcet consistent voting rule satisfying participation.*

The proof is the subject of Exercise 9.6, showing also that with three candidates, Condorcet consistency and participation are compatible.

We conclude this section by stating one of the most interesting results of the theory of voting. It says that reinforcement is essentially enough to characterize the scoring methods.

We need to introduce an additional continuity property.

> *Continuity:* Say that the electorate N_1 elects candidate a from A whereas a disjoint electorate N_2 elects a different candidate b. Then we can replicate the electorate N_1 sufficiently many times – say, m – so that the combined electorate $(mN_1) \cup N_2$ chooses a.

This is a mild requirement: If a coalition of voters contains a sufficiently small fraction of the total voters, it should not be able to influence the final outcome. Notice that reinforcement implies that the set of winning candidates is not affected when we replicate the electorate.

Theorem 9.4 (Young [1975]).   *A voting correspondence is a scoring method (Definition 9.3 where ties are not broken) if and only if it satisfies the four following properties:*

> *anonymity, neutrality, reinforcement, and continuity*

We omit the difficult proof.

Weber [1978] compares deterministic voting rules by means of their "effectiveness," that is, the expected satisfaction enjoyed by voters whose utilities for candidates are independently and uniformly distributed. He finds that Borda's method is nearly optimal when the number of voters is large.

In the next chapter, we will consider voting rules of which the outcome is a lottery over the set of candidates. Scoring methods generalize to this context and are then characterized by a strategyproofness argument (see Remark 10.2 and Exercise 10.9).

9.4   Sequential majority comparisons

Despite the problems uncovered in the previous section, Condorcet consistency is widely regarded as a compelling democratic principle.

Of course, Condorcet consistent voting rules differ at those profiles where a Condorcet winner does not exist. The Copeland and Simpson rules (Definitions 9.4 and 9.5) resolve the problem by calling each and every pair of candidates for a majority vote. In practice, this is a lengthy process, to which simpler algorithms must be preferred. Here is one familiar method used in the U.S. Congress to vote upon a motion and its proposed amendments. It is known as the amendment procedure (see Riker [1982], p. 70, for details):

$$(7)$$

Voting by successive elimination: First a majority vote decides to eliminate a or b, then a majority vote is called to eliminate the survivor from the first round or c, and so on. In case of ties, the lower candidate loses.

In the amendment procedure, a would be the amendment, b the amendment to the amendment, c the original motion, and d the status quo.

This method satisfies the Condorcet consistency axiom: If a is a Condorcet winner, he wins. Actually, it is consistent with majority comparisons in an even stronger sense:

Smith's consistency: If the set A of candidates splits into two disjoint subsets B_1, B_2 and every $b_1 \in B_1$ beats (by a strict majority) every $b_2 \in B_2$, then an outcome from B_1 should be elected.

On the other hand, voting by successive elimination is inherently not neutral. The order of elimination obviously matters to the outcome. To see this, consider the following five-voter profile:

No. of voters:	1	2	1	1
	d	a	d	b
	b	b	c	c
	a	c	a	d
	c	d	b	a

The corresponding majority comparisons are collected in the following "majority tournament":

$$(8)$$

where we read a beats b, b beats c, b beats d, and so on.

Now suppose the chairman of the committee has the power to set the agenda, namely, the ordering in which candidates will be successively compared. It is easy to realize that he can then force the election of whichever candidate he wishes. For instance, to get c elected, the following agenda will do:

Similarly, we have

elects *d*   elects *a*   elects *b*

Thus, by setting the agenda, the chairman actually controls the election outcome. Although not all profiles endow the agenda setter with absolute power, at any profile where no Condorcet winners exist, the choice of the agenda does influence the election; see Exercise 9.10, question (d).

In addition to the lack of neutrality, the successive elimination method may violate Pareto optimality. Consider the following three-voter profile:

1	1	1
b	*a*	*c*
a	*d*	*b*
d	*c*	*a*
c	*b*	*d*

and the successive elimination ordering *abcd* [as in (7)]. Then *b* beats *a*, next *c* beats *b*, next *d* beats *c*, and so *d* is finally elected. Yet *a* is unanimously preferred to *d*!

Thus, voting by successive elimination is inherently unfair (lack of neutrality). The candidate entering last (*d* in the example) has an obvious advantage, for he wins by defeating only one opponent. By contrast, any one of the two candidates entering first (*a* and *b* in our example) must defeat every other outcome (namely, be a Condorcet winner) to win.

This defect can be solved easily in the four-candidate case. Consider the following elimination tournament:

$$
\begin{array}{cccc}
a & b & c & d
\end{array}
$$

(9)

Parallel-elimination rule: Oppose first *a* to *b* and *c* to *d* by a majority vote. The two winners meet in the final majority vote. In case of ties the first candidate in alphabetic order wins.

Again, this method is Condorcet consistent. Moreover, the elected candidate *x* must win at least two majority contests to be elected. Suppose first these two votes are not tied (x wins by a strict majority). Then x cannot be Pareto inferior to some candidate y, for y would be a Condorcet winner. Thus, the parallel-elimination method chooses a Pareto-optimal outcome in the (most frequent) case where no binary vote results in a draw. However, Pareto optimality may be violated when ties occur. Consider the following four-voter profile:

No. of voters:	2	2
	d	c
	a	d
	c	a
	b	b

Here a wins against b, but the tie-breaking rule sees c beat d, then a beat c. The winner a is Pareto dominated by d.

We run into a general question: For an arbitrary number of candidates, can we design a pattern of successive eliminations along a well-constructed tree that would elect a Pareto-optimal outcome at all profiles?

To state the question with the proper degree of generality, we attach to every preference profile its *majority tournament,* namely, the binary relation T resulting from majority comparisons: aTb means a majority prefers a to b. For simplicity, we suppose throughout the rest of this chapter that none of the pairwise majority comparisons is tied. Thus, for any two candidates a, b, exactly one of aTb or bTa holds. Our assumption is true, for instance, if the number of voters is odd and reporting indifference is not permitted.

Denote by A the set of candidates. A *binary tree* on A is a finite tree where each nonterminal node (including the origin) has exactly two successors, each terminal node (zero successor) has attached to it a candidate (an element of A), and each candidate appears at least on one terminal node.

For instance, here is a binary tree on $A = \{a, b, c, d\}$:

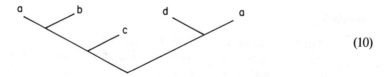

$$(10)$$

To a binary tree on A, we associate the following voting rule. Given any preference profile, compute its majority tournament T. Then solve the tree according to T:

(i) Pick a nonterminal node n whose two successors m, m' are terminal nodes (such a node exists; consider a path with maximal length going upward from the origin and take the node next to the last).

(ii) If x, x' are the candidates attached to m, m', call y the majority winner:

$$y = \begin{cases} x & \text{if } xTx' \text{ or } x = x' \\ x' & \text{otherwise} \end{cases}$$

(iii) Delete the two branches nm and nm', thus making n a terminal node with attached candidate y.

(iv) Repeat this operation until a tree with one single node (the origin of Γ) is left. Its attached candidate is elected.

For instance, with the tree (10) and tournament aTb, aTc, bTd, cTd, dTa, we get the following elimination process of which d is the winner:

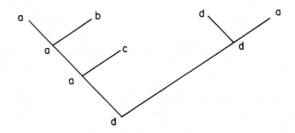

It is easy to check that any binary tree generates a Condorcet consistent (even a Smith consistent) voting method. Other basic properties such as Pareto optimality (see the preceding) and monotonicity (see what follows) are not always satisfied.

Among binary trees on A, the simplest are those where each candidate is attached to *exactly one* terminal node. We call them *knock-out elimination trees*. For instance, voting by successive elimination (7) and parallel elimination (9) are knock-out trees, but the tree (10) is not.

Lemma 9.1

(a) *When A contains three candidates, the successive elimination tree is the unique knock-out tree. The corresponding voting rule is Pareto optimal (under our assumption that all majority comparisons are strict).*

(b) *When A contains four candidates, successive elimination and parallel elimination are the only two knock-out trees. The former violates Pareto optimality; the latter does not.*

(c) *When A contains five candidates or more, any knock-out elimination tree will select a Pareto-inferior candidate at some profiles.*

Proof: Statement (b) is already proven, and the proof of statement (a) is quite similar. To prove statement (c), observe that in any binary tree with five terminal nodes or more, there exists a path of length 3 or more. We can find a node n following the origin 0 and a nonterminal node n' following n:

$$(11)$$

Partition A into four subsets: B contains the candidates attached to a node following the branch at 0 not containing n; C contains those following the branch at n not containing n'; and E and D correspond to the two branches from n' [see (11)]. Pick an outcome b in B, c in C, d in D, and e in E. Then consider a profile where all candidates but b, c, d, e are Pareto inferior (every agent prefers any one of these four to anyone else). At such a profile the binary tree voting method reduces to successive elimination:

Hence, it is not Pareto optimal [statement (b)]. Q.E.D.

Thus, a binary tree generating a Pareto-optimal voting rule must be more complicated than a knock-out tree. However, by multiplying the terminal nodes at which the same candidate is attached, we run the risk of violating yet another basic requirement, namely, monotonicity. Indeed, as the example of Exercise 9.4 shows, some of those binary trees generate a nonmonotonic voting rule (although all knock-out elimination trees yield monotonic rules).

Fortunately, there exists a binary tree defined for any number of candidates and avoiding both dangers. The corresponding sequence of majority comparisons generates a Pareto-optimal, anonymous, and monotonic voting rule. This remarkable tree is called the *multistage elimination* tree.

There is one such tree for each particular ordering of the candidates. We denote by $\Gamma_p(1, 2, ..., p)$ the tree corresponding to the ordering $A = \{1, 2, ..., p\}$. It is defined by induction on the size of A:

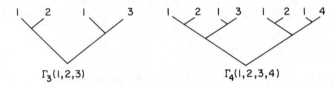

Thus, for three and four candidates, we have:

The tree among p candidates has 2^{p-1} terminal nodes; candidate 1 is attached to 2^{p-2} terminal nodes, whereas candidate p is attached to just one such node. Yet, to be finally elected, even p must win $p-1$ duels (although he may face the same opponent many times).

Although the tree involved in multistage elimination is big, its solution – namely, the computation of the winning candidate – is given by a very simple algorithm.

Theorem 9.5 (Shepsle and Weingast [1984]). *Given are the multistage elimination tree $\Gamma_p(1, 2, ..., p)$ and a preference profile with associated majority tournament T. The elected candidate a^* is given by the following algorithm:*

$$\alpha_1 = 1$$

$$for\ i = 2, ..., p: \quad \alpha_i = \begin{cases} i & if\ iT\alpha_{i-1},\ iT\alpha_{i-2},\ ...,\ iT\alpha_1 \\ \alpha_{i-1} & if\ \alpha_j T\alpha_i\ for\ some\ j,\ 1 \le j \le i-1 \end{cases} \quad (12)$$

$$\alpha_p = a^*$$

Proof: By induction on p. For $p = 1, 2$ the claim is obvious. Suppose it is true up to $p-1$ and consider a tournament T on $\{1, 2, ..., p\}$. Denote by T^{-p} ($T^{-(p-1)}$) the restriction of T to $\{1, 2, ..., p-1\}$ (to $\{1, 2, ..., p-2, p\}$). Denote by β_{p-1} the outcome of $\Gamma_{p-1}(1, 2, ..., p-1)$ on T^{-p} with associated sequence $\beta_1, ..., \beta_{p-1}$ in (12). Similarly, γ_{p-1} is the outcome of $\Gamma_{p-1}(1, 2, ..., p-2, p)$ on $T^{-(p-1)}$ with associated sequence $\gamma_1, ..., \gamma_{p-1}$. By the inductive definition of $\Gamma_p(1, 2, ..., p)$, its outcome a on tournament T is given by

$$a = \begin{cases} \beta_{p-1} & \text{if } \beta_{p-1}T\gamma_{p-1} \\ \gamma_{p-1} & \text{if } \gamma_{p-1}T\beta_{p-1} \end{cases} \tag{13}$$

Now consider the sequence $\alpha_1, \dots, \alpha_p$ defined by (12). By construction, we have

$$\{\text{for } i = 1, \dots, p-2: \ \alpha_i = \beta_i = \gamma_i\} \quad \text{and} \quad \{\alpha_{p-1} = \beta_{p-1}\}$$

In order to prove $\alpha_p = a$, we distinguish three cases.

Case 1: $\gamma_{p-1} = \gamma_{p-2}$. Then for some i, $1 \le i \le p-2$, $\gamma_i Tp$. Since $\alpha_i = \gamma_i$ this implies $\alpha_p = \alpha_{p-1}$. On the other hand, $\beta_{p-1}T\beta_{p-2}$ [by (12) again with the convention xTx], so from $\gamma_{p-1} = \beta_{p-2}$ we get $\beta_{p-1}T\gamma_{p-1}$. Therefore, by (13) $a = \beta_{p-1}$, so $a = \alpha_{p-1} = \alpha_p$, and we are done.

Case 2: $\gamma_{p-1} = p$ *and* $\beta_{p-1} = \beta_{p-2}$. In this case p beats any α_i, $1 \le i \le p-2$ (definition of γ_{p-1}) *and* β_{p-1} is one of them. So p beats $\alpha_1, \dots, \alpha_{p-1}$. Hence, $\alpha_p = p$. On the other hand, $\gamma_{p-1} = p$ beats $\beta_{p-1} = \alpha_{p-2}$, so by (13) we get $a = p$.

Case 3: $\gamma_{p-1} = p$ *and* $\beta_{p-1} = p-1$. Here both p and $p-1$ beat $\{\alpha_1, \dots, \alpha_{p-2}\}$. Thus, $\alpha_p = p$ if $pT(p-1)$ and $\alpha_p = (p-1)$ if $(p-1)Tp$. By (13), on the other hand, a is just the same. Q.E.D.

Corollary to Theorem 9.5. *The candidate a elected by the multistage elimination tree at tournament T satisfies*

for all $b \in A$, $b \ne a$: $\{aTb\}$ *and/or* $\{$*for some c, aTc and cTb*$\}$ (14)

In particular, a is Pareto optimal. Moreover, the multistage elimination tree defines a monotonic voting method.

Proof: To prove (14), denote by a the outcome of (12). Suppose a is ranked i and consider a different b ranked j. Suppose first $j < i$. If $\alpha_j = j$, then by (12) we have aTb. If $\alpha_j = \alpha_{j-1}$, then b is beaten by some $c = \alpha_k$, $k < j$ whereas a beats c, thus proving (14). Suppose next $j > i$. Then j is beaten by one of $\alpha_1, \dots, \alpha_i = a$ whereas a beat $\alpha_1, \dots, \alpha_{i-1}$; so conclusion (14) follows.

Deduce from (14) that a is Pareto optimal. If b is Pareto superior to a, then aTb is impossible, so there exists c such that aTc – a strict majority prefers a to c – and cTb – a strict majority prefers c to b. As two strict majorities must intersect, we find a voter preferring a to b, a contradiction.

To prove monotonicity, consider two profiles u and u' differing only inasmuch as the relative position of a in u is better. The corresponding tournaments T and T' differ only inasmuch as some (maybe none) relations bTa become aTb. Check then that if a wins algorithm (12) for T, it must win it for T' as well. Q.E.D.

The set of candidates satisfying (14) is called the *uncovered set* of the tournament T (Miller [1980]). It is a singleton if and only if T has a Condorcet winner, otherwise it contains at least three elements; see Exercise 9.11 and the articles by Banks [1985] and Moulin [1986c] for more details.

Among Condorcet consistent voting rules, we have discovered three methods meeting the fundamental requirements of Pareto optimality, anonymity, and monotonicity: the set of Copeland winners, the set of Simpson winners, and the multistage elimination tree. The former two are neutral but may have ties (the tie-breaking rule will destroy neutrality). Notice that the multistage elimination winner is quicker to compute because algorithm (12) on average does not have to compare more than half of the $\frac{1}{2}p(p-1)$ pairs, whereas to compute the Copeland and Simpson winners requires the entire majority tournament. Actually, Moulin [1986c] shows that no binary tree exists of which the winner is always a Copeland (Simpson) winner. This result is explained in Exercise 9.8.

EXERCISES

9.1 **A curious profile** (Straffin [1980]). Consider the following profile, with nine voters and five candidates:

No. of voters:	1	4	1	3
	a	c	e	e
	b	d	a	a
	c	b	d	b
	d	e	b	d
	e	a	c	c

(a) Construct the majority tournament. Identify the Copeland winner and the Simpson winner.

(b) Compute the Borda winner. Show that the Borda scores rank the candidates in the reverse of the Copeland scores.

(c) Find a scoring method that uniquely elects c, one for b, and one for d.

9.2 **The alternative-vote method.** Consider the following profile with 17 voters and 7 candidates, suggested by Dummett [1984], p. 172:

Name of voter:	1	2	3	4	5	6	7	8	9	10	11	12	13	14	15	16	17
	a	a	a	b	b	b	b	c	c	c	c	d	d	d	e	e	f
	g	b	c	f	g	d	a	d	e	g	g	f	g	g	g	f	g
	f	e	b	g	f	c	c	g	g	f	f	g	e	f	f	g	a
	e	d	f	e	e	a	d	f	f	e	e	e	f	e	b	a	e
	d	g	g	d	c	e	e	e	d	d	d	c	b	a	d	d	d
	c	f	e	c	d	f	g	a	b	a	b	a	c	c	c	c	c
	b	c	d	a	a	g	f	b	a	b	a	b	a	b	a	b	b

Show that the alternative-vote method (see Section 9.2) would eliminate successively g, f, e, d, c, and b, making a the winner. Check that
Borda scores are in perfect contradiction of this: that is, g has the highest score, f is second, then e, and so on. Check also that the Copeland
scores coincide with Borda scores except for the relative rankings of a
and b.

9.3 More on scoring methods

(a) A Condorcet winner (loser) cannot be a Borda loser (winner). To prove
the claim, fix a preference profile with n voters and p candidates. Denote by $\beta(a)$ the Borda score of candidate a and by $N(a, b)$ the number
of voters preferring a to b. Then prove the formula

$$\beta(a) = \sum_{b \neq a} N(a, b)$$

Check that if a is a Condorcet winner, we must have $\beta(a) > n \cdot (p-1)/2$,
whereas $n \cdot (p-1)/2$ is precisely the average Borda score.

(b) Consider a strictly increasing vector of scores $s_0 < s_1 < \cdots < s_{p-1}$. Show
that if candidate a is an s winner, its associated vector $r(a)$ [(3)] is Pareto optimal: There is no other outcome b such that $r_k(b) \geq r_k(a)$ for all
$k = 1, \ldots, p-1$ with at least one strict inequality. *Hint*: Define $d_k = s_k - s_{k-1}$ for $k = 1, \ldots, p-1$. Then show that the s score $\sigma(a)$ of candidate a is given by

$$\sigma(a) = n \cdot s_0 + \sum_{k=1}^{p-1} d_{p-k} \cdot r_k(a)$$

(c) Consider an arbitrary vector of scores (Definition 9.3). Show that if a is
an s winner, the vector $r(a)$ is weakly Pareto optimal: There is no candidate b such that $r_k(b) > r_k(a)$ for all $k = 1, \ldots, p-1$.

9.4 Condorcet consistency and monotonicity

(a) The Nanson method consists of successively eliminating the Borda losers (computing fresh scores after each round of elimination, just as the
alternative-vote method does for plurality). Show that this method is
Condorcet consistent [use question (a) of Exercise 9.3]. Yet it is not
monotonic by virtue of example (6).

(b) Consider the following elimination tree on a set of candidates $\{a, b, c, d\}$:

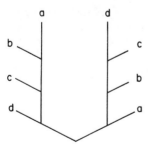

This is a Condorcet consistent voting rule. Check that it is also Pareto optimal (assuming, as in Section 9.4, that all pairwise comparisons are strict). Next show that the rule is not monotonic by considering the two following three-voter profiles:

b	d	c		a	d	c
a	a	b	and	b	a	b
c	c	d		c	c	d
d	b	a		d	b	a

(c)   Show that all knock-out elimination trees yield a monotonic voting rule.

9.5

(a)   In voting by successive elimination, prove that candidate a_1 (or a_2) is elected only if he is a Condorcet winner:

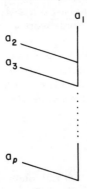

Hence, they are at a disadvantage. Prove that the later a candidate enters, the better his chances of winning in the following sense: If a_k is elected at a given profile, then he is still elected when the candidates enter as

$$a_1, a_2, \ldots, a_{k-1}, a_{k+1}, a_k, a_{k+2}, \ldots, a_n$$

(b)   In voting by multistage elimination, prove that the first candidate is elected only if he is a Condorcet winner. Prove as above that the later a candidate enters, the better his chances of winning [use algorithm (12)].

9.6   Proof of Theorem 9.3 (Moulin [in press])

(a)   Show that any scoring voting rule where ties are broken by a fixed ordering of the candidates satisfies participation.

However, successively eliminating candidates by means of scoring methods may lead to the no-show paradox. To check this, use plurality with runoff on the following profile:

No. of voters:	3	4	4
	a	b	c
	c	a	b
	b	c	a

Check that if two voters with preferences $b > a > c$ did not show up, their utility would increase.

(b) Consider the case with three candidates and show that the Simpson voting rule (with ties broken by a fixed ordering of A) satisfies participation.

However, not every Condorcet consistent rule does. For instance, consider successive elimination

at the following profile:

No. of voters	1	2	2	2
	c	a	b	c
	b	c	a	a
	a	b	c	b

Check that the two voters with preferences $c > a > b$ are better off staying home.

(c) *Proof of statement (b) in Theorem 9.3.* Consider a Condorcet consistent voting rule defined for electorates of all sizes and satisfying participation. For a given electorate N with size n, denote by $t(a)$ the Simpson score of candidate a (see Definition 9.5):

$$t(a) = \min_{x \neq a} N(a, x)$$

Next pick two candidates a, b and assume

$$t(b) \geq N(a, b) + 1 \tag{15}$$

Then augment N by m identical voters, $m = n - 2t(b) + 1$, who have a on top and b second. Check that in the augmented profile with $n + m$ voters, b is the Condorcet winner. Yet by participation, if a was elected in the initial profile over N, it should still be elected in the augmented profile. We have proven the following property for all a, b:

$$t(b) \geq N(a, b) + 1 \Rightarrow a \text{ is not elected} \tag{16}$$

Use this to show that a must be elected at the following profile with 15 voters and 4 candidates:

No. of voters:	3	3	5	4
	a	a	d	b
	d	d	b	c
	c	b	c	a
	b	c	a	d

Next add 4 voters with identical preferences $c > a > b > d$. Use (16) again to show that neither a nor c can be elected in the augmented profile with 19 voters. Conclude to a contradiction.

9.7   Tournaments and majority relation (McGarvey [1953]). Consider a tournament T (complete antisymmetric relation) on a set A of candidates. Construct a profile of preferences over A of which the majority comparisons yield exactly tournament T. *Hint:* If p is the number of candidates, a profile with $p(p-1)$ voters will do.

Stearns [1959] improves substantially McGarvey's result by showing that for every tournament T over p candidates, one can construct a preference profile with at most $p+2$ voters (or $p+1$ if p is odd) of which the associated majority tournament is precisely T.

9.8   Copeland winners and binary elimination tournaments (Moulin [1986c])

(a)   When A contains four candidates, the parallel elimination method [(9)] must elect a Copeland winner from every tournament. Yet when A has eight or more elements, it is impossible to construct a binary tree that would do the same. This will be proven after the next three questions.

(b)   Consider the following tournament T among eight candidates a, b, c, d, e, x, y, z: T coincides with the ordering $a>b>c>d>e>x>y>z$ except for

$$zTa, \quad zTb, \quad zTc, \quad zTd, \quad zTe \tag{17}$$

Show that a is the unique Copeland winner.

(c)   Consider an arbitrary binary tree on A and suppose that it selects a at tournament T. Change T into another tournament T' by changing only some relations within the set *abcde*. Denoting $B=\{abcde\}$, this means that T' satisfies

$$\text{for all } \alpha \in B: \quad \alpha Tx, \; \alpha Ty, \; zT\alpha, \quad xTy, \; xTz, \; yTz \tag{18}$$

Show that the outcome elected by our tree T' must be in B.

(d)   Consider the particular tournament T' defined by (18) and

$$aTb, \; aTc, \; dTa, \; eTa; \quad bTc, \; bTd, \; eTb; \quad cTd, \; cTe, \; dTe$$

Compute its Copeland winner. Comparing with question (c), conclude the following: With at least eight candidates no binary tree exists that would elect a Copeland winner from every tournament.

9.9   Unavoidable ties in voting rules. Given are the set A of outcomes with cardinality p and the set N of voters with cardinality n. Denote by $L(A)$ the set of linear orderings of A. Thus, a deterministic voting rule is a mapping S from $L(A)^N$ into A. We look for anonymous and neutral voting rules.

S is *anonymous* if S is a symmetrical function of its n variables (the individual orderings).

S is *neutral* if for a one-to-one mapping σ from A into itself and each profile u we have

$$S(u^\sigma) = \sigma[S(u)]$$

where in the profile u^σ, agent i prefers a to b if and only if in profile u agent i prefers $\sigma^{-1}(a)$ to $\sigma^{-1}(b)$.

(a) Show that there exists on A, N a single-valued voting rule that is Pareto optimal, anonymous, and neutral *if and only if n* has no prime factor less than or equal to p. *Hint for "if":* Use a repeated version of plurality voting. First keep all plurality winners, next all plurality winners among these, and so on.

(b) If $n = 2$, $p = 3$, we can find an anonymous, neutral, and single-valued voting rule [yet it will not be Pareto optimal in view of question (a)]. Here is one: If u_1 and u_2 agree on their top candidate, take it as $S(u_1, u_2)$. Otherwise, elect the remaining (possibly Pareto inferior) candidate.

In general, show that there exists on A, N a deterministic voting rule that is anonymous and neutral if and only if p cannot be written as the sum of nontrivial dividers of n (a nontrivial divider of n is a divider different from 1, possibly n itself). *Hint:* Fix n and set D_n to be the set of integers q that can be written as the sum of nontrivial dividers of n, with the convention $0 \in D_n$. The proof goes by induction on p. Assume $p \notin D_n$ and fix a profile u. For all t, $0 \le t \le n$, denote by A_t the (possibly empty) subset of outcomes that are ranked first by exactly t agents. Since p is not in D_n, and $p = \sum_{0 \le t \le n} |A_t|$, at least one t exists such that $|A_t| \notin D_n$, and $|A_t| < p$. Take the largest such t and apply the induction assumption.

This proves the "if" statement. To prove "only if," suppose $p \in D_n$. It can be written as $p = q_1 p_1 + \cdots + p_k q_k$, where $q_1 \cdots q_k$ are nonzero integers and $p_1, \ldots, p_k$ are pairwise distinct prime dividers of n. Hence, the product $(p_1 \cdots p_k)$ is a divider of n. Construct a profile among $p_1 \cdots p_k$ agents and $p_1 + \cdots + p_k$ outcomes that cannot be decisively arbitrated upon under anonymity and neutrality; next replicate agents and outcomes.

9.10 **The top cycle.** Given is a tournament T on the set A containing p candidates. Denote by T^* the transitive closure of T, namely, the complete and transitive relation defined by

aT^*b if and only if there is an integer q and a sequence $a = a_0, a_1, \ldots, a_q = b$, such that $a_i T a_{i+1}$ for all $i = 0, 1, \ldots, q-1$.

The top cycle of T is the nonempty set of maximal elements of relation T^*; it is denoted tc(T):

$a \in \text{tc}(T) \Leftrightarrow aT^*b$ for all $b \ne a$

(a) Check that the top cycle of a tournament T is a singleton if and only if it is the Condorcet winner of T (aTb for all $b \ne a$). For instance, in the tournament (8) the top cycle is the whole set A.

(b) Show that tc(T) is the smallest subset B of A with respect to inclusion satisfying

for all $a \in B$, $b \notin B$: aTb

Deduce that tc(T) never contains exactly two elements.

(c) If tc(T) is not a singleton, it is a T cycle with size at least 3. That is, one can order tc(T) as tc(T) = $\{a_1, \ldots, a_k\}$, where

$a_i T a_{i+1}, \; i=1, \ldots, k-1 \quad \text{and} \quad a_k T a_1$

Hint: If T has no Condorcet winner, every outcome in $\mathrm{tc}(T)$ is beaten by at least one other outcome in $\mathrm{tc}(T)$. Consider an inclusion maximal T cycle in $\mathrm{tc}(T)$ and prove it must be $\mathrm{tc}(T)$ itself.

(d)   Show that any binary tree on A elects from tournament T a candidate in the top cycle of T. Consider the successive elimination trees [as in question (a) of Exercise 9.5] for all possible orderings of the candidates. Fix a tournament T and show that by varying this ordering, all outcomes in the top cycle can be elected.

9.11   The uncovered set (Miller [1980]). Given a tournament T on A, define its covering relation by

$\{b \text{ covers } a\}$ if and only if $\{a \neq b, \; bTa, \text{ and for all } c \in A: \; aTc \Rightarrow bTc\}$

The covering relation is transitive yet not necessarily complete. The uncovered set of T, denoted $\mathrm{uc}(T)$, consists of its maximal elements:

$\{a \in \mathrm{uc}(T)\}$ if and only if $\{\text{for no } b \in A, \; b \text{ covers } a\}$

(a)   Prove that an outcome a is in the uncovered set if and only if it satisfies property (14). Show that (i) the uncovered set is a subset of the top cycle (Exercise 9.10) and (ii) the uncovered set contains all Copeland winners of T.

(b)   If T is tournament (8), show that the uncovered set is $\{a, b, d\}$. Next consider the tournament T on $A = \{1, 2, \ldots, n\}$ that coincides with the ordering $1 > 2 > \cdots > n$ except for $nT1$. Show that its uncovered set is $\{1, 2, n\}$ and compare it with the top cycle.

(c)   Show that the uncovered set is a singleton if and only if it is the Condorcet winner of T. Otherwise the restriction of T to $\mathrm{uc}(T)$ has no Condorcet winner, and hence $\mathrm{uc}(T)$ contains at least three elements. *Hint:* Every outcome outside $\mathrm{uc}(T)$ must be covered by an outcome inside $\mathrm{uc}(T)$. Suppose next that T has no Condorcet winner, yet $a \in \mathrm{uc}(T)$ beats every other outcome in $\mathrm{uc}(T)$. Set $B = \{b \mid b \neq a, bTa\}$: an outcome in B is covered by some outcome in $\mathrm{uc}(T)$. Contradiction.

(d)   We know (Corollary to Theorem 9.5) that the multistage elimination method elects a candidate in the uncovered set (for any ordering of A).

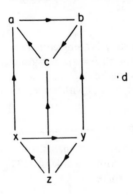

We show now by an example that by varying the ordering of A, one may not reach all outcomes of uc(T).

Our graph (bottom of page 254) depicts the tournament T on $A = \{a, b, c, d, x, y, z\}$ with the convention that every nonmarked arrow goes down (e.g., aTd, dTy, and cTx). Check that the uncovered set is $\{a, b, c, d\}$. Then show that d will never be elected by algorithm (12) no matter how we order A.

CHAPTER 10

Strategyproofness and core stability

Overview

In plurality voting it is sometimes rational to cast one's vote for another candidate than one's first-best choice: If I know that my most preferred candidate a will not pass because b and c are both going to get more votes, then I had better help whomever of b, c I like more. In any voting method when a voter realizes that his own vote may influence the final outcome, he thinks twice before casting it. Maybe the naive ballot suggested by his true preferences does not serve his interest best. Rather than passively reporting his opinion about candidates, he acts as a player in the game of election, trying to maximize the returns from his vote.

In real-world elections it is impossible to distinguish a strategically biased report of a voters' preferences from a truthful one. One's opinion is private information *de jure,* and hence an openly untruthful report is a perfectly legal move.

Several early analysts of voting methods were aware of their strategic aspects, thought of as the nuisance of a dishonest vote; see the quotation by Borda in Straffin [1980] or by Dodgson in Farquharson [1969]. A mathematically rigorous attack of the problem has come only in the last 15 years. The seminal question is this: Can we design a *strategyproof* voting rule, namely, such that each individual voter would always want to report his opinion truthfully while isolated in the voting booth?

For a binary choice (only two candidates) majority voting is strategyproof. But with three candidates or more the only strategyproof voting rules are dictatorial. This important result was proven by Gibbard [1973] and Satterthwaite [1975].

The Gibbard–Satterthwaite theorem is a very general statement. A dictatorial rule leaves all the decision power in the hands of a single voter (the same at all profiles). Surely we dismiss such a rule as the most unfair possible. Yet for every nondictatorial voting rule there exists some preference profile at which some agent benefits by not reporting truthfully his preferences. Therefore, voting is not a faithful device to collect information about voters' preferences; some strategic noise will blur the information-gathering process. We state and prove the theorem in Section 10.1. The proof is quite similar to that of Arrow's theorem (Theorem 11.2). We also discuss a variant of the theorem for *probabilistic* voting rules, where the outcome of the voting rule is a lottery over the candidates (so the final election involves some element of chance). Although one can find strategyproof probabilistic voting rules that are anonymous and neutral, they are grossly inefficient (see Remark 10.2).

How severe is the Gibbard–Satterthwaite impossibility result? A key feature of the theorem is that all preference profiles are admissible inputs of the voting rule (this is the unrestricted-domain assumption). When the context allows us to restrict the domain of preferences, the threat of strategic manipulation may disappear. For instance, suppose that the preference profile varies in a domain where the voting paradox never occurs, that is, where a Condorcet winner always exists. Then majority voting (electing precisely the Condorcet winner) is a strategyproof rule and is even robust to manipulations by any coalition of voters. We prove this important result in Section 10.2 (Lemma 10.3). Then we study the prominent example of restricted domain avoiding the voting paradox, namely, *single peaked* preferences. Suppose that the set A of outcomes (candidates) can be linearly ordered, as when politicians are arrayed from left to right. A preference on the ordered set A is single peaked if it is increasing before the peak and decreasing after the peak. We discuss several economic examples in Section 10.2.

From Section 10.3 on, we go back to the unrestricted domain of preferences. In Section 10.3 we consider manipulations by coalitions of voters. Is it possible for a coalition of voters to jointly agree on some voting strategy that increases the utility of every coalition member, no matter how hard voters outside the coalition try to block this move? Formally, this amounts to looking for an outcome in the *core* of the (NTU) cooperative game generated by the winning coalitions of the voting rule (a coalition is winning if it can force the election of any candidate it wishes). If the voting rule selects a candidate in the core for every profile, then coalitions are not likely to form, and we conclude to a strategically robust method (although core stability does not imply strategyproofness).

Nakamura's theorem (Theorem 10.2) characterizes the cooperative games for which the core is always nonempty. For instance, with p candidates and n voters, core stability is possible if no winning coalition contains less than $n \cdot (p-1)/p$ voters (this critical quota cannot be lowered). We discuss this result and related results in the spatial model of voting, where the candidates form a subset of some Euclidean space, and voters have spherical preferences (i.e., the disutility of a voter for a particular candidate is measured by the distance of this candidate to the voter's ideal point).

Section 10.4 introduces a strengthening of the core property where the allocation of power to various coalitions specifies the number of candidates that each coalition of a given size can block (this is the veto function). The corresponding core property is more demanding than with winning coalitions only, and hence the set of stable outcomes is smaller. There is a (unique) largest anonymous veto function yielding a nonempty core at every profile. It endows each coalition with a veto power nearly proportional to its size (Theorem 10.3). We see this result as a mathematical formulation of a "minority principle" seeking to protect the rights of small coalitions rather than give dictatorial power to any majority coalition.

Finally, in Section 10.5 we put our results in the perspective of the literature on implementation and strategic voting.

10.1   The Gibbard–Satterthwaite theorem

Say that A is the finite set of outcomes (candidates) and denote by $L(A)$ the set of linear orderings (complete, transitive, asymmetric relations) on A. Let N be the finite set of agents (voters) with current element i. Voter i's opinion is described by an element u_i of $L(A)$, that is, an ordering of A (indifferences are excluded). As usual, it is written as a utility function, for example, $u_i(a) > u_i(b) > u_i(c) > u_i(d)$ means a is top, b is second, and so on.

A *voting rule* is a single-valued mapping S from $L(A)^N$ onto A associating to each preference profile $u = (u_i, i \in N)$ the elected outcome $S(u)$. That S is single valued is essential to the definition of strategyproofness [property (1)]. The assumption that S is onto means that no candidate is a priori discarded: For each candidate a, there is a profile u such that $S(u) = a$. Say that the voting rule S is *strategyproof* if for all profiles $u \in L(A)^N$ and all agents i, we have

$$\text{for all } v_i \in L(A): \quad u_i(S(u)) \geq u_i(S(v_i, u_{-i})) \tag{1}$$

Here v_i is a preference (possibly different from the true one) that agent i might report instead of the sincere one u_i. If he does so, every other report remaining fixed, the reported profile is (v_i, u_{-i}) with the jth component u_j for all $j \neq i$. Inequality (1) says that misreporting does not pay.

For binary choices (A contains two candidates), strategyproofness is equivalent to monotonicity and is therefore satisfied by many nondictatorial voting rules (e.g., majority voting; see the details in Section 11.1). When three candidates or more are on stage, the picture is quite different.

Theorem 10.1 (Gibbard [1973], Satterthwaite [1975]). *If A contains at least three outcomes, a voting rule S is strategyproof **if and only if** it is dictatorial:* $S = S^{i^*}$ *for some agent* i^* *– the dictator – where*

$$\text{for all } u \in L(A)^N: \quad S^{i^*}(u) = \text{top } u_{i^*}.$$

The proof uses the auxiliary concept of strong monotonicity. We will use the following notations. Given two profiles u, v and outcome a, we say that *a keeps or improves its relative position from u to v* if

$$u_i(a) > u_i(b) \Rightarrow v_i(a) > v_i(b) \quad \text{for all } i, \text{ all } b \neq a$$

Next we say that *v is deduced from u by lifting a* if

  (i) u and v coincide on $A/\{a\}$: $u_i(b) > u_i(c) \Leftrightarrow v_i(b) > v_i(c)$ for all i, all $b, c \neq a$;
  (ii) a keeps or improves its relative position from u to v; and
  (iii) $v \neq u$, and hence the position of a improves for at least one agent.

Definition 10.1. *A voting rule S is **strongly monotonic** if for all profiles* u, v *and outcome a,*

$$\{v \text{ is deduced from } u \text{ by lifting } a\} \Rightarrow \{S(v) = S(u) \text{ and/or } S(v) = a\} \quad (2)$$

If a voting rule is strongly monotonic, a push-up to any candidate (who may or may not be initially elected) can ensure the election of this very candidate or confirm the candidate previously elected; but it cannot allow the election of a *third* candidate. In short, campaigning for one candidate can only help that very candidate.

Compare property (2) with the monotonicity property introduced in Section 9.2, which reads

$$\{v \text{ is deduced from } u \text{ by lifting } a \text{ and } S(u) = a\} \Rightarrow \{S(v) = a\}$$

Strong monotonicity thus implies monotonicity. The next two lemmas show that strong monotonicity is actually *much* stronger than ordinary monotonicity.

Lemma 10.1. *A voting rule S is strongly monotonic if and only if, for all* u, v *and all a, we have:*

$$\{a = S(u) \text{ and } a \text{ keeps or improves its relative position from } u \text{ to } v\}$$
$$\Rightarrow \{a = S(v)\} \quad (3)$$

The straightforward proof of Lemma 10.1 is the subject of Exercise 10.2.

Keeping the relative position of a from u to v consists of shuffling in each voter's preferences the candidates better than a and those worse than a. For instance, if u_i is worth

$$u_i(b) > u_i(d) > u_i(a) > u_i(e) > u_i(c) > u_i(f)$$

then we may change it to any v_i where the two top candidates are a, b (in an arbitrary order) and the bottom three are c, e, f. This shows already the force of strong monotonicity. The fact that a is elected depends only upon the subsets of candidates that the various voters prefer to a.

Lemma 10.2 (Muller and Satterthwaite [1977]).   *Suppose A contains three outcomes or more. Then a voting rule S is strongly monotonic if and only if it is dictatorial.*

Proof: Fix an agent i^* and check that the dictatorial rule $S(u) = top(u_{i^*})$ is strongly monotonic. This proves the "if" statement. To prove "only if," we fix a strongly monotonic voting rule.

   Notation: $N(u, a, b)$ is the (possibly empty) subset of voters preferring a to b at profile u.

   Step 1: For all coalitions T and outcomes a, b, set

$$U(T, a, b) = \{u \in L(A)^N \mid \text{for } i \in T, \ a \text{ is on top of } u_i \text{ and } b \text{ is second};$$

$$\text{for } i \in N/T, \ b \text{ is on top of } u_i \text{ and } a \text{ is second}\}$$

We prove the equivalence of the three following statements:

   (i) $S(U(T, a, b)) = \{a\}$.
   (ii)   There exists $u \in L(A)^N$: $N(u, a, b) = T$ and $S(u) = a$.
   (iii)   For all $u \in L(A)^N$: $N(u, a, b) = T \Rightarrow S(u) \neq b$.

Clearly, (i) $\Rightarrow$ (ii) [take any $u \in U(T, a, b)$]. Next suppose (ii) holds but (iii) fails. For some u, $N(u, a, b) = T$ and $S(u) = a$, whereas for some v, $N(v, a, b) = T$ and $S(v) = b$. By lifting a and b on top while preserving the relative position of a versus b, we transform u into some $u' \in U(T, a, b)$ and v into some $v' \in U(T, a, b)$. This is a contradiction since from u' to v', a keeps its relative position. Finally assume (iii) and consider a profile u in $U(T, a, b)$. By (iii), $S(u) \neq b$, whereas the only two Pareto-optimal outcomes at u are a, b. So if S elects a Pareto-optimal candidate, it must be $S(u) = a$, and (i) is proved.

   We check now Pareto optimality of S. Since S is onto, for all $a \in A$ there is a profile u such that $S(u) = a$. By lifting a on top of each preference in u, we preserve its election, so by strong monotonicity we get

$$\{a \text{ is on top of every } u_i\} \Rightarrow \{S(u) = a\} \qquad (4)$$

Next consider a profile u where a is Pareto superior to b. If $S(u) = b$, by lifting a and b on top while preserving the relative position of a versus b, we should not threaten the election of b, which contradicts (4). This concludes the proof that (i), (ii), and (iii) are equivalent.

Denote by $B(a, b)$ the set of coalitions that satisfy (i)–(iii). We have proved already $N \in B(a, b)$ for all a, b.

Step 2: The proof is parallel to that of Arrow's theorem (Theorem 11.2). Choose T inclusion minimal in $\bigcup B(x, y)$, $(x, y) \in A \times A$. So T is in some $B(a, b)$.

Suppose T is not a singleton. We can partition T as $T_1 \cup T_2$ where neither T_1 nor T_2 belongs to $B(x, y)$ for any x, y. Then pick a third outcome c, different from a and b, and construct a profile as follows:

T_1	T_2	$N-T$
a	c	b
b	a	c
c	b	a

where every other outcome is Pareto inferior to a, b, and c. Because $N(u, a, b) = T$ and $T \in B(a, b)$, (iii) implies $S(u) \neq b$. As $N(u, a, c) = T_1$ and $T_1 \notin B(a, c)$, (ii) implies $S(u) \neq a$. As $N(u, c, b) = T_2$ and $T_2 \notin B(c, b)$, (ii) implies $S(u) \neq c$. Hence, a contradiction exists of the Pareto optimality of S. Therefore T is a singleton, say, $T = \{1\}$.

Check next $\{1\} \in B(x, y)$ for all $x, y \in A$. Choose a third outcome d and consider a profile where a, b, d are Pareto superior to every other outcome, and moreover,

1	$N/\{1\}$
a	b
b	d
d	a

$$\tag{5}$$

As $N(u, a, b) = \{1\}$ and $\{1\} \in B(a, b)$, we have $S(u) \neq b$. Also $S(u) \neq d$ since d is Pareto inferior to b. Hence, $S(u) = a$. Since $N(u, a, d) = \{1\}$, (ii) implies $\{1\} \in B(a, d)$. To prove $\{1\} \in B(c, d)$ for all c, use a similar argument [a profile such as the one of formula (7) in Chapter 11 will do].

It remains to check that agent 1 is a dictator. Fix a preference $u_1 \in L(A)$ with top outcome a. Consider a profile u_1, v_{-1} where each v_i, $i \neq 1$, has a on bottom. Then $N(u, a, b) = \{1\}$ for all $b \neq a$, so $S(u_1, v_{-1}) \neq b$ by (iii), implying $S(u_1, v_{-1}) = a$.

Finally take any profile u_{-1} for the coalition $N/\{1\}$. As a keeps or improves its relative position from (u_1, v_{-1}) to (u_1, u_{-1}), we must have $S(u_1, u_{-1}) = a$. This concludes the proof that agent 1 is a dictator.

Q.E.D.

Proof of Theorem 10.1:   The "if" statement (a dictatorial rule is strategyproof) is clear. To prove "only if," let S be a strategyproof voting rule. We prove that S is strongly monotonic. To that end we fix a profile u and an agent i as well as another preference v_i of agent i deduced from u_i by lifting a. We must prove that $S(v_i, u_{-i})$ must be $S(u)$ and/or a.

Suppose first $S(u) = b \neq a$. If $S(v_i, u_{-i}) = c$, and $c \neq b, a$, we have *either* $u_i(b) > u_i(c)$ and $v_i(b) > v_i(c)$ *or* $u_i(b) < u_i(c)$ and $v_i(b) < v_i(c)$ (since the relative position of b versus c has not changed). In the former case

$$v_i(S_i(u_i, u_{-i})) > v_i(S_i(v_i, u_{-i}))$$

so agent i manipulates at (v_i, u_{-i}) by reporting u_i. In the latter case

$$u_i(S_i(v_i, u_{-i})) > u_i(S_i(u_i, u_{-i}))$$

so agent i manipulates at (u_i, u_{-i}) by reporting v_i.

Suppose next $S(u) = a$. If $S(v_i, u_{-i}) = b \neq a$, we have *either* $u_i(b) > u_i(a)$ *or* $u_i(b) < u_i(a)$ and $v_i(b) < v_i(a)$ (since v_i is deduced from u_i by lifting a). In the former case, agent i manipulates at (u_i, u_{-i}) by reporting v_i. In the latter case, he manipulates at (v_i, u_{-i}) by reporting u_i.

Q.E.D.

Remark 10.1:   Theorem 10.1 generalizes to an arbitrary game form, that is, a decision mechanism where each agent is endowed with an arbitrary message space (his message may be more complicated than simply reporting his preferences). The notion of dominant strategy then replaces that of truthful report of preferences. A dominant strategy is a message that is best independently of the other voters' messages. Given a game form onto A, every voter has dominant strategy at every profile if and only if the game form is dictatorial (for a precise statement and proof, see e.g., Moulin [1983], Chapter 4). This generalization is useful to the strategic analysis of voting games.

Remark 10.2 Probabilistic voting: Consider a game form that elicits from each voter a report of his preferences and deduces from these reports a *lottery* over the set A of outcomes. A typical example is *random dictator:* Each voter casts a ballot with the name of one candidate, and then a ballot is drawn at random with equal probability, thus determining the winner. This method is a probabilistic version of plurality voting.

In random dictator, each voter's dominant strategy is to nominate his top candidate, and hence the method *is* strategyproof. Notice also that it is anonymous and neutral. Thus, with probabilistic voting, strategyproofness *is* compatible with a fair distribution of the decision power (each voter has, ex ante, the same influence over the outcome of the lottery). The random dictator method, however, is not Pareto optimal. Assuming that voters are endowed with von Neumann–Morgenstern utility functions, the uniform lottery over the voters' top candidates is typically Pareto dominated (ex ante).

Gibbard [1977, 1978] and Hylland [1980] give a precise characterization of the strategyproof probabilistic voting rules. It turns out that the probability mixtures of dictatorial methods are the only strategyproof rules satisfying a mild attainability condition (see Exercise 10.9 for details). Those methods are constructed by picking an arbitrary probability distribution $I = (I_i, i \in N)$ over N ($I_i \geq 0$ for all i, and $\sum_{i=1}^{n} I_i = 1$). Each voter i casts a vote for a candidate, say a_i. The winner is drawn at random among the a_i according to the probability distribution I.

Barbera [1979], on the other hand, drops the attainability condition and describes the set of anonymous, neutral, and strategyproof probabilistic voting rules. This set contains some probabilistic version of the scoring methods and of the Copeland and Simpson methods. Both Hylland's and Barbera's results are described (but not proven) in Exercise 10.9.

10.2   Single-peaked preferences and Condorcet winners

When the domain of preferences is suitably restricted, nondictatorial voting rules may exist. This is true in particular when the restricted domain guarantees existence of a Condorcet winner.

Lemma 10.3.   *Given are an electorate N with an odd number of agents and a restricted domain $D \subset L(A)$ such that for all $u \in D^N$, a Condorcet winner (necessarily unique) exists. Then the voting rule associating to each profile in D^N its Condorcet winner is strategyproof. It is even coalitionally strategyproof: No coalition of agents can jointly misreport its preferences and make every coalition member better off.*

Proof: We denote by CW(u) the Condorcet winner at profile $u \in D^N$.

Suppose there is a profile $u \in D^N$, a coalition T, and a joint lie $v_T \in D^T$ such that

$$\mathrm{CW}(u) = a, \qquad \mathrm{CW}(v_T, u_{N/T}) = b$$

and yet

$$u_i(a) < u_i(b) \quad \text{for all } i \in T \tag{6}$$

By definition of the Condorcet winner, $N(u; a, b)$ is a strict majority, and by (6), $(N(v_T, u_{N/T}); a, b)$ contains $N(u, a, b)$. Hence, b cannot be a Condorcet winner at $(v_T, u_{N/T})$.   Q.E.D.

The main example of a successful restriction of the domain is that of single-peaked preferences. Suppose A, the set of outcomes, is linearly ordered as $a_1 < a_2 < \cdots < a_p$. We say that a preference v on A is *single peaked* if there is an outcome a^*, called the *peak* of v, such that v is strictly increasing before a^* and strictly decreasing after it:

$$a < b \leq a^* \Rightarrow u(a) < u(b), \quad \text{all } a, b$$
$$a^* \leq a < b \Rightarrow u(a) > u(b) \tag{7}$$

For instance, if the peak is $a^* = a_1$, the corresponding single-peaked preference is exactly the opposite of the fixed ordering of A; if the peak is $a^* = a_p$, the single-peaked preference coincides with the ordering of A.

Note that indifferences across the peak could be allowed. They are ruled out for simplicity.

We denote by $SP(A)$ the set of single-peaked preferences for the fixed ordering $a_1, \ldots, a_p$.

Examples where the single-peaked assumption is plausible are numerous. In political models, the candidates are often ordered by a one-dimensional criterion, as in the left–right scale (see Black [1958]). The single-peakedness assumption means that each voter has an ideal point on the left–right scale and prefers a candidate to the left (right) of this point to a candidate still more to the left (right). A second example is the location of a facility in a linear city. Presumably, most consumers want the facility as close as possible to their residence, and hence their preferences are single peaked. This example can be generalized to a tree (see what follows).

In economic models the outcome to be voted upon is often a numerical index, such as the ratio of taxation or the quantity of public goods to be supplied; see Example 10.2. Then single peakedness follows from the quasiconcavity of preferences.

Lemma 10.4. *Given is an ordering of the outcomes in A and the corresponding single-peaked domain $SP(A)$. If the number of voters is **odd**, there is a unique Condorcet winner at any profile u in $SP(A)^N$. It is the median peak of the individual preferences.*

Proof: Denote by a_i^* the peak of agent i's preferences and rank the agents by increasing peaks – along the given ordering of A:

$$a_1^* \leq a_2^* \leq \cdots \leq a_n^*$$

As n is odd, the number $m = \frac{1}{2}(n+1)$ is an integer, and a_m^* is the *median* peak. The agents whose peak is not smaller than a_m^*, call them rightist, form a strict majority (since $m - 1 < \frac{1}{2}n$) and those whose peak is not greater than a_m^*, call them leftist, form another majority (since $m > \frac{1}{2}n$).

Note that the median agent m itself is both a leftist and a rightist.

When we oppose outcome a_m^* to a greater outcome a, $a_m^* < a$, all leftist support a_m^* by definition of single-peakedness [(7)]. When a_m^* is opposed to a smaller outcome, all rightist support a_m^*; whence the desired conclusion.   Q.E.D.

When there is an even number of voters, existence of a strict Condorcet winner does not hold anymore, yet the conclusions of Lemma 10.3 and 10.4 can be essentially preserved. Consider the following example with 6 voters and 10 outcomes:

$$A = \{1, 2, \ldots, 10\}, \quad a_1^* = 1, \quad a_2^* = 3, \quad a_3^* = 3, \quad a_4^* = 6, \quad a_5^* = a_6^* = 7$$

Outcome 3 is a Condorcet winner in a weak sense: In pairwise majority comparisons, he beats outcomes 1, 2, and 7–10 but he is tied with 4–6 (with voters 1–3 opposed to voters 4–6). Thus, no other outcome overrules outcome 3 by a strict majority. The same applies to outcomes 4–6.

Lemma 10.5. *Say that an outcome is a* **weak Condorcet winner** *if there is no other outcome that is preferred by a strict majority.*

Given a single-peaked domain $\mathrm{SP}(A)$, *consider a profile in* $\mathrm{SP}(A)^N$, *where N has an even number of agents. Rank the agents' peak increasingly:*

$$a_1^* \le a_2^* \le \cdots \le a_n^*$$

Then all outcomes between $a_{n/2}^*$ *and* $a_{n/2+1}^*$ *(including those two bounds) are weak Condorcet winners.*

The easy proof is omitted. Within the interval $[a_{n/2}^*, a_{n/2+1}^*]$ of weak Condorcet winners, it is easy to pick a strategyproof selection. For instance, we can pick $a_{n/2}^*$ (the leftist Condorcet winner). This is a (coalitionally) strategyproof voting rule as one can check directly or deduce from Lemma 10.4 because $a_{n/2}^*$ is the strict Condorcet winner of a $(n+1)$-agent profile in $\mathrm{SP}(A)^N$, where the $(n+1)$th agent has its peak at a_1. See Exercise 10.3 for details.

We now give an application of Lemma 10.5 to a familiar cost-sharing problem.

Example 10.1. Provision of a public good with fixed cost sharing
Consider the public good production economy $(b_1, \ldots, b_n; c)$ of Section 7.1 (quasi-linear case).

Assume that the benefit functions b_i are all strictly concave and that the cost function c is convex.

Consider the uniform cost-sharing rule. If the level of public good is $x \ge 0$, agent i's net utility (possibly negative) is worth

$$b_i(x) - \frac{1}{n} c(x) \tag{8}$$

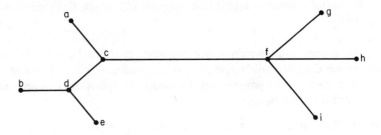

Figure 10.1.

This is a strictly concave function of x. Therefore, on any interval $[0, a]$ of possible levels of production, agent i's preference is single peaked with its peak at the maximum of (8) – unique by the strict concavity assumption. Thus, a very simple strategyproof and budget-balanced mechanism – ask each agent to report his peak – produces the level of public good corresponding to the median of the reported peaks (if n is even, take the leftist Condorcet winners $a^*_{n/2}$) and divides the cost of the public good equally.

This mechanism does not, however, produce the Pareto-optimal level except by coincidence, and it may imply a net loss for individual agents (lack of individual rationality).

Another domain guaranteeing the existence of a Condorcet winner (at least in the weak sense) for every profile is the set of single-peaked preferences *on a tree* (Demange [1982]). Suppose the outcomes of A are the nodes of a tree, namely, a connected graph without cycles. An example is illustrated in Figure 10.1. If we pick two nodes on a tree, there is a unique path connecting them. Thus, the statement "node x lies between nodes y and z" is meaningful (on the figure c is between e and g, but a is not). Given such a tree, say that the preference ordering u_i is single peaked if its top outcome x^* is such that

> for all x, y distinct, and both different from x^*:
> $\{x \text{ is between } x^* \text{ and } y\} \Rightarrow \{u_i(x) > u_i(y)\}$ (9)

A typical example is the location of a public facility problem (Example 1.1, Exercise 1.1). If an agent is located at node x^*, his disutility for various locations is measured by the distance from x^* to the location, thus satisfying (9). On the contrary, a preference such as $f > h > d > c > \cdots$ (see the preceding) is not single peaked.

The results of Lemmas 10.3 and 10.4 generalize: For any profile of single-peaked preferences on a given tree, a strict (weak) Condorcet winner exists when the number of agents is odd (even). Moreover, in case the agents' disutilities equal the distance from their peak, the Condorcet winner(s) coincides with the solution of the utilitarian program (minimizing the sum of distances to the individual peaks). See Exercise 10.4 for details.

Remark 10.3:   When preferences are single peaked (for a given ordering of A), the Condorcet winner defines a strategyproof voting rule. Over the same domain there are many other strategyproof rules. One example is the leftist rule, where each agent reports his own peak, and the smallest peak (w.r.t. the given ordering of A) is elected.

The class of such strategyproof rules, however, is entirely described as *generalized Condorcet winners* in the following sense. Given our n voters, fix arbitrarily $n-1$ outcomes representing the peaks of some $n-1$ *phantom* voters. Then ask every *real* voter to cast a vote for his preferred outcome and add the $n-1$ peaks of the phantom voters in the urn; elect the overall Condorcet winner from the $2n-1$ ballots (it is unique since $2n-1$ is odd). This method is (coalitionally) strategyproof among the real agents.

It turns out that this class of voting rules captures all strategyproof rules in the single-peaked framework (Moulin [1980a]). Exercise 10.3 gives more examples of generalized Condorcet winners.

Remark 10.4:   There are other restricted domains of preferences on which nondictatorial strategyproof voting rules exist. However, the characterization of those domains does not lead to examples as easy to interpret as the single-peaked domain. The abstract rules due to Kalaï and Muller [1977] and others are reviewed in the very good paper by Muller and Satterthwaite [1985]. They have yet to find their applications.

10.3   Core stability

We are now back to unrestricted domains of preferences. A strategyproof voting rule prevents manipulations by a single deviating voter. If I know that the others will report truthfully, can I find a profitable misreport? In view of the negative Gibbard and Satterthwaite theorem, only a more modest stability requirement can be satisfied by reasonable (e.g., anonymous) voting rules.

In the next two sections we deem a manipulation *safe* if the player(s) undertaking it are positively certain to benefit from it, no matter how the nonmanipulating voters react to it (i.e., even if those voters carry out an incredible threat). This provision makes profitable manipulations more difficult. On the other hand, we allow coalitions to form and jointly coordinate their misreport, thus broadening the scope for strategic maneuvers.

For a given voting rule at a given profile, the property that no coalition of voters has a safe and profitable deviation is a core property in a game without transferable utility (see Section 4.4). Consider, for instance, a Condorcet consistent rule. There a united majority can force the election of any outcome it wishes. Therefore, only two cases are essentially possible. If a (strict) Condorcet winner exists, then it is the unique core outcome; on the other hand, if every outcome is defeated by some other outcome in a majority comparison, then the core is empty. Thus, the core requirement either determines the outcome or cannot be met.

Definition 10.2. *Consider an arbitrary voting rule S (a mapping from $L(A)^N$ into A). Say that a coalition T of voters is **winning** if for every candidate a, coalition T has a message $v_T \in L(A)^T$ that forces the election of a:*

$$\text{for all } v_{N/T} \in L(A)^{N\backslash T}: \quad S(v_T, v_{N\backslash T}) = a$$

We denote by $W(S)$ the set of winning coalitions of the voting rule S.

Thus, a winning coalition is endowed by the voting rule with full decision power provided that the members of the coalition can coordinate their messages. Of course, at a particular preference profile, a given winning coalition may form or not, depending upon their conflicting opinions.

As noted, in any Condorcet consistent rule, a coalition T is winning if it contains a strict majority of voters. Reporting preferences v_T showing the same top candidate a on top of each v_i, $i \in T$, makes a the Condorcet winner no matter how the voters in $N\backslash T$ report. Note that if $|N|$ is odd, majority coalitions are the only winning coalition as well, whereas if $|N|$ is even, some coalitions containing half of the voters may be winning too, depending upon the particular Condorcet consistent rule.

For a second example, take a Borda method. At every profile it elects a Borda winner. There we claim that any coalition T containing strictly more than *two-thirds* of the voters is winning. Indeed, pick a candidate a and consider a message v_T where a is the top candidate of each v_i and the other candidates are shuffled in such a way that they all receive the same Borda score from T. Suppose, for simplicity, that $|T|$ is even. Then make half of the voters in T have a certain preference on $A\backslash a$ and the other half have the exact reverse preference. With the usual convention that the Borda scores are $0, 1, \ldots, p-1$, the T score of candidate a is thus $|T|\cdot(p-1)$, whereas that of any other candidate is $|T|\cdot(p-2)/2$. From coalition $N\backslash T$, a candidate receives at most the score $(n-|T|)\cdot(p-1)$, so that a will always be the unique Borda winner if

$$|T|\cdot(p-2)/2 + (n-|T|)\cdot(p-1) < |T|\cdot(p-1)$$

This inequality follows from $\frac{2}{3}\cdot n<|T|$, as was to be proved. In the case where $|T|$ is odd, one must construct a T message where a is on top and every other candidate receives almost the same Borda score; see Exercise 10.7 for details. There it is shown also that coalitions with less than two-thirds of the votes are not winning.

The set $W(S)$ of winning coalitions for the rule S is a *simple game* in the game-theoretic jargon (see Owen [1982], Chapter 8). If S is monotonic (see Section 9.2), the winning coalitions are monotonic, too:

$$\{T\in W(S) \text{ and } T\subset T'\} \Rightarrow \{T'\in W(S)\} \tag{10}$$

If S is onto A (see Definition 10.1), the grand coalition N is winning: $N\in W(S)$.

Definition 10.3. *Given a voting rule S and a preference profile $u \in L(A)^N$, we say that candidate a is **dominated** if there exists a candidate b and a winning coalition T that unanimously prefers b to a:*

$$\exists T\in W(S),\ \exists b\in A\setminus a:\ u_i(b)>u_i(a) \quad \text{for all } i\in T$$

The core of S at u is the (possibly empty) set of undominated candidates. It is denoted $C_S(u)$. We say that a voting rule is core stable if its core $C_S(u)$ is nonempty at every profile u.

The core stability of a voting rule depends only upon the simple game of its winning coalitions. There is a very simple test to check the core stability of that game. The *Nakamura number* of the simple game $W(S)$ is the minimal number v of winning coalitions with empty intersection. If all the coalitions in $W(S)$ have a nonempty intersection, we set $v = +\infty$. Otherwise, v is the smallest number such that one can find v coalitions in $W(S)$ with empty intersection.

Theorem 10.2 (Nakamura [1979]). *The voting rule S is core stable if and only if the Nakamura number of its associated simple game is strictly greater than the number of candidates.*

We prove this result in the next chapter, where it is formulated in the context of preference aggregation (Theorem 11.4).

Consider a Condorcet consistent rule. Its winning coalitions are all coalitions with more than half of the voters. Hence, the Nakamura number is 3 as soon as $|N|\geq 3$ (with the exception of $|N|=4$ for which $v=4$). Thus, a Condorcet consistent rule is *not* core stable as soon as A contains three candidates or more (a reformulation of the voting paradox).

Next consider a Borda method, of which the winning coalitions must contain more than two-thirds of the voters. The Nakamura number is then 4 as soon as $|N| \geq 10$. Any three coalitions with more than two-thirds of the voters must have a nonempty intersection, and we can find four such coalitions with empty intersection (see Exercise 10.7 for a detailed computation of the Nakamura number of the Borda methods).

Consider next an anonymous simple game $W(S)$, that is, a quota game. A coalition is winning if and only if it contains at least q voters, where q is the *quota*. Any anonymous voting rule (as well as some non-anonymous ones) yields a quota game of winning coalitions. It is easy to compute the Nakamura number of the q-quota game:

$$\nu = [n/n - q]$$

where $n = |N|$ and $[x]$ is the smallest integer greater than or equal to x. To check this, set $t^* = [n/n - q]$ and note that finding (in N) t coalitions of size q with an empty intersection is the same as finding t coalitions of size $n - q$ with union N. The latter is possible if and only if $t(n-1) \geq n \Leftrightarrow t \geq t^*$.

By Nakamura's theorem, a voting rule with associated quota q is core stable if and only if

$$p < [n/n - q] \Leftrightarrow n \cdot (p-1)/p < q$$

where $p = |A|$. Thus, core stability requires a fairly high quota. With 3 candidates it must be no less than 67 percent, with 5 candidates no less than 81 percent, and with 20 candidates no less than 96 percent! With a high quota, a winning coalition forms only when agents are almost unanimous in rejecting a particular outcome; consequently, the core is typically a large subset of the Pareto set.

In the next section we refine the description of coalitional power (from the game of winning coalitions to the veto function), thereby narrowing the set of core-stable outcomes.

Remark 10.5:   In political science, the model of *spatial voting* is often used to describe the competition of politicians for voters. The main postulates are (i) each candidate is identified by a point in some Euclidean space E^K representing his *position* on the K issues constituting the political "horizon" and (ii) each voter has an ideal point in E^K representing his opinion on these issues, and he compares various candidates by the distance (for some metric in E^K) from his ideal point to their positions. In this model, the core of simple games (made up of winning coalitions) has been extensively studied. Majority games rarely are core stable (Plott [1967]), but quota games fare better. Any quota greater than $\{K/(K+1)\} \cdot n$ allows core stability (Greenberg [1979]). These results have recently been generalized to arbitrary simple games, thus providing a counterpart to Nakamura's theorem in the spatial voting context; see Schofield [1984], Le-Breton [1987], and McKelvey and Schofield [1987].

Remark 10.6: Other cooperative stability concepts have been explored, such as the von Neumann–Morgenstern solution sets (Wilson [1971]) and some variants of the bargaining set (Rubinstein [1980]). Under those weaker stability requirements, many outcomes are stable even under the majority rule.

10.4 The minority principle

When a Condorcet winner does not exist, the core of the majority simple game is empty. Therefore, the corresponding voting game is cooperatively unstable. In the hard sciences unstable states of the world are typically (but not necessarily) transient and unobservable. In the social sciences, the dominant paradigm sees stability as a desirable feature for a collective decision process. Instability is bad because it makes the outcome less predictable, and our job as scholars more difficult. But serious justification for the desirability of stable outcomes is seldom given. It is not hard to realize that instability has its own appeal and can be seriously preferred to stability. The core stability in voting is a very good case in point.

In political philosophy, the pluralist and normative traditions diverge widely in their interpretation of the voting paradox. The pluralist tradition (see the article by Miller [1983] for historical references) gathers most supporters of the majority principle. It postulates that the opinion of any majority of voters should prevail. Formally, this corresponds to the Condorcet consistency axiom (Chapter 9) and implies cooperative instability when a Condorcet winner fails to exist.

The normative tradition (with such diverse supporters as the philosopher Rousseau, the utopian political thinker Proudhon, as well as some modern social choice theorists) argues, on the contrary, that the majority principle makes any homogeneous coalition controlling 50 percent of the electorate an actual dictator, allowing them to ignore the opinion of the antagonistic minority, which may be as large as 49 percent. Presumably, voters within this minority will experience frustration and possibly be tempted to defect from the social conventions carried by the particular voting rule: "Cependant une minorité ne peut pas être a la merci d'une majorité: la justice, qui est la negation de la force, veut que la minorité ait ses garanties" (Proudhon [1861]) (yet a minority should not be at the mercy of a majority; justice is the negation of force, and demands to protect the minority).

To contrast these two views, think first of a profile with no Condorcet winner. For the normativist, if the voting rule actually endows any majority with full decision power, then Condorcet cycles generate a cooperative unstability threatening the very roots of social consensus. By all means, the social rules should avoid such "explosive" configurations by bringing about within the decision rule itself some stable compromises upon which the collective tensions will come to rest. But the pluralists deny that cooperative stability is at all desirable. They argue that Condorcet cycles are the best protection for minorities, who can always live in the hope of belonging tomorrow to the ever-changing ruling majority (see Miller [1983]).

The remedy to the tyranny of the majority is the *minority principle,* requiring that *all* coalitions, however small, should be given some fraction of the decision power. One measure of this power is the ability to veto certain subsets of outcomes (see Theorem 10.2). We illustrate the principle by an example where a Condorcet winner does exist.

We have 10 voters and 8 outcomes. Two homogeneous coalitions, with 6 and 4 members, respectively, have exactly opposite preferences:

No. of voters:	6	4
	a	*h*
	b	*g*
	c	*f*
	d	*e*
	e	*d*
	f	*c*
	g	*b*
	h	*a*

Although the Condorcet winner is *a* (the favorite of the majority), the minority principle allows the four-voter coalition to oppose any three outcomes – *a*, *b*, *c* – whereas the six-voter coalition can oppose (veto) any four outcomes – *e*, *f*, *g*, *h*. Thus, *d* emerges as the fair compromise: The majority opinion is more influential but not tyrannical.

The formal definition of the minority principle rests upon the concept of veto function.

Definition 10.4.   *Given the set of outcomes A and a society N with respective cardinalities p, n, an **anonymous veto function** is a nondecreasing function v from $\{1, \ldots, n\}$ to $\{0, \ldots, p-1\}$, where $v(t) = k$ is interpreted as follows: any coalition with size t can veto any subset with at most k outcomes.*

Note that an anonymous veto function does not immediately suggest a precise game form, where the coalitions of agents are endowed with this distribution of veto power. We come back to this point after stating Theorem 10.3.

To any anonymous veto function corresponds a finer core property than to winning coalitions. The idea is that a coalition T blocks the election of outcome a if there is a subset B of outcomes that does not contain a such that T can force the final outcome within B (T can veto the complement of B) and wishes to do so since every agent in T prefers every outcome in B to a.

Denote by $\Pr(T, a, u)$ the (possibly empty) subset of outcomes strictly preferred to a by all members of coalition T at profile u. Thus coalition T blocks a if (and only if) T can veto $A/\Pr(T, a, u)$, that is, $v(|T|) \geq p - |\Pr(T, a, u)|$.

Definition 10.5. *Fix A, N and an anonymous veto function v. Given a profile $u \in L(A)^N$, the **core** of v is denoted by $C_v(u)$. It contains outcome a if and only if*

$$\text{for all } T \subset N: \quad |\Pr(T, a, u)| + v(t) \leq p - 1, \quad \text{where } t = |T|$$

*We say that an anonymous veto function v is **stable** if for every profile $u \in L(A)^N$ the associated core is nonempty:*

$$\text{for all } u \in L(A)^N: \quad C_v(u) \neq \varnothing$$

Before characterizing stable anonymous veto functions, we compute the veto function of our two principal examples of voting rules.

Example 10.2. Veto function of Condorcet consistent voting rules
In any Condorcet consistent rule (i.e., electing the Condorcet winner whenever there is one), a strict majority coalition (i.e., a coalition T such that $|T| > \frac{1}{2}n$) has full control of the outcome whereas a minority ($|T| < \frac{1}{2}n$) has none. Hence, its veto function tells us no more than the winning coalitions do:

$$v(t) = \begin{cases} 0 & \text{if } t \leq \frac{1}{2}n \\ p - 1 & \text{if } t > \frac{1}{2}n \end{cases}$$

Example 10.3. Veto function of Borda's method
Fix A with $|A| = p$ and N with $|N| = n$. For any profile $u \in L(A)^N$, denote by $B(u) \subset A$ the set of Borda winners, that is, those outcomes with maximal Borda score. Say that coalition T can veto a subset C of outcomes if there is a message $u_T \in L(A)^T$ such that

$$B(u_T, u_{N/T}) \cap C = \varnothing \quad \text{for all } u_{N/T} \in L(A)^{N/T} \tag{11}$$

Since B is neutral and anonymous, only the size t of T and that of C matter. Thus, there is for all t, $1 \leq t \leq n$, a number $v(t)$, $0 \leq v(t) \leq p - 1$, such that any t coalition can veto any $v(t)$ subset but no $v(t)+1$ subset. Actually, $v(t)$ is determined, with an error of at most 1, by the following inequalities:

$$
\begin{array}{ll}
v(t) = 0 & \text{if } t < \tfrac{1}{2}n \\
[z(t)-1/t] \le v(t) \le [z(t)] & \text{if } \tfrac{1}{2}n \le t \le \tfrac{2}{3}n \\
v(t) = p-1 & \text{if } \tfrac{2}{3}n < t
\end{array}
\tag{12}
$$

where $z(t) = 2(2-n/t)(p-1)$ and $[x]$ denotes the smallest integer bounded below by x (x rounded up). Inequalities (12) are proven in Exercise 10.7. Any strict minority has zero power whereas any strict two-thirds majority has full veto power.

We now turn to the characterization of stable anonymous veto functions.

Theorem 10.3 (Moulin [1981]).   *For fixed n, p define the **proportional veto function** by*

$$
v_{n,p}(t) = \left[p \cdot \frac{t}{n} \right] - 1, \quad all \ t = 1, 2, \dots, n
\tag{13}
$$

where $[x]$ is the smallest integer bounded below by x. Hence, $v_{n,p}(t)$ is the greatest integer strictly less than $p \cdot t/n$. For all n, p we have

(a)   *The proportional veto function $v_{n,p}$ is stable. For every profile u, denote by $C_{n,p}(u)$ the associated core.*

(b)   *An anonymous veto function is stable if and only if it is bounded above by the proportional veto function:*

$$
\{v \ stable\} \Leftrightarrow \{ for \ all \ t = 1, \dots, n\colon v(t) \le v_{n,p}(t)\}
$$

The proportional distribution of power (as precisely described by the proportional veto function $v_{n,p}$) is the optimal distribution of coalitional power if one wants, first, to guarantee the core stability of at least one outcome and, second, to make the set of stable outcomes as small as possible. Namely, $v \le v_{n,p}$ implies that $C_{n,p}(u)$ is a subset of $C_v(u)$ for each profile u.

To allocate veto power across coalitions is to arbitrate a trade-off: If we give too much veto power, cooperatively stable outcomes will disappear, yet if we give too little, stable outcomes will be too many. This dilemma has a unique solution, which we call the *minority principle:* Any coalition with x percent of the voters must be able to veto any subset with less than x percent of the candidates. The point is to give *some* decision power (some right to veto some outcomes) to *all* coalitions, however small.

For instance, take $n = p = 5$, so that the proportional veto function is

$$v_{5,5}(t) = t - 1, \quad \text{all } t = 1, 2, ..., 5$$

Consider the profile with five candidates and five voters:

Name of voter:	1, 2	3	4	5	
	a	e	d	c	
	b	a	e	d	
	c	b	a	e	(14)
	d	c	b	a	
	e	d	c	b	

Here e is blocked by $T = \{1, 2\}$, d is blocked by $\{1, 2, 3\}$ (vetoing $\{d, e\}$), c is blocked by $\{1, 2, 3, 4\}$ (vetoing $\{c, d, e\}$), and b is blocked by N (a is Pareto superior to b). So the proportional veto core is $\{a\}$. By contrast, there is no Condorcet winner.

To implement the minority principle, we need a voting rule endowing each and every coalition with the very veto power ascribed by the proportional veto function.

Consider for simplicity the case $n = p - 1$, where the proportional veto function is worth

$$v_{n, n+1}(t) = t$$

Fix an arbitrary ordering of the voters, say, $N = \{1, 2, ..., n\}$. Then define a voting rule as follows:

> *Voting by successive veto:* Voters report their complete preference ordering. Voter 1's least preferred outcome is eliminated first, next voter 2's least preferred outcome among the remaining outcomes is eliminated, and so on, until only one outcome is left after all voters have exercised their veto. This outcome is elected.

This voting rule endows a coalition T of size t with the power to veto any subset C of size t: To do this, each agent in T reports a different outcome of C as the bottom of his preferences. Note that although the voting rule is not anonymous, its veto power is.

For arbitrary integers n and p it is possible to adapt voting by successive veto so as to endow each coalition with precisely the veto power ascribed by the proportional veto function. The idea is to replicate the candidates and endow each voter with veto tokens that eliminate only one replicate at a time; see Exercise 10.8.

Veto functions also admit non-anonymous and nonneutral generalizations, known as *effectivity functions* (Moulin and Peleg [1982]). The main result (Peleg [1982]) characterizes stable effectivity functions (i.e., with a nonempty core at every profile). It is a powerful generalization of Theorem 10.3. For an account of the theory of effectivity functions, see Peleg [1984a], Moulin [1983], and Ichiishi [1986].

10.5   Strategic voting and implementation theory

In this chapter we have considered two forms of strategic stability: Strategyproofness eliminates noncooperative deviations whereas core stability takes care of cooperative deviations. In our normative perspective, both properties are meaningful axioms that one may want to require of a voting rule.

Better insights into the strategic properties of voting rules necessitate the full catalog of game-theoretic concepts. The viewpoint is now positive: Given this particular voting rule, what can we say about that specific equilibrium behavior? To capture the richness of strategic manipulations, it is also necessary to enlarge the set of voting rules by allowing mechanisms where an agent's strategy set is more complex than simply reporting his own preferences. For instance, voting by sequential majority comparisons along a given tree (see Section 10.4) yields a game form where an agent casting successive votes is fully aware of other agents' earlier votes, and this may influence his decision at later stages.

The most successful equilibrium concepts turn out to be the sophisticated (or subgame perfect) equilibrium and the strong equilibrium. The former was introduced by Farquharson [1969] and investigated by McKelvey and Niemi [1978] and Moulin [1979, 1983], among others; the latter was proposed by Peleg [1978] and further studied by Maskin [1979], Moulin and Peleg [1982], and Dutta [1980].

The most interesting methods are voting by sequential majority comparisons (Miller [1977, 1980]) or by successive eliminations of candidates (voting by veto, introduced by Mueller [1978], see Section 10.4). In those methods, the sophisticated equilibrium is typically unique and well behaved, and in voting by veto, it selects an outcome in the core.

The Nash equilibrium concept, surprisingly, does not pinpoint any particular practical voting method. In fact, it is easy to show that in most familiar methods, *all* candidates are elected by some Nash equilibrium message. This is true in particular with plurality, with Borda, and with any Condorcet consistent method (when we have three voters or more). To obtain interesting results with Nash equilibrium, one must take the more abstract viewpoint of implementation theory.

Maskin [1977] shows that the Nash equilibrium outcomes of any voting mechanism yield a strongly monotonic correspondence, and this property almost characterizes the correspondences that can be obtained in this way.

This was among the first results on the implementation problem, providing an explicit cooking recipe of a mechanism of which the Nash equilibrium outcomes would exactly recover a given correspondence. The proposed mechanism, however, is practically useless as it requires each agent to report the entire preference profile, and a Nash equilibrium obtains only if all reports agree completely. The results on implementation using the Nash equilibrium as well as the subgame perfect and strong equilibrium concepts are reviewed in the excellent survey article by Maskin [1985] and described in more detail in two books, Moulin [1983] and Peleg [1984a].

EXERCISES

10.1 Strategic voting in plurality and Borda

(a) The rule is plurality voting, and ties are broken lexicographically (if b and c are tied, b wins). We have seven voters and the profile is:

No. of voters:	2	3	2
	a	c	b
	d	b	d
	b	d	a
	c	a	c

Who can profitably misreport his preference and how? Answer first for individual agents, next for coalitions. Which outcomes, if any, are in the core?

(b) The rule is Borda, and ties, again, are broken lexicographically. Answer the same questions as in (a) with four candidates and four voters:

Name of voter:	1	2	3	4
	d	c	b	a
	b	a	a	d
	c	d	c	b
	a	b	d	c

(c) There are three voters or more, and the rule is either plurality voting or Borda or a Condorcet consistent voting rule. Show that at any given profile, *all* outcomes are Nash equilibrium outcomes. *Hint for Borda:* Given any outcome a, construct a profile where a is on top of every preference and every other outcome receives no more than $\frac{1}{2}n(p-1)$ (with the usual convention that the bottom outcome gets 0 points and the top one gets $p-1$ points).

(d) For which scoring method does the property of question (c) hold?

10.2 More on strong monotonicity

(a) *Proof of Lemma 10.1.* Say that profile v is deduced from profile u by an *elementary improvement of outcome a* if v is deduced from u by lifting

a in only one agent's opinion and by making a jump above only one out-come (e.g., from $c>b>a>d$ to $c>a>b>d$). Check that a voting rule S is strongly monotonic if and only if (2) holds for every elementary improvement. Suppose S satisfies (3) and consider v deduced from u by an elementary improvement of a in which a jumps above b. Set $c=S(v)$ and show that c equals $S(u)$ or a by distinguishing the cases $c=b$ and $c\neq b$. Suppose S is strongly monotonic and show that if v is deduced from u by an elementary improvement of a in which a jumps above b, then $\{x=S(u)\}$ implies $\{x=S(v)\}$ for all x except possibly b.

(b)   Suppose that S is a Condorcet consistent voting rule and that we have at least three outcomes and at least five voters. Show, without invoking Lemma 10.2, that S is not strongly monotonic. *Hint:* Pick three outcomes and construct a profile u with only three types of preferences,

$$a>b>c>x$$
$$c>a>b>x$$
$$b>c>a>x \quad \text{for all } a,b,c$$

and a Condorcet cycle among a,b,c. By lifting up c above b in all preferences of the first type, show that $S(u)$ cannot contain a. Show next that $S(u)$ cannot contain a Pareto-inferior outcome either; consider the profile v deduced from u by lifting outcome a on top of each preference.

(c)   Show, without invoking Lemma 10.2, that a Borda voting rule (ties broken arbitrarily) cannot be strongly monotonic. Assume at least three outcomes and at least five voters. *Hint:* Pick two integers such that $1\leq n_1\leq n_2$ and $2n_2+n_1=n$. Then consider a profile with

n_1 voters like $c>b>a>x$ for all $x\neq a,b,c$
n_2 voters like $a>c>b>x$
n_2 voters like $b>a>c>x$

Compute the Borda winner. Then lift up outcome b above c for the n_1 voters of the first type and n_2 voters with $a>c>b$.

10.3   Generalized Condorcet winners (Moulin [1980a]). The set of outcomes is ordered as $A=\{a_1,\ldots,a_p\}$, and the corresponding single-peaked domain is denoted $SP(A)$. Given a society N with n voters, we fix $n-1$ outcomes $\alpha_1,\ldots,\alpha_{n-1}$ interpreted as the peaks of some phantom voters. Define the generalized majority rule as follows: Each voter reports his peak a_i^*. The median of the $2n-1$ peaks $(a_1^*,\ldots,a_n^*,\alpha_1,\ldots,\alpha_{n-1})$ is then elected.

(a)   Show that this voting rule is anonymous and coalitionally strategyproof (and in particular, efficient).

(b)   Show that if $\alpha_j=a_1$ or a_p for each $j=1,\ldots,n-1$ (each phantom voter is either a leftist or a rightist), the corresponding generalized majority rule is a *positional dictator:* It selects the kth ranked among the reported peaks for some integer $k=1,\ldots,n$. For instance, if $k=1$, we have the leftist rule selecting the smallest reported peak w.r.t. the fixed ordering of A.

(c) Suppose $A = \{1, 2, ..., 20\}$ and there are 100 voters. Spread the phantom peaks (almost) uniformly in A. For instance, each outcome has five except outcome 10 with only four.

Suppose the preference profile among the 100 voters is made up of 40 leftist ($a_i^* = 1$) and 60 rightist ($a_i^* = 20$). Show that our generalized majority rule would select outcome $a = 8$, whereas any positional dictator method would select either $a = 1$ or $a = 20$.

Compute the outcome elected by our generalized majority rule when there are x leftist and $100 - x$ rightist voters ($x = 1, ..., 99$).

10.4 Single-peaked preferences on a tree (Demange [1982]). The outcomes are the nodes of a tree (connected graph with no cycle), and each agent in N has a single-peaked preference on this tree [(9)]. Agent i's peak is denoted a_i^*.

(a) Show that Lemmas 10.4 and 10.5 generalize: There is a strict Condorcet winner if n is odd, and at least one weak Condorcet winner if n is even. *Hint:* Use an induction on the number of nodes of the tree. Find a terminal node of the tree (i.e., a node that is not between any other two nodes) where no more than half of the agents have their peak. Then delete that node and use the induction assumption.

(b) Suppose next that an agent's disutility is measured by the distance from his peak. Show that a location is a Condorcet winner if and only if it is a utilitarian solution (minimizing the sum of distances; see Exercise 1.1). Does the equivalence extend to locations on a loop (see Exercise 1.2)?

10.5 Strategyproof voting on cyclic domains (Kim and Roush [1980]). This is another restricted domain of preferences where nondictatorial strategyproof voting rules exist. Let $A = \{1, 2, ..., p\}$ be given and let Z be the domain consisting of the following linear orders:

$1 > 2 > \cdots > p, \quad 2 > 3 > \cdots > p > 1, \quad 3 > 4 > \cdots > 1 > 2$
$p > 1 > \cdots > p-2 > p-1$

Show that a voting rule S with two players on Z (S is a mapping from $Z \times Z$ into A) is strategyproof if and only if there is a sequence $c_1, c_2, ..., c_p$ in A such that

$c_i \le c_{i+1} + 1, \quad$ all $i = 1, ..., p, \quad$ (where $p + 1 = 1$)

and S takes the form

$S(a_1, a_2) = a_2 \quad$ if $\quad a_1 \le a_2 \le a_1 + c_{a_1} - 1 \pmod{p}$

where we identify a preference in Z with its peak $a_i \in A$.

10.6 Two examples of the proportional veto core. In profile (14) there is no Condorcet winner whereas the veto core is a singleton. Show that in the following example there is a Condorcet winner and a unique outcome in the veto core, but they are different:

Three voters, four outcomes:

d	a	a
c	d	c
b	b	b
a	c	d

In our next example, we have three outcomes in the veto core and a Condorcet winner outside the core. Compute them.

Five voters, six outcomes:

No. of voters:	1	1	1	2
	a	a	a	f
	b	c	d	e
	c	d	e	d
	d	e	b	c
	e	b	c	b
	f	f	f	a

10.7 Veto function of Borda's rule (Moulin [1985a]). We wish to prove inequalities (12).

(a) Show that any strict minority has zero veto power.

(b) Show that every coalition T of size t, $t > \frac{2}{3} \cdot n$, has full veto power. If t is even, we can repeat the argument of Section 10.3. If t is odd, show that T has a message where a given candidate is on top of every preference, whereas no other candidates score above $t \cdot (p-2)/2 + 1$. Then use the same argument as when t is even.

(c) We now assume $n/2 \le t \le \frac{2}{3} \cdot n$ and prove the left inequality in (12). Pick a coalition T with size t and denote $C = \{a_1, a_2, \ldots, a_k\}$ a subset of outcomes that T (viewed as a simple decision maker controlling the T message u_T) wishes to veto. The best way to do so is to send a message u_T where C is at bottom of all u_i yet its outcomes are shuffled in such a way that they all receive the same Borda score (or nearly the same) over T.

Suppose $t = 2t'$ is even. Show that T has a message u_T from which all outcomes in C receive the Borda score $t'(k-1)$ yet the Borda score of a_p is $t(p-1)$ (the Borda scores assigned by each individual are $(0, 1, \ldots, p-1)$). Deduce that C is actually eliminated by u_T if

$$t'(k-1) + (n-t)(p-1) < 2t'(p-1)$$

This proves the left inequality of (12) when t is even.

Suppose next that t is odd. Show that T has some u_T from which no outcome in C gets a score above $\frac{1}{2}t(k-1) + 1$ whereas a_p gets $t(p-1)$.

(d) For $n/2 \le t \le \frac{2}{3} \cdot n$, show the right inequality in (12) by similar techniques. For instance, if t is even, show that for every message u_T by coalition T, there is at least one element of C with a Borda score not smaller than $t' \cdot (k-1)$.

(e) Use the approximation (12) for computing the possible size (s) of winning coalitions in a Borda method. Do this for every number of voters

$n \geq 3$. Deduce the possible values of the Nakamura number in a Borda method (for all $n \geq 3$).

10.8 **Voting by fractional veto** (Moulin [1980b]). Suppose we have p candidates and n voters, and denote by d the largest common divisor of n and p. There exist two integers R, K such that

$$Rn = Kp - d$$

Assume that each outcome is replicated K times, and each voter is endowed with R veto tokens. Given a preference profile, eliminate first R among the worst elements for u_1 in the set $K \cdot A$ (with cardinality $K \cdot p$), where each of the p original outcomes has K copies. Note that preference u_1 is indifferent between any two copies of the same outcome.

Next eliminate R among the worst elements for u_2 in the remaining elements of $K \cdot A$ and so on. After each voter has exercised his veto rights, we are left with d outcomes in $K \cdot A$, among which the final outcome is elected. Show that if R and K are large enough, any such voting rule endows the various coalitions with at least the proportional veto (13). Show that if $d = 1$, this voting rule yields exactly the proportional veto function.

10.9 **Probabilistic voting rules** (Barbera [1979], Hylland [1980]). Given the finite set A of outcomes (candidates), we let $P(A)$ be the set of lotteries on A (the unit simplex of E^A) and U be the set of von Neumann–Morgenstern utility functions on A [thus U is E^A where we identify two utility functions inducing the same preferences over $P(A)$]. Given the set N of voters, a probabilistic voting rule is a mapping π from U^N into $P(A)$. We say that π is *strategyproof* if for all $i \in N$, all $u \in U^N$, and all $v_i \in U$, we have

$$u_i \cdot \pi(u_i, u_{-i}) \geq u_i \cdot \pi(v_i, u_{-i}) \tag{15}$$

where the dot means the scalar product in E^A. We say that a voting rule π is *dictatorial* if for all $u \in U^N$, the probability distribution $\pi(u)$ weighs positively only the top outcome (s) of u_i.

(a) *Hylland's theorem.* Say that π satisfies *attainability* if for every outcome a in A there exists a profile u in U^N such that the distribution $\pi(u)$ is concentrated on a.

The theorem says that if π is strategyproof and satisfies the attainability condition, then π is a probability mixture (with fixed coefficients) of dictatorial voting rules.

Show the converse property: If π is a probability mixture of dictatorial rules, then π is strategyproof at every profile where every voter has a unique top outcome, and π satisfies attainability. Can you define π at those profiles where some voter(s) have more than one top outcome so as to make it strategyproof [i.e., π satisfies (15) on the whole domain U]?

(b) *Barbera's positional scoring methods.* Denote by U_0^N the set of utility profiles $u \in U^N$ such that no agent is ever indifferent between two deterministic outcomes $[u_i(a) \neq u_i(b)]$. Denote by U_*^N the subset of those utility profiles u such that each utility function u_i is a one-to-one mapping from A into $\{0, 1, ..., p-1\}$. We think of u_i as representing an *ordinal* preference over A.

Fix a vector of scores $s \in E^p$ as follows:

$$0 \leq s_0 \leq \cdots \leq s_{p-1} \quad \text{and} \quad s_0 + \cdots + s_{p-1} = 1/n$$

and define a probabilistic rule π as follows: For all $u \in U_0^N$, pick $u^* \in U_*^N$, representing the same ordinal preferences as u; then

$$\pi(u)(a) = \sum_{i \in N} s_{u_i^*}(a) \quad \text{for all } a \in A$$

Show that the positional scoring method π is strategyproof on U_0^N. Check that in general it violates attainability but that it is always anonymous and neutral.

(c) *Barbera's "supporting size methods."* Fix a vector of weights $t \in E^{n+1}$ as follows:

$$0 \leq t_0 \leq \cdots \leq t_n \quad \text{and} \quad t_i + t_{n-i} = 2p(p-1), \quad \text{all } i = 1, ..., n$$

and define a probabilistic rule π as follows:

for all $u \in U_0^N$: $\quad \pi(u)(a) = \sum_{b \in A \setminus a} t_{|N(u,a,b)|} \quad \text{for all } a \in A$

where we denote by $N(u, a, b)$ the set of voters preferring a to b at u. Show that the supporting size method π is strategyproof on U_0^N, as well as anonymous and neutral, but that it violates attainability.

(d) *Barbera's simple methods.* Consider a positional scoring method (supporting size method) of which the vector of scores (vector of weights) is an arithmetic progression. Show that it is a supporting size method (positional scoring method) as well.

Call *simple* a probabilistic voting rule on U_0^N that is both positional scoring and supporting size. Show that all simple rules are given by the following formula for some fixed number q, $0 \leq q \leq 2/p(p-1)n$:

$$\pi(u)(a) = r + q \cdot \sum_{b \in A \setminus a} |N(u,a,b)| = r + q \cdot \sum_{i \in N} u_i^*(a)$$

where $r = 1/p - n(p-1)q/2$. Note that the simple method where the lottery $\pi(u)$ depends most upon u (attains the largest subset of lotteries) corresponds to $\bar{q} = 2/p(p-1)n$. In the corresponding method, even an outcome a that is unanimously viewed as the top outcome $[u_i(a) > u_i(b)$, all i, all $b \neq a]$ is chosen with a probability as low as $2/p$. Comparing with the draw of an outcome at random (with uniform probability), an outcome can at most double its chances of winning, and this only if it is unanimously best.

(e) *Statement of Barbera's characterization result.* A probabilistic voting rule on U_*^N is strategyproof, anonymous, and neutral if and only if it is a probability mixture of a positional scoring and a supporting size method (Theorem 1 in Barbera [1979]).

CHAPTER 11

Aggregation of preferences

Overview

A voting rule compromises between the voters' conflicting claims by picking a single outcome from each preference profile. In his very influential book, Arrow [1963] proposed a more ambitious goal to the social planner, that of aggregating the preference profile into a complete ordering of outcomes. This ordering is meant to reflect the level of social welfare at any one of the outcomes, including the suboptimal ones. If exogenous constraints prevent the planner from implementing a socially best outcome [i.e., a maximal outcome of the social welfare ordering (SWO)], the social ordering allows him to distinguish the welfare-improving changes of outcomes from those that decrease social welfare.

The thrust of Arrow's approach is his axiom independence of irrelevant alternatives (AIIA). It states that the (social) welfare comparisons within any given subset of outcomes should not depend upon individual preferences outside this subset. Hence, AIIA limits the information one may use when comparing two outcomes a and b: The voter's preferences among these two (who prefers a to b, who prefers b to a, who is indifferent?) should be all that matters to form the social preference about a, b. The bite of the axiom is to reduce the task of defining an ordering of all outcomes to that of solving all pairwise comparisons and to check if those comparisons together form a transitive SWO. But pairwise comparisons are easy to solve. For instance, if we require anonymity and neutrality, the only sensible method is majority voting (see Section 11.1 for a detailed analysis of the binary case). Hence, the possibility of the voting paradox (Section 9.1) is a rudimentary version of Arrow's theorem: We cannot deduce a transitive SWO from binary majority comparisons. Of course, the real Arrow theorem does not use any anonymity, neutrality, or monotonicity assumption and rests on a much deeper mathematical argument.

The first half of Chapter 11 is devoted to Arrow's impossibility theorem (Theorem 11.2) and its two main variants, namely, the possibility results for quasi-transitive social welfare (Theorem 11.3) and acyclic social welfare (ASW) (Theorem 11.4). We consider first a binary choice (two candidates only) and state May's theorem (Theorem 11.1) as the axiomatic justification of the majority rule.

Starting with Section 11.2, we look at decision problems involving three outcomes (candidates) or more. In Section 11.2 we state and prove Arrow's theorem: If we require the social welfare binary comparisons to form a complete ordering (both the strict preference and the indifference relations must be transitive), then the only (Pareto-optimal) aggregation methods satisfying AIIA are dictatorial. In Section 11.3 we merely require the social welfare relation to be a quasi ordering (the strict binary preferences are transitive but not necessarily so for the binary indifferences). The aggregation methods satisfying AIIA are then characterized as *oligarchic:* There is a subset of voters (the oligarchy) such that a is socially preferred to b if and only if all oligarchs prefer a to b (Theorem 11.3).

In Section 11.4 we weaken even further the assumption on the social welfare relation; we only ask that it should be acyclic (its strict component has no cycles). This is the minimal requirement to guarantee the existence of at least one maximal element out of every subset of outcomes, thus making (social) choice always possible. The set of acyclic aggregation methods satisfying AIIA is fairly complex, but the subset of its neutral and monotonic elements admits a simple characterization (Nakamura's Theorem 11.4), and so does the subset of anonymous methods (Exercise 11.4).

The Arrowian approach to aggregation of preferences is disappointing because it forces a severe trade-off between decisiveness (the set of maximal elements of the social ordering should be small, if possible it should be a singleton) and anonymity (each agent's preferences should have an equal influence on the social preferences). Full decisiveness yields a dictatorial method, whereas anonymity brings a very undecisive method, rejecting an outcome a only if some other outcome b is preferred to a by a very large fraction of the voters (see Corollary to Theorem 11.4 for the exact quota). If one believes that actual preference aggregation methods must or do satisfy AIIA, the sequence of Theorems 11.2–11.4 explains their intrinsic limits.

A way to overcome the impossibility result is to restrict the domain of individual preferences. In Section 11.5 we consider an abstract domain restriction on which an aggregation method satisfying AIIA exists. We observe that such a method induces a (coalitionally) strategyproof voting rule on every issue (subset of outcomes); this property actually character-izes the AIIA axiom (Theorem 11.5). The result explains why the proof of the Gibbard–Satterthwaite theorem (Theorem 10.1) and that of Arrow's theorem (Theorem 11.2) are technically so similar.

Section 11.6 is devoted to the most successful domain restriction, name-ly, single-peakedness. There the ordinary majority relation is a viable Arrowian aggregator. Under the assumption of anonymity and monoton-icity, all Arrowian aggregators (SWOs satisfying Arrow's IIA) are charac-terized as a class of generalized majority relations (Theorem 11.6). Those include the positional dictators as well as other methods.

In Section 11.7 we take a different look at the rationality properties underlying social welfare relations (whether transitive, quasi-transitive, or acyclic). We investigate the dependence of the chosen outcome(s) with respect to the *issue* (set of feasible outcomes) captured in the concept of choice function.

We conclude this chapter on a more optimistic note, by discussing in Section 11.8 a very appealing Condorcet consistent aggregation method that falls only a little short of satisfying the AIIA axiom. The idea of this method goes back to Condorcet himself, but it was not formally defined until 1959. It consists of seeking a SWO that differs as little as possible from the (weighted) tournament of binary comparisons. Although the social ordering may be hard to compute, the method admits a remark-able axiomatic characterization similar to that of scoring methods (Theo-rem 9.4).

11.1 Binary choice: the majority rule and other methods

When only two decisions (candidates) are at stake, majority voting is the uniquely fair voting method. This follows from the three requirements of anonymity, neutrality, and monotonicity.

Let a, b be the two candidates and $N = \{1, \ldots, n\}$ be the finite set of voters. Each voter has a strict preference for one candidate (indifferences are ruled out; see Remark 11.1). Therefore, a preference profile is an ele-ment $u = (u_1, \ldots, u_n)$ of $\{a, b\}^N$. Of course, $u_i = a$ means voter i prefers a to b.

A voting rule is any correspondence S from $\{a, b\}^N$ into $\{a, b\}$ associ-ating to any profile u a nonempty subset $S(u)$ of $\{a, b\}$. Here $S(u)$ is the *choice set* at profile u. Hence $S(u) = \{b\}$ reads: At profile u, candidate b is uniquely elected, whereas $S(u) = \{a, b\}$ means a tie. Collective indiffer-ences are allowed, but individual indifferences are not. This is actually the most general formulation of the voting problem (again, see Remark 11.1).

In this framework the two basic equity requirements read as follows:

> *Anonymity:* S is a symmetrical mapping of its n variables.
> *Neutrality:* Permuting every agent's opinion permutes the choice set. If σ exchanges a and b, $S(\sigma(u_1), \ldots, \sigma(u_n)) = \sigma(S(u_1, \ldots, u_n))$.

A voting rule is anonymous and neutral if and only if the fact that a candidate is in the choice set or not depends only upon the number of its supporters (and this dependence is the same for each candidate). This allows for silly voting rules such as: If no more than 40 percent and no less than 20 percent vote a, choose a; otherwise choose b. Such a rule is silly because it is not monotonic.

> *Monotonicity:* A new supporter can do no harm. If two profiles u, v are such that $u_j = v_j$ (all $j \neq i$) and $u_i = a$, $v_i = b$, then $\{b \in S(u) \Rightarrow b \in S(v)\}$ and $\{a \in S(v) \Rightarrow a \in S(u)\}$.

Lemma 11.1.   *The voting rule S is anonymous, neutral, and monotonic if and only if there is some integer q, $0 \leq q \leq \frac{1}{2}(n+1)$, such that for all $x \in \{a, b\}$, all $u \in \{a, b\}^N$,*

$$x \in S(u) \Leftrightarrow |\{i \in N \mid u_i = x\}| \geq q \tag{1}$$

The obvious proof is omitted. For each q property, (1) defines a voting rule S_q that we call the q-quota rule. The majority rule S^* is the most decisive (i.e., the smallest w.r.t. inclusion) of these rules, namely, $S^* = S_{n/2}$ if n is even, and $S^* = S_{n+1/2}$ if n is odd.

Theorem 11.1 (May [1952]).   *There is exactly one voting rule that is together anonymous, neutral, and strictly monotonic:*

> *Strict monotonicity: For all u, v such that $u_j = v_j$ (all $j \neq i$) and $u_i = a$, $v_i = b$: $\{b \in S(u) \Rightarrow S(v) = \{b\}\}$ and $\{a \in S(v) \Rightarrow S(u) = \{a\}\}$.*

It is the majority rule S^*: $x \in S^*(u)$ if and only if at least as many agents favor x as y, where $\{x, y\} = \{a, b\}$.

Proof: If n is even, the only strictly monotonic q-quota rule is for $q = \frac{1}{2}n$. If n is odd, it is the one for $q = \frac{1}{2}(n+1)$. Notice that the latter is always single valued whereas the former is not.   Q.E.D.

An important consequence of monotonicity is *strategyproofness:* No voter has a (strategic) incentive to lie, namely, to cast the opposite opinion from his true one. For instance, the silly 20–40 percent rule is not strategyproof: If I like a better than b but I know that a is guaranteed to receive nearly 40 percent of the votes, I help a more by voting for b.

May's theorem generalizes when we drop the anonymity or neutrality requirement. This is important when collective choice involves voters with different relative weights (as in the U.N. security council) or when the two alternatives should not be treated equally (as when a two-thirds majority is required to overrule the status quo).

(i) *Relaxing neutrality:* Consider the generalized quota rules $S_{p,q}$ defined for all pairs p, q of nonnegative integers such that $p + q \leq n + 1$:

$a \in S_{p,q}(u)$ iff   at least p agents vote a

$b \in S_{p,q}(u)$ iff   at least q agents vote b

The $S_{p,q}$ are all monotonic and anonymous. The converse is true: All monotonic and anonymous voting rules can be written in this way. Moreover, the strictly monotonic and anonymous voting rules are the $S_{p,q}$, where $p + q = n$ or $p + q = n + 1$. Observe finally that $S_{p,q}$ is single valued (elects a unique candidate at all profiles) if and only if $p + q = n + 1$. Hence, strict monotonicity, anonymity, and single valuedness are always compatible.

(ii) *Relaxing anonymity:* Consider a *simple game* ω over N, namely, a subset ω of nonempty subsets of N such that

$$T \in \omega, \ T \subset T' \ \Rightarrow \ T' \in \omega, \quad \text{all } T, T' \in 2^N \setminus \varnothing \qquad (2)$$

Suppose, moreover, that ω satisfies

$$T \in \omega \Rightarrow N \setminus T \notin \omega, \quad \text{all } T \in 2^N \setminus \varnothing \qquad (3)$$

Interpret $T \in \omega$ as "coalition T is winning," namely, if all voters in T support a candidate, this candidate is uniquely chosen. A typical example is *weighted majority:* Give nonnegative weights $w_1, \ldots, w_n$ to the voters, pick a quota q, and define:

$$T \in \omega \quad \text{iff} \quad \sum_{i \in T} w_i > q \qquad (4)$$

This defines a simple game satisfying (3) provided that $2q \geq w_1 + \cdots + w_n$. Note that not all simple games satisfying (3) can be obtained as weighted majority games (counterexamples require at least six voters).

Now let ω be any simple game satisfying (3). Define the voting rule S_ω as follows:

for all candidates x and profiles u: $x \in S_\omega(u)$ iff $\{i \in N \mid u_i = x\} \in \omega$

This rule is monotonic and neutral. Conversely, all monotonic and neutral voting rules are described in this way. Moreover, a monotonic and neutral voting rule is single valued if and only if the simple game ω is *strong:*

$$T \in \omega \Leftrightarrow N \setminus T \notin \omega$$

Similarly, a strictly monotonic and neutral voting rule is represented by a simple game ω satisfying (2), (3), and the following additional property:

$$\{T \notin \omega, N \setminus T \notin \omega\} \Rightarrow \{T' \in \omega \text{ for all } T' \subsetneq T\}$$

Remark 11.1. On the matter of indifferences: All our subsequent voting rules for three outcomes or more allow indifferences in the social choice but exclude them from individual messages. One may want to allow individuals to report indifferences as well. This in turn *narrows down* the set of reasonable voting rules. Indeed, these "new" rules are defined on a *larger* domain, and therefore each new voting rule defines an old rule, but it is not always clear that every old rule can be consistently extended into a new one; when it can, the extension is generally not unique. Exercise 11.2 explores the generalization of May's theorem when agents may report indifferences.

11.2   Social welfare preorderings: dictators

The set A of outcomes contains now three elements or more. Each voter has preferences on A described by an ordering u_i of A; u_i is a complete, transitive, and asymmetric relation on A (indifferences are excluded). For convenience, u_i is written as a utility function; $u_i(a) > u_i(b)$ means a is preferred to b by agent i. We denote by $L(A)$ the set of orderings of A. As usual, the set of voters is denoted by N. A preference profile assigns to each agent i a preference u_i; it is an element $u = (u_i)_{i \in N}$ of $L(A)^N$.

A *social welfare preordering* (SWP) is a mapping R from preference profiles into *preorderings* on A (a preordering is a complete and transitive relation on A; indifferences are allowed). Thus R aggregates the profile u into a collective preference $R(u)$. The relation $aR(u)b$ reads: outcome a is socially preferred or indifferent to outcome b.

The SWP has an immediate anthropomorphic appeal just as in the welfarist context (Chapter 2). The collective preference $R(u)$ is of the same nature as any individual preference (except for possible indifferences). In general, there is no "real" agent endowed precisely with the preference $R(u)$, but conceivably a shrewd politician could adopt it as his program and become the ideal representative of the people's opinions.

If collective decisions are at all consistent with the social ordering $R(u)$, our society N has but one possible choice set when confronted with a *smaller* issue B, that is, a subset B (of A) of feasible outcomes. It chooses those outcomes that are best in B according to $R(u)$:

$$\max_B R(u) = \{a \in B \mid \text{for all } b \in B, \, aR(u)b\} \tag{5}$$

The point of AIIA is to make sure that the choice set $\max_B R(u)$ depends upon the preference profile over B *only*. Outcomes outside B (irrelevant since the choice must be made within B) should not affect the choice inside B. An example with Borda's ranking illustrates the problem.

There are four outcomes and three voters. On the following profile the Borda scores generate the social ordering $b > a > d > c$:

Points	Voter 1	Voter 2	Voter 3	Borda scores
3	a	d	b	b: 6
2	b	a	c	a: 5
1	c	b	d	d: 4
0	d	c	a	c: 3

Here b is the undisputed winner for the issue $\{a, b, c, d\}$. Yet if the issue shrinks to $B = \{a, b, d\}$, the election of b (as suggested by the preceding) makes voters 1 and 2 bitter. They argue it is unfair to favor b while the preferences over $\{a, b, d\}$ are

1	2	3
a	d	b
b	a	d
d	b	a

whereupon *any* anonymous and neutral rule makes a, b, d a tie since preferences are deduced from one another by cyclical permutation. If the issue should shrink to $\{a, b\}$, our plaintiffs have an even stronger argument against election of b since a majority favors a over b.

To introduce the axiom that rules out these inconsistencies, we need one piece of notation:

for all profiles $u \in L(A)^N$ and all $a, b \in A$, $a \neq b$: $N(u, a, b) = \{i \in N \mid u_i(a) > u_i(b)\}$

Definition 11.1. *Let R be a SWP over A, N. We say that R satisfies AIIA if we have*

for all $a, b \in A$ and all profiles $u, v \in L(A)^N$: $N(u, a, b) = N(v, a, b) \Rightarrow \{aR(u)b \Leftrightarrow aR(v)b\}$

In words, collective preferences over any pair $\{a, b\}$ depend only upon individual preferences over that pair. Equivalently, the choice set from any issue B [the set $\max_B R(u)$ given by (5)] depends only upon the restriction of individual preferences to B.

When this axiom is violated, manipulations of the SWP by the authority choosing the issue and by agents misreporting their preferences about irrelevant alternatives (i.e., candidates outside the issue) are inevitable. See Theorem 11.5 for a precise statement.

On the contrary, when the axiom does hold, the choice of the maximal universe A encompassing all conceivable outcomes is not conflictual; any constraint narrowing down the set of actual candidates is consistent with informational decentralization. Also the cost of finding out individual preferences is minimal since only opinions about ultimately feasible outcomes matter.

Notation: $P(u)$ denotes the strict component of $R(u)$: $aP(u)b$ if and only if $\{aR(u)b$ and no $bR(u)a\}$.

Theorem 11.2 (Arrow [1951, 1963]).   *Let A contain at least three outcomes. Let R be a SWP consistent with the Pareto relation, namely, satisfying:*

> **Unanimity:** *for all profiles u and outcomes a, b:*
> $\{N(u, a, b) = N\} \Rightarrow aP(u)b$

*Then R satisfies the AIIA axiom **if and only if** it is dictatorial:*

> *There is an agent $i \in N$ (the dictator) such that $R(u) = u_i$*
> *for all u.*

Proof: Given is a SWP R satisfying AIIA and unanimity. For any given outcomes a, b, define $B(a, b)$ to be the following subset of 2^N:

$$T \in B(a, b) \text{ iff } \{\text{for all } u \in L(A)^N: N(u, a, b) = T \Rightarrow aP(u)b\}$$

From AIIA, an equivalent definition of $B(a, b)$ is

$$T \in B(a, b) \text{ iff } \{\text{for some } u \in L(A)^N: N(u, a, b) = T \text{ and } aP(u)b\}$$

The proof parallels that of Lemma 10.2. Choose T inclusion minimal in $\bigcup_{(x,y) \in A \times A} B(x, y)$. So T belongs to some $B(a, b)$. We claim that T is a singleton.

Suppose it is not. We can partition T as $T_1 \cup T_2$ where neither T_1 nor T_2 belongs to $B(x, y)$ for any x, y. Pick an outcome $c \neq a, b$ and construct a profile as follows:

T_1	T_2	N/T
a	c	b
b	a	c
c	b	a

(6)

Here and in the rest of the proof, we do not specify the profile on $A \setminus \{a, b, c\}$. By AIIA, this does not matter.

As $N(u, a, b) = T$, we have $aP(u)b$. As $N(u, a, c) = T_1$ and $T_1 \notin B(a, c)$, we have $cR(u)a$. As $N(u, c, b) = T_2$ and $T_2 \notin B(c, b)$, we have $bR(u)c$, hence a contradiction. Thus, we have found a pair a, b and a single agent, say, 1, such that $\{1\} \in B(a, b)$.

Check next that $\{1\} \in B(c, d)$ for *all* outcomes c, d. Indeed, for any c different from a and b, consider a profile such as:

$$
\begin{array}{cc}
1 & N/\{1\} \\
\\
c & b \\
a & c \\
b & a
\end{array}
\qquad (7)
$$

From $\{1\} \in B(a, b)$ follows $aP(u)b$, and from unanimity follows $cP(u)a$. Hence, $cP(u)b$ implies $\{1\} \in B(c, b)$ since $N(u, c, b) = \{1\}$. Thus, $\{1\}$ belongs to $B(c, b)$ for all $c \neq b$. To show that it belongs to $B(c, d)$ for all $d \neq c$, use a profile similar to profile (5) in Chapter 10.

It remains to check that agent 1 is a dictator, namely, for all a, b and all profiles u,

$$u_1(a) > u_1(b) \Rightarrow aP(u)b$$

Fix a, b, and u such that $u_1(a) > u_1(b)$. Pick a third outcome c and consider the following profile v:

$$v_1(a) > v_1(c) > v_1(b)$$

for all $i \neq 1$ such that $u_i(a) > u_i(b)$: $\quad v_i(c) > v_i(a) > v_i(b)$

for all i such that $u_i(b) > u_i(a)$: $\quad v_i(c) > v_i(b) > v_i(a)$

Since $N(v, a, c) = \{1\}$, we have $aP(v)c$. Since $N(v, c, b) = N$, unanimity implies $cP(v)b$. Hence, $aP(v)b$. As $N(u, a, b) = N(v, a, b)$, the AIIA axiom implies $aP(u)b$, as was to be proved. Q.E.D.

Remark 11.2: Without the unanimity assumption, the impossibility result is essentially preserved. In addition to dictatorial SWP, the equally stupid antidictatorial SWP emerges: An agent is chosen whose opinion is exactly opposite to the collective preference. Wilson [1972] proves that there are no other SWOs satisfying the AIIA property.

11.3 Social welfare quasi orderings: oligarchies

We give a second chance to the aggregation viewpoint by relaxing slightly the assumption that the social preference relation be transitive. We require only that its strict component be transitive (whereas indifferences need not be) and discover more aggregation methods meeting AIIA.

Definition 11.2.   *A **quasi ordering** is a complete binary relation on A of which the strict component is transitive. A social welfare quasi ordering is a mapping associating to each preference profile $u \in L(A)^N$ a collective quasi ordering $R(u)$.*

Theorem 11.3.   *Fix a coalition $T^* \subset N$ – the oligarchy – and to each preference profile associate the collective quasi ordering $R_{T^*}(u)$ defined as follows:*

$$aR_{T^*}(u)b \quad \textit{iff} \quad N(u; b, a) \text{ does not contain } T^*$$

Equivalently, $R_{T^*}(u)$ is defined by its transitive strict component P_{T^*}:

$$aP_{T^*}(u) \quad \textit{iff} \quad \{\textit{for all } i \in T^*, \ u_i(a) > u_i(b)\}$$

The social welfare quasi ordering R_{T^*} satisfies AIIA and unanimity. Conversely, every social welfare quasi ordering satisfying AIIA and unanimity takes this form.

In a way this result is more encouraging than Arrow's impossibility result. A quasi-transitive social welfare is compatible with an arbitrary allocation of decision power. Yet in an oligarchy this allocation is quite coarse. An agent either has no power at all or a full veto power. By declaring a preferred or indifferent to b, an oligarch forces a to be collectively preferred or indifferent to b. In particular, the only anonymous social welfare quasi ordering endows all players with full veto power ($T^* = N$). It is the unanimous aggregation method declaring all Pareto-optimal outcomes indiscriminately best.

Thus, oligarchies achieve decisiveness at the cost of anonymity, and vice versa.

Proof of Theorem 11.3:   Given is a social welfare quasi ordering R satisfying AIIA and unanimity. Define $B(a, b)$ as in the proof of Theorem 11.2. By the unanimity assumption, the grand coalition N belongs to $B(a, b)$ for all a, b. As in the previous proof, we show that $B(a, b) = B$ is independent of both a and b. We check, for instance, $B(a, b)$ for all triples a, b, c. Pick $T \in B(a, b)$ and consider a profile where

T	N/T
a	b
b	c
c	a

From $N(u; a, b) = T$ follows $aP(u)b$ and from $N(u, b, c) = N$ we obtain $bP(u)c$. Hence, $aP(u)c$ so that $T \in B(a, c)$, as claimed. The proof that $B(a, b) = B(c, b)$ is similar.

Denote $B = B(a, b)$, all a, b. We claim that B is stable by intersection. Take T, T' in B and construct a profile u such that

$T \cap T'$	T/T'	T'/T	$N/(T \cup T')$	
a	c	b	c	
b	a	c	b	(8)
c	b	a	a	

We have $N(u, a, b) = T$ and hence $aP(u)b$. Also, $N(u, b, c) = T'$ and hence $bP(u)c$. Thus, $aP(u)c$ whereas $N(u; a, c) = T \cap T'$, implying $T \cap T' \in B$ and establishing the claim.

Denote by T^* the overall intersection of the coalitions in B. It remains to check that $R = R_{T^*}$. This amounts to proving, for all outcomes a, b and profiles u,

$$aP(u)b \quad \text{iff} \quad T^* \subset N(u, a, b)$$

Suppose $aP(u)b$. By definition of B, we have $N(u, a, b) \in B$, so $N(u, a, b)$ contains T^* since T^* is the smallest element in B.

Conversely, suppose $T^* \subset N(u, a, b)$. We need to prove that $N(u, a, b)$ is in B. To do this, pick a third outcome c and construct an auxiliary profile v such that:

T^*	$N(u, a, b)/T^*$	$N/N(u, a, b)$
a	a	b
c	b	a
b	c	c

As $N(v, a, c) = N$, we have $aP(v)c$. As $N(v, cb) = T^*$, we get $cP(v)b$. Hence, $aP(v)b$ so that $N(v, a, b) = N(u, a, b)$ belongs to B.   Q.E.D.

Remark 11.3. About the paternity of Theorem 11.3: Sen [1970] was the first to observe that anonymous quasi-transitive social welfare exists. The characterization result was proven by Gibbard [1969] and later refined by Guha [1972]. See also Brown [1975].

11.4   Acyclic social welfare

From the collective preference we demand even less than transitivity of its strict component: only that its strict component displays no cycles, no "Condorcet effect." Thus, the aggregation loses some degree of "rationality" (in the sense of Section 11.7), but it is still possible to find a maximal element of the social welfare relation on every subset of outcomes.

Definition 11.3.   *An acyclic relation on A is a complete binary relation R of which the strict component P has no cycles:*

*There is no sequence $a_0, a_1, \ldots, a_T$ such that $a_t P a_{t+1}$,
$t = 0, \ldots, T-1$, and $a_T P a_0$.*

An acyclic social welfare (ASW) is a mapping R aggregating a profile $u \in L(A)^N$ into an acyclic relation $R(u)$.

If $R(u)$ is an acyclic relation, over any issue B (subset of A) it has at least one maximal element, that is, an outcome a such that $aR(u)b$ for all $b \in B$. The maximal elements of $R(u)$ over B form the choice set of the collective preference (see Section 11.7).

Acyclic social welfares are numerous and hard to describe in full generality (see Remark 11.4 for general references). It is thus interesting – and not too difficult – to characterize those that are, in addition, monotonic and neutral (Theorem 11.4) or monotonic and anonymous (Exercise 11.4). Note that for quasi-transitive social welfares, the monotonicity and neutrality assumptions follow from AIIA and unanimity.

Monotonicity: For all a and u, v: $\{u$ and v coincide on $A \setminus \{a\}$ and $[u_i(a) > u_i(b) \Rightarrow v_i(a) > v_i(b)$, all b, all $i]\} \Rightarrow$ (9)
$\{aR(u)b \Rightarrow aR(v)b$, all $b\}$

In words, if the only change from u to v has been to improve the relative position of a, then the position of a in $R(u)$ does not deteriorate.

Neutrality: For any permutation σ of A: $\{aR(u^\sigma)b \Leftrightarrow \sigma(a)R(u)\sigma(b)$, all a, b, and $u\}$, where the notation u^σ reads $u_i^\sigma(a) = u_i(\sigma(a))$.

As usual, neutrality rules out discrimination among candidates on the face of their name.

Lemma 11.2. *Let R be a neutral, monotonic social welfare satisfying AIIA. Then there exists a simple game ω [(2)] satisfying*

$$T \in \omega \Rightarrow N \setminus T \notin \omega, \quad \text{all } T$$

which completely describes R in the following sense:

$$\text{for all } a, b \text{ and all } u: \quad aR(u)b \Leftrightarrow N(u, b, a) \notin \omega \qquad (10)$$

Proof: A social welfare R associates a complete binary relation $R(u)$ to every profile $u \in L(A)^N$. Denote by $P(u)$ the strict component of $R(u)$. If R satisfies AIIA, the property $aR(u)b$ depends on $N(u, b, a)$ only, so we define $\omega \subset 2^N$ as follows: ω contains T if and only if, for all u, a, b such that $N(u, b, a) = T$, we have $bP(u)a$. Equivalently, ω contains T if and only if there exist u, a, b such that $N(u, b, a) = T$ and $bP(u)a$.

Since $P(u)$ is asymmetric, we cannot have at the same time T and $N \setminus T$ both in ω. Finally, monotonicity of R implies property (2), and the proof is complete. Q.E.D.

For a given profile u, the collective strict preference is also called the *dominance relation: a dominates b if and only if $N(u, a, b) \in \omega$*: The agents who prefer a to b form a winning coalition. Given a profile u and an issue B, the *core* of ω is the set of outcomes of B not dominated in B, or maximal outcomes of $R(u)$ on B.

The interesting question now is this: Given a simple game ω satisfying (3), when does relation (10) define an ASW (necessarily neutral and monotonic)? This reduces easily to the following question: Which are the simple games ω such that at any profile u the associated dominance relation has no cycles?

The difficulty is related to a generalized version of the Condorcet paradox. Suppose the simple game ω is *strong;* namely, from any bipartition $(T, N/T)$, exactly one coalition is winning:

$$T \in \omega \Leftrightarrow N/T \notin \omega \quad \text{for all } T \tag{11}$$

(If the size of N is odd, the majority coalitions are an example of a strong simple game.)

Lemma 11.3. *If N contains three agents or more,* (11) *implies that **either** ω is dictatorial (there is an $i^* \in N$ such that $T \in \omega$ if and only if T contains i^*) **or** there is a tripartition $N = T_1 \cup T_2 \cup T_3$ such that each of the three coalitions $T_i \cup T_j$ is winning.*

Proof: Pick an inclusion minimal winning coalition T^*. Suppose first it is a singleton: $T^* = \{i^*\}$. Then by (2) every coalition containing i^* is winning, and by (11) every coalition not containing i^* is losing. Then ω is dictatorial.

Suppose next T^* is not a singleton, so it can be partitioned as $T^* = T_1 \cup T_2$ (where both T_i are nonempty). By inclusion minimality of T^*, each T_i is a losing coalition, and hence by (11) its complement must be winning. Setting $T_3 = N/T^*$, we have the desired tripartition.

This establishes that at least one of the two statements in the lemma must be true. It is obvious that they cannot be true together. Q.E.D.

If a strong simple game is not dictatorial, we can pick T_i, $i = 1, 2, 3$, as in Lemma 11.3 and construct a profile u exhibiting a Condorcet paradox:

T_1	T_2	T_3
a	c	b
b	a	c
c	b	a

By construction, a dominates b, b dominates c, and c dominates a. Thus, the strict preference associated with ω has a cycle. We conclude that if the dominance relation associated with a simple game is always acyclic, the simple game must be dictatorial, or not strong. The next result makes this statement much more precise.

Definition 11.4.   *Given a simple game ω on N, its Nakamura number $\nu(\omega)$ is the minimal number of winning coalitions with empty intersection:*

$$\nu = +\infty \quad if \bigcap_{T \in W} T \neq \varnothing$$

$$\nu = \inf\left\{ \frac{|J|}{J} \subset \omega \ and \bigcap_{T \in J} T = \varnothing \right\}$$

Theorem 11.4 (Nakamura [1979]).   *Given A, the two following statements on (A, ω) are equivalent:*

(i) $|A| < \nu(\omega)$.

(ii)   *For all u in $L(A)^N$, the relation $R_\omega(u)$ is acyclic on A: $aR_\omega(u)b \Leftrightarrow N(u, b, a) \notin \omega$.*

Proof: Suppose $|A| < \nu(\omega)$ and (ii) fails. For some profile u the strict component of relation $R_\omega(u)$ has a cycle $a_1, ..., a_K$, $a_{K+1} = a_1$, that is, $N(u; a_1, a_2) \in \omega, ..., N(u; a_k, a_{k+1}) \in \omega, ..., N(u; a_K, a_1) \in \omega$. Since $K < \nu$, there exists an agent $i \in \bigcap_{k=1,...,K} N(a_k, a_{k+1})$. This implies a contradiction:

$$u_i(a_1) < u_i(a_2) < u_i(a_3) < \cdots < u_i(a_K) < u_i(a_1)$$

Conversely, suppose that $\nu \leq |A|$. We construct a profile u such that $R_\omega(u)$ is cyclic. Denoting $p = |A|$, we find a sequence $T_1, ..., T_p$ of winning coalitions with an empty intersection:

$$T_k \in \omega, \quad all \ k = 1, ..., p \ and \bigcap_{k=1,...,p} T_k = \varnothing$$

Since $\bigcup_{k=1,...,p} T_k^c = N$, we can find a sequence $R_1, ..., R_p$ of pairwise disjoint (possibly empty) coalitions such that

$$R_k \subset T_k^c, \quad k = 1, ..., p \ and \bigcup_{k=1,...,p} R_k = N$$

Next, order arbitrarily the outcomes as $A = \{b_1, ..., b_p\}$. Since T_k is winning, $R_k^c = \bigcup_{k' \neq k} R_{k'}$ is winning as well. We now construct a profile u such that

on R_1: $b_1 < b_2 < \cdots < b_p$

on R_2: $b_2 < b_3 < \cdots < b_p < b_1$

on R_k: $b_k < b_{k+1} < \cdots < b_p < b_1 < \cdots < b_{k-1}$

on R_p: $b_p < b_1 < \cdots < b_{p-1}$

We check that $R_\omega(u)$ is cyclic:

$$N(b_2, b_1) = R_2^c \Rightarrow b_2 \, P_\omega(u) b_1$$
$$N(b_k, b_{k+1}) = R_{k+1}^c \Rightarrow b_{k+1} \, P_\omega(u) b_k$$
$$N(b_p, b_1) = R_1^c \Rightarrow b_1 \, P_\omega(u) b_p \qquad\qquad \text{Q.E.D.}$$

As an application of Theorem 11.4, we characterize the ASWs that are anonymous, neutral, and monotonic. Since an anonymous simple game is just a quota game ω_q, $\omega_q = \{T/|T| \geq q\}$ for some integer q, $0 \leq q \leq n$, this amounts to computing the Nakamura number of a quota game and plugging it into condition (i) of Theorem 11.4. We have done this in Chapter 10 already (see the comments after Theorem 10.2 at the end of Section 11.3):

$$\nu(\omega_q) = \left[\frac{n}{n-q} \right]$$

where $[x]$ is the smallest integer greater than or equal to x.

Corollary 1 to Theorem 11.4. *If we have p outcomes and n voters, the dominance relation of a q-quota game is acyclic if and only if*

$$p < \left[\frac{n}{n-q} \right] \Leftrightarrow q > n \cdot \frac{p-1}{p} \qquad\qquad (12)$$

Every anonymous, neutral, and monotonic social welfare is described as a q-quota game (in the sense that the q-dominance relation is the strict component of the social welfare relation, and the core of the quota game is the set of maximal elements of that relation). The smaller the quota, the smaller the core and the more decisive the social welfare. But acyclicity imposes a very high lower bound on this quota. For instance, if we have five outcomes, we need a quota q above $0.8n$ (e.g., 81 voters out of 100); in the presence of 10 outcomes this quota must exceed $0.9n$; and so on. In particular, a Borda winner always belongs to the q core when q satisfies (12). (Exercise: Why?)

Here is another interesting corollary of Theorem 11.4 and Lemma 11.2.

Corollary 2 to Theorem 11.4.   *Suppose p, the number of candidates, is not smaller than n, the number of voters, $p \geq n$. Let R be a neutral, monotonic, and acyclic social welfare satisfying AIIA. Then there exists a **vetoer**, namely, an agent contained in every winning coalition of the simple game ω [defined by (10)].*

Proof: Assume that ω has no vetoer. For all $i \in N$ we can find a coalition T_i in ω not containing i. Therefore, the Nakamura number $\nu(\omega)$ is at most n (take the intersection of the T_i). Since $n \leq p$, we get $\nu(\omega) \leq p$, and by Theorem 11.4, R cannot be acyclic.   Q.E.D.

A vetoer can block any collective strict preference: $aP(u)b$ requires that the vetoer also prefers a to b.

Next it is possible to characterize anonymous, monotonic (not necessarily neutral) ASW. This result is described in Exercise 11.4.

From Theorems 11.2–11.4 emerges a *trilemma* between rationality, decisiveness, and equity (anonymity plus neutrality), among methods satisfying AIIA. For instance, the ordinary majority tournament yields equitable and decisive solutions (as in Section 9.4) but cannot avoid cycles and hence falls short of rationality (in the sense of Section 11.7).

Next denote by q^* the smallest integer greater than $n \cdot [(p-1)/p]$. Then, the q^*-quota game has an acyclic dominance relation; it is a rational, equitable, but poorly decisive collective preference. The dictatorial methods are perfectly rational and decisive, but they grossly ignore anonymity. If we insist on anonymity, the only rational and decisive methods are imposed (electing the same outcome no matter what) or binary (only two outcomes can possibly be elected). Those methods grossly violate neutrality.

Remark 11.4. About the literature: Acyclic social welfares were first studied by Mas-Colell and Sonnenschein [1972] and Brown [1975]. Blau and Deb [1977] proved Corollary 2, and Blair and Pollack [1979, 1982] gave further results about the vetoers. These papers, all in the social choice tradition, miss the simplicity of Nakamura's result because they do not use explicitly the representation of ASW by simple games.

11.5   Restricted domain: equivalence of AIIA and strategyproofness

The proofs of Gibbard and Satterthwaite's theorem (Theorem 10.1) and Arrow's theorem (Theorem 11.2) are parallel. Our next result explains why, on any domain of preferences, the AIIA axiom is essentially equivalent to strategyproofness of the choice function on any issue.

Theorem 11.5 (Blair and Muller [1983]). *Fix the sets A of outcomes and N of agents and a preference domain $D \subset L(A)$. Given is a SWO R, associating to each profile $u \in D^N$ an **ordering** $R(u) \in L(A)$ (indifferences are ruled out). For each issue B (subset of A), consider the voting rule picking the (unique) maximal element for R on B.*

Then the two following statements are equivalent:

(i) *R is monotonic [(9)] and satisfies AIIA; and*
(ii) *for all fixed issues $B \subset A$, the voting rule $S(\cdot, B)$ is strategyproof on D^N.*

Proof: (i) $\Rightarrow$ (ii). Fix B and suppose $S(\cdot, B)$ is not strategyproof. For some agent i, some $u_i, v_i \in L(A)$, and some $u_{-i} \in L(A)^{N/i}$, we have

$$u_i(S(u_i, u_{-i}); B) < u_i(S(v_i, u_{-i}); B) \tag{13}$$

Denote $a = S((u_i, u_{-i}); B)$ and $b = S((v_i, u_{-i}); B)$. These two outcomes are necessarily distinct and both in B. Furthermore, $aR(u_i, u_{-i})b$, whereas $bR(v_i, u_{-i})a$. By (13), $N((u_i, u_{-i}); a, b)$ does not contain i, whence it is contained in (perhaps equal to) $N((v_i, u_{-i}); a, b)$. Since $aR(u)b$ depends on $N(u, a, b)$ only (AIIA), monotonicity now implies that $aR(u_i, u_{-i})b \Rightarrow aR(v_i, u_{-i})b$, the desired contradiction.

We prove (ii) $\Rightarrow$ (i). Suppose first R does not satisfy AIIA. For some issue B, we can find two profiles $u, v \in D^N$ such that u, v coincide on B and $R(u), R(v)$ do not coincide on B. In particular, we can find a, b both in B such that

$$N(u; a, b) = N(v; a, b) \quad \text{and} \quad aR(u)b, \ bR(v)a \tag{14}$$

As $aR(u)b$, we get $S(u; \{a, b\}) = a$. We claim that $S((v_1, u_{-1}); \{a, b\}) = a$ as well. Indeed, suppose $S((v_1, u_{-1}); \{a, b\}) = b$. Since u_1 and v_1 agree in comparing a and b, strategyproofness of $S(\cdot; \{a, b\})$ would be contradicted: If $u_1(a) > u_1(b)$, then agent 1 with true preferences v_1 manipulates successfully by reporting u_1; if $u_1(a) < u_1(b)$, agent 1 with true u_1 manipulates by reporting v_1. A similar argument shows successively

$$a = S((v_1, u_{-1}); \{a, b\}) = S((v_1, v_2, u_{-1,2}); \{a, b\})$$

and so on, until $a = S((v_{-n}, u_n); \{a, b\}) = S(v; \{a, b\})$. This is a contradiction of (14), and the AIIA property is established.

We check next that R is monotonic. Because R satisfies AIIA, it is enough to prove that for all pairs of outcomes a, b, the following *cannot* happen:

At profile u we have $aR(u)b$; one agent i supporting b against a in u $[u_i(b) > u_i(a)]$ changes to a supporter of a [his ordering is now v_i such that $v_i(a) > v_i(b)$], yet at the new profile (v_i, u_{-i}) we have $bR(v_i, u_{-i})a$.

This would indeed contradict strategyproofness of $S(\cdot, \{a, b\})$ for if agent i's true preference is v_i, he would prefer reporting u_i.   Q.E.D.

Remark 11.5:   When property (i) is satisfied, the voting rules $S(\cdot, B)$ are even robust against manipulations by coalitions (as in Lemma 10.3). Given B, a profile $u \in D^N$ and a coalition $T \subset N$, there is no joint misreport $v_T \in D^T$ such that

$$S(u; B) = a, \quad S((v_T, u_{N/T}); B) = b, \quad \text{and} \quad u_i(b) > u_i(a) \quad \text{for all } i \in T$$

The proof copies the preceding one. Suppose coalition T has a profitable manipulation v_T at profile u. Then $N(u; a, b) \subset N((v_T, u_{N/T}); a, b)$ since all agents in T prefer b to a. Hence, $aR(v_T, u_{N/T})b$ by monotonicity and AIIA, which yields the desired contradiction.

Notice that coalitional strategyproofness gives in particular Pareto optimality if the voting rule $S(\cdot, B)$ is *onto* B (take $T = N$).

The main example of a restricted domain where successful Arrowian aggregators exist is single-peaked preferences, studied in the next section. Two more examples are provided in Exercises 11.6 and 11.7. There are several abstract characterizations of domain restrictions guaranteeing the existence of nondictatorial SWPs; see Kalaï and Muller [1977] and Blair and Muller [1983], among others. This literature is reviewed in Muller and Satterthwaite [1985].

Another trend of literature studies the restrictions guaranteeing transitivity of the majority relation. The original contributions are by Inada [1969] and Sen and Pattanaik [1969]; see Gaertner [1979] for a survey of the literature. All these results again are quite abstract, and none of them has produced the readily applicable and intuitive test that makes single peakedness so appealing.

11.6   Social welfare orderings on the single-peaked domain

We fix an ordering of A, $A = \{a_1, \ldots, a_p\}$, and denote by $SP(A)$ the corresponding domain of single-peaked preferences [see condition (7) in Chapter 10]. We already know that Condorcet winners always exist on this domain (Lemmas 10.4 and 10.5) and yield strategyproof voting rules (Lemma 10.3). We now show that the Condorcet paradox does not occur, namely, that the majority relation yields a social welfare (quasi) ordering.

Definition 11.5. *Given a profile u for society N, we denote by $M(u)$ the majority relation, $aM(u)b$ if and only if $|N(u, a, b)| \geq |N(u, b, a)|$, and by $M^*(u)$ its asymmetric component, $aM^*(u)b$ if and only if $|N(u, a, b)| > |N(u, b, a)|$. We say that an outcome is a (weak) Condorcet winner at profile u on A if it is a maximal element of $M(u)$ and denote by $CW(u)$ the set of Condorcet winners at u.*

Lemma 11.4. *If the size of N is odd, the majority relation is a social welfare ordering satisfying AIIA and monotonicity on $SP(A)^N$. Moreover, for all single-peaked profiles $u \in SP(A)^N$, the associated majority relation $M(u)$ is single peaked, and its peak is the (unique) Condorcet winner at u.*

Proof: Since n is odd and individual indifferences are excluded, the strict majority relation $M^*(u)$ coincides with $M(u)$. We check first its transitivity. Suppose it fails. Then there exists a triple a, b, c such that $aM^*(u)b$, $bM^*(u)c$, and $cM^*(u)a$. Since the intersection of two strict majorities is nonempty, at least one agent has $u_i(a) > u_i(b) > u_i(c)$. Hence, for the given ordering of A, c cannot be in between a and b (this would contradict single peakedness of u_i). Next at least one agent has $u_j(b) > u_j(c) > u_j(a)$, so a cannot be in between b and c; similarly, b cannot be in between a and c, and we have a contradiction.

Check that the top outcome for $M^*(u)$ is the Condorcet winner, or median peak $a = a_k$. By construction of a_k, $\{a_k, a_{k+1}, ..., a_p\}$ contains a strict majority of peaks, implying that for $i < j \leq k$, $a_j M^*(u)a_i$. By a symmetrical argument, for $k < i < j$ we get $a_i M^*(u)a_j$.

We have proved that $M(u) = M^*(u)$ is a single-peaked ordering for all u. It is now obvious that $M(u)$ satisfies AIIA and monotonicity.

$$Q.E.D.$$

When the size n of society is even, the majority relation is not necessarily transitive, as the following example with four voters and three outcomes shows:

$A = \{a_1, a_2, a_3\}$	No. of voters:	1	1	2
		c	b	a
		b	c	b
		a	a	c

For the majority relation c and a are indifferent, and so are a and b, yet b is strictly preferred to c.

It is easy to show that the strict component M^* of the majority relation is transitive when the number of agents is even (see Exercise 11.5). Thus, the majority relation always yields a social welfare quasi ordering on $SP(A)^N$ satisfying AIIA and monotonicity.

In order to recover a SWO when n is even, it is necessary to break ties in a systematic way. For instance, we can decide to favor always the smallest outcome with respect to the given ordering of A. This gives the leftist majority relation:

$$aM_\ell(u)b \quad \text{iff} \quad \{|N(u;a,b)| > |N(u;b,a)| \text{ or}$$
$$|N(u,a,b)| = |N(u;b,a)| \text{ and } a \text{ is before } b\} \qquad (15)$$

This relation is a single-peaked ordering, and $M_\ell(u)$ is a SWO on $\text{SP}(A)^N$ satisfying AIIA and monotonicity. To summarize, the majority relation is an aggregation method with remarkable properties:

(α)   It aggregates any profile of single-peaked preferences into a single-peaked collective preference.

(β)   It is monotonic and satisfies AIIA and hence induces strategy-proof voting rules on every issue (Theorem 11.5).

(γ)   It is anonymous and unanimous [if all agents prefer a to b at u, so does $R(u)$].

Notice that neutrality is meaningless in the single-peaked framework because of the given ordering of the outcomes.

Is there an analogous result to May's theorem (Theorem 11.1) for single-peaked preferences? In other words, is the majority rule the only SWO (on the domain SP) meeting all properties α, β, γ?

Strictly speaking, the answer is no. However, the class of all aggregation methods characterized by α, β, γ consists of simple generalizations of the majority rule.

Definition 11.6 (Moulin [1984b]).   *Given society N with size n, a generalized majority relation on A is a relation M_v taking the form*

$$M_v(u) = M(u_1, \dots, u_n; v_1, \dots, v_{n-1}), \quad \text{all } u \in \text{SP}(A)^N$$

where $v_1, \dots, v_{n-1} \in \text{SP}(A)$ are $n-1$ fixed single-peaked preferences, called **phantom voters.**

Given u, the generalized Condorcet winner associated with M_v is thus the median of the peaks of $u_1, \dots, u_n, v_1, \dots, v_{n-1}$.

Thus, the (strategyproof) voting rule associated with M_v is fairly simple: Each agent casts his peak, next the $n-1$ fixed ballots (the preferences $v_1, \dots, v_{n-1}$) are thrown into the urn, and finally the overall median is elected (see Exercise 11.3).

Example 11.1. Positional dictators
Call r the rightist preference in $\text{SP}(A)$, namely, the ordering $a_1 < a_2 < \cdots < a_p$. Call ℓ the leftist preference, namely, the reverse ordering $a_p < a_{p-1} < \cdots < a_1$.

Suppose first all phantom voters are rightist, $v_1 = \cdots = v_{n-1} = r$. Then $M_v(u)$ is the relation $a M_v b$ if and only if $\{a > b$ and at least one agent prefers a to $b\}$ or $\{a < b$ and all agents prefer a to $b\}$. Its generalized Condorcet winner is the greatest peak of a real voter for the given ordering. This SWO is called the rightist dictator. Symmetrically, when all voters are leftist, $v_1 = \cdots = v_{n-1} = 1$, we obtain the leftist dictator.

Suppose next the phantom voters split into $k-1$ leftist and $n-k$ rightist. This is the k-positional dictator. The elected outcome is the kth ranked agent's peak w.r.t. the fixed ordering of A. Indeed, this agent has k fellow agents at least as rightist (including himself) and $n-k+1$ at least as leftist. Adding the phantom voters' ballots, this gives n votes at least as rightist and n votes at least as leftist.

Other examples of generalized majority relations obtain by spreading the phantom voters among all possible single-peaked orderings; see Exercise 11.3, question (c).

By Lemma 11.4, a generalized majority relation M_v is a SWO on $SP(A)^N$ satisfying the three requirements α, β, γ. The converse is true as well.

Theorem 11.6. *Let A with its fixed ordering and society N be given. Let R be a SWO on single-peaked preferences [a mapping $u \to R(u)$ from $SP(A)^N$ into $SP(A)$]. Suppose R is unanimous, anonymous, and monotonic and satisfies AIIA. Then R is a generalized majority relation: There exist $v_1, \ldots, v_{n-1} \in SP(A)$ such that*

$$R(u) = M(u_1, \ldots, u_n, v_1, \ldots, v_{n-1}) \quad \text{for all } u \in SP(A)^N$$

This result generalizes earlier results in Moulin [1984b]; its original proof is given in full.

Proof: Let R be a SWO on $SP(A)^N$ satisfying the premises of the theorem. First, as in the nonneutral version of May's theorem (see Section 11.1), we deduce from AIIA, anonymity, and monotonicity that for each pair of outcomes a, b there exists an integer $n_{a,b}$ such that

$$\text{for all } u \in SP(A)^N: \quad aR(u)b \text{ iff } |N(u, a, b)| \geq n_{a,b} \quad (16)$$

Since $R(u)$ is an ordering, we have

$$|N(u, a, b)| \geq n_{a,b} \Leftrightarrow |N(u, b, a)| < n_{b,a} \quad (17)$$

Since agents are never indifferent, $|N(u, a, b)| + |N(u, b, a)| = n$. Hence, (17) amounts to

$$n_{a,b} + n_{b,a} = n+1 \quad \text{for all } a \neq b \quad (18)$$

Since R is unanimous for all pairs a, b, we have

$$n_{a,b} \leq n \quad \text{for all } a \neq b \quad (19)$$

We exploit now the single peakedness of $R(u)$. Fix any three outcomes a, b, c such that $a < b < c$. Then we have

$$aR(u)b \Rightarrow aR(u)c \tag{20}$$

$$cR(u)b \Rightarrow cR(u)a \tag{21}$$

Consider a profile u with $n_{a,b}$ leftist and $n - n_{a,b}$ rightist. Then $N(u, a, b) = N(u, a, c) = n_{a,b}$, and (20) implies $n_{a,b} \geq n_{a,c}$. Similarly, consider a profile u' with $n_{c,b}$ rightist and $n - n_{c,b}$ leftist, so that $N(u', c, b) = N(u', c, a) = n_{c,b}$. Then (21) implies $n_{c,b} \geq n_{c,a}$. In view of (17), this is equivalent to $n_{a,c} \geq n_{b,c}$. We have just proved

$$a < b < c \Rightarrow n_{a,b} \geq n_{a,c} \text{ and } n_{a,c} \geq n_{b,c} \tag{22}$$

Now consider a generalized majority relation $u \to M(u, v)$, where we fix $n - 1$ phantom voters $v = (v_1, \ldots, v_{n-1}) \in \text{SP}(A)^{n-1}$. By definition, for all outcomes a, b

$$aM(u, v)b \quad \text{iff} \quad |N(u, a, b)| + |N(v, a, b)| \geq n \tag{23}$$

Comparing (16) and (23), we conclude that R is a generalized majority relation if and only if we can find $v \in \text{SP}(A)^{n-1}$ such that

$$\text{for all } a, b, \ a \neq b: \quad |N(v, a, b)| = n - n_{a,b}$$

Set $m_{a,b} = n - n_{a,b}$. Let us gather the properties of $m_{a,b}$. For simplicity, we assume that $A = \{1, 2, \ldots, p\}$, and the natural ordering is our fixed ordering of A. In view of (18), (19), and (22), the integers $m_{k,\ell}$, $k \neq \ell$, satisfy

$$0 \leq m_{k,\ell} \leq n - 1, \quad m_{k,\ell} + m_{\ell,k} = n - 1$$
$$k > \ell \Rightarrow m_{k,\ell} \geq m_{k,\ell+1} \text{ and } m_{k-1,\ell} \geq m_{k,\ell} \tag{24}$$

To complete the proof, we must construct $n - 1$ phantom voters $v_1, \ldots, v_{n-1}$, all single peaked, such that $|N(v, k, \ell)| = m_{k,\ell}$ for all k, ℓ. We do so by induction on p.

If $p = 2$, the construction is obvious. Suppose now the claim is proved up to p and consider A with $p + 1$ outcomes, with the coefficients $m_{k,\ell}$, $1 \leq k, \ell \leq p + 1$, satisfying (24). The restriction $m_{k,\ell}$, $1 \leq k, \ell \leq p$, defines $n - 1$ phantom voters $v_1, \ldots, v_{n-1}$ on $\{1, \ldots, p\}$ such that $|N(v, k; \ell)| = m_{k,\ell}$ for $1 \leq k, \ell \leq p$. It remains to extend the v_k to $\{1, \ldots, p+1\}$ while preserving this equality.

Observe first that $m_{p+1,p}$ is the number of phantom voters with peak at $p + 1$. In $v_1, \ldots, v_{n-1}$ over $\{1, \ldots, p\}$ there are $m_{p,p-1}$ voters with peak at p. By (24), $m_{p+1,p} \leq m_{p,p-1}$, so we can pick $m_{p+1,p}$ among the phantom voters with peak at p and extend them into rightist voters on $\{1, \ldots, p+1\}$. The remaining $r_p = m_{p,p-1} - m_{p+1,p}$ have their peak at p. We shall denote by r_ℓ the number of voters with their peak at ℓ, $1 \le \ell \le p$. By single peak-edness, we have

$$r_\ell = m_{\ell,\ell-1} - m_{\ell+1,\ell} \quad \text{all } \ell = 1, \dots, p$$

(with the convention $m_{1,0} = n-1$).

To complete the construction of our fixed ballots, we need to determine for a voter with peak at ℓ, say, the relative position of $p+1$ with respect to outcomes $1, \dots, k-1$. Thus, for all $k = 1, \dots, p$ and all $\ell = 1, \dots, k$, we denote by $r_{\ell,k}$ the number of agents with peak at ℓ and $p+1$ ranked between $k-1$ and k. (Of course, by $r_{\ell,1}$ we mean those with peak at ℓ and $p+1$ at bottom.)

Once all numbers $r_{\ell,k}$ are chosen consistently with the given $m_{\ell,k}$, the phantom voters are entirely determined on $\{1, \dots, p+1\}$. The induction formula relating the $m_{p+1,k}$, $k = 1, \dots, p$, to these unknown numbers is

$$m_{p+1,k} = m_{p+1,k+1} + \sum_{\ell=k+1}^{p} r_{\ell,k}, \quad \text{all } k = 0, \dots, p-1$$

(with the convention $m_{p+1,0} = n-1$). This system together with the equations

$$\sum_{k=0}^{\ell-1} r_{\ell,k} = r_\ell, \quad \text{all } \ell = 1, \dots, p$$

are the only constraints in the choice of the $p(p+1)/2$ unknown $r_{\ell,k}$ (for $1 \le \ell \le p$, $0 \le k \le p-1$, and $k+1 \le \ell$). Define the integers β_k [nonnegative by (24)]:

$$\beta_k = m_{p+1,k} - m_{p+1,k+1}$$

We must now prove the existence of a solution $r_{\ell,k}$ in nonnegative integers of the system

$$\sum_{k=0}^{\ell-1} r_{\ell k} = r_\ell, \text{ all } \ell = 1, \dots, p, \qquad \sum_{\ell=k+1}^{p} r_{\ell k} = \beta_k, \text{ all } k = 0, \dots, p-1$$

It is straightforward to check that a solution exists if and only if

$$\sum_{\ell=1}^{p} r_\ell = \sum_{k=0}^{p-1} \beta_k \qquad (25)$$

and

$$\sum_{\ell=1}^{\ell^*} r_\ell \le \sum_{k=0}^{\ell^*-1} \beta_k \quad \text{for all } \ell^* = 1, \dots, p \qquad (26)$$

Compute $\sum_{\ell=1}^{\ell^*} r_\ell = m_{1,0} - m_{\ell^*+1,\ell^*} = n-1 - m_{\ell^*+1,\ell^*}$. Also, $\sum_{k=0}^{\ell^*-1} \beta_k = m_{p+1,0} - m_{p+1,\ell^*} = n-1 - m_{p+1,\ell^*}$. Thus, inequalities (26) and equation (25) follow from (24).   Q.E.D.

11.7   Rationalizable choice functions

Requiring that the collective preference be a preordering, a quasi ordering, or an acyclic relation affects critically the class of AIIA aggregation methods. Therefore, it is important to understand in depth the various degrees of choice rationality implied by each of these three assumptions. To do this, we need the formalism of the choice function.

Society faces a finite set A of conceivable outcomes. Exogenous constraints determine a subset $B \subset A$ of actual candidates; B is the *issue*. Within the issue B, one must designate the choice set $S(B) \subset B$. The choice set must contain at least one outcome; if it has more than one, they are viewed as equally good choices (outcomes are mutually exclusive; only one is eventually chosen by some unspecified tie-breaking device). The mapping S is called a *choice function*.

The simplest way to construct a choice function is by ordering the elements of A. Let R be an ordering on A, namely, a complete, asymmetric, and transitive binary relation on A. An ordering amounts to ranking the candidates of A; the associated choice function selects in B the unique outcome with higher rank. However, it is not necessary that R be an ordering to interpret it as preferences in binary comparisons. It is enough that for all issues B, the subset of maximal elements of R be nonempty.

Lemma 11.5.   *Given a complete binary relation R on A, its maximal elements over an issue B are given by*

$$\max_B R = \{a \in B \mid \text{for all } b \in A \colon aRb\} = \{a \in B \mid \text{for no } b \in A \colon bPa\} \qquad (27)$$

The subset $\max_B R$ is nonempty for all issues B if and only if the relation R is acyclic.

The obvious proof is omitted.

To an acyclic relation R is associated the choice function $S(B) = \max_B R$. The interesting question is the converse: Given a choice function S, can we find a binary relation such that $S(B) = \max_B R$, all $B \subset A$? If we can, we say that R *rationalizes* S. Rationalizable choice functions are interesting (i) because they are easy to describe (a binary relation on A is determined by only $p \cdot (p-1)/2$ pairwise comparisons, whereas a choice function involves nearly 2^p free parameters where $p = |A|$); (ii) because they are easily interpreted.

A first remark is in order: If a choice function S is at all rationalizable, it must be by the relation R_S, called the *base* relation of S and defined by

$$aR_S b \quad \text{iff} \quad a \in S(ab), \quad \text{for all } a, b \in A$$

To check this, apply (27) to $B = \{a, b\}$.

Since S is nonempty valued, R_S is complete. Yet it is not always acyclic. Even if it is, it does not necessarily rationalize S.

We introduce two functional properties of choice functions:

Chernoff: $B \subset B' \Rightarrow S(B') \cap B \subset S(B)$, all B, B'

This axiom says that a best choice in some issue is still best if the issue shrinks. It implies, in particular, $S(S(B)) = S(B)$ for all B. It was originally proposed in Chernoff (1954). Exercise 11.8 provides several equivalent formulations.

Expansion: $S(B) \cap S(B') \subset S(B \cup B')$, all B, B'

If a is a best choice against two different issues, it is still a best choice against their union; joining forces against a does not pay.

Theorem 11.7 (Sen [1971]). *A choice function is rationalizable if and only if it satisfies Chernoff and expansion.*

Proof: "Only if" is straightforward. For instance, we check expansion. Let S be rationalized by R and $a \in S(B) \cap S(B')$. This means that for no $b \in B$ or $b \in B'$ do we have bPa. So $a \in S(B \cup B')$. Incidentally, we prove more, namely, for $a \in B \cap B'$, $a \in S(B) \cap S(B')$ if and only if $a \in S(B \cup B')$. This property, by itself, characterizes rationalizability (see Exercise 11.10).

"If": Let S satisfy Chernoff and expansion. Take first $B \subset A$ and $a \in S(B)$. If $a \notin S(ab)$ for some $b \in B$, then by Chernoff $S(B) \cap \{ab\} \subset S(ab) = \{b\}$, a contradiction. This proves aR_Sb for all $b \in B$. Next suppose a is such that aR_Sb for all $b \in B$ or, equivalently, $a \in S(ab)$ for all $b \in B$. Apply successively expansion to deduce:

$$a \in S(ab) \cap S(ac) \Rightarrow a \in S(abc)$$
$$a \in S(abc), \; a \in S(ad) \Rightarrow a \in S(abcd), \text{ and so on}$$

This proves $a \in S(B)$. Hence, R_S rationalizes S. In passing, we note an equivalent formulation of expansion:

$$\bigcap_{1 \leq k \leq K} S(B_k) \subset S\left(\bigcup_{1 \leq k \leq K} B_k \right) \qquad\qquad \text{Q.E.D.}$$

The case of single-valued choice functions yields a simpler result. If S is single valued, its base relation is asymmetric:

for $a \neq b$: $aR_Sb \Rightarrow a \in S(ab) \Rightarrow b \notin S(ab) \Rightarrow aP_Sb$

A complete, asymmetric, acyclic binary relation is just an ordering. We thus have the following:

Corollary to Theorem 11.7.   *Let S be a single-valued choice function. Then S is rationalizable if and only if it satisfies Chernoff. In that case its base relation is an ordering.*

Proof: By single-valuedness, Chernoff is rewritten as

$$B \subset B' \text{ and } S(B') \in B \Rightarrow S(B) = S(B') \tag{28}$$

Similarly, expansion is now

$$S(B) = S(B') = \{a\} \Rightarrow S(B \cup B') = \{a\} \tag{29}$$

Check that (28) implies (29).   Q.E.D.

We turn now to choice functions rationalizable by preorderings and/or quasi orderings. The characterization of preordering rationalizability is given first. It relies on a strengthening of Chernoff's condition:

NIIA: $\{B \subset B', S(B') \cap B \neq 0 \Rightarrow S(B') \cap B = S(B)\}$, all B, B'

When an issue shrinks and the smaller issue contains some element of the original choice set, the new choice set is made of these elements only. Contrary to Chernoff's condition, NIIA does not allow new outcomes to enter the choice set as the issue shrinks. (This axiom has been used already for welfarist social choice functions; see Section 3.2.)

Lemma 11.6.   *The NIIA axiom is equivalently formulated as the weak axiom of revealed preferences (WARP):*

$$\{a \in S(B), \ b \in B/S(B)\} \Rightarrow \text{no} \{a \in B', \ b \in S(B')\}, \text{ all } a, b, B, B'$$

WARP says that if outcome b was rejected once when a was chosen, then whenever a and b are both in the issue, b will never be chosen.

Proof: Suppose that S satisfies NIIA and assume $a \in S(B)$, $b \in B/S(B)$. Then $\{ab\} \subset B$ and $S(B) \cap \{ab\} \neq \varnothing$ so by NIIA, $S(ab) = S(B) \cap \{ab\} = \{a\}$. Suppose next that $a \in B'$ and $b \in S(B')$ for some other issue B'. Then (again by NIIA),

$$\{\{ab\} \subset B' \text{ and } S(B') \cap \{ab\} \neq \varnothing\} \Rightarrow S(ab) = S(B') \cap \{ab\}$$

so that $S(ab)$ contains b, a contradiction. Conversely, suppose S satisfies WARP and assume $B \subset B'$, $S(B') \cap B \neq \varnothing$. Denote a^* an element in $C = S(B') \cap B$. Suppose there exists $a \in S(B)$, $a \notin C$. Then $a \notin S(B')$ so we have $\{a^* \in S(B'), \ a \in B' \setminus S(B')\}$ and yet $\{a^* \in B, \ a \in S(B)\}$, contradicting WARP. This proves $S(B) \subset C$. Conversely, suppose $a \in C$, $a \notin S(B)$ and pick some $b \in S(B)$. Then we have $\{b \in S(B), a \in B \setminus S(B)\}$ and yet $\{b \in B', a \in S(B')\}$, contradicting WARP again.   Q.E.D.

Theorem 11.8 (Arrow [1959]). *A choice function satisfies NIIA if and only if it is rationalized by a preordering.*

Proof: First NIIA implies expansion. For any B, B', $S(B \cup B')$ intersects B and/or B'. Say that $S(B \cup B') \cap B \neq \varnothing$. Then by NIIA, $S(B) = S(B \cup B') \cap B$, and hence $S(B) \subset S(B \cup B')$ so that $S(B) \cap S(B') \subset S(B \cup B')$. The case $S(B \cup B') \cap B' \neq \varnothing$ is similar.

Let S be a choice function satisfying NIIA. Since S satisfies Chernoff and expansion, it is rationalized by its base relation R_S (Theorem 11.7). We only have to prove that R_S is transitive. Suppose it is not. We can choose a, b, c such that

$$a \in S(ab), \quad b \in S(bc), \quad \{c\} = S(ac)$$

Consider $S(abc)$. It does not contain a. Otherwise, by Chernoff,

$$a \in S(abc) \cap \{ac\} \subset S(ac)$$

contradicting $a \notin S(ac)$. It does not contain b; otherwise, by NIIA,

$$S(abc) \cap \{ab\} \neq \varnothing \Rightarrow S(ab) = S(abc) \cap \{ab\}$$

Thus, $a \in S(ab)$ implies $a \in S(abc)$, a contradiction. It does not contain c either. Otherwise, by NIIA,

$$S(abc) \cap \{bc\} \neq \varnothing \Rightarrow S(bc) = S(abc) \cap \{bc\}$$

Thus, $b \in S(bc)$ implies $b \in S(abc)$, a contradiction. This proves that R_S is transitive. Conversely, we let the reader check that the choice function associated with a preordering satisfies NIIA. Q.E.D.

Our next axiom is again a contraction property, relating the choice set within a particular issue to the choice set of smaller issues.

Aizerman: $\{S(B') \subset B \subset B'\} \Rightarrow \{S(B) \subset S(B')\}$, all B, B'

Deleting from a given issue some outcomes outside the choice set cannot make new outcomes chosen. Although this axiom has been in the literature for a while (e.g., see Fishburn [1973]), its prominent role was recognized only recently (Aizerman and Malishevski [1981]). Together with the Chernoff and expansion axioms, this axiom characterizes all choice functions that are quasi-transitively rationalizable.

Theorem 11.9 (Schwartz [1976]). *A choice function satisfies {Chernoff, expansion, and Aizerman} if and only if it is rationalized by a quasi ordering.*

Proof: "Only if." By Theorem 11.6, it is enough to prove that if S is rationalized by its base relation R_S and S satisfies Aizerman, then R_S is a quasi ordering. In other words, we want

$$[S(ab) = \{a\}, \ S(bc) = \{b\}] \Rightarrow [S(ac) = \{a\}] \qquad (30)$$

Since S is rationalizable, $S(ab) = \{a\}$ and $S(bc) = \{b\}$ imply $S(abc) = \{a\}$. Next, by Aizerman,

$$S(abc) \subset \{ac\} \subset \{abc\} \Rightarrow S(ac) \subset S(abc) = \{a\}$$

proving (30). Conversely, let S be rationalized by the quasi ordering R; we prove it satisfies Aizerman. Fix an issue B' and pick $a \in B' \setminus S(B') = B' \setminus \max_{B'} R$. By definition of the maximal elements, there is $a_1 \in B'$ such that $a_1 P a$. We claim that a_1 can be taken in $S(B')$. To prove this, construct inductively a sequence $a = a_0, a_1, \ldots, a_t$, where $a_t \in B'$ and $a_t P a_{t-1}$. By transitivity of P, the sequence cannot cycle, so by finiteness of A, it must stop. When it stops, we have reached a maximal element of R on B', namely, $a_t \in S(B')$. By transitivity of P, we conclude $a_t P a$, and the claim is proved.

We take now some issue B such that $S(B') \subset B \subset B'$. By the preceding argument, any outcome $a \in B/S(B')$ is such that bPa for some $b \in S(B')$. Therefore, a is outside $\max_B R = S(B)$. This proves

$$B \setminus S(B') \subset B \setminus S(B) \Rightarrow S(B) \subset S(B') \qquad \text{Q.E.D.}$$

Interestingly, a quasi ordering R can always be represented as the Pareto relation of finitely many orderings of A: There exist an integer ν and ν orderings $R_1, \ldots, R_\nu$ such that

$$aRb \quad \text{iff} \quad \{\text{for some } i = 1, \ldots, \nu, \ aR_i b\}$$

(see, e.g., F. Roberts [1979]). Thus, quasi-ordering rationalization is equivalent to some Pareto rationalization. Note that an oligarchic social welfare (Theorem 11.3) is precisely the Pareto relation of the oligarchs' preferences.

The three axioms Chernoff, expansion, and Aizerman are of the same vein, yet they are not logically related (when A contains at least three outcomes); one can find a choice function satisfying precisely any subset of those three (see Aizerman and Malishevski [1981]). These eight examples will be easily constructed in a set A of size 3 by the patient reader. Notice, however, that for single-valued choice functions, Chernoff and Aizerman coincide and imply expansion. (See Corollary to Theorem 11.7.)

11.8   Condorcet's aggregation method

This section is built upon the remarkable interpretation of Condorcet's manuscript by Young [1985d].

Faced with the problem of choosing some collective preference, Condorcet always supposes that there exists some *objective* ranking of the candidates that can be inferred from the profile of individual preferences. He posits a simple binomial model of voter error. In every binary comparison, each voter has a probability greater than one-half of ordering the candidates correctly. All voters are assumed to be equally able, and there is no correlation between judgments on different pairs. In the case of a binary choice, the most likely choice is clearly that of the majority. This observation is due to Condorcet, for whom it was the main justification of the majority principle.

Note that if different voter-experts are known to be of different competence in comparing outcomes, the most likely correct choice is not so clear. It turns out to be determined by a weighted majority of the experts' opinions where the weights of the experts vary as $\log[p_i/(1-p_i)]$ if p_i is expert i's probability of giving the correct answer (see Nitzan and Paroush [1982] and Shapley and Grofman [1984]).

For the case where all voters have equal competence, we describe Condorcet's idea for pooling the various opinions of our voters over three candidates or more. From the binary case he deduces that the relevant data is contained in the majority tournament that results from taking all pairwise votes, keeping track of the scores. He then proposes that the candidates be ranked according to "the most probable combination of opinions" (see the *Essai,* 1785, p. 125). In modern statistical terminology this is a maximum-likelihood criterion (see Young [1986]).

If the majority relation is transitive at a particular profile, it is obviously the most probable ordering. What if the majority relation has a cycle? Then one must choose this ordering of the candidates that is supported by the maximum number of pairwise opinions. Consider, for instance, Condorcet's original example of the voting paradox:

No. of voters:	23	17	2	10	8
	a	*b*	*b*	*c*	*c*
	b	*c*	*a*	*a*	*b*
	c	*a*	*c*	*b*	*a*

Here *a* beats *b*, 33 to 27; *b* beats *c*, 42 to 18; and *c* beats *a*, 35 to 25. According to the maximum-likelihood criterion, this cycle should be broken at its weakest link (*a* over *b*), which yields the ordering $b > c > a$ with support $42 + 35 + 27 = 104$, whereas an ordering such as $a > b > c$ scores only $33 + 42 + 25 = 100$, and every other ordering scores even less.

Condorcet, however, wrongly suggested that the idea of deleting the weakest pairwise majority could be used successively with an arbitrary number of candidates to find the most probable ordering. This heuristic argument is not valid with four candidates or more. Consider the following example with four candidates and 100 voters due to Young [1986]. The table shows the number of voters supporting each row candidate over each column candidate:

	a	b	c	d
a	–	76	38	34
b	24	–	36	68
c	62	64	–	30
d	66	32	70	–

Majority comparisons yield the cycle $a > b > d > c > a$. According to Condorcet's heuristic, we break this cycle at its weakest link (c over a, 62), thus keeping $a > c$ in the final ordering. We are left now with two cycles $a > b > d > a$ and $b > d > c > b$. The weakest proposition is $c > b$ (supported by only 64 voters). Thus, reverse it to $b > c$ in the final ordering. Finally, break the cycle $a > b > d > a$ at $d > a$ (supported by 66 voters), which yields the final ordering $a > b > d > c$. Note that the *total* support for this ordering – namely, the number of binary votes agreeing with one of the six binary propositions in this ordering – is 322. Yet the ordering $d > c > a > b$ collects a total support of 370 and should therefore be selected by the maximum-likelihood method.

The correct method, maximizing total support for the $p \cdot (p-1)/2$ binary propositions contained in an ordering, is sometimes attributed to Kemeny [1959], but its clearest exposition is due to Young. It can be axiomatically characterized by a combination of the reinforcement axiom (see Section 9.3) and of a weakening of AIIA; see Young and Levenglick [1978]. The only drawback of this aggregation method is the difficulty in computing it when the number of candidates grows.

EXERCISES

11.1 Borda ranking and AIIA axiom (Fishburn [1984]). This example shows that the Borda ranking can be dramatically dependent upon irrelevant alternatives. It involves four candidates and seven voters:

No. of voters:	3	2	2
	c	b	a
	b	a	d
	a	d	c
	d	c	b

Show that the Borda ranking is $a > b > c > d$. However, if the loser d is removed and Borda scores are computed anew among the three remaining candidates, check that the ordering of a, b, c is completely turned around.

11.2 Reporting indifferences in a binary choice (generalization of May's theorem). Say that voters report a, b, or $*$ (meaning indifference between a and b). A profile u is now an element in $\{a, b, *\}^N$, and a voting rule maps profiles into nonempty subsets of $\{a, b\}$. The definition of monotonicity becomes a bit more complicated. Fix a voter i, a candidate $x \in \{a, b\}$, and two profiles u, v such that $u_j = v_j$, all $j \neq i$, $u_i = x$, $v_i = *$:

$$\{x \in S(v) \Rightarrow x \in S(u)\} \text{ and } \{y \in S(u) \Rightarrow y \in S(v)\}, \quad \text{where } \{x, y\} = \{a, b\}$$

Similarly, for strict monotonicity, under the same premises we require

$$\{x \in S(v) \Rightarrow S(u) = \{x\}\} \text{ and } \{y \in S(u) \Rightarrow S(v) = \{y\}\}$$

(a) Show that May's theorem (Theorem 11.1) generalizes. There is a unique voting rule that is anonymous, neutral, and strictly monotonic, namely, the maority rule S^*:

$$x \in S^*(u) \quad \text{iff at least as many agents vote } x \text{ as } y$$

(b) When we relax strict monotonicity, the picture becomes more complicated. At profile u we denote by n_x the number of agents voting $x, x = a, b$. Denote

$$E = \{(\ell, m) \mid \ell, m \text{ are nonnegative integers, and } \ell + m \leq n\}$$

Fix a subset F of E such that

$$\ell \geq m \Rightarrow (\ell, m) \in F \quad \text{and} \quad \{(\ell, m) \in F, \ell \leq \ell', m \geq m'\} \Rightarrow \{(\ell', m') \in F\}$$

To F associate the following voting rule:

$$x \in S(u) \text{ iff } (n_x, n_y) \in F, \quad \text{where } \{x, y\} = \{a, b\}$$

Prove that this rule is anonymous, neutral, and monotonic.

(c) Conversely, show that all anonymous, neutral, and monotonic rules take this form.

11.3 A variant of Arrow's theorem. Let R be an ASW that satisfies AIIA and is strictly monotonic [this says: if the only change from u to v is to improve the relative position of a, and indeed there is a change $(u \neq v)$, then $aR(u)b \Rightarrow aP(v)b$]. Prove that R must be dictatorial if A contains at least three outcomes.

11.4 Acyclic and anonymous social welfare (Moulin [1985c]). Throughout the exercise we fix R, an anonymous and monotonic ASW satisfying AIIA. We suppose that R is nonimposed: For all a, b there exists u such that $aR(u)b$.

(a) Show that for all a, b there exists an integer $\pi_{a,b}$, $0 \leq \pi_{a,b} \leq n$, $n = |N|$, such that

$$aR(u)b \Leftrightarrow |N(u, a, b)| \geq \pi_{a,b} \quad \text{for all } u \qquad (31)$$

Thus, for each pairwise comparison a versus b we have a blocking *quota* $\pi_{a,b}$.

(b)   We address the converse question: Which conditions on the integers $(\pi_{a,b}; a, b \in A, a \neq b)$ guarantee acyclicity of the social welfare relation defined by (31)?

We fix a mapping π associating to each pair (a, b) of distinct outcomes a nonnegative integer $\pi_{a,b}$. Define an integer $\lambda(\pi)$ as follows:

$$\lambda(\pi) = \sup\left\{\left(\sum_{k=1}^{K} \pi_{a_k a_{k+1}}\right) - K\right\}$$

where the supremum is taken over all $K \leq |A|$ and all sequences $a_1, \ldots, a_K$ of distinct elements of A, with the convention $a_{K+1} = a_1$.

Show that if $\lambda(\pi)$ is strictly smaller than n, the social welfare relation R defined by (31) is acyclic.

Hint: Check first that $\pi_{a,b} \leq n+1$ and deduce that $R(u)$ is complete. Next suppose that the strict component $P(u)$ has a cycle $a_1, \ldots, a_K$:

$$a_{k+1} P(u) a_k, \quad \text{all } k = 1, \ldots, K, \text{ where } a_{K+1} = a_1$$

Deduce from the assumptions

$$\sum_{k=1}^{K} |N(u, a_k, a_{k+1})| \leq n-1$$

and derive a contradiction.

(c)   Conversely, prove that if the social welfare relation defined by (31) is acyclic for all u, then we must have $\lambda(\pi) < n$.

Hint: Check first $\pi_{a,b} + \pi_{b,a} - 2 < n$. Next pick a finite sequence $a_1, \ldots, a_K$ of distinct outcomes and suppose

$$\sum_{k=1}^{K} (\pi_{a_k a_{k+1}} - 1) \geq n$$

Prove the existence of K pairwise disjoint coalitions $R_1, \ldots, R_K$ such that

$$\bigcup_{k=1}^{K} R_k = N \text{ and } |R_k| \leq \pi_{a_k a_{k+1}} - 1 \quad \text{for all } k = 1, \ldots, K$$

Then construct a profile u such that $N(u, a_k, a_{k+1}) = R_{k+1}$ for all $k = 1, \ldots, K$ and derive a contradiction.

(d)   An example for $|A| = 4$ illustrates the result. Here $n = 100$ and the entry row x, column y is $\pi_{x,y}$.

	a	b	c	d	
a	–	20	10	15	
b	60	–	21	33	
c	30	8	–	22	$(n = 100)$
d	40	11	20	–	

To be in the choice set, a needs to be preferred or indifferent to b by at least 20 agents, to c by at least 10 agents, and to d by at least 15 agents. Check that the constraint $\lambda(\pi) < n$ is tight on all cycles of length 4. Thus, one cannot increase *any* of the numbers $\pi_{x,y}$ without destroying acyclicity.

(e) Instead of the blocking quotas $\pi_{a,b}$, use the winning quotas $w_{a,b}$:

$$aP(u)b \Leftrightarrow |N(u,a,b)| \geq w_{a,b}$$

Show that the preceding equivalence defines an acyclic relation if and only if over any cycle of length K (in A) the sum of the winning quotas is at least $kn-n+1$ (this interpretation is due to D. Blair, private communication).

11.5 More on the majority relation and single-peaked preferences. Given is an ordering of A, $A = \{a_1, \ldots, a_p\}$, and SP(A) the corresponding domain of single-peaked preferences. Show that when the size of N is even, the majority relation $M(u)$ at any profile $u \in \mathrm{SP}(A)^N$ is a quasi ordering (Definition 11.2). *Hint:* Denoting by $M_\ell(u)$, $M_r(u)$, respectively, the leftist and rightist majority relations [see (15)], show that $M(u)$ is the Pareto relation deduced from M_ℓ, M_r:

$$aM(u)b \quad \text{iff} \quad aM_\ell(u)b \text{ and/or } aM_r(u)b$$

11.6 A sufficient condition for transitivity of the majority relation. Given is an ordering $N = \{1, 2, \ldots, n\}$ of the set of agents. We consider a profile $u \in L(A)^N$ satisfying the following property. For all $i, j, k \in N$ and all $a, b \in A$,

$$\{i < k < j \text{ and } u_i(a) > u_i(b), u_j(a) > u_j(b)\} \Rightarrow \{u_k(a) > u_k(b)\}$$

Show that the associated majority relation is an ordering if n is odd and a quasi ordering if n is even.

11.7 Dichotomous preferences and approval voting (Brams and Fishburn [1978]). Let $D(A)$ be the set of dichotomous preferences on A, namely, preorderings with exactly two indifference classes:

$u_i \in D(A)$ if and only if for some subset B_i, $\varnothing \neq B_i \subset A$, u_i is indifferent within B_i as well as within $A \setminus B_i$, and $u_i(B_i) > u_i(A \setminus B_i)$

Given society N, call approval voting the following SWP:

$$aR(u)b \quad \text{iff} \quad |\{i \in N \mid a \in B_i\}| \geq |\{i \in N \mid b \in B_i\}|$$

Show that it is the only SWP satisfying on $D(A)^N$ anonymity, neutrality, AIIA, and strict monotonicity (to be defined properly).

11.8 Equivalent formulations of Chernoff's axiom. Chernoff's condition is equivalent to any one of the eight following properties:

(i) $S(B \cup B') \subset S(B) \cup B'$, all B, B'
(ii) $S(B \cup B') \subset S(B) \cup S(B')$
(iii) $S(B \cup B') \subset S(S(B) \cup B')$
(iv) $S(B \cup B') \subset S(S(B) \cup S(B'))$
(v)   Same as above, stated for all pairs B, B' of *disjoint* subsets of A.

11.9 A consequence of Chernoff's axiom. Let S be a choice function satisfying Chernoff. Prove the existence of at least one ordering R such that for all $B \subset A$: $\max_{B} R \in S(B)$

Hint: Construct a sequence $a_1 \in S(A)$, $a_2 \in S(A/\{a_1\})$, $a_3 \in S(A/\{a_1, a_2\})$, and so on. Then define R as the ordering with a_1 on top, a_2 second, and so on.

11.10 One more characterization of rationality (Schwartz [1976]). Prove that S is rationalizable if and only if

$$S(B) \cap S(B') = S(B \cup B') \cap B \cap B',   \text{all } B, B'$$

11.11 One more characterization of rationalizability by a preordering (Sen [1971]). Prove that S is rationalizable by a preordering if and only if it satisfies Chernoff's condition *and* the following condition:

Sen: $\{B \subset B' \text{ and } S(B') \cap S(B) \neq \varnothing\} \Rightarrow S(B) \subset S(B')$, all B, B'

11.12 Plott's path independence (Plott [1973]). Consider the following property of a choice function S, called path independence:

$$S(B \cup B') = S(S(B) \cup B'),   \text{all } B, B'$$

This allows us to decompose the choice problem over a (large) issue into choices over smaller issues. We can cut *any* piece out of the original issue and replace it by its own choice set. Hence, the original choice problem can be converted to an arbitrary path of smaller problems.

(i)   Fix an integer $K \geq 2$. Show that path independence is equivalent to the following condition:

$$S\left(\bigcup_{1 \leq k \leq K} B_k\right) = S\left(\bigcup_{1 \leq k \leq K} S(B_k)\right)   \text{for all } B_1, \ldots, B_K$$

(ii) Prove that S satisfies path independence if and only if it satisfies Chernoff and Aizerman.

Bibliography

Aczél, J. 1966. *Lectures on Functional Equations and Their Applications.* New York: Academic.

Aizerman, M. A., and A. V. Malishevski. 1981. General theory of best variant choice, *IEEE Transactions on Automatic Control,* **26**, 1030–41.

Arrow, K. 1959. Rational choice functions and orderings, *Econometrica,* **26**, 121–7.
1963. *Social Choice and Individual Values,* 2nd ed. (1st ed., 1951). New York: John Wiley.

Arrow, K., and M. Intriligator, eds. 1981. *Handbook of Mathematical Economics.* Amsterdam: North-Holland.

d'Aspremont, C. 1985. Axioms for social welfare orderings, in *Social Goals and Social Organizations,* L. Hurwicz, D. Schmeidler, and H. Sonnenschein, eds. Cambridge: Cambridge University Press.

d'Aspremont, C., and L. Gevers. 1977. Equity and the informational basis of collective choice, *Review of Economic Studies,* **44**(2), 199–209.

Atkinson, A. B. 1970. On the measurement of inequality, *Journal of Economic Theory,* **2**, 244–63.

Aumann, R. J. 1976. Lectures on Game Theory, mimeo, Stanford University.
1985. An axiomatization of the non-transferable utility value, *Econometrica,* **53**(3), 667–78.

Aumann, R. J., and M. Maschler. 1985. Game theoretic analysis of a bankruptcy problem from the Talmud, *Journal of Economic Theory,* **36**, 195–213.

Aumann, R., and L. Shapley. 1974. *Values of Non-atomic Games.* Princeton, NJ: Princeton University Press.

Banker, R. 1981. Equity consideration in traditional full-cost allocation practices: an axiomatic perspective, in *Joint Cost Allocations,* S. Moriarty, ed. Norman: University of Oklahoma.

Banks, J. S. 1985. Sophisticated voting outcomes and agenda control, *Social Choice and Welfare,* **1**(4), 295–306.

Barbera, S. 1979. Majority and positional voting in a probabilistic framework, *Review of Economic Studies,* **46**, 389–97.

Baumol, W., J. Panzar, and R. Willig. 1982. *Contestable Markets and the Theory of Industry Structure.* New York: Harcourt Brace Jovanovich.

Binmore, K., A. Rubinstein, and A. Wolinsky. 1986. Nash bargaining solution in economic modelling, *Rand Journal of Economics,* **17**, 176–88.

Black, D. 1958. *The Theory of Committees and Elections.* Cambridge: Cambridge University Press.

Blackorby, C., and D. Donaldson. 1984. Social criteria for evaluating population change, *Journal of Public Economics*, **25**, 13–33.

Blackorby, C., D. Primont, and R. Russell. 1978. *Duality, Separability and Functional Structure*. Amsterdam: North-Holland.

Blair, D., and E. Muller. 1983. Essential aggregation procedures on restricted domains of preferences, *Journal of Economic Theory*, **30**, 34–53.

Blair, D., and R. Pollak. 1979. Collective rationality and dictatorship: the scope of the Arrow theorem, *Journal of Economic Theory*, **21**, 186–94.

1982. Acyclic collective choice rules, *Econometrica*, **50**, 931–4.

Blau, J., and R. Deb. 1977. Social decision functions and the veto, *Econometrica*, **45**, 871–9.

Bondavera, O. N. 1962. Teoriia iadra v igre n lits, *Vestnik Leningrad University, Mathematics, Mechanics, Astronomy*, **13**, 141–2.

Borda, J. C. de. 1781. Mémoire sur les élections au Scrutin, *Histoire de l'Academie Royale des Sciences, Paris*.

Border, K. 1985. *Fixed Points Theorems with Application to Economics and Game Theory*. Cambridge: Cambridge University Press.

Brams, S., and P. Fishburn. 1978. Approval voting, *American Political Science Review*, **72**(3), 831–47.

1983. Paradoxes of preferential voting, *Mathematics Magazine*, **56**(5), 207–14.

Brown, D. J. 1975. Aggregation of preferences, *Quarterly Journal of Economics*, **89**, 456–69.

Champsaur, P., and J. C. Rochet. 1983. On planning procedures which are locally strategyproof, *Journal of Economic Theory*, **30**(2), 283–99.

Chernoff, H. 1954. Rational selection of decision functions, *Econometrica*, **22**, 422–43.

Chun, Y. 1986. The solidarity axiom for quasi-linear social choice problems, *Social Choice and Welfare*, **3**, 297–310.

1988. The proportional solution for rights problems, *Mathematical Social Sciences*, **15**(3).

Chun, Y., and W. Thomson. 1990. Bargaining with Uncertain Disagreement Points, *Econometrica*, 58, 4, 951–959.

Clarke, E. H. 1971. Multipart pricing of public goods, *Public Choice*, **11**, 17–33.

Condorcet, Marquis de, 1785. Essai sur l'application de l'analyse à la probabilité des decisions rendues à la pluralité des voix, Paris.

Dasgupta, P., P. Hammond, and E. Maskin. 1979. The implementation of social choice rules, *Review of Economic Studies*, **46**, 185–216.

Debreu, G. 1960. Topological methods in cardinal utility theory, in *Mathematical Methods in the Social Sciences*, K. Arrow, S. Karlin, and P. Suppes, eds. Stanford: Stanford University Press.

Debreu, G., and H. Scarf. 1963. A limit theorem on the core of an economy, *International Economic Review*, **4**, 235–46.

Demange, G. 1982. Single peaked orders on a tree, *Mathematical Social Sciences*, **3**(4), 389–96.

1987. Non Manipulable Cores, *Econometrica*, , 55, 5, 1057–1074.

Dubins, L. F. 1977. Group decision devices, *American Mathematical Monthly*, May, pp. 350–6.

Dummett, M. 1984. *Voting Procedures*. Oxford: Oxford University Press.

Dutta, B. 1980. On the possibility of consistent voting procedures, *Review of Economic Studies*, **47**, 603–16.

Erdös, P., and L. Moser. 1964. On the representation of directed graphs as unions of orderings, *Publication of the Mathematics Institute of the Hungarian Academy of Sciences,* **9,** 125–32.

Farquharson, R. 1969. *Theory of Voting.* New Haven: Yale University Press.

Faulhaber, G. 1975. Cross-subsidization: pricing in public enterprises, *American Economic Review,* **65,** 966–77.

Feldman, A. 1980. *Welfare Economics and Social Choice Theory.* Boston: Kluwer, Nijhoff.

Fishburn, P. C. 1973. *The Theory of Social Choice.* Princeton: Princeton University Press.

1982. Monotonicity paradoxes in the theory of elections, *Discrete Applied Mathematics,* **4,** 119–34.

1984. Discrete mathematics in voting and group choice, *SIAM Journal of Algebraic and Discrete Methods,* **5,** 263–75.

Foley, D. 1967. Resource allocation and the public sector, *Yale Economic Essays,* **7**(1), 45–98.

1970. Lindahl's solution and the core of an economy with public goods, *Econometrica,* **38,** 66–72.

Foster, J. 1985. Inequality measurement, in *Fair Allocation,* H. P. Young, ed., AMS Short Course Lecture Notes, Vol. 33. Providence: The American Mathematical Society.

Gaertner, W. 1979. An analysis and comparison of several necessary and sufficient conditions for transitivity under the majority rule, in *Aggregation and Revelation of Preferences,* J. J. Laffont, ed. Amsterdam: North-Holland.

Gehrlein, W., B. Gopinath, J. C. Lagarias, and P. C. Fishburn. 1982. Optimal pairs of score vectors for positional scoring rules, *Applied Mathematics and Optimization,* **8,** 309–24.

Gibbard, A. 1969. Social Choice and the Arrow Condition, mimeo.

1973. Manipulation of voting schemes: a general result, *Econometrica,* **41,** 587–601.

1977. Manipulation of schemes that mix voting with chance, *Econometrica,* **45,** 665–81.

1978. Straightforwardness of game forms with lotteries as outcomes, *Econometrica,* **46,** 595–614.

Gillies, D. B. 1959. Solutions to general non-zero sum games, in *Contribution to the Theory of Games IV,* Tucker and Luce, eds., Annals of Mathematics Studies, Vol. 40. Princeton: Princeton University Press, pp. 47–85.

Gorman, W. M. 1968. The structure of utility functions, *Review of Economic Studies,* **35,** 369–90.

Green, J., E. Kohlberg, and J. J. Laffont. 1976. Partial equilibrium approach to the free rider problem, *Journal of Public Economics,* **6,** 375–94.

Green, J., and J. J. Laffont. 1979. Incentives in public decision making, in *Studies in Public Economics,* Vol. 1. Amsterdam: North-Holland.

Greenberg, J. 1979. Consistent majority rules over compact sets of alternatives, *Econometrica,* **47,** 627–36.

Groves, T. 1973. Incentives in teams, *Econometrica,* **41,** 617–63.

Groves, T., and J. Ledyard. 1977. Optimal allocation of public goods: a solution to the free rider problem, *Econometrica,* **45,** 783–809.

Groves, T., and M. Loeb. 1975. Incentives and public inputs, *Journal of Public Economics,* **4,** 211–26.

320   **Bibliography**

Guha, A. S. 1972. Neutrality, monotonicity and the right of veto, *Econometrica,* **40,** 821–6.

Hammond, P. 1976. Equity, Arrow's conditions and Rawls' difference principle, *Econometrica,* **44**(4), 793–804.

Hardy, G. H., J. E. Littlewood, and G. Pölya. 1934/1952. *Inequalities.* Cambridge: Cambridge University Press.

Harsanyi, J. C. 1955. Cardinal welfare, individualistic ethics, and interpersonal comparisons of utility, *Journal of Political Economy,* **63,** 309–21.

  1963. A simplified bargaining model for the N-person cooperative games, *International Economic Review,* **4,** 194–220.

  1975. Can the maximin principle serve as a basis for morality? *American Political Science Review,* **69,** 594–606.

  1977. *Rational Behavior and Bargaining Equilibrium in Games and Social Situations.* Cambridge: Cambridge University Press.

Hart, S. 1985. An axiomatization of Harsanyi's non-transferable utility solution, *Econometrica,* **53**(6), 1295–1314.

Hart, S., and A. Mas-Colell, 1989, Potential , value, and consistency, *Econometrica,* 57, 3, 589–614.

Hurwicz, L. 1979. Outcome functions yielding Walrasian and Lindahl allocations at Nash equilibrium points, *Review of Economic Studies,* **46,** 217–25.

Hylland, A. 1980. Strategy-Proofness of Voting Procedures with Lotteries as Outcomes and Infinite Sets of Strategies, mimeo, University of Oslo.

Ichiishi, T. 1981. Super modularity: applications to convex games and to the greedy algorithm for LP, *Journal of Economic Theory,* **25,** 283–6.

  1983. *Game Theory for Economic Analysis.* New York: Academic.

  1986. The effectivity function approach to the core, in *Contributions to Mathematical Economics in Honor of Gerard Debreu,* W. Hildenbrand and A. Mas-Colell, eds. Amsterdam: North-Holland.

  Forthcoming. On Peleg's theorem for stability of convex effectivity functions, *European Journal of Political Economy,* Special Issue on Economic Design.

Inada, K. I. 1969. The simple majority decision rule, *Econometrica,* **32,** 490–506.

Kalaï, E. 1977. Proportional solutions to bargaining situations: interpersonal utility comparisons, *Econometrica,* **45**(7), 1623–30.

  1985. Solutions to the bargaining problem, in *Social Goals and Social Organization,* L. Hurwicz, D. Schmeidler, and H. Sonnenschein, eds. Cambridge: Cambridge University Press.

Kalaï, E., and E. Muller. 1977. Characterization of domains admitting nondictatorial social welfare functions and nonmanipulable voting procedures, *Journal of Economic Theory,* **16,** 457–69.

Kalaï, E., and D. Samet. 1985. Monotonic solutions to general cooperative games, *Econometrica,* **53**(2), 307–28.

Kalaï, E., and M. Smorodinsky. 1975. Other solutions to Nash's bargaining problem, *Econometrica,* **43**(3), 513–18.

Kaneko, M. 1977. The ratio equilibrium and a voting game in a public good economy, *Journal of Economic Theory,* **16**(2), 123–36.

  1984. Reformulation of the Nash social welfare function for a continuum of individuals, *Social Choice and Welfare,* **1,** 33–43.

Kelly, J. S. 1986. Condorcet winner proportions, *Social Choice and Welfare,* **3,** 311–14.

Kemeny, J. 1959. Mathematics without numbers, *Daedalus,* **88,** 571–91.

Kern, R. 1985. The Shapley transfer value without zero weight, *International Journal of Game Theory,* **14**(2), 73–92.

Kim, K. W., and F. Roush. 1980. Special domains and nonmanipulability, *Mathematical Social Sciences,* **1**(1), 85–92.

Kim, T. 1986. A Stable Nash Mechanism Implementing Lindahl Allocations for Quasi-Linear Environments, mimeo, University of Minnesota.

Kolm, S. C. 1968. The optimal production of social justice, in *Public Economics,* H. Guitton and J. Margolis, eds. London: Macmillan.

1972. Justice et Equité, Monograph of the CNRS, Paris, CNRS.

1976. Unequal inequalities, *Journal of Economic Theory,* **12**(3), 416–42; **13**(1), 82–111.

Laffont, J. J., and E. Maskin. 1980. A differential approach to dominant strategy mechanisms, *Econometrica,* **48**(6), 1507–20.

LeBreton, M. 1987. On the Core of Voting Games, *Social Choice and* , 4, 295 – 303.

Legros, P. 1981. A Note on the Nucleolus of Three Person Games, mimeo, University of Paris.

Lensberg, T. 1987. Stability and collective rationality, *Econometrica,* **55**(4), 935–62.

Littlechild, S. C., and G. Owen. 1973. A simple expression for the Shapley value in a special case, *Management Science,* **20**, 370–2.

Loehman, E., and A. Whinston. 1974. An axiomatic approach to cost allocation for public investment, *Public Finance Quarterly,* **2**, 236–51.

McGarvey, D. C. 1953. A theorem on the construction of voting paradoxes, *Econometrica,* **21**, 608–10.

McKelvey, R. D., and R. G. Niemi. 1978. A multistage game representation of sophisticated voting for binary procedures, *Journal of Economic Theory,* **18**, 1–22.

McKelvey, R., and N. Schofield. 1987. Generalized Symmetry Conditions at a Core Point, *Econometrica,* **55**, 4, 923–934.

Maschler, M., and M. A. Perles. 1981(a). The super-additive solution for the Nash bargaining game, *International Journal of Game Theory,* **10**(314), 163–93.

1981(b). The present status of the super-additive solution, in *Essays in Game Theory and Mathematical Economics in Honor of Oskar Morgenstern,* R. J. Aumann, ed. Mannheim: Bibliographisches Institut.

Mas-Colell, A. 1980. Remarks on the game-theoretic analysis of a simple distribution of surplus problem, *International Journal of Game Theory,* **9**(3), 125–40.

Mas-Colell, A., and J. Silvestre. 1989. Cost Share Equilibria: A Lindahlian Approach, *Journal of Economic Theory,* **47**, 239–56.

Mas-Colell, A., and H. Sonnenschein. 1972. General possibility theorems for group decision functions, *Review of Economic Studies,* **39**, 185–92.

Maskin, E. 1977. Nash Equilibrium and Welfare Optimality, mimeo, Massachusetts Institute of Technology.

1979. Implementation and strong Nash equilibrium, in *Aggregation and Revelation of Preferences,* J. J. Laffont, ed. Amsterdam: North-Holland.

1985. The theory of implementation in Nash equilibrium, in *Social Goals and Social Organizations,* L. Hurwicz, D. Schmeidler, and H. Sonnenschein, eds. Cambridge: Cambridge University Press.

May, K. 1952. A set of independent necessary and sufficient conditions for simple majority decision, *Econometrica,* **20**, 680–4.

Megiddo, N. 1974. On the nonmonotonicity of the bargaining set, the kernel, and the nucleolus of a game, *SIAM Journal on Applied Mathematics,* **27**, 355-8.

Miller, N. 1977. Graph-theoretical approaches to the theory of voting, *American Journal of Political Science,* **21**, 769-803.

1980. A new solution set for tournaments and majority voting: further graph-theoretical approaches to the theory of voting, *American Journal of Political Science,* **24**, 68-9.

1983. Pluralism and social choice, *American Political Science Review,* **77**, 734-5.

Milleron, J. C. 1972. Theory of value with public goods: a survey article, *Journal of Economic Theory,* **5**, 419-77.

Mirman, L. J., Y. Tauman, and I. Zang. 1985. Supportability, sustainability and subsidy-free prices, *Rand Journal of Economics,* **16**(1), 114-26.

Mirrlees, J. 1974. Notes on welfare economics, information and uncertainty, in *Essays on Economic Behaviour under uncertainty,* T. Balch, D. McFadden, and S. Wu, eds. Amsterdam: North-Holland.

Moulin, L. 1953. Les origines religieuses des techniques electorales et deliberatives modernes, *Revue d'Histoire Politique et Constitutionnelle.*

Moulin, H. 1979. Dominance solvable voting schemes, *Econometrica,* **47**(6), 1337-51.

1980(a). On strategy-proofness and single peakedness, *Public Choice,* **35**, 437-55.

1980(b). Implementing efficient, anonymous and neutral social choice functions, *Journal of Mathematical Economics,* **7**, 249-69.

1981(a). Implementing just and efficient decision making, *Journal of Public Economics,* **16**, 193-213.

1981(b). The proportional veto principle, *Review of Economic Studies,* **48**, 407-16.

1983. *The Strategy of Social Choice,* Advanced Textbooks in Economics, No. 18. Amsterdam: North-Holland.

1984(a). The conditional auction for sharing a surplus, *Review of Economic Studies,* **51**, 157-70.

1984(b). Generalized Condorcet winners for single peaked and single plateau preferences, *Social Choice and Welfare,* **1**, 127-47.

1985(a). Fairness and strategy in voting, in *Fair Allocation,* H. P. Young, ed., AMS Short Course Lecture Notes, Vol. 33. Providence, RI: American Mathematical Society.

1985(b). Egalitarianism and utilitarianism in quasi-linear bargaining, *Econometrica,* **53**(1), 49-67.

1985(c). From social welfare orderings to acyclic aggregation of preferences, *Mathematical Social Sciences,* **9**, 1-17.

1985(d). The separability axiom and equal sharing methods, *Journal of Economic Theory,* **36**(1), 120-48.

1986(a). *Game Theory for the Social Sciences,* 2nd ed. New York: New York University Press.

1986(b). Characterizations of the pivotal mechanism, *Journal of Public Economics,* **31**, 53-78.

1986(c). Choosing from a tournament, *Social Choice and Welfare,* **3**, 271-91.

1987(a). Equal or proportional division of a surplus, and other methods, *International Journal of Game Theory,* **16**(3), 161-86.

1987(b). Egalitarian equivalent cost-sharing of a public good, *Econometrica,* **55**(4), 963–77.

1987(c). A core selection for pricing a single output monopoly, *Rand Journal of Economics,* **18**(3), 397–407.

1987(d). The pure compensation problem: egalitarianism versus laissez-fairism, *Quarterly Journal of Economics,* **102**, 769–83.

Forthcoming. Common property of resources: can everyone benefit from growth? *Journal of Mathematical Economics.*

1988. Condorcet's principle implies the no show paradox, *Journal of Economic Theory,* **45**, *1*, 53–64.

Moulin, H., and B. Peleg. 1982. Core of effectivity functions and implementation theory, *Journal of Mathematical Economics,* **10**, 115–45.

Mueller, D. 1978. Voting by veto, *Journal of Public Economics,* **10**, 57–75.

1979. *Public Choice,* Cambridge Surveys of Economic Literature. Cambridge: Cambridge University Press.

Muller, E., and M. Satterthwaite. 1977. The equivalence of strong positive association and strategy-proofness, *Journal of Economic Theory,* **14**, 412–18.

1985. Strategyproofness: the existence of dominant strategy mechanisms, in *Social Goals and Social Organization,* L. Hurwicz, D. Schmeidler, and H. Sonnenschein, eds. Cambridge: Cambridge University Press.

Musgrave, R., and A. Peacock, eds. 1958. *Classics in the Theory of Public Finance.* London: Macmillan.

Myerson, R. 1977. Graphs and cooperation in games, *Mathematics of Operations Research,* **2**, 225–9.

1981. Utilitarianism, egalitarianism and the timing effect in social choice problems, *Econometrica,* **49**(4), 883–97.

Nakamura, K. 1979. The vetoers in a simple game with ordinal preferences, *International Journal of Game Theory,* **8**, 55–61.

Nash, J. F. 1950. The bargaining problem, *Econometrica,* **28**, 155–62.

Nitzan, S., and J. Paroush. 1982. Optimal decision rules in uncertain dichotomous choice situations, *International Economic Review,* **23**(2), 289–97.

O'Neill, B. 1982. A problem of rights arbitration in the Talmud, *Mathematical Social Science,* **2**, 345–71.

Owen, G. 1982. *Game Theory,* 2nd ed. New York: Academic.

Peleg, B. 1978. Consistent voting systems, *Econometrica,* **46**, 153–61.

1982. Convex Effectivity Functions, mimeo, The Hebrew University of Jerusalem.

1984(a). *Game Theoretic Analysis of Voting in Committees.* Cambridge: Cambridge University Press.

1986. A Proof That the Core of an Ordinal Convex Game is a Von Neumann Morgenstern Solution, *Mathematical Social Sciences* , **11**, 83–87.

1985. An Axiomatization of the Core of Cooperative Games Without Side Payments, *Journal of Mathematical Economics* , **14**, 203–14.

1986. On the reduced game property and its converse, *International Journal of Game Theory,* **15**(3), 187–200.

Peters, H. 1986(a). Simultaneity of issues and additivity in bargaining, *Econometrica,* **54**, 153–69.

1986(b). Characterizations of Bargaining Solutions by Properties of Their Status Quo Sets, mimeo, Rijksuniversiteit Limburg, The Netherlands.

1986(c). Bargaining Game Theory. Ph.D. Thesis, Catholic University of Nijmegen, The Netherlands.

Peters, H., and P. Wakker. 1987. Independence of Irrelevant Alternatives and Revealed Group Preferences, mimeo, Limburg Rijksuniversiteit.

Plott, C. R. 1967. A notion of equilibrium and its possibility under majority rule, *American Economic Review,* **57,** 787–806.

1973. Path independence, rationality and social choice, *Econometrica,* **41**(6), 1075–91.

Proudhon, P. J. 1861. *Essais de Philosophie Pratique,* Paris.

Rawls, J. 1971. *A Theory of Justice.* Cambridge, MA: Belknap.

Riker, W. 1982. *Liberalism Against Populism.* San Francisco: Freeman.

Rob, R. 1982. Asymptotic efficiency of the demand-revealing mechanism, *Journal of Economic Theory,* **28,** 208–20.

Roberts, F. J. 1979. Measurement theory, in *Encyclopedia of Mathematics and Applications,* Vol. 7, F. Rota, ed. London: Addison-Wesley.

Roberts, K. 1979. The characterization of implementable choice rules, in *Aggregation and Revelation of Preferences,* J. J. Laffont, ed. Studies in Public Economics. Amsterdam: North-Holland.

1980(a). Possibility theorems with interpersonally comparable welfare levels, *Review of Economic Studies,* **47,** 409–20.

1980(b). Interpersonal comparability and social choice theory, *Review of Economic Studies,* **47,** 421–39.

Rockafellar, R. T. 1970. *Convex Analysis.* Princeton: Princeton University Press.

Roth, A. 1979. *Axiomatic Models of Bargaining.* Berlin and New York: Springer-Verlag.

Rubinstein, A. 1980. Stability of decision systems under majority rule, *Journal of Economic Theory,* **23,** 150–9.

1982. Perfect equilibrium in a bargaining model, *Econometrica,* **50,** 97–109.

Satterthwaite, M. A. 1975. Strategy-proofness and Arrow's conditions: existence and correspondence theorems for voting procedures and social welfare functions, *Journal of Economic Theory,* **10,** 198–217.

Scarf, H. 1967. The core of an *N* person game, *Econometrica,* **35,** 50–69.

1986. Notes on the core of a productive economy, in *Contributions to Mathematical Economics in Honor of Gerard Debreu,* W. Hildenbrand and A. Mas-Colell, eds. Amsterdam: North-Holland.

Schmeidler, D. 1969. The nucleolus of a characteristic function game, *SIAM Journal on Applied Mathematics,* **17,** 1163–70.

Schofield, N. 1984. Social equilibrium and cycles on compact sets, *Journal of Economic Theory,* **33,** 59–71.

Schokkaert, E., and B. Overlaet, 1986. Moral Intuitions and Economic Models of Distributive Justice, mimeo, K. V. Leuven.

Schwartz, T. 1976. Choice functions, rationality conditions and variations on the weak axiom of revealed preferences, *Journal of Economic Theory,* **13,** 414–27.

Sen, A. K. 1970. *Collective Choice and Social Welfare.* San Francisco: Holden Day.

1971. Choice functions and revealed preferences, *Review of Economic Studies,* **38,** 307–17.

1973. *On Economic Inequality.* Oxford: Clarendon.

1977. On weights and measures: informational constraints in social welfare analysis, *Econometrica,* **45**(7), 1539–72.

Sen, A. K., and P. K. Pattanaik. 1969. Necessary and sufficient conditions for rational choice under majority decision, *Journal of Economic Theory,* **1,** 178–202.

Sen, A. K., and B. Williams, eds. 1982. *Utilitarianism and Beyond.* Cambridge: Cambridge University Press.

Shapley, L. S. 1953. A value for *N*-person games, in *Contributions to the Theory of Games II,* H. W. Kuhn and A. W. Tucker, eds. Annals of Mathematics Studies No. 28. Princeton: Princeton University Press, pp. 307–17.

1969. Utility comparison and the theory of games, in *La Decision,* G.Th. Guilbaud, ed. Paris: CNRS, pp. 251–63.

1971. Core of convex games, *International Journal of Game Theory,* **1,** 11–26.

Shapley, L., and B. Grofman. 1984. Optimizing group judgmental accuracy in the presence of interdependencies, *Public Choice,* **43**(3), 329–44.

Sharkey, W. W. 1979. Existence of a core when there are increasing returns, *Econometrica,* **47**(4), 869–76.

1981. Convex games without side-payments, *International Journal of Game Theory,* **11,** 101–6.

1982. *The Theory of Natural Monopoly.* Cambridge: Cambridge University Press.

Sharkey, W. W., and L. G. Telser. 1978. Supportable cost functions for the multi-product firm, *Journal of Economic Theory,* **18,** 23–37.

Shepsle, K., and B. Weingast. 1984. Uncovered sets and sophisticated voting outcomes, with implications for agenda institutions, *American Journal of Political Science,* **28**(1), 49–75.

Shorrocks, A. F. 1984. Inequality decomposition by population subgroups, *Econometrica,* **52,** 1369–86.

1985. Aggregation Issues in Inequality Measurement, mimeo, the Australian National University, Canberra.

Shubik, M. 1962. Incentives, decentralized controls, the assignment of joint costs and internal pricing, *Management Science,* **8**(3), 325–43.

Smith, J. 1973. Aggregation of preferences with variable electorate, *Econometrica,* **41**(6), 1027–41.

Sobolev, A. I. 1975. Characterization of the principle of optimality for cooperative games through functional equations, in *Mathematical Methods in the Social Sciences,* Vipusk 6, N. N. Vorby'ev, ed. USSR: Vilnius, pp. 92–151 (in Russian).

Stearns, R. 1959. The voting problem, *American Mathematics Monthly,* **66,** 761–3.

Straffin, P. D. 1980. *Topics in the Theory of Voting,* The UMAP Expository Monograph Series. Boston: Birkhaüser.

Straffin, P. D., and J. P. Heaney. 1981. Game theory and the Tennessee Valley Authority, *International Journal of Game Theory,* **10**(1), 35–43.

Suzumura, K. 1983. *Rational Choice, Collective Decisions, and Social Welfare.* Cambridge: Cambridge University Press.

Thomson, W. 1983(a). The fair division of a fixed supply among a growing population, *Mathematics of Operations Research,* **8,** 319–26.

1983(b). Problems of fair division and the egalitarian solution, *Journal of Economic Theory,* **31,** 211–26.

Forthcoming. *Bargaining Theory: the Axiomatic Approach,* New York: Academic.

Thomson, W., and R. B. Myerson. 1980. Monotonicity and independence axioms, *International Journal of Game Theory,* **9,** 37–49.

Thomson, W., and H. Varian. 1985. Theories of justice based on symmetry, in *Social goals and Social Organization,* L. Hurwicz, D. Schmeidler, and H. Sonnenschein, eds. Cambridge: Cambridge University Press.

Tideman, T. N., and G. Tullock. 1976. A new and superior principle for collective choice, *Journal of Political Economy,* **84,** 1145–59.

Tocqueville, A. de. 1860. *De la Démocratie en Amérique.* Paris.

Vilkov, V. B. 1977. Convex games without side-payments, *Vestnik Leningradskiva Universitata,* **7,** 21–4 (in Russian).

von Neumann, J., and O. Morgenstern. 1947. *Theory of Games and Economic Behavior,* 2nd ed. Princeton: Princeton University Press.

Weber, R. J. 1978. Reproducing Voting Systems, mimeo, Cowles Foundation, New Haven.

Wilson, R. 1971. Stable coalition proposals in majority rule voting, *Journal of Economic Theory,* **3,** 254–71.

    1972. Social choice without the Pareto principle, *Journal of Economic Theory,* **5,** 478–86.

Yaari, M. 1978. Separably concave utilities and the principle of diminishing eagerness to trade, *Journal of Economic Theory,* **18,** 102–18.

    1981. Rawls, Edgeworth, Shapley, Nash: theories of distributive justice reexamined, *Journal of Economic Theory,* **24**(1), 1–39.

Yaari, M., and M. Bar-Hillel. On dividing justly, *Social Choice and Welfare,* **1,** 1–24.

Young, H. P. 1974. An axiomatization of Borda's rule, *Journal of Economic Theory,* **9,** 43–52.

    1975. Social choice scoring functions, *SIAM Journal of Applied Mathematics,* **28,** 824–38.

    1985(a). Monotonic solutions of cooperative games, *International Journal of Game Theory,* **14**(2), 65–72.

    1985(b). Cost allocation, in *Fair Allocation,* H. P. Young, ed., AMS Short Course Lecture Notes, Vol. 33. Providence: American Mathematical Society.

    1986. Optimal ranking and choice from pairwise comparisons, in *Information Pooling and Group Decision-Making,* B. Grofman and G. Owen, eds. Greenwich, CT: JAI.

    1987. On dividing an amount according to individual claims or liabilities, *Mathematics of Operations Research,* **12,** 397–414.

    1988. Condorcet's Theory of Voting, mimeo, University of Maryland.

Young, H. P., and A. Levenglick. 1978. A consistent extension of Condorcet's election principle, *SIAM Journal of Applied Mathematics, Part C,* **35,** 285–300.

Author index

Aczel, J., 159
Aizerman, M. A., 309, 310
Arrow, K., ix, 3, 6, 225, 283, 290, 309
Atkinson, A. B., 50, 52
Aumann, R. J., 120, 136, 138, 155, 156, 157

Banker, R., 157, 159
Banks, J. S., 248
Barbera, S., 263, 281, 282
Baumol, W., 89, 99, 166
Binmore, K., 66
Black, D., 264
Blackorby, C., 44, 57
Blair, D., 298, 299, 300
Blau, J., 298
Bondavera, O. N., 96
Borda, J. C., 6, 225
Brams, S., 239, 315
Brown, D. J., 293, 298

Champsaur, P., 219
Chernoff, H., 307
Chun, Y., 62, 157
Clarke, E. H., 203
Condorcet, M., 6, 30, 225

d'Aspremont, C., 7, 36, 40
Deb, R., 298
Debreu, G., 35, 44, 60, 88
Demange, G., 172, 226, 279
Donaldson, D., 57
Dubins, L. F., 205
Dummett, M., 248
Dutta, B., 276

Farquharson, R., 256, 276
Faulhaber, G., 87

Feldman, A., 7
Fishburn, P., 231, 236, 239, 309, 312, 315
Foley, D., 88, 180
Foster, J., 7, 33, 50, 52

Gaertner, W., 300
Gevers, L., 36, 40
Gibbard, A., 3, 256, 259, 263, 293
Gillies, D. B., 94
Gorman, W. M., 44
Green, J., 7, 204, 205, 209, 210
Greenberg, J., 270
Groves, T., 203, 207, 213
Guha, A. S., 293

Hammond, P., 40
Hardy, G. H., 50
Harsanyi, J. C., 23, 120, 140
Hart, S., 120
Heaney, J. P., 109
Hurwicz, L., 213
Hylland, A., 263, 281

Ichiishi, T., 7, 103, 114, 140, 276
Inada, K. I., 300

Kalai, E., 7, 63, 67, 70, 81, 120, 140, 267, 300
Kaneko, M., 60, 180, 181
Kelly, J. S., 230
Kemeny, J., 312
Kern, R., 116
Kim, K. W., 279
Kim, T., 213
Kohlberg, E., 204
Kolm, S. C., 7, 50, 52

327

Subject index